No Wonder They Call Him the Savior

Six Hours One Friday

And the Angels Were Silent

CHRONICLES OF THE CROSS

NO WONDER THEY CALL HIM THE SAVIOR

SIX HOURS ONE FRIDAY

AND THE ANGELS WERE SILENT

MAX LUCADO

THOMAS NELSON
Since 1798

NASHVILLE   DALLAS   MEXICO CITY   RIO DE JANEIRO   BEIJING

Thomas Nelson, Inc., titles may be purchased in bulk for educational, business, fundraising, or sales promotional use. For information, please e-mail SpecialMarkets@ThomasNelson.com.

ISBN 978-0-8499-2091-2 (hc)

Printed in the United States of America.

08 09 10 11 12 13 QWM 9 8 7 6 5 4 3 2 1

No Wonder They Call Him the Savior

CHRONICLES OF THE CROSS

Max Lucado

THOMAS NELSON

Since 1798

NASHVILLE   DALLAS   MEXICO CITY   RIO DE JANEIRO   BEIJING

Published in Nashville, Tennessee, by Thomas Nelson. Thomas Nelson is a registered trademark of Thomas Nelson, Inc.

Thomas Nelson, Inc., titles may be purchased in bulk for educational, business, fund-raising, or sales promotional use. For information, please e-mail SpecialMarkets@ThomasNelson.com.

Unless otherwise indicated, Scripture quotations used in this book are from *The Holy Bible,* New International Version (NIV) © 1973, 1984, by International Bible Society, used by permission of Zondervan Publishing House.

Scripture references marked RSV are from the *Revised Standard Version* © 1946, 1952 by the Division of Christian Education of the National Council of the Churches of Christ in the United States of America.

Scripture references marked TEV are from *The Good News Bible: The Bible in Today's English Version* © 1976 by American Bible Society.

Scripture references marked NEB are from *The New English Bible* © 1961, 1970 by Oxford University Press and Cambridge University Press.

"The Boxer" © 1968 by Paul Simon. Used by permission.

Library of Congress Cataloging-in-Publication Data

Lucado, Max.
    No wonder they call him the Savior / by Max Lucado.
      p. cm.
    Originally published: Sisters, Or. : Multnomah Books, 1996.
    ISBN 978-0-8499-0855-2 (tradepaper)
    ISBN 978-0-8499-1814-8 (hardcover)
    ISBN 978-0-8499-9065-6 (special edition)
    ISBN 978-0-8499-2098-1 (SE)
    1. Jesus Christ—Passion—Meditations. I. Title.
BT431.3.L85 2004
232.96—dc22

2003022808

Printed in the United States of America

To Denalyn
with love eternal

CONTENTS

PART III
THE CROSS: ITS WISDOM

ACKNOWLEDGMENTS

A warm thank you to:

Dr. Tom Olbricht—for showing me what matters.

Dr. Carl Brecheen—for seeds planted in a hungry heart.

Jim Hackney—for your insights into our Master's sufferings.

Janine, Sue, Doris, and Paul—for your typing and encouragement.

Bob and Elsie Forcum—or your partnership in the gospel.

Randy Mayeux and Jim Woodroof—for your constructive comments and brotherly support.

Liz Heaney—for your keen editorial skills and creativity.

Multnomah Press, the original publisher of this book—thanks for taking a chance on a young author.

And most of all to Jesus Christ—please accept this offering of gratitude.

INTRODUCTION

The Brazilians taught me the beauty of a blessing. Here is a scene repeated in Brazil thousands of times daily . . . It's early morning. Time for young Marcos to leave for school. As he gathers his books and heads for the door, he pauses by his father's chair. He searches his father's face. *Ben o, Pai?* Marcos asks. (*Blessing, Father?*)

The father raises his hand. *Deus te aben oe, meu filho*, he assures. (*God bless you, my son.*)

Marcos smiles and hurries out the door.

This scene came to mind as I thought about the rerelease of *No Wonder They Call Him the Savior*. I wrote this book in Brazil. My years in Rio de Janeiro gave birth to many of these thoughts. The church we served was young (so were we) and hungry for the cross (we were, too). Many of my messages centered around the Savior.

May God bless you as you read them. Just as the Brazilian children seek blessings from their fathers, so may you seek his. He'll give it, you know. He always has. That's why we call him Father.

MAX LUCADO

THE PART
THAT MATTERS

"I just want to know what counts." Deep Irish brogue. Dark, deep eyes. The statement was sincere. "Don't talk to me of religion, I've been down that road. And please, stay off theology. I have a degree in that. Get to the heart of it, okay? I want to know what counts."

His name was Ian. He was a student at a Canadian university where I was visiting. Through a series of events he found out I was a Christian and I found out he wanted to be but was disenchanted.

"I grew up in the church," he explained. "I wanted to go into the ministry. I took all the courses, the theology, the languages, the exegesis. But I quit. Something just didn't click."

"It's in there somewhere," he spoke with earnestness. "At least I think it is."

I looked up from my coffee as he began to stir his. Then he summarized his frustration with one question.

"What *really* matters? What counts? Tell me. Skip the periphery. Go to the essence. Tell me the part that matters."

The part that matters.

I looked at Ian for a long time. The question hung in the air. What should I have said? What could I have said? I could have told him about church. I could've given him a doctrinal answer or read him something classic like the Twenty-third Psalm, "The LORD is my shepherd . . . " But that all seemed too small. Maybe some thoughts on sexuality or prayer or the Golden Rule. No, Ian wanted the treasure—he wanted the meat.

Stop and empathize for a second. Can you hear his question? Can you taste his frustration? "Don't give me religion," he was saying. "Give me what matters."

What does matter?

In your Bible of over a thousand pages, what matters? Among all the do's and don'ts and shoulds and shouldn'ts, what is essential? What is indispensable? The Old Testament? The New? Grace? Baptism?

What would you have said to Ian? Would you have spoken on the evil of the world or maybe the eminence of heaven? Would you have quoted John 3:16 or Acts 2:38 or maybe read 1 Corinthians 13?

What really matters?

You've probably wrestled with this question. Maybe you've gone through the acts of religion and faith and yet found yourself more often than not at a dry well. Prayers seem empty. Goals seem unthinkable. Christianity becomes a warped record full of highs and lows and off-key notes.

Is this all there is? Sunday attendance. Pretty songs. Faithful tithings. Golden crosses. Three-piece suits. Big choirs. Leather Bibles. It is nice and all, but . . . where is the heart of it?

I stirred my coffee. Ian stirred his. I had no answer. All my verses so obediently memorized seemed inappropriate. All my canned responses seemed timid.

Yet now, years later, I know what I would share with him.

Think about these words from Paul in 1 Corinthians, chapter 15.

> For I delivered to you as of *first importance* what I also received, that Christ died for our sins in accordance with the scriptures.

"First importance" he says.

Read on:

> That he was buried, that he was raised on the third day in accordance with the scriptures, and that he appeared to Cephas, then to the twelve.[1]

There it is. Almost too simple. Jesus was killed, buried, and resurrected. Surprised? The part that matters is the cross. No more and no less.

The cross.

It rests on the time line of history like a compelling diamond. Its tragedy summons all sufferers. Its absurdity attracts all cynics. Its hope lures all searchers.

And according to Paul, the cross is what counts.

My, what a piece of wood! History has idolized it and despised it, gold-plated it and burned it, worn and trashed it. History has done everything to it but ignore it.

That's the one option that the cross does not offer.

No one can ignore it! You can't ignore a piece of lumber that suspends the greatest claim in history. A crucified carpenter claiming that he is God on earth? Divine? Eternal? The death-slayer?

No wonder Paul called it "the core of the gospel." Its bottom line is sobering: if the account is true, it is history's hinge. Period. If not, it is history's hoax.

That's why the cross is what matters. That's why if I had that cup of coffee to drink with Ian again I would tell him about it. I'd

tell of the drama on that windy April day, the day when the kingdom of death was repossessed and hope took up the payments. I'd
tell of Peter's tumble, Pilate's hesitancy, and John's loyalty. We'd
read about the foggy garden of decision and the incandescent
room of the resurrection. We'd discuss the final words uttered so
deliberately by this self-sacrificing Messiah.

And finally, we'd look at the Messiah himself. A blue-collar
Jew whose claim altered a world and whose promise has never
been equaled.

No wonder they call him the Savior.

I'm wondering if I might not be addressing some readers who
have the same question that Ian had. Oh, the cross is nothing
new to you. You have seen it. You have worn it. You have thought
about it. You have read about it. Maybe you have even prayed to
it. But do you know it?

Any serious study of the Christian claim is, at its essence, a
study of the cross. To accept or reject Christ without a careful
examination of Calvary is like deciding on a car without looking
at the engine. Being religious without knowing the cross is like
owning a Mercedes with no motor. Pretty package, but where is
your power?

Will you do me a favor? Get yourself some coffee, get comfortable, and give me an hour of your time. Take a good look at
the cross with me. Let's examine this hour in history. Let's look at
the witnesses. Let's listen to the voices. Let's watch the faces. And
most of all, let's observe the one they call the Savior. And let's see
if we can find the part that matters.

PART ONE

THE CROSS:

ITS WORDS

FINAL WORDS, FINAL ACTS

In a recent trip to my hometown I took some time to go see a tree. "A live oak tree," my dad had called it (with the accent on "live"). It was nothing more than a sapling, so thin I could wrap my hand around it and touch my middle finger to my thumb. The West Texas wind scattered the fall leaves and caused me to zip up my coat. There is nothing colder than a prairie wind, especially in a cemetery.

"A special tree," I said to myself, "with a special job." I looked around. The cemetery was lined with elms but no oaks. The ground was dotted with tombstones but no trees. Just this one. A special tree for a special man.

About three years ago Daddy began noticing a steady weakening of his muscles. It began in his hands. He then felt it in his calves. Next his arms thinned a bit.

He mentioned his condition to my brother-in-law, who is a physician. My brother-in-law, alarmed, sent him to a specialist. The specialist conducted a lengthy battery of tests—blood, neurological, and muscular—and he reached his conclusion. Lou Gehrig's disease. A devastating crippler. No one knows the cause or the cure. The only sure thing about it is its cruelty and accuracy.

I looked down at the plot of ground that would someday entomb my father. Daddy always wanted to be buried under an oak tree so he bought this one. "Special order from the valley," he had boasted. "Had to get special permission from the city council to put it here." (That wasn't hard in this dusty oil field town where everybody knows everybody.)

The lump got tighter in my throat. A lesser man might have been angry. Another man might have given up. But Daddy didn't. He knew that his days were numbered so he began to get his house in order.

The tree was only one of the preparations he made. He improved the house for Mom by installing a sprinkler system and a garage door opener and by painting the trim. He got the will updated. He verified the insurance and retirement policies. He bought some stock to go toward his grandchildren's education. He planned his funeral. He bought cemetery plots for himself and Mom. He prepared his kids through words of assurance and letters of love. And last of all, he bought the tree. A live oak tree. (Pronounced with an accent on "live.")

Final acts. Final hours. Final words.

They reflect a life well lived. So do the last words of our Master. When on the edge of death, Jesus, too, got his house in order:

> A final prayer of forgiveness.
> A plea honored.
> A request of love.
> A question of suffering.
> A confession of humanity.
> A call of deliverance.
> A cry of completion.

Words of chance muttered by a desperate martyr? No. Words of intent, painted by the Divine Deliverer on the canvas of sacrifice.

Final words. Final acts. Each one is a window through which the cross can be better understood. Each one opens a treasury of promises. "So that is where you learned it," I said aloud as though speaking to my father. I smiled to myself and thought, "It's much easier to die like Jesus if you have lived like him for a lifetime."

The final hours are passing now. The gentle flame on his candle grows weaker and weaker. He lies in peace. His body dying, his spirit living. No longer can he get out of bed. He has chosen to live his last days at home. It won't be long. Death's windy draft will soon exhaust the flickering candle and it will be over.

I looked one last time at the slender oak. I touched it as if it had been hearing my thoughts. "Grow," I whispered. "Grow strong. Stand tall. Yours is a valued treasure."

As I drove home through the ragged oil field patchwork, I kept thinking about that tree. Though feeble, the decades will find it strong. Though slender, the years will add thickness and strength. Its last years will be its best. Just like my father's. Just like my Master's. "It is much easier to die like Jesus if you have lived like him for a lifetime."

"Grow, young tree." My eyes were misting. "Stand strong. Yours is a valued treasure."

He was awake when I got home. I leaned over his bed. "I checked on the tree," I told him. "It's growing."

He smiled.

CHAPTER 2

WORDS THAT WOUND

"Father, forgive them."
LUKE 23:34

The dialogue that Friday morning was bitter.

From the onlookers, "Come down from the cross if you are the Son of God!"

From the religious leaders, "He saved others but he can't save himself."

From the soldiers, "If you are the king of the Jews, save yourself."

Bitter words. Acidic with sarcasm. Hateful. Irreverent. Wasn't it enough that he was being crucified? Wasn't it enough that he was being shamed as a criminal? Were the nails insufficient? Was the crown of thorns too soft? Had the flogging been too short?

For some, apparently so.

Peter, a writer not normally given to using many descriptive verbs, says that the passers-by "hurled" insults at the crucified Christ.[1] They didn't just yell or speak or scream. They "hurled" verbal stones. They had every intention of hurting and bruising. "We've broken the body, now let's break the spirit!" So they strung their bows with self-righteousness and launched stinging arrows of pure poison.

Of all the scenes around the cross, this one angers me the most. What kind of people, I ask myself, would mock a dying man? Who would be so base as to pour the salt of scorn upon open wounds? How low and perverted to sneer at one who is laced with pain. Who would make fun of a person who is seated in an electric chair? Or who would point and laugh at a criminal who has a hangman's noose around his neck?

You can be sure that Satan and his demons were the cause of such filth.

And then the criminal on cross number two throws his punch.

"Aren't you the Christ? Save yourself and us!"

The words thrown that day were meant to wound. And there is nothing more painful than words meant to hurt. That's why James called the tongue a fire. Its burns are every bit as destructive and disastrous as those of a blowtorch.

But I'm not telling you anything new. No doubt you've had your share of words that wound. You've felt the sting of a well-aimed gibe. Maybe you're still feeling it. Someone you love or respect slams you to the floor with a slur or slip of the tongue. And there you lie, wounded and bleeding. Perhaps the words were intended to hurt you, perhaps not; but that doesn't matter. The wound is deep. The injuries are internal. Broken heart, wounded pride, bruised feelings.

Or maybe your wound is old. Though the arrow was extracted long ago, the arrowhead is still lodged . . . hidden under your skin. The old pain flares unpredictably and decisively, reminding you of harsh words yet unforgiven.

If you have suffered or are suffering because of someone else's words, you'll be glad to know that there is a balm for this laceration. Meditate on these words from 1 Peter 2:23.

When they hurled their insults at him, he did not retaliate; when he suffered, he made no threats. Instead, he entrusted himself to him who judges justly.

Did you see what Jesus did not do? He did not retaliate. He did not bite back. He did not say, "I'll get you!" "Come on up here and say that to my face!" "Just wait until after the resurrection, buddy!" No, these statements were not found on Christ's lips.

Did you see what Jesus did do? He "entrusted himself to him who judges justly." Or said more simply, he left the judging to God. He did not take on the task of seeking revenge. He demanded no apology. He hired no bounty hunters and sent out no posse. He, to the astounding contrary, spoke on their defense. "Father, forgive them, for they do not know what they are doing."[2]

Yes, the dialogue that Friday morning was bitter. The verbal stones were meant to sting. How Jesus, with a body wracked with pain, eyes blinded by his own blood, and lungs yearning for air, could speak on behalf of some heartless thugs is beyond my comprehension. Never, never have I seen such love. If ever a person deserved a shot at revenge, Jesus did. But he didn't take it. Instead he died for them. How could he do it? I don't know. But I do know that all of a sudden my wounds seem very painless. My grudges and hard feelings are suddenly childish.

Sometimes I wonder if we don't see Christ's love as much in the people he tolerated as in the pain he endured.

Amazing Grace.

VIGILANTE VENGEANCE

"They do not know what they are doing."
LUKE 23:34

Thirty-seven years old. Thin, almost frail. Balding and bespectacled. An electronics buff. Law-abiding and timid. Certainly not a description you would give a vigilante. Certainly not the person you would cast to play Robin Hood or the Lone Ranger.

But that didn't bother the American public. When Bernhard Hugo Goetz blasted four would-be muggers in a New York subway, he instantly became a hero. A popular actress sent him a "love and kisses" telegram. "Thug-buster" T-shirts began to appear on the streets of New York City. A rock group wrote a song in his honor. People gave and raised money to go toward his defense. Radio talk shows were deluged with callers. "They won't let it go," said one radio host.

It's not hard to see why.

Bernhard Goetz was an American fantasy come true. He did what every citizen wants to do. He fought back. He "kicked the bully in the shins." He "punched the villain in the nose." He "clobbered evil over the head." This unassuming hero embodied a nationwide, even worldwide anger: a passion for revenge.

The outpouring of support gives clear evidence. People are mad. People are angry. There is a pent-up, boiling rage that causes us to toast a man who fearlessly (or fearfully) says, "I ain't taking it no more!" and then comes out with a hot pistol in each hand.

We're tired. We're tired of being bullied, harassed, and intimidated. We're weary of the serial murderer, rapists, and hired assassins.

We're angry at someone, but we don't know who. We're scared of something, but we don't know what. We want to fight back, but we don't know how. And then, when a modern-day Wyatt Earp walks onto the scene, we applaud him. He is speaking for us! "That-a-way to go, Thug-Buster; that's the way to do it!"

Or is it? Is that really the way to do it? Let's think about our anger for just a minute.

Anger. It's a peculiar yet predictable emotion. It begins as a drop of water. An irritant. A frustration. Nothing big, just an aggravation. Someone gets your parking place. Someone pulls in front of you on the freeway. A waitress is slow and you are in a hurry. The toast burns. Drops of water. Drip. Drip. Drip. Drip.

Yet, get enough of these seemingly innocent drops of anger and before long you've got a bucket full of rage. Walking revenge. Blind bitterness. Unharnessed hatred. We trust no one and bare our teeth at anyone who gets near. We become walking time bombs that, given just the right tension and fear, could explode like Mr. Goetz.

Now, is that any way to live? What good has hatred ever brought? What hope has anger ever created? What problems have ever been resolved by revenge?

No one can blame the American public for applauding the man who fought back. Yet, as the glamour fades on such acts, reality makes us ask the questions:

What good was done? Is that really the way to reduce the crime rate? Are subways forever safer? Are the streets now free of fear? No. Anger doesn't do that. Anger only feeds a primitive lust for revenge that feeds our anger that feeds our revenge that feeds our anger—you get the picture. Vigilantes are not the answer.

Yet, what do we do? We can't deny that our anger exists. How do we harness it? A good option is found in Luke 23:34. Here, Jesus speaks about the mob that killed him. "Father forgive them, for they do not know what they are doing."

Have you ever wondered how Jesus kept from retaliating? Have you ever asked how he kept his control? Here's the answer. It's the second part of his statement: "for they do not know what they are doing." Look carefully. It's as if Jesus considered this bloodthirsty, death-hungry crowd not as murderers, but as victims. It's as if he saw in their faces not hatred but confusion. It's as if he regarded them not as a militant mob but, as he put it, as "sheep without a shepherd."

"They don't know what they are doing."

And when you think about it, they didn't. They hadn't the faintest idea what they were doing. They were a stir-crazy mob, mad at something they couldn't see so they took it out on, of all people, God. But they didn't know what they were doing.

And for the most part, neither do we. We are still, as much as we hate to admit it, shepherdless sheep. All we know is that we were born out of one eternity and are frighteningly close to another. We play tag with the fuzzy realities of death and pain. We can't answer our own questions about love and hurt. We can't solve the riddle of aging. We don't know how to heal our own bodies or get along with our own mates. We can't keep ourselves out of war. We can't even keep ourselves fed.

Paul spoke for humanity when he confessed, "I do not know what I am doing."[1]

Now, I know that doesn't justify anything. That doesn't justify hit-and-run drivers or kiddie-porn peddlers or heroin dealers. But it does help explain why they do the miserable things they do.

My point is this: Uncontrolled anger won't better our world, but sympathetic understanding will. Once we see the world and ourselves for what we are, we can help. Once we understand ourselves we begin to operate not from a posture of anger but of compassion and concern. We look at the world not with bitter frowns but with extended hands. We realize that the lights are out and a lot of people are stumbling in the darkness. So we light candles.

As Michelangelo said, "we criticize by creating." Instead of fighting back we help out. We go to the ghettos. We teach in the schools. We build hospitals and help orphans . . . and we put away our guns.

"They do not know what they are doing."

There is something about understanding the world that makes us want to save it, even to die for it. Anger? Anger never did anyone any good. Understanding? Well, the results are not as quick as the vigilante's bullet, but they are certainly much more constructive.

CHAPTER 4

THE TALE OF THE CRUCIFIED CROOK

"I tell you the truth, today you will be with me in paradise."
LUKE 23:43

The only thing more outlandish than the request was that it was granted. Just trying to picture the scene is enough to short-circuit the most fanciful of imaginations; a flat-nosed ex-con asking God's son for eternal life? But trying to imagine the appeal being honored, well, that steps beyond the realm of reality and enters absurdity.

But as absurd as it may appear, that's exactly what happened. He who deserved hell got heaven, and we are left with a puzzling riddle. What, for goodness' sake, was Jesus trying to teach us? What was he trying to prove by pardoning this strong-arm, who in all probability had never said grace, much less done anything to deserve it?

Well, I've got a theory. But to explain it, I've got to tell you a tale that you may not believe.

It seems a couple of prowlers broke into a department store in a large city. They successfully entered the store, stayed long enough to do what they came to do, and escaped unnoticed. What is unusual about the story is what these fellows did. They took nothing. Absolutely nothing. No merchandise was stolen. No items were removed. But what they did do was ridiculous.

Instead of stealing anything, they changed the cost of everything. Price tags were swapped. Values were exchanged. These clever pranksters took the tag off a $395.00 camera and stuck it on a $5.00 box of stationery. The $5.95 sticker on a paperback book was removed and placed on an outboard motor. They repriced everything in the store!

Crazy? You bet. But the craziest part of this story took place the next morning. (You are not going to believe this.) The store opened as usual. Employees went to work. Customers began to shop. The place functioned as normal for four hours before anyone noticed what had happened.

Four hours! Some people got some great bargains. Others got fleeced. For four solid hours no one noticed that all the values had been swapped.

Hard to believe? It shouldn't be—we see the same thing happening every day. We are deluged by a distorted value system. We see the most valuable things in our lives peddled for pennies and we see the cheapest smut go for millions.

The examples are abundant and besetting. Here are a few that I've encountered in the last week.

The salesman who defended his illegal practices by saying, "Let's not confuse business with ethics."

The military men who sold top-secret information (as well as their integrity) for $6,000.

The cabinet member of a large nation who was caught illegally dealing in semi-precious stones. His cabinet position? Minister of *Justice.*

The father who confessed to the murder of his twelve-year-old daughter. The reason he killed her? She refused to go to bed with him.

Why do we do what we do? Why do we take blatantly black-and-white and paint it gray? Why are priceless mores trashed while senseless standards are obeyed? What causes us to elevate the body and degrade the soul? What causes us to pamper the skin while we pollute the heart?

Our values are messed up. Someone broke into the store and exchanged all the price tags. Thrills are going for top dollar and the value of human beings is at an all-time low.

One doesn't have to be a philosopher to determine what caused such a sag in the market. It all began when someone convinced us that the human race is headed nowhere. That man has no *destiny*. That we are in a cycle. That there is no reason or rhyme to this absurd existence. Somewhere we got the idea that we are meaninglessly trapped on a puny mudheap that has no destination. The earth is just a spinning mausoleum and the universe is purposeless. The creation was incidental and humanity has no direction.

Pretty gloomy, huh?

The second verse is even worse. If man has no destiny, then he has no *duty*. No obligation, no responsibility. If man has no destiny, then he has no guidelines or goals. If man has no destiny, then who is to say what is right or wrong? Who is to say that a husband can't leave his wife and family? Who is to say you can't abort a fetus? What is wrong with shacking up? Who says I can't step on someone's neck to get to the top? It's your value system against mine. No absolutes. No principles. No ethics. No standards. Life is reduced to weekends, paychecks, and quick thrills. The bottom line is disaster.

"The existentialist," writes existentialist Jean-Paul Sartre, "finds it extremely embarrassing that God does not exist, for there disappears with him all possibility of finding values in an intelligible heaven. . . . Everything is indeed permitted if God does not exist, and man is in consequence forlorn, for he cannot find anything to depend on within or without himself."[1]

If man has no duty or destiny, the next logical step is that man has no *value*. If man has no future, he isn't worth much. He is worth, in fact, about as much as a tree or a rock. No difference. There is no reason to be here, therefore, there is no value.

And you've seen the results of this. Our system goes haywire. We feel useless and worthless. We freak out. We play games. We create false value systems. We say that you are valuable if you are pretty. We say that you are valuable if you can produce. We say that you are valuable if you can slam-dunk a basketball or snag a pop fly. You are valuable if your name has a "Dr." in front of it or Ph.D. on the end of it. You are valuable if you have a six-figure salary and drive a foreign car.

Value is now measured by two criteria, appearance and performance.

Pretty tough system, isn't it? Where does that leave the retarded? Or the ugly or uneducated? Where does that place the aged or the handicapped? What hope does that offer the unborn child? Not much. Not much at all. We become nameless numbers on mislaid lists.

Now please understand, this is man's value system. It is not God's. His plan is much brighter. God, with eyes twinkling, steps up to the philosopher's blackboard, erases the never-ending, ever-repeating circle of history and replaces it with a line; a hopefilled, promising, slender line. And, looking over his shoulder to see if the class is watching, he draws an arrow on the end.

In God's book man is heading somewhere. He has an amazing destiny. We are being prepared to walk down the church aisle and become the bride of Jesus. We are going to live with him. Share the throne with him. Reign with him. We count. We are valuable. And what's more, our worth is built in! Our value is inborn.

You see, if there was anything that Jesus wanted everyone to understand it was this: A person is worth something simply because he is a person. That is why he treated people like he did. Think about it. The girl caught making undercover thunder with someone she shouldn't—he forgave her. The untouchable leper who asked for cleansing—he touched him. And the blind welfare case that cluttered the roadside—he honored him. And the worn-out old windbag addicted to self-pity near the pool of Siloam— he healed him!

And don't forget the classic case study on the value of a person by Luke. It is called "The Tale of the Crucified Crook."

If anyone was ever worthless, this one was. If any man ever deserved dying, this man probably did. If any fellow was ever a loser, this fellow was at the top of the list.

Perhaps that is why Jesus chose him to show us what he thinks of the human race.

Maybe this criminal had heard the Messiah speak. Maybe he had seen him love the lowly. Maybe he had watched him dine with the punks, pickpockets, and potmouths on the streets. Or maybe not. Maybe the only thing he knew about this Messiah was what he now saw: a beaten, slashed, nail-suspended preacher. His face crimson with blood, his bones peeking through torn flesh, his lungs gasping for air.

Something, though, told him he had never been in better company. And somehow he realized that even though all he had was prayer, he had finally met the One to whom he should pray.

"Any chance that you could put in a good word for me?" (Loose translation.)

"Consider it done."

Now why did Jesus do that? What in the world did he have to gain by promising this desperado a place of honor at the banquet table? What in the world could this chiseling quisling ever offer in return? I mean, the Samaritan woman I can understand. She could go back and tell the tale. And Zacchaeus had some money that he could give. But this guy? What is he going to do? Nothing!

That's the point. Listen closely. Jesus' love does not depend upon what we do for him. Not at all. In the eyes of the King, you have value simply because you are. You don't have to look nice or perform well. Your value is inborn.

Period.

Think about that for just a minute. You are valuable just because you exist. Not because of what you do or what you have done, but simply because you are. Remember that. Remember that the next time you are left bobbing in the wake of someone's steamboat ambition. Remember that the next time some trickster tries to hang a bargain basement price tag on your self-worth. The next time someone tries to pass you off as a cheap buy, just think about the way Jesus honors you . . . and smile.

I do. I smile because I know I don't deserve love like that. None of us do. When you get right down to it, any contribution that any of us make is pretty puny. All of us—even the purest of us—deserve heaven about as much as that crook did. All of us are signing on Jesus' credit card, not ours.

And it also makes me smile to think that there is a grinning ex-con walking the golden streets who knows more about grace than a thousand theologians. No one else would have given him a prayer. But in the end that is all that he had. And in the end, that is all it took.

No wonder they call him the Savior.

LEAVING
IS LOVING

"Woman, behold, your son."
JOHN 19:26, RSV

The gospel is full of rhetorical challenges that test our faith
and buck against human nature.

"It is more blessed to give than to receive."[1]

"For whoever wants to save his life will lose it, but whoever
loses his life for me will save it."[2]

"Only in his home town and in his own house is a prophet
without honor."[3]

But no statement is as confusing or frightening as the one in
Matthew 19:29. "And everyone who has left houses or brothers
or sisters or father or mother or children or fields for my sake will
receive a hundred times as much and will inherit eternal life."

The part about leaving land and fields I can understand. It is
the other part that causes me to cringe. It's the part about leaving
mom and dad, saying good-bye to brothers and sisters, placing a
farewell kiss on a son or daughter. It is easy to parallel discipleship
with poverty or public disgrace, but leaving my family? Why do I

have to be willing to leave those I love? Can sacrifice get any more sacrificial than that?

"Woman, behold your son."

Mary is older now. The hair at her temples is gray. Wrinkles have replaced her youthful skin. Her hands are calloused. She has raised a houseful of children. And now she beholds the crucifixion of her firstborn.

One wonders what memories she conjures up as she witnesses his torture. The long ride to Bethlehem, perhaps. A baby's bed made from cow's hay. Fugitives in Egypt. At home in Nazareth. Panic in Jerusalem. "I thought he was with you!" Carpentry lessons. Dinner table laughter.

And then the morning Jesus came in from the shop early, his eyes firmer, his voice more direct. He had heard the news. "John is preaching in the desert." Her son took off his nail apron, dusted off his hands, and with one last look said good-bye to his mother. They both knew it would never be the same again. In that last look they shared a secret, the full extent of which was too painful to say aloud.

Mary learned that day the heartache that comes from saying good-bye. From then on she was to love her son from a distance; on the edge of the crowd, outside of a packed house, on the shore of the sea. Maybe she was even there when the enigmatic promise was made, "Anyone who has left . . . mother . . . for my sake."

Mary wasn't the first one to be called to say good-bye to loved ones for sake of the kingdom. Joseph was called to be an orphan in Egypt. Jonah was called to be a foreigner in Nineveh. Hannah sent her firstborn son away to serve in the temple. Daniel was sent from Jerusalem to Babylon. Nehemiah was sent from Susa to Jerusalem. Abraham was sent to sacrifice his own son. Paul had to say good-bye to his heritage. The Bible is bound together with good-bye trails and stained with farewell tears.

In fact, it seems that *good-bye* is a word all too prevalent in the Christian's vocabulary. Missionaries know it well. Those who send them know it, too. The doctor who leaves the city to work in the jungle hospital has said it. So has the Bible translator who lives far from home. Those who feed the hungry, those who teach the lost, those who help the poor all know the word good-bye.

Airports. Luggage. Embraces. Taillights. "Wave to grandma." Tears. Bus terminals. Ship docks. "Good-bye, Daddy." Tight throats. Ticket counters. Misty eyes. "Write me!"

Question: What kind of God would put people through such agony? What kind of God would give you families and then ask you to leave them? What kind of God would give you friends and then ask you to say good-bye?

Answer: A God who knows that the deepest love is built not on passion and romance but on a common mission and sacrifice.

Answer: A God who knows that we are only pilgrims and that eternity is so close that any "Good-bye" is in reality a "See you tomorrow."

Answer: A God who did it himself.

"Woman, behold your son."

John fastened his arm around Mary a little tighter. Jesus was asking him to be the son that a mother needs and that in some ways he never was.

Jesus looked at Mary. His ache was from a pain far greater than that of the nails and thorns. In their silent glance they again shared a secret. And he said good-bye.

THE CRY
OF LONELINESS

"My God, my God, why have you forsaken me?"
MATTHEW 27:46

For those of us who endured it, the summer of 1980 in Miami was nothing to smile about. The Florida heat scorched the city during the day and baked it at night. Riots, looting, and racial tension threatened to snap the frayed emotions of the people. Everything soared: unemployment, inflation, the crime rate, and especially the thermometer. Somewhere in the midst of it all, a *Miami Herald* reporter captured a story that left the entire Gold Coast breathless. It was the story of Judith Bucknell. Attractive, young, successful, and dead.

Judith Bucknell was homicide number one hundred and six that year. She was killed on a steamy June 9th evening. Age: 38. Weight: 109 pounds. Stabbed seven times. Strangled.

She kept a diary. Had she not kept this diary perhaps the memory of her would have been buried with her body. But the diary exists; a painful epitaph to a lonely life. The correspondent made this comment about her writings:

In her diaries, Judy created a character and a voice. The character is herself, wistful, struggling, weary; the voice is yearning. Judith Bucknell has failed to connect; age 38, many lovers, much love offered, none returned.[1]

Her struggles weren't unusual. She worried about getting old, getting fat, getting married, getting pregnant, and getting by. She lived in stylish Coconut Grove (Coconut Grove is where you live if you are lonely but act happy).

Judy was the paragon of the confused human being. Half of her life was fantasy, half was nightmare. Successful as a secretary, but a loser at love. Her diary was replete with entries such as the following:

> Where are the men with the flowers and champagne and music? Where are the men who call and ask for a genuine, actual date? Where are the men who would like to share more than my bed, my booze, my food. . . . I would like to have in my life, once before I pass through my life, the kind of sexual relationship which is part of a loving relationship.[2]

She never did.

Judy was not a prostitute. She was not on drugs or on welfare. She never went to jail. She was not a social outcast. She was respectable. She jogged. She hosted parties. She wore designer clothes and had an apartment that overlooked the bay. And she was very lonely. "I see people together and I'm so jealous I want to throw up. What about me! What about me!" Though surrounded by people, she was on an island. Though she had many acquaintances, she had few friends. Though she had many lovers (fifty-nine in fifty-six months), she had little love.

24

"Who is going to love Judy Bucknell?" the diary continues. "I feel so old. Unloved. Unwanted. Abandoned. Used up. I want to cry and sleep forever."[3]

A clear message came from her aching words. Though her body died on June 9th from the wounds of a knife, her heart had died long before . . . from loneliness.

"I'm alone," she wrote, "and I want to share something with somebody."[4]

Loneliness.

It's a cry. A moan, a wail. It's a gasp whose origin is the recesses of our souls.

Can you hear it? The abandoned child. The divorcée. The quiet home. The empty mailbox. The long days. The longer nights. A one-night stand. A forgotten birthday. A silent phone.

Cries of loneliness. Listen again. Tune out the traffic and turn down the TV. The cry is there. Our cities are full of Judy Bucknells. You can hear their cries. You can hear them in the convalescent home among the sighs and the shuffling feet. You can hear them in the prisons among the moans of shame and the calls for mercy. You can hear them if you walk the manicured streets of suburban America, among the aborted ambitions and aging homecoming queens. Listen for it in the halls of our high schools where peer pressure weeds out the "have-nots" from the "haves."

This moan in a minor key knows all spectrums of society. From the top to the bottom. From the failures to the famous. From the poor to the rich. From the married to the single. Judy Bucknell was not alone.

Many of you have been spared this cruel cry. Oh, you have been homesick or upset a time or two. But despair? Far from it. Suicide? Of course not. Be thankful that it hasn't knocked on your door. Pray that it never will. If you have yet to fight this battle, you are welcome to read on if you wish, but I'm really writing to someone else.

I am writing to those who know this cry firsthand. I'm writing to those of you whose days are bookended with broken hearts and long evenings. I'm writing to those of you who can find a lonely person simply by looking in the mirror.

For you, loneliness is a way of life. The sleepless nights. The lonely bed. The distrust. The fear of tomorrow. The unending hurt.

When did it begin? In your childhood? At the divorce? At retirement? At the cemetery? When the kids left home?

Maybe you, like Judy Bucknell, have fooled everyone. No one knows that you are lonely. On the outside you are packaged perfectly. Your smile is quick. Your job is stable. Your clothes are sharp. Your waist is thin. Your calendar is full. Your walk brisk. Your talk impressive. But when you look in the mirror, you fool no one. When you are alone, the duplicity ceases and the pain surfaces.

Or maybe you don't try to hide it. Maybe you have always been outside the circle looking in, and everyone knows it. Your conversation is a bit awkward. Your companionship is seldom requested. Your clothes are dull. Your looks are common. Ziggy is your hero and Charlie Brown is your mentor.

Am I striking a chord? If I am, if you have nodded or sighed in understanding, I have an important message for you.

The most gut-wrenching cry of loneliness in history came not from a prisoner or a widow or a patient. It came from a hill, from a cross, from a Messiah.

"My God, my God," he screamed, "why did you abandon me!"[5]

Never have words carried so much hurt. Never has one being been so lonely.

The crowd quietens as the priest receives the goat; the pure, unspotted goat. In somber ceremony he places his hands on the young animal. As the people witness, the priest makes his proclamation. "The sins of the people be upon you." The innocent animal receives the sins of the Israelites. All the lusting, adultery, and cheating are transferred from the sinners to this goat, to this scapegoat.

He is then carried to the edge of the wilderness and released. Banished. Sin must be purged, so the scapegoat is abandoned. "Run, goat! Run!"

The people are relieved.

Yahweh is appeased.

The sinbearer is alone.[6]

And now on Skull's hill, the sinbearer is again alone. Every lie ever told, every object ever coveted, every promise ever broken is on his shoulders. He is sin.

God turns away. "Run, goat! Run!"

The despair is darker than the sky. The two who have been one are now two. Jesus, who had been with God for eternity, is now alone. The Christ, who was an expression of God, is abandoned. The Trinity is dismantled. The Godhead is disjointed. The unity is dissolved.

It is more than Jesus can take. He withstood the beatings and remained strong at the mock trials. He watched in silence as those he loved ran away. He did not retaliate when the insults were hurled nor did he scream when the nails pierced his wrists.

But when God turned his head, that was more than he could handle.

"My God!" The wail rises from parched lips. The holy heart is broken. The sinbearer screams as he wanders in the eternal wasteland. Out of the silent sky come the words screamed by all who walk in the desert of loneliness. "Why? Why did you abandon me?"

I can't understand it. I honestly cannot. Why did Jesus do it? Oh, I know, I know. I have heard the official answers. "To gratify the old law." "To fulfill prophecy." And these answers are right. They are. But there is something more here. Something very compassionate. Something yearning. Something personal.

What is it?

I may be wrong, but I keep thinking of the diary. "I feel abandoned," she wrote. "Who is going to love Judith Bucknell?" And I keep thinking of the parents of the dead child. Or the friend at the hospital bedside. Or the elderly in the nursing home. Or the orphans. Or the cancer ward.

I keep thinking of all the people who cast despairing eyes toward the dark heavens and cry "Why?"

And I imagine him. I imagine him listening. I picture his eyes misting and a pierced hand brushing away a tear. And although he may offer no answer, although he may solve no dilemma, although the question may freeze painfully in midair, he who also was once alone, understands.

CHAPTER 7

I THIRST

Later, knowing that all was now completed, and so that the Scripture would be fulfilled, Jesus said, "I am thirsty."

JOHN 19:28

I

I'm tired," he sighed. So he stopped. "You go on and get the food. I'll rest right here." He was tired. Bone-tired. His feet were hurting. His face was hot. The noon sun was sizzling. He wanted to rest. So he stopped at the well, waved on his disciples, stretched a bit, and sat down. But before he could close his eyes, here came a Samaritan woman. She was alone. Maybe it was the bags under her eyes or the way she stooped that made him forget how weary he was. "How strange that she should be here at midday."

II

"I'm sleepy." He stretched. He yawned. It had been a long day. The crowd had been large, so large that preaching on the beach had proved to be an occupational hazard, so he had taught from the bow of a fishing boat. And now night had fallen and Jesus was sleepy. "If you guys don't mind, I'm going to catch a few winks." So he did. On a cloud-covered night on the Sea of Galilee, God went to sleep. Someone rustled him up a pillow and he went to the boat's driest point and sacked out. So deep was his sleep, the thunder did not wake him. Nor did the tossing of the boat. Nor did the salty spray of the storm-blown waves. Only the screams of some breathless disciples could penetrate his slumber.

III

"I'm angry." He didn't have to say it; you could see it in his eyes. Face red. Blood vessels bulging. Fists clenched. "I ain't taking this no more!" And what was a temple became a one-sided barroom brawl. What was a normal day at the market became a one-man riot. And what was a smile on the face of the Son of God became a scowl. "Get out of here!" The only thing that flew higher than the tables were the doves flapping their way to freedom. An angry Messiah made his point: don't go making money off religion, or God will make hay of you!

We are indebted to Matthew, Mark, Luke, and John for choosing to include these tidbits of humanity. They didn't have to, you know. But they did—and at just the right times.

Just as his divinity is becoming unapproachable, just when his holiness is becoming untouchable, just when his perfection becomes inimitable, the phone rings and a voice whispers, "He was human. Don't forget. He had flesh."

Just at the right time we are reminded that the one to whom we pray knows our feelings. He knows temptation. He has felt discouraged. He has been hungry and sleepy and tired. He knows what we feel like when the alarm clock goes off. He knows what we feel like when our children want different things at the same time. He nods in understanding when we pray in anger. He is touched when we tell him there is more to do than can ever be done. He smiles when we confess our weariness.

But we are most indebted to John for choosing to include verse 28 of chapter 19. It reads simply:

"I'm thirsty."

That's not The Christ that's thirsty. That's the carpenter. And those are words of humanity in the midst of divinity.

This phrase messes up your sermon outline. The other six statements are more "in character." They are cries we would expect: forgiving sinners, promising paradise, caring for his mother, even the cry "My God, My God, why have you forsaken me" is one of power.

But, "I thirst"?

Just when we had it all figured out. Just when the cross was all packaged and defined. Just when the manuscript was finished. Just when we had invented all those nice clean "ation" words like sanctification, justification, propitiation, and purification. Just when we put our big golden cross on our big golden steeple, he reminds us that "the Word became flesh."

He wants us to remember that he, too, was human. He wants us to know that he, too, knew the drone of the humdrum and the weariness that comes with long days. He wants us to remember that our trailblazer didn't wear bulletproof vests or rubber gloves or an impenetrable suit of armor. No, he pioneered our salvation through the world that you and I face daily.

He is the King of Kings, the Lord of Lords, and the Word of Life. More than ever he is the Morning Star, the Horn of Salvation, and the Prince of Peace.

But there are some hours when we are restored by remembering that God became flesh and dwelt among us. Our Master knew what it meant to be a crucified carpenter who got thirsty.

CHAPTER 8

CREATIVE COMPASSION

"It is finished."
JOHN 19:30

I n the beginning God *created* the heavens and the earth."[1] That's what it says. "God *created* the heavens and the earth." It doesn't say, "God *made* the heavens and the earth." Nor does it say that he "xeroxed" the heavens and the earth. Or "built" or "developed" or "mass-produced." No, the word is "created."

And that one word says a lot. Creating is something far different than constructing. The difference is pretty obvious. Constructing something engages only the hands while creating something engages the heart and the soul.

You've probably noticed this in your own life. Think about something you've created. A painting perhaps. Or a song. Those lines of poetry you never showed to anyone. Or even the doghouse in the backyard.

How do you feel toward that creation? Good? I hope so. Proud? Even protective? You should. Part of you lives in that project. When you create something you are putting yourself into it.

It's far greater than an ordinary assignment or task; it's an expression of you!

Now, imagine God's creativity. Of all we don't know about the creation, there is one thing we do know—he did it with a smile. He must've had a blast. Painting the stripes on the zebra, hanging the stars in the sky, putting the gold in the sunset. What creativity! Stretching the neck of the giraffe, putting the flutter in the mockingbird's wings, planting the giggle in the hyena.

What a time he had. Like a whistling carpenter in his workshop, he loved every bit of it. He poured himself into the work. So intent was his creativity that he took a day off at the end of the week just to rest.

And then, as a finale to a brilliant performance, he made man. With his typical creative flair, he began with a useless mound of dirt and ended up with an invaluable species called a human. A human who had the unique honor to bear the stamp, "In His Image."

At this point in the story one would be tempted to jump and clap. "Bravo!" "Encore!" "Unmatchable!" "Beautiful!"

But the applause would be premature. The Divine Artist has yet to unveil his greatest creation.

As the story unfolds, a devil of a snake feeds man a line and an apple, and gullible Adam swallows them both. This one act of rebellion sets in motion a dramatic and erratic courtship between God and man. Though the characters and scenes change, the scenario repeats itself endlessly. God, still the compassionate Creator, woos his creation. Man, the creation, alternately reaches out in repentance and runs in rebellion.

It is within this simple script that God's creativity flourishes. If you thought he was imaginative with the sea and the stars, just wait until you read what he does to get his creation to listen to him!

For example:

> A ninety-year-old woman gets pregnant.
> A woman turns to salt.
> A flood blankets the earth.
> A bush burns (but doesn't burn up!).
> The Red Sea splits in two.
> The walls of Jericho fall.
> The sky rains fire.
> A donkey speaks.

Talk about special effects! But these acts, be they ever ingenious, still couldn't compare with what was to come.

Nearing the climax of the story, God, motivated by love and directed by divinity, surprised everyone. He became a man. In an untouchable mystery, he disguised himself as a carpenter and lived in a dusty Judaean village. Determined to prove his love for his creation, he walked incognito through his own world. His callused hands touched wounds and his compassionate words touched hearts. He became one of us.

Have you ever seen such determination? Have you ever witnessed such a desire to communicate? If one thing didn't work, he'd try another. If one approach failed, he'd try a new one. His mind never stopped. "In the past God spoke . . . at *many* times and in *various* ways," writes the author of Hebrews, "but in these last days he has spoken to us by his Son."[2]

But as beautiful as this act of incarnation was, it was not the zenith. Like a master painter God reserved his masterpiece until the end. All the earlier acts of love had been leading to this one. The angels hushed and the heavens paused to witness the finale. God unveils the canvas and the ultimate act of creative compassion is revealed.

God on a cross.

The Creator being sacrificed for the creation. God convincing man once and for all that forgiveness still follows failure.

I wonder if, while on the cross, the Creator allowed his thoughts to wander back to the beginning. One wonders if he allowed the myriad of faces and acts to parade in his memory. Did he reminisce about the creation of the sky and sea? Did he relive the conversations with Abraham and Moses? Did he remember the plagues and the promises, the wilderness and the wanderings? We don't know.

We do know, however, what he said.

"It is finished."

The mission was finished. All that the master painter needed to do was done and was done in splendor. His creation could now come home.

"It is finished!" he cried.

And the great Creator went home.

(He's not resting, though. Word has it that his tireless hands are preparing a city so glorious that even the angels get goosebumps upon seeing it. Considering what he has done so far, that is one creation I plan to see.)

CHAPTER 9

IT IS FINISHED

"It is finished."
JOHN 19:30

Several years ago, Paul Simon and Art Garfunkel enchanted us all with the song of a poor boy who went to New York on a dream and fell victim to the harsh life of the city. Penniless, with only strangers as friends, he spent his days "laying low, seeking out the poorer quarters where the ragged people go, looking for the places only they would know."[1]

It's easy to picture this young lad, dirty face and worn clothes, looking for work and finding none. He trudges the sidewalks and battles the cold, and dreams of going somewhere "where the New York City winters aren't bleeding me, leading me home."

He entertains thoughts of quitting. Going home. Giving up—something he never thought he would do.

But just when he picks up the towel to throw it into the ring he encounters a boxer. Remember these words?

In the clearing stands a boxer and a fighter by his trade, and he carries a reminder of every blow that laid him down or cut him till he cried out in his anger and his shame—'I am leaving, I am leaving!' but the fighter still remains.[2]

"The fighter still remains." There is something magnetic in that phrase. It rings with a trueness.

Those who can remain like the boxer are a rare breed. I don't necessarily mean win, I just mean remain. Hang in there. Finish. Stick to it until it is done. But unfortunately, very few of us do that. Our human tendency is to quit too soon. Our human tendency is to stop before we cross the finish line.

Our inability to finish what we start is seen in the smallest of things:

> A partly mowed lawn.
> A half-read book.
> Letters begun but never completed.
> An abandoned diet.
> A car up on blocks.

Or, it shows up in life's most painful areas:

> An abandoned child.
> A cold faith.
> A job hopper.
> A wrecked marriage.
> An unevangelized world.

Am I touching some painful sores? Any chance I'm addressing someone who is considering giving up? If I am, I want to encourage you to remain. I want to encourage you to remember Jesus' determination on the cross.

Jesus didn't quit. But don't think for one minute that he wasn't tempted to. Watch him wince as he hears his apostles backbite and quarrel. Look at him weep as he sits at Lazarus's tomb or hear him wail as he claws the ground of Gethsemane.

Did he ever want to quit? You bet.

That's why his words are so splendid.

"It is finished."

Stop and listen. Can you imagine the cry from the cross? The sky is dark. The other two victims are moaning. The jeering mouths are silent. Perhaps there is thunder. Perhaps there is weeping. Perhaps there is silence. Then Jesus draws in a deep breath, pushes his feet down on that Roman nail, and cries, "It is finished!"

What was finished?

The history-long plan of redeeming man was finished. The message of God to man was finished. The works done by Jesus as a man on earth were finished. The task of selecting and training ambassadors was finished. The job was finished. The song had been sung. The blood had been poured. The sacrifice had been made. The sting of death had been removed. It was over.

A cry of defeat? Hardly. Had his hands not been fastened down I dare say that a triumphant fist would have punched the dark sky. No, this is no cry of despair. It is a cry of completion. A cry of victory. A cry of fulfillment. Yes, even a cry of relief.

The fighter remained. And thank God that he did. Thank God that he endured.

Are you close to quitting? Please don't do it. Are you discouraged as a parent? Hang in there. Are you weary with doing good? Do just a little more. Are you pessimistic about your job? Roll up your sleeves and go at it again. No communication in your marriage? Give it one more shot. Can't resist temptation? Accept God's forgiveness and go one more round. Is your day framed with sorrow and disappointment? Are your tomorrows turning into nevers? Is hope a forgotten word?

Remember, a finisher is not one with no wounds or weariness.

Quite to the contrary, he, like the boxer, is scarred and bloody. Mother Teresa is credited with saying, "God didn't call us to be successful, just faithful." The fighter, like our Master, is pierced and full of pain. He, like Paul, may even be bound and beaten. But he remains.

The Land of Promise, says Jesus, awaits those who endure.[3] It is not just for those who make the victory laps or drink champagne. No sir. The Land of Promise is for those who simply remain to the end.

Let's endure.

Listen to this chorus of verses designed to give us staying power:

Consider it pure joy, my brothers, whenever you face trials of many kinds, because you know that the testing of your faith develops perseverance.[4]

Therefore lift your drooping hands and strengthen your weak knees, and make straight paths for your feet, so that what is lame may not be put out of joint but rather be healed.[5]

Let us not become weary in doing good, for at the proper time we will reap a harvest if we do not give up.[6]

I have fought the good fight, I have finished the race, I have kept the faith. Now there is in store for me the crown of righteousness, which the Lord, the righteous Judge, will award to me on that day—and not only to me, but also to all who have longed for his appearing.[7]

Blessed is the man who perseveres under trial, because when he has stood the test, he will receive the crown of life that God has promised to those who love him.[8]

Thank you, Paul Simon. Thank you, apostle Paul. Thank you, apostle James. But most of all, thank you, Lord Jesus, for teaching us to remain, to endure, and in the end, to finish.

CHAPTER 10

TAKE ME HOME

"Father, into your hands I commit my spirit."
LUKE 23:46

Were it a war—this would be the aftermath.
Were it a symphony—this would be the second
between the final note and the first applause.
Were it a journey—this would be the sight of home.
Were it a storm—this would be the sun, piercing the clouds.
But it wasn't. It was a Messiah. And this was a sigh of joy.

"Father!" (The voice is hoarse.)
The voice that called forth the dead,
the voice that taught the willing,
the voice that screamed at God,
now says, "Father!" "Father."

The two are again one.
The abandoned is now found.
The schism is now bridged.

"Father." He smiles weakly. "It's over."
Satan's vultures have been scattered.
Hell's demons have been jailed.
Death has been damned.
The sun is out,
The Son is out.

It's over.
An angel sighs. A star wipes away a tear.

"Take me home."
Yes, take him home.
Take this prince to his king.
Take this son to his father.
Take this pilgrim to his home.
(He deserves a rest.)

"Take me home."
Come ten thousand angels! Come and take this wounded
    troubadour to
the cradle of his Father's arms!

Farewell manger's infant.
Bless You holy ambassador.
Go Home death slayer.
Rest well sweet soldier.

The battle is over.

PART TWO

THE CROSS:

ITS WITNESSES

CHAPTER 11

WHO WOULD HAVE BELIEVED?

I t's Friday morning. The news is blazing across the Jerusalem streets like a West Texas brush fire. "The Nazarene is being executed!" From Solomon's Porch to the Golden Gate people are passing the word. "Have you heard? They've got the Galilean." "I knew he would go too far." "They've got him? I don't believe it!" "They say one of his own men turned him in."

Nicodemus is about to go AWOL.
Graves are about to pop open.
An earthquake is about to shake the city.
The temple curtains are about to be torn in two.
Shock, bewilderment, confusion.

A few weep. A few smile. A few walk up the hill to watch the spectacle. A few are irritated that the sanctity of the Passover is being violated by a bunch of social activists. Someone wonders aloud if this was the same man who was celebrated just a few days ago on a carpet of palm leaves. "A lot can happen in seven days," he comments.

A lot can happen in just one day.

Just ask Mary. Who could have convinced this mother

yesterday that today would find her a few feet from the torn body of her son? And who could have convinced John on Thursday that he was twenty-four hours away from anointing the corpse of his hero? And Pilate? Who could have convinced Pilate that he was about to pass judgment on the Son of God!

A lot can happen in twenty-four hours.

Peter can tell you. If you had told this proud, devoted disciple yesterday that this morning would find him in the pit of guilt and shame, he would have proclaimed his loyalty. Or the other ten apostles can tell you. For them the same twenty-four hours brought both boasting and betrayal. And Judas . . . oh, pitiful Judas! Yesterday he was determined and defiant. This morning he is dead at his own belt. His dangling body eclipses the morning sun.

No one has been left untouched. No one.

The immensity of the Nazarene's execution makes it impossible to ignore. See the women arguing on the street corner? Lay odds that the subject is the Nazarene. Those two women at the market? They are giving their opinion on the self-proclaimed Messiah. The countless pilgrims who are entering Jerusalem for the Passover? They will go home with a spellbinding story of the "teacher who was raised from the dead." Everybody has an opinion. Everyone is choosing a side. You can't be neutral on an issue like this one. Apathy? Not this time. It's one side or the other. All have to choose.

And choose they did.

For every cunning Caiaphas there was a daring Nicodemus. For every cynical Herod there was a questioning Pilate. For every pot-mouthed thief there was a truth-seeking one. For every turncoat Judas there was a faithful John.

There was something about the crucifixion that made every

witness either step toward it or away from it. It simultaneously compelled and repelled.

And today, two thousand years later, the same is true. It's the watershed. It's the Continental Divide. It's Normandy. And you are either on one side or the other. A choice is demanded. We can do what we want with the cross. We can examine its history. We can study its theology. We can reflect upon its prophecies. Yet the one thing we can't do is walk away in neutral. No fence sitting is permitted. The cross, in its absurd splendor, doesn't allow that. That is one luxury that God, in his awful mercy, doesn't permit.

On which side are you?

CHAPTER 12

FACES IN THE CROWD

Two types of people were touched by the cross: those touched by choice and those touched by chance. Among the latter, some intriguing tales are still told.

I

Take Malchus, for example. As a servant of the high priest, he was only doing his job at the Garden. Yet, this routine raid would have been his last if he had not been quick to duck. The torches gave just enough light for him to see the flash of the sword and "swoosh!" Malchus leans back enough to save his neck but not his ear. Peter gets a rebuke and Malchus gets a healing touch, and the event is history.

History, that is, to everyone but Malchus. Had it not been for the telltale bloodstain on his cloak, he might have awakened the next morning talking about a crazy dream he'd had. Some believe that Malchus was later numbered among the believers at Jerusalem. We don't know for sure. But we can be sure of one thing: from that night on, whenever Malchus would hear people talk about the carpenter who rose from the dead, he wouldn't scoff. No, he'd tug at his earlobe and know that it was possible.

II

It happened too fast. One minute Barabbas was in his cell on death row playing tic-tac-toe on the dirt walls, and the next he was outside squinting his eyes at the bright sun.

"You're free to go."

Barabbas scratches his beard. "What?"

"You're free. They took the Nazarene instead of you."

Barabbas has often been compared to humanity, and rightly so. In many ways he stands for us: a prisoner who was freed because someone he had never seen took his place.

But I think Barabbas was probably smarter than we are in one respect.

As far as we know, he took his sudden freedom for what it was, an undeserved gift. Someone tossed him a life preserver and he grabbed it, no questions asked. You couldn't imagine him pulling some of our stunts. We take our free gift and try to earn it or diagnose it or pay for it instead of simply saying "thank you" and accepting it.

Ironic as it may appear, one of the hardest things to do is to be saved by grace. There's something in us that reacts to God's free gift. We have some weird compulsion to create laws, systems, and regulations that will make us "worthy" of our gift.

Why do we do that? The only reason I can figure is pride. To accept grace means to accept its necessity, and most folks don't like to do that. To accept grace also means that one realizes his despair, and most people aren't too keen on doing that either.

Barabbas, though, knew better. Hopelessly stranded on death row, he wasn't about to balk at a granted stay of execution. Maybe he didn't understand mercy and surely he didn't deserve it, but he wasn't about to refuse it. We might do well to realize that our plight isn't too different than that of Barabbas's. We, too, are prisoners with no chance for appeal. But why some prefer to stay in prison while the cell door has been unlocked is a mystery worth pondering.

III

If it is true that a picture paints a thousand words, then there was a Roman centurion who got a dictionary full. All he did was see Jesus suffer. He never heard him preach or saw him heal or followed him through the crowds. He never witnessed him still the wind; he only witnessed the way he died. But that was all it took to cause this weather-worn soldier to take a giant step in faith. "Surely this was a righteous man."[1]

That says a lot, doesn't it? It says the rubber of faith meets the road of reality under hardship. It says the trueness of one's belief is revealed in pain. Genuineness and character are unveiled in misfortune. Faith is at its best, not in three-piece suits on Sunday mornings or at V.B.S. on summer days, but at hospital bedsides, cancer wards, and cemeteries.

Maybe that's what moved this old, crusty soldier. Serenity in suffering is a stirring testimony. Anybody can preach a sermon on a mount surrounded by daisies. But only one with a gut full of faith can *live* a sermon on a mountain of pain.

CHAPTER 13

WELL . . .
ALMOST

*A*lmost. It's a sad word in any man's dictionary. "Almost."
It runs herd with "nearly," "next time," "if only," and "just
about." It's a word that smacks of missed opportunities,
aborted efforts, and fumbled chances. It's honorable mention,
right field, on the bench, runner-up, and burnt cookies.

Almost. The one that got away. The sale that nearly closed.
The gamble that almost paid off. Almost.

How many people do you know whose claim to fame is an
almost?

"Did I ever tell you about the time I almost was selected as the
Employee of the Year?"

"They say he almost made the big leagues."

"I caught a catfish that was taller than me! Well . . . almost."

As long as there have been people, there have been almosts.
People who *almost* won the battle, who *almost* climbed the mountain, who *almost* found the treasure.

One of the most famous "almost's" is found in the Bible.
Pilate. Yet, what he missed was far more significant than a catfish
or an award.

He almost performed what would have been history's greatest
act of mercy. He almost pardoned the Prince of Peace. He almost

released the Son of God. He almost opted to acquit the Christ. Almost. He had the power. He had the choice. He wore the signet ring. The option to free God's Son was his . . . and he did it . . . almost.

Almost. How many times do these six ugly letters find their way into despairing epitaphs?

"He almost got it together."

"She almost chose not to leave him."

"They almost tried one more time."

"We almost worked it out."

"He almost became a Christian."

What is it that makes *almost* such a potent word? Why is there such a wide gap between "he almost" and "he did"?

In the case of Pilate, we don't have to look far to find an answer. It is Dr. Luke's acute commentary in chapter 23 that provides the reason. Let's tune in at verse 22:

A third time he [Pilate] said to them [the crowd], "Why, what evil has he done? I have found in him no crime deserving death; I will therefore chastise him and release him." But they were urgent, demanding with loud cries that he should be crucified. *And their voices prevailed.* (RSV italics mine)

You're right, Luke. *Their* voices prevailed. And, as a result, Pilate's pride prevailed. Pilate's fear prevailed. Pilate's power-hunger prevailed.

"Their" voices were not the only voices, you know. There were at least three others Pilate could have heard.

He could have heard the voice of Jesus. Pilate stood eye to eye with him. Five times he postponed the decision hoping to gratify the mob with policies or lashings.[1] Yet Jesus was always sent back

56

to him. Three times he stood eye to eye with this compelling Nazarene who had come to reveal the truth. "What is truth?" Pilate asked rhetorically (or was it honestly?). Jesus' silence was much louder than the crowd's demands. But Pilate didn't listen.

He could have heard the voice of his wife. She pleaded with him to "have nothing to do with that righteous man for I have suffered much over him today in a dream."[2] One has to pause and wonder about the origin of such a dream that would cause a lady of purple to call a small-town Galilean righteous. But Pilate didn't.

Or he could have heard his own voice. Surely he could see through the facade. "Ananias, Caiaphas, cut the phony allegiance, you slobs; I know where your interests are." Surely his conscience was speaking to him. "There is nothing wrong with this man. A bit mysterious maybe, but that's no reason to string him up."

He could have heard other voices. But he didn't. He almost did. But he didn't. Satan's voices prevailed.

His voice often does prevail. Have you heard his wooings?

"One time won't hurt."

"She'll never know."

"Other people do much worse things."

"At least you're not being hypocritical."

His rhetoric of rationalization never ends. The father of lies croons and woos like a traveling peddler, promising the moon and delivering disaster. "Step right up. Taste my brew of pleasure and sing my song of sensuality. After all, who knows about tomorrow?"

God, meanwhile, never enters a shouting match with Satan. Truth need not scream. He stands permanently, quietly pleading, ever present. No tricks, no side shows, no temptations, just open proof.

People's reactions vary. Some flow immediately to the peddler of poison. Others turn quickly to the Prince of Peace. Most of us, however, are caught somewhere in between, lingering on the edge of Satan's crowd yet hovering within earshot of the message of God.

Pilate learned the hard way that this stance of "almost" is suicidal. The other voices will win. Their lure is too strong. Their call too compelling. And Pilate also learned that there is no darker hell than the one of remorse. Washing your hands a thousand times won't free you from the guilt of an opportunity ignored. It's one thing to forgive yourself for something you did. It is something else to try to forgive yourself for something that you might have done, but didn't.

Jesus knew that all along. For our own good, he demanded and demands absolute obedience. He never has had room for "almost" in his vocabulary. You are either with him or against him. With Jesus "nearly" has to become "certainly." "Sometimes" has to become "always." "If only" has to become "regardless." And "next time" has to become "this time."

No, Jesus never had room for "almost" and he still doesn't. "Almost" may count in horseshoes and hand grenades, but with the Master, it is just as good as a "never."

THE TEN
WHO RAN

There is something striking in the simple fact that the disciples got together again. I mean, they had to have been embarrassed. As they sat gawking at each other that Sunday, they must have felt a bit foolish. Only two nights earlier the kitchen had gotten hot and they had taken off. It was as if someone threw a pan of scalding water on a bunch of cats. Bam! Off they scampered. They didn't stop until they had ducked into every available hole in Jerusalem.

Have you ever wondered what the disciples did that weekend? I have. I've wondered if any walked the streets or thought of going home. I've wondered what they said when people asked them what happened. "Uh . . . well . . . you see . . . " I've wondered if they stayed in pairs or small groups or alone. I've wondered what they thought, what they felt.

"We had to run! They would have killed us all!"

"I don't understand what happened."

"I let him down."

"He should have warned us!"

I have wondered where they were when the sky turned black. I've wondered, were they near the temple when the curtain ripped or near the cemetery when the graves opened? I've wondered if any of them even dared to sneak back up to the hillside and stand at the edge of the crowd and stare at the three silhouettes on the hill.

No one knows. Those hours are left to speculation. Any guilt, any fear, any doubts are all unrecorded.

But we do know one thing. They came back. Slowly. One by one. They came back. Matthew, Nathaniel, Andrew. They came out of hiding. Out of the shadows. James, Peter, Thaddeus. Perhaps some were already on their way home, back to Galilee, but they turned around and came back. Perhaps others had given up in disgust, but they changed their minds. Maybe others were flooded with shame, but still they returned.

One by one, they appeared at that same upper room. (They must have been relieved to see others already there.)

From all sections of the city they appeared. Too convicted to go home, yet too confused to go on. Each with a desperate hope that it had all been a nightmare or a cruel joke. Each hoping to find some kind of solace in numbers. They came back. Something in their nature refused to let them give up. Something in those words spoken by the Master pulled them back together.

It certainly was an awkward position in which to be. Caught on that uneven ground between failure and forgiveness. Suspended somewhere between "I can't believe I did it" and "I'll never do it again." Too ashamed to ask for forgiveness, yet too loyal to give up. Too guilty to be counted in, but too faithful to be counted out.

I guess we've all been there. I dare say that all of us have witnessed our sandcastle promises swept away by the pounding waves of panic and insecurity. I imagine that all of us have seen our words of promise and obedience ripped into ribbons by the chainsaw of fear and fright. And I haven't met a person yet who hasn't done the very thing he swore he would never do. We've all walked the streets of Jerusalem.

Why did the disciples come back? What made them return? Rumors of the resurrection? That had to be part of it. Those who walked next to Jesus had learned to expect him to do the unusual. They had seen him forgive a woman who had five husbands, honor a pint-size thief disguised as a tax collector, and love a streetwalker whose reputation would have brought blushes to the faces of Bonnie and Clyde. They'd seen him scare the devil out of some demoniacs and put the fear of God in some churchgoers. Traditions had tumbled, lepers had leaped, sinners had sung, Pharisees had fumed, multitudes had been moved. You just don't pack up the bags and go home after three years like that.

Maybe he really had risen from the dead.

But it was more than just rumors of an empty tomb that brought them back. There was something in their hearts that wouldn't let them live with their betrayal. For as responsible as their excuses were, they weren't good enough to erase the bottom line of the story: they had betrayed their Master. When Jesus needed them they had scampered. And now they were having to deal with the shame.

Seeking forgiveness, but not knowing where to look for it, they came back. They gravitated to that same upper room that contained the sweet memories of broken bread and symbolic wine. The simple fact that they returned says something about their leader. It says something about Jesus that those who knew him best could not stand to be in his disfavor. For the original twelve there were only two options—surrender or suicide. Yet, it also says something about Jesus that those who knew him best knew that although they had done exactly what they had promised they wouldn't, they could still find forgiveness.

So they came back. Each with a scrapbook full of memories and a thin thread of hope. Each knowing that it is all over, but in his heart hoping that the impossible will happen once more. "If I had just one more chance."

There they sat. What little conversation there is focuses on the rumors of an empty tomb. Someone sighs. Someone locks the door. Someone shuffles his feet.

And just when the gloom gets good and thick, just when their wishful thinking is falling victim to logic, just when someone says, "How I'd give my immortal soul to see him one more time," a familiar face walks through the wall.

My, what an ending. Or, better said, what a beginning! Don't miss the promise unveiled in this story. For those of us who, like the apostles, have turned and run when we should have stood and fought, this passage is pregnant with hope. A repentant heart is all he demands. Come out of the shadows! Be done with your hiding! A repentant heart is enough to summon the Son of God himself to walk through our walls of guilt and shame. He who forgave his followers stands ready to forgive the rest of us. All we have to do is come back.

No wonder they call him the Savior.

THE ONE
WHO STAYED

I've always perceived John as a fellow who viewed life simply. "Right is right and wrong is wrong, and things aren't nearly as complicated as we make them out to be."

For example, defining Jesus would be a challenge to the best of writers, but John handles the task with casual analogy. The Messiah, in a word, was "the Word." A walking message. A love letter. Be he a fiery verb or a tender adjective, he was, quite simply, a word.

And life? Well, life is divided into two sections, light and darkness. If you are in one, you are not in the other and vice versa.

Next question?

"The devil is the father of lies and the Messiah is the father of truth. God is love and you are in his corner if you love too. In fact, most problems are solved by loving one another."

And sometimes, when the theology gets a bit thick, John pauses just long enough to offer a word of explanation. Because of this patient storytelling, we have the classic commentary, "God so loved the world that he gave his one and only Son."

But I like John most for the way he loved Jesus. His relationship with Jesus was, again, rather simple. To John, Jesus was a good friend with a good heart and a good idea. A once-upon-a-time storyteller with a somewhere-over-the-rainbow promise.

One gets the impression that to John, Jesus was above all a loyal companion. Messiah? Yes. Son of God? Indeed. Miracle worker? That, too. But more than anything Jesus was a pal. Someone you could go camping with or bowling with or count the stars with.

Simple. To John, Jesus wasn't a treatise on social activism, nor was he a license for blowing up abortion clinics or living in a desert. Jesus was a friend.

Now what do you do with a friend? (Well, that's rather simple too.) You stick by him.

Maybe that is why John is the only one of the twelve who was at the cross. He came to say good-bye. By his own admission he hadn't quite put the pieces together yet. But that didn't really matter. As far as he was concerned, his closest friend was in trouble and he came to help.

"Can you take care of my mother?"

Of course. That's what friends are for.

John teaches us that the strongest relationship with Christ may not necessarily be a complicated one. He teaches us that the greatest webs of loyalty are spun, not with airtight theologies or foolproof philosophies, but with friendships; stubborn, selfless, joyful friendships.

After witnessing this stubborn love, we are left with a burning desire to have one like it. We are left feeling that if we could have been in anyone's sandals that day, we would have been in young John's and would have been the one to offer a smile of loyalty to this dear Lord.

CHAPTER 16

THE HILL
OF REGRET

While Jesus was climbing up the hill of Calvary, Judas was climbing another hill; the hill of regret. He walked it alone. Its trail was rock-strewn with shame and hurt. Its landscape was as barren as his soul. Thorns of remorse tore at his ankles and calves. The lips that had kissed a king were cracked with grief. And on his shoulders he bore a burden that bowed his back—his own failure.

Why Judas betrayed his master is really not important. Whether motivated by anger or greed, the end result was the same—regret.

A few years ago I visited the Supreme Court. As I sat in the visitor's chambers, I observed the splendor of the scene. The chief justice was flanked by his colleagues. Robed in honor, they were the apex of justice. They represented the efforts of countless minds through thousands of decades. Here was man's best effort to deal with his own failures.

How pointless it would be, I thought to myself, if I approached the bench and requested forgiveness for my mistakes. Forgiveness for talking back to my fifth grade teacher. Forgiveness for being disloyal to my friends. Forgiveness for pledging "I won't" on Sunday and saying "I will" on Monday.

Forgiveness for the countless hours I have spent wandering in society's gutters.

It would be pointless because the judge could do nothing. Maybe a few days in jail to appease my guilt, but forgiveness? It wasn't his to give. Maybe that's why so many of us spend so many hours on the hill of regret. We haven't found a way to forgive ourselves.

So up the hill we trudge. Weary, wounded hearts wrestling with unresolved mistakes. Sighs of anxiety. Tears of frustration. Words of rationalization. Moans of doubt. For some the pain is on the surface. For others the hurt is submerged, buried in a rarely touched substrata of bad memories. Parents, lovers, professionals. Some trying to forget, others trying to remember, all trying to cope. We walk silently in single file with leg irons of guilt. Paul was the man who posed the question that is on all of our lips, "Who will rescue me from this body of death?"[1]

At the trail's end there are two trees.

One is weathered and leafless. It is dead but still sturdy. Its bark is gone, leaving smooth wood bleached white by the years. Twigs and buds no longer sprout, only bare branches fork from the trunk. On the strongest of these branches is tied a hangman's noose. It was here that Judas dealt with his failure.

If only Judas had looked at the adjacent tree. It is also dead; its wood is also smooth. But there is no noose tied to its cross-beam. No more death on this tree. Once was enough. One death for all.

Those of us who have also betrayed Jesus know better than to be too hard on Judas for choosing the tree he did. To think that Jesus would really unburden our shoulders and unshackle our legs after all we've done to him is not easy to believe. In fact, it takes just as much faith to believe that Jesus can look past my betrayals as it does to believe that he rose from the dead. Both are just as miraculous.

What a pair, these two trees. Only a few feet from the tree of despair stands the tree of hope. Life so paradoxically close to death. Goodness within arm's reach of darkness. A hangman's noose and a life preserver swinging in the same shadow.

But here they stand.

One can't help but be a bit stunned by the inconceivability of it all. Why does Jesus stand on life's most barren hill and await me with outstretched, nail-pierced hands? A "crazy, holy grace" it has been called.[2] A type of grace that doesn't hold up to logic. But then I guess grace doesn't have to be logical. If it did, it wouldn't be grace.

CHAPTER 17

THE GOSPEL OF
THE SECOND CHANCE

I t was like discovering the prize in a box of Crackerjacks or
spotting a little pearl in a box of buttons or stumbling across
a ten dollar bill in a drawer full of envelopes.

It was small enough to overlook. Only two words. I know I'd
read that passage a hundred times. But I'd never seen it. Maybe I'd
passed over it in the excitement of the resurrection. Or, since
Mark's account of the resurrection is by far the briefest of the four,
maybe I'd just not paid too much attention. Or, maybe since it's
in the last chapter of the gospel, my weary eyes had always read
too quickly to note this little phrase.

But I won't miss it again. It's highlighted in yellow and under-
lined in red. You might want to do the same. Look in Mark, chapter 16. Read the first five verses about the women's surprise when
they find the stone moved to the side. Then feast on that beautiful phrase spoken by the angel, "He is not here, he is risen," but
don't pause for too long. Go a bit further. Get your pencil ready
and enjoy this jewel in the seventh verse (here it comes). The verse
reads like this: "But go, tell his disciples and Peter that he is going
before you to Galilee."

Did you see it? Read it again. (This time I italicized the
words.)

"But go, tell his disciples *and Peter* that he is going before you to Galilee."

Now tell me if that's not a hidden treasure.

If I might paraphrase the words, "Don't stay here, go tell the disciples," a pause, then a smile, "and especially tell Peter, that he is going before you to Galilee."

What a line. It's as if all of heaven had watched Peter fall—and it's as if all of heaven wanted to help him back up again. "Be sure and tell Peter that he's not left out. Tell him that one failure doesn't make a flop."

Whew!

No wonder they call it the gospel of the second chance.

Not many second chances exist in the world today. Just ask the kid who didn't make the little league team or the fellow who got the pink slip or the mother of three who got dumped for a "pretty little thing."

Not many second chances. Nowadays it's more like, "It's now or never." "Around here we don't tolerate incompetence." "Gotta get tough to get along." "Not much room at the top." "Three strikes and you're out." "It's a dog-eat-dog world!"

Jesus has a simple answer to our masochistic mania. "It's a dog-eat-dog world?" he would say. "Then don't live with the dogs." That makes sense doesn't it? Why let a bunch of other failures tell you how much of a failure you are?

Sure you can have a second chance.

Just ask Peter. One minute he felt lower than a snake's belly and the next minute he was the high hog at the trough. Even the angels wanted this distraught netcaster to know that it wasn't over. The message came loud and clear from the celestial Throne Room through the divine courier. "Be sure and tell Peter that he gets to bat again."

Those who know these types of things say that the Gospel of Mark is really the transcribed notes and dictated thoughts of Peter. If this is true, then it was Peter himself who included these two words! And if these really are his words, I can't help but imagine that the old fisherman had to brush away a tear and swallow a lump when he got to this point in the story.

It's not every day that you get a second chance. Peter must have known that. The next time he saw Jesus, he got so excited that he barely got his britches on before he jumped into the cold water of the Sea of Galilee. It was also enough, so they say, to cause this backwoods Galilean to carry the gospel of the second chance all the way to Rome where they killed him. If you've ever wondered what would cause a man to be willing to be crucified upside down, maybe now you know.

It's not every day that you find someone who will give you a second chance—much less someone who will give you a second chance every day.

But in Jesus, Peter found both.

CHAPTER 18

LEAVE ROOM
FOR THE MAGIC

Thomas. He defies tidy summary.

Oh, I know we've labeled him. Somewhere in some sermon somebody called him "Doubting Thomas." And the nickname stuck. And it's true, he *did* doubt. It's just that there was more to it than that. There was more to his questioning than a simple lack of faith. It was more due to a lack of imagination. You see it in more than just the resurrection story.

Consider, for instance, the time that Jesus was talking in all eloquence about the home he was going to prepare. Though the imagery wasn't easy for Thomas to grasp, he was doing his best. You can see his eyes filling his face as he tries to envision a big white house on St. Thomas Avenue. And just when Thomas is about to get the picture, Jesus assumes, "You know the way that I am going." Thomas blinks a time or two, looks around at the other blank faces, and then bursts out with candid aplomb, "Lord, we don't know where you are going, so how can we know the way?"[1] Thomas didn't mind speaking his mind. If you don't understand something, say so! His imagination would only stretch so far.

And then there was the time that Jesus told his disciples he was going to go be with Lazarus even though Lazarus was already

dead and buried. Thomas couldn't imagine what Jesus was referring to, but if Jesus was wanting to go back into the arena with
those Jews who had tried once before to stone him, Thomas
wasn't going to let him face them alone. So he patted his trusty
sidearm and said, "Let's die with him!"[2] Thomas had spent his life
waiting on the Messiah, and now that the Messiah was here,
Thomas was willing to spend his life for him. Not much imagination, but a lot of loyalty.

Perhaps it is this trait of loyalty that explains why Thomas
wasn't in the Upper Room when Jesus appeared to the other
apostles. You see, I think Thomas took the death of Jesus pretty
hard. Even though he couldn't quite comprehend all the
metaphors that Jesus at times employed, he was still willing to go
to the end with him. But he had never expected that the end
would come so abruptly and prematurely. As a result, Thomas was
left with a crossword puzzle full of unanswered riddles.

On the one hand, the idea of a resurrected Jesus was too far-
fetched for dogmatic Thomas. His limited creativity left little
room for magic or razzle dazzle. Besides, he wasn't about to set
himself up to be disappointed again. One disappointment was
enough, thank you. Yet, on the other hand, his loyalty made him
yearn to believe. As long as there was the slimmest thread of
hope, he wanted to be counted in.

His turmoil, then, came from a fusion between his lack of
imagination and his unwavering loyalty. He was too honest with
life to be gullible and yet was too loyal to Jesus to be unfaithful. In
the end, it was this realistic devotion that caused him to utter the
now famous condition, "Unless I see the nail marks in his hands
and put my fingers where the nails were, I will not believe it."[3]

So, I guess you could say that he did doubt. But it was a different kind of doubting that springs not from timidity or mistrust,

but from a reluctance to believe the impossible and a simple fear of being hurt twice.

Most of us are the same way, aren't we? In our world of budgets, long-range planning and computers, don't we find it hard to trust in the unbelievable? Don't most of us tend to scrutinize life behind furrowed brows and walk with cautious steps? It's hard for us to imagine that God can surprise us. To make a little room for miracles today, well, it's not sound thinking.

As a result, we, like Thomas, find it hard to believe that God can do the very thing that he is best at; replacing death with life. Our infertile imaginations bear little hope that the improbable will occur. We then, like Thomas, let our dreams fall victim to doubt.

We make the same mistake that Thomas made: we forget that "impossible" is one of God's favorite words.

How about you? How is your imagination these days? When was the last time you let some of your dreams elbow out your logic? When was the last time you imagined the unimaginable? When was the last time you dreamed of an entire world united in peace or all believers united in fellowship? When was the last time you dared dream of the day when every mouth will be fed and every nation dwell in peace? When was the last time you dreamed about every creature on earth hearing about the Messiah? Has it been awhile since you claimed God's promise to do "more than all we ask or imagine?"[4]

Though it went against every logical bone in his body, Thomas said he would believe if he could have just a little proof. And Jesus (who is ever so patient with our doubting), gave Thomas exactly what he requested. He extended his hands one more time. And was Thomas ever surprised. He did a double take, fell flat on his face, and cried, "My Lord and my God!"[5]

Jesus must have smiled.

He knew he had a winner in Thomas. Anytime you mix loyalty with a little imagination, you've got a man of God on your hands. A man who will die for a truth. Just look at Thomas. Legend has him hopping a freighter to India where they had to kill him to get him to quit talking about his home prepared in the world to come and his friend who came back from the dead.

A Candle
in the Cavern

They are coming as friends—secret friends—but friends nonetheless. "You can take him down now, soldier. I'll take care of him."

The afternoon sun is high as they stand silently on the hill. It is much quieter than it was earlier. Most of the crowd has left. The two thieves gasp and groan as they hang near death. A soldier leans a ladder against the center tree, ascends it and removes the stake that holds the beam to the upright part of the cross. Two of the other soldiers, glad that the day's work is nearing completion, assist with the heavy chore of laying the cypress crosspiece and body on the ground.

"Careful now," says Joseph.

The five-inch nails are wrenched from the hard wood, freeing the limp hands. The body that encased a Savior is lifted and laid on a large rock.

"He's yours," says the sentry. The cross is set aside, soon to be carried into the supply room until it is needed again.

The two are not accustomed to this type of work. Yet their hands move quickly to their tasks.

Joseph of Arimathea kneels behind the head of Jesus and tenderly wipes the wounded face. With a soft, wet cloth he cleans the blood that came in the garden, that came from the lashings and from the crown of thorns. With this done, he closes the eyes tight.

Nicodemus unrolls some linen sheeting that Joseph brought and places it on the rock beside the body. The two Jewish leaders lift the lifeless body of Jesus and set it on the linen. Parts of the body are now anointed with perfumed spices. As Nicodemus touches the cheeks of the Master with aloe, the emotion he has been containing escapes. His own tear falls on the face of the crucified King. He pauses to brush away another. The middle-aged Jew looks longingly at the young Galilean.

It's a bit ironic that the burial of Jesus should be conducted, not by those who had boasted they would never leave, but by two members of the Sanhedrin—two representatives of the religious group that killed the Messiah.

But then again, of all who were indebted to this broken body, none were as much as these two. Many had been freed from the deep pits of slavery and sickness. Many had been found in the darkest of tunnels, tunnels of perversion and death. But no tunnel was ever darker than the tunnel from which these two had been rescued.

The tunnel of religion.

They don't come any darker. Its caverns are many and its pitfalls are deep. Its subterranean stench reeks with the spirit of good intentions. Its endless maze of channels are cluttered with the disoriented. Its paths are covered with cracked wineskins and spilt wine.

You wouldn't want to carry a young faith into this tunnel. Young minds probing with questions quickly stale in the numbing darkness. Fresh insights are squelched in order to protect fragile traditions. Originality is discouraged. Curiosity is stifled. Priorities are reshuffled.

Christ had nothing but stinging words of rebuke for those who dwell in the caverns. "Hypocrites," he called them. Godless actors. Fence builders. Inflexible judges. Unauthorized hedge trimmers. Hair splitters. "Blind guides." "White-washed tombs." "Snakes." "Vipers." Bang! Bang! Bang! Jesus had no room for those who specialized in making religion a warlord, and faith a footrace. No room at all.[1]

Joseph and Nicodemus were tired of it too. They had seen it for themselves. They had seen the list of rules and regulations. They had watched the people tremble under unbearable burdens. They had heard the hours of senseless wrangling over legalistic details. They had worn the robes and sat at the places of honor and seen the Word of God be made void. They had seen religion become the crutch that cripples.

And they wanted out.

It was a sizable risk. The high society of Jerusalem wasn't going to look too kindly on two of their religious leaders burying a revolutionist. But for Joseph and Nicodemus the choice was obvious. The stories this young preacher from Nazareth told rang with the truth that they had never heard in the cavern. And, besides, they'd much rather save their souls than their skin.

So they lifted the body slowly and carried it to the unused tomb. In so doing, they lit a candle in the cavern.

Supposing these two have been observing the religious world during the last two thousand years, they have probably found things to be not too terribly different. There is still a sizable amount of evil that wears the robe of religion and uses the Bible as a sledgehammer. It is still fashionable to have sacred titles and wear holy chains. And it is still often the case that one has to find faith in spite of the church instead of in the church.

But they have also observed that just when the religious get too much religion and the righteous get too right, God finds somebody in the cavern who will light a candle. It was lit by Luther at Wittenburg, by Latimer in London, and by Tyndale in Germany. John Knox fanned the flame as a galley slave and Alexander Campbell did the same as a preacher.

It's not easy to light a candle in a dark cavern. Yet, those of us whose lives have been enlightened because of these courageous men are eternally grateful. And of all the acts of enlightenment, there is no doubt which one was the noblest.

"You can take him down now, soldier. I'll take care of him."

MINIATURE MESSENGERS

Befficiation we bid good-bye to those present at the cross, I have one more introduction to make. This introduction is very special.

There was one group in attendance that day whose role was critical. They didn't speak much, but they were there. Few noticed them, but that's not surprising. Their very nature is so silent they are often overlooked. In fact, the gospel writers scarcely gave them a reference. But we know they were there. They had to be. They had a job to do.

Yes, this representation did much more than witness the divine drama; they expressed it. They captured it. They displayed the despair of Peter; they betrayed the guilt of Pilate and unveiled the anguish of Judas. They transmitted John's confusion and translated Mary's compassion.

Their prime role, however, was with that of the Messiah. With utter delicacy and tenderness, they offered relief to his pain and expression to his yearning.

Who am I describing? You may be surprised.

Tears.

Those tiny drops of humanity. Those round, wet balls of fluid that tumble from our eyes, creep down our cheeks, and splash on the floor of our hearts. They were there that day. They are always present at such times. They should be, that's their job. They are miniature messengers; on call twenty-four hours a day to substitute for crippled words. They drip, drop, and pour from the corner of our souls, carrying with them the deepest emotions we possess. They tumble down our faces with announcements that range from the most blissful joy to darkest despair.

The principle is simple; when words are most empty, tears are most apt.

A tearstain on a letter says much more than the sum of all its words. A tear falling on a casket says what a spoken farewell never could. What summons a mother's compassion and concern more quickly than a tear on a child's cheek? What gives more support than a sympathetic tear on the face of a friend?

Words failed the day the Savior was slain. They failed miserably. What words could have been uttered? What phrases could have possibly expressed the feelings of those involved?

That task, my friend, was left for the tears.

What do you do when words won't come? When all the nouns and verbs lay deflated at your feet, with what do you communicate? When even the loftiest statements stumble, what do you do? Are you one of the fortunate who isn't ashamed to let a tear take over? Can you be so happy that your eyes water and your throat swells? Can you be so proud that your pupils blur and your vision mists? And in sorrow, do you let your tears decompress that tight chest and untie that knot in your throat?

Or do you reroute your tears and let them only fall on the inside?

Not many of us are good at showing our feelings, you know. Especially us fellows. Oh, we can yell and curse and smoke, yes sir!

But tears? "Save those for the weak-kneed and timid. I've got a world to conquer!"

We would do well, guys, to pause and look at the tearstained faces that appear at the cross.

Peter. The burly fisherman. Strong enough to yank a full net out of the sea. Brave enough to weather the toughest storm. The man who only hours before had bared his sword against the entire Roman guard. But now look at him. Weeping, no . . . *wailing*. Huddled in a corner with his face hidden in his callused hands. Would a real man be doing this? Admitting his fault? Confessing his failure? Begging forgiveness? Or would a real man bottle it up . . . justify it . . . rationalize it . . . keep a "stiff upper lip" and stand his ground? Has Peter lost his manhood? We know better don't we? Maybe he's less a man of the world, but less a man of God? No way.

And John, look at his tears. His face swollen with sorrow as he stands eye-level with the bloody feet of his Master. Is his emotion a lack of courage? Is his despair a lack of guts?

And the tears of Jesus. They came in the garden. I'm sure they came on the cross. Are they a sign of weakness? Do those stains on his cheeks mean he had no fire in his belly or grit in his gut?

Of course not.

Here's the point. It's not just tears that are the issue, it's what they represent. They represent the heart, the spirit, and the soul of a person. To put a lock and key on your emotions is to bury part of your Christlikeness!

Especially when you come to Calvary.

You can't go to the cross with just your head and not your heart. It doesn't work that way. Calvary is not a mental trip. It's not an intellectual exercise. It's not a divine calculation or a cold theological principle.

It's a heart-splitting hour of emotion.

Don't walk away from it dry-eyed and unstirred. Don't just straighten your tie and clear your throat. Don't allow yourself to descend Calvary cool and collected.

Please . . . pause. Look again.

Those are nails in those hands.

That's *God* on that cross.

It's us who put him there.

Peter knew it. John knew it. Mary knew it.

They knew a great price was being paid. They knew who really pierced his side. They also somehow knew that history was being remade.

That's why they wept.

They *saw* the Savior.

God, may we never be so "educated," may we never be so "mature," may we never be so "religious" that we can see your passion without tears.

PART THREE

THE CROSS:

ITS WISDOM

ALIVE!

Road. Dark. Stars. Shadows. Four. Sandals. Robes. Quiet. Suspense. Grove. Trees. Alone. Questions. Anguish. "Father!" Sweat. God. Man. God-Man. Prostrate. Blood. "NO!" "Yes." Angels. Comfort.

Footsteps. Torches. Voices. Romans. Surprise. Swords. Kiss. Confusion. Betrayal. Fearful. Run! Bound. Wrists. Marching.

Courtyard. Priests. Lamps. Sanhedrin. Caiaphas. Sneer. Silk. Arrogance. Beard. Plotting. Barefoot. Rope. Calm. Shove. Kick. Annas. Indignant. Messiah? Trial. Nazarene. Confident. Question. Answer. Punch!

Peter. "Me?" Rooster. Thrice. Guilt.

Proceedings. Court. Rejection. Prosecute. Weary. Pale. Witnesses. Liars. Inconsistent. Silence. Stares. "Blasphemer!" Anger. Waiting. Bruised. Dirty. Fatigued. Guards. Spit. Blindfold. Mocking. Blows. Fire. Twilight.

Sunrise. Golden. Jerusalem. Temple. Passover. Lambs. Lamb. Worshipers. Priests. Messiah. Hearing. Fraud. Prisoner. Waiting. Standing. Shifting. Strategy. "Pilate!" Trap. Murmurs. Exit.

Stirring. Parade. Crowd. Swell. Romans. Pilate. Toga. Annoyed. Nervous. Officers. Tunics. Spears. Silence. "Charge?" "Blasphemy." Indifference. Ignore. (Wife. Dream.) Worry. Interview. Lips. Pain. Determined. "King?" "Heaven." "Truth."

"Truth?" Sarcasm. (Fear.) "Innocent!" Roar. Voices. "Galilean!" "Galilee?" "Herod!"

9:00 A.M. Marchers. Palace. Herod. Fox. Schemer. Paunchy. Crown. Cape. Scepter. Hall. Elegance. Silence. Manipulate. Useless. Vexed. Revile. Taunt. "King?" Robe. Theatrical. Cynical. Hateful. "Pilate!"

Marching. Uproar. Prisoner. Hushed. Pilate. "Innocent!" Bedlam. "Barabbas!" Riot. Despair. Christ. Bare. Rings. Wall. Back. Whip. Slash. Scourge. Tear. Bone. Moan. Flesh. Rhythm. Silence. Whip! Silence. Whip! Silence. Whip! Thorns. Stinging. Blind. Laughter. Jeering. Scepter. Slap. Governor. Distraught. (Almost.) Eyes. Jesus. Decision. Power. Freedom? Threats. Looks. Yelling. Weak. Basin. Water. Swayed. Compromise. Blood. Guilt.

Soldiers. Thieves. Crosspiece. Shoulder. Heavy. Beam. Heavy. Sun. Stagger. Incline. Houses. Shops. Faces. Mourners. Murmurs. Pilgrims. Women. Tumble. Cobblestone. Exhaustion. Gasping. Simon. Pathetic. Golgotha.

Skull. Calvary. Crosses. Execution. Death. Noon. Tears. Observers. Wails. Wine. Nude. Bruised. Swollen. Crossbeam. Sign. Ground. Nails. Pound. Pound. Pound. Pierced. Contorted. Thirst. Terrible. Grace. Writhing. Raised. Mounted. Hung. Suspended. Spasms. Heaving. Sarcasm. Sponge. Tears. Taunts. Forgiveness. Dice. Gambling. Darkness.

Absurdity.

Death. Life.

Pain. Peace.

Condemn. Promise.

Nowhere. Somewhere.

Him. Us.

"Father!" Robbers. Paradise. Wailing. Weeping. Stunned.

"Mother." Compassion. Darkness. "My God!" Afraid. Scapegoat. Wilderness. Vinegar. "Father." Silence. Sigh. Death. Relief.

Earthquake. Cemetery. Tombs. Bodies. Mystery. Curtain. Spear. Blood. Water. Spices. Linen. Tomb. Fear. Waiting. Despair. Stone. Mary. Running. Maybe? Peter. John. Belief. Enlightenment. Truth. Mankind. Alive. Alive. Alive!

OPEN ARMS

They aren't exactly what you'd call a list of "Who's Who in Purity and Sainthood." In fact, some of their antics and attitudes would make you think of the Saturday night crowd at the county jail. What few halos there are among this befuddled bunch could probably use a bit of straightening and polish. Yet, strange as it may seem it is this very humanness that makes these people refreshing. They are so refreshing that should you ever need a reminder of God's tolerance, you'd find it in these people. If you ever wonder how in the world God could use you to change the world, look at these people.

What people? The people God used to change history. A rag-bag of ne'er-do-wells and has-beens who found hope, not in their performance, but in God's proverbially open arms.

Let's start with Abraham. Though eulogized by Paul for his faith, this Father of a Nation wasn't without his weaknesses. He had a fibbing tongue that wouldn't stop! One time, in order to save his neck, he let the word get out that Sarah wasn't his wife but his sister, which was only half true.[1] And then, not long later, he did it again! "And there Abraham said of his wife Sarah, 'She is my sister.'"[2]

Twice he traded in his integrity for security. That's what you call confidence in God's promises? Can you build a nation on that kind of faith? God can. God took what was good and forgave what was bad and used "old forked tongue" to start a nation.

Another household name is Moses. Definitely one of history's greatest. But until he was eighty years old he looked like he wouldn't amount to much more than a once-upon-a-time prince turned outlaw. Would you choose a wanted murderer to lead a nation out of bondage? Would you call upon a fugitive to carry the Ten Commandments? God did. And he called him, of all places, right out of the sheep pasture. Called his name through a burning bush. Scared old Moses right out of his shoes! There, with knees knocking and "Who me?" written all over his face, Moses agreed to go back into the ring.

And what can you say about a fellow whose lust got so lusty that he got a woman pregnant, tried to blame it on her husband, had her husband killed, and then went on living like nothing ever happened? Well, you could say he was a man after God's own heart. David's track record left little to be desired, but his repentant spirit was unquestionable.

Then comes Jonah. God's ambassador to Nineveh. Jonah, however, had other ideas. He had no desire to go to that heathen city. So he hopped on another boat while God wasn't looking (or at least that's what Jonah thought). God put him in a whale's belly to bring him back to his senses. But even the whale couldn't stomach this missionary for too long. A good burp and Jonah went flying over the surf and landed big-eyed and repentant on the beach. (Which just goes to show that you can't keep a good man down.)

And on and on the stories go: Elijah, the prophet who pouted; Solomon, the king who knew too much; Jacob, the wheeler-dealer; Gomer, the prostitute; Sarah, the woman who giggled at God. One story after another of God using man's best and overcoming man's worst.

Even the genealogy of Jesus is salted with a dubious character or two—Tamar the adulteress, Rahab the harlot, and Bathsheba, who tended to take baths in questionable locations.

The reassuring lesson is clear. God used (and uses!) people to change the world. *People!* Not saints or superhumans or geniuses, but people. Crooks, creeps, lovers, and liars—he uses them all. And what they may lack in perfection, God makes up for in love.

Jesus later summarized God's stubborn love with a parable. He told about a teenager who decided that life at the farm was too slow for his tastes. So with pockets full of inheritance money, he set out to find the big time. What he found instead were hangovers, fair-weather friends, and long unemployment lines. When he had had just about as much of the pig's life as he could take, he swallowed his pride, dug his hands deep into his empty pockets, and began the long walk home; all the while rehearsing a speech that he planned to give to his father.

He never used it. Just when he got to the top of the hill, his father, who'd been waiting at the gate, saw him. The boy's words of apology were quickly muffled by the father's words of forgiveness. And the boy's weary body fell into his father's opened arms.

The same open arms welcomed him that had welcomed Abraham, Moses, David, and Jonah. No wagging fingers. No clenched fists. No "I told you so!" slaps or "Where have you been?" interrogations. No crossed arms. No black eyes or fat lips. No. Only sweet, open arms. If you ever wonder how God can use you to make a difference in your world, just look at those he has already used and take heart. Look at the forgiveness found in those open arms and take courage.

And, by the way, never were those arms opened so wide as they were on the Roman cross. One arm extending back into history and the other reaching into the future. An embrace of forgiveness offered for anyone who'll come. A hen gathering her chicks. A father receiving his own. A redeemer redeeming the world.

No wonder they call him the Savior.

CHAPTER 23

A Street Vendor Named Contentment

Ahhh . . . an hour of contentment. A precious moment of peace. A few minutes of relaxation. Each of us has a setting in which contentment pays a visit.

Early in the morning while the coffee is hot and everyone else is asleep.

Late at night as you kiss your six-year-old's sleepy eyes.

In a boat on a lake when memories of a life well lived are vivid.

In the companionship of a well-worn, dog-eared, even tear-stained Bible.

In the arms of a spouse.

At Thanksgiving dinner or sitting near the Christmas tree.

An hour of contentment. An hour when deadlines are forgotten and strivings have ceased. An hour when what we have overshadows what we want. An hour when we realize that a lifetime of blood-sweating and headhunting can't give us what the cross gave us in one day—a clean conscience and a new start.

But unfortunately, in our squirrel cages of schedules, contests, and side-glancing, hours like these are about as common as one-legged monkeys. In our world, contentment is a strange street vendor, roaming, looking for a home, but seldom finding an open door. This old salesman moves slowly from house to house, tapping on windows, knocking on doors, offering his wares: an hour of peace, a smile of acceptance, a sigh of relief. But his goods are seldom taken. We are too busy to be content. (Which is crazy, since the reason we kill ourselves today is because we think it will make us content tomorrow.)

"Not now, thank you. I've too much to do," we say. "Too many marks to be made, too many achievements to be achieved, too many dollars to be saved, too many promotions to be earned. And besides, if I'm content, someone might think I've lost my ambition."

So the street vendor named Contentment moves on. When I asked him why so few welcomed him into their homes, his answer left me convicted. "I charge a high price, you know. My fee is steep. I ask people to trade in their schedules, frustrations, and anxieties. I demand that they put a torch to their fourteen-hour days and sleepless nights. You'd think I'd have more buyers." He scratched his beard, then added pensively, "But people seem strangely proud of their ulcers and headaches."

Can I say something a bit personal? I'd like to give a testimony. A live one. I'm here to tell you that I welcomed this bearded friend into my living room this morning.

It wasn't easy.

My list of things was, for the most part, undone. My responsibilities were just as burdensome as ever. Calls to be made. Letters to be written. Checkbooks to be balanced.

But a funny thing happened on the way to the rat race that made me slip into neutral. Just as I got my sleeves rolled up, just as the old engine was starting to purr, just as I was getting up a good head of steam, my infant daughter, Jenna, needed to be held.

She had a stomachache. Mom was in the bath so it fell to Daddy to pick her up.

She's three weeks old today. At first I started trying to do things with one hand and hold her with the other. You're smiling. You've tried that too? Just when I realized that it was impossible, I also realized that it was not at all what I was wanting to do.

I sat down and held her tight little tummy against my chest. She began to relax. A big sigh escaped her lungs. Her whimpers became gurgles. She slid down my chest until her little ear was right on top of my heart. That's when her arms went limp and she fell asleep.

And that's when the street vendor knocked at my door.

Good-bye, schedule. See you later, routine. Come back tomorrow, deadlines . . . hello Contentment, come on in.

So here we sit, Contentment, my daughter, and I. Pen in hand, note pad on Jenna's back. She'll never remember this moment and I'll never forget it. The sweet fragrance of a moment captured fills the room. The taste of an opportunity seized sweetens my mouth. The sunlight of a lesson learned illuminates my understanding. This is one moment that didn't get away.

The tasks? They'll get done. The calls? They'll get made. The letters? They'll be written. And you know what? They'll get done with a smile.

I don't do this enough, but I'm going to do it more. In fact, I'm thinking of giving that street vendor a key to my door. "By the way, Contentment, what are you doing this afternoon?"

CHAPTER 24

CLOSE TO THE CROSS— BUT FAR FROM CHRIST

There was some dice-throwing that went on at the foot of the cross.

Imagine this scene. The soldiers are huddled in a circle, their eyes turned downward. The criminal above them is forgotten. They gamble for some used clothes. The tunic, the cloak, the sandals are all up for grabs. Each soldier lays his luck on the hard earth, hoping to expand his wardrobe at the expense of a cross-killed carpenter.

I've wondered what that scene must have looked like to Jesus. As he looked downward past his bloody feet at the circle of gamblers, what did he think? What emotions did he feel? He must have been amazed. Here are common soldiers witnessing the world's most uncommon event and they don't even know it. As far as they're concerned, it's just another Friday morning and he is just another criminal. "Come on, hurry up; it's my turn!"

"All right, all right—this throw is for the sandals."

Casting lots for the possessions of Christ. Heads ducked. Eyes downward. Cross forgotten.

The symbolism is striking. Do you see it?

It makes me think of us. The religious. Those who claim heritage at the cross. I'm thinking of all of us. Every believer in the land. The stuffy. The loose. The strict. The simple. Upper church. Lower church. "Spirit-filled." Millenialists. Evangelical. Political. Mystical. Literal. Cynical. Robes. Collars. Three-piece suits. Born-againers. Ameners.

I'm thinking of us.

I'm thinking that we aren't so unlike those soldiers. (I'm sorry to say.)

We, too, play games at the foot of the cross. We compete for members. We scramble for status. We deal out judgments and condemnations. Competition. Selfishness. Personal gain. It's all there. We don't like what the other did so we take the sandal we won and walk away in a huff.

So close to the timber yet so far from the blood.

We are so close to the world's most uncommon event, but we act like common crapshooters huddled in bickering groups and fighting over silly opinions.

How many pulpit hours have been wasted on preaching the trivial? How many churches have tumbled at the throes of miniscuity? How many leaders have saddled their pet peeves, drawn their swords of bitterness and launched into battle against brethren over issues that are not worth discussing?

So close to the cross but so far from the Christ.

We specialize in "I am right" rallies. We write books about what the other does wrong. We major in finding gossip and become experts in unveiling weaknesses. We split into little huddles and then, God forbid, we split again.

Another name. Another doctrine. Another "error." Another denomination. Another poker game. Our Lord must be amazed.

"Those selfish soldiers," we smirk with our thumbs in lapels. "They were so close to the cross and yet so far from the Christ." And yet, are we so different? Our divisions are so numerous that we can't be cataloged. There are so many offshoots that even the offshoots have shoots!

Now . . . really.

Are our differences that divisive? Are our opinions that obtrusive? Are our walls that wide? Is it *that* impossible to find a common cause?

"May they all be one," Jesus prayed.

One. Not one in groups of two thousand. But one in One. *One* church. *One* faith. *One* Lord. Not Baptist, not Methodist, not Adventist. Just Christians. No denominations. No hierarchies. No traditions. Just Christ.

Too idealistic? Impossible to achieve? I don't think so. Harder things have been done, you know. For example, once upon a tree, a Creator gave his life for his creation. Maybe all we need are a few hearts that are willing to follow suit.

What about you? Can you build a bridge? Toss a rope? Span a chasm? Pray for oneness? Can you be the soldier who snaps to his senses, jumps to his feet, and reminds the rest of us, "Hey, that's God on that cross!"

The similarity between the soldier's game and our game is scary. What did Jesus think? What does he think today? There is still dice-throwing going on. And it is at the foot of the cross.

CHAPTER 25

THE FOG OF
THE BROKEN HEART

The fog of the broken heart.

It's a dark fog that slyly imprisons the soul and refuses easy escape. It's a silent mist that eclipses the sun and beckons the darkness. It's a heavy cloud that honors no hour and respects no person. Depression, discouragement, disappointment, doubt . . . all are companions of this dreaded presence.

The fog of the broken heart disorients our life. It makes it hard to see the road. Dim your lights. Wipe off the windshield. Slow down. Do what you wish, nothing helps. When this fog encircles us, our vision is blocked and tomorrow is a forever away. When this billowy blackness envelopes us, the most earnest words of help and hope are but vacant phrases.

If you have ever been betrayed by a friend, you know what I mean. If you have ever been dumped by a spouse or abandoned by a parent, you have seen this fog. If you have ever placed a spade of dirt on a loved one's casket or kept vigil at a dear one's bedside, you, too, recognize this cloud.

If you have been in this fog, or are in it now, you can be sure of one thing—you are not alone. Even the saltiest of sea captains have lost their bearings because of the appearance of this unwanted cloud. Like the comedian said, "If broken hearts were commercials, we'd all be on TV."

Think back over the last two or three months. How many broken hearts did you encounter? How many wounded spirits did you witness? How many stories of tragedy did you read about?

My own reflection is sobering:

The woman who lost her husband and son in a freak car wreck.

The attractive mother of three who was abandoned by her husband.

The child who was hit and killed by a passing garbage truck as he was getting off the school bus. His mother who was waiting for him, witnessed the tragedy.

The parents who found their teenager dead in the forest behind their home. He had hung himself from a tree with his own belt.

The list goes on and on, doesn't it? Foggy tragedies. How they blind our vision and destroy our dreams. Forget any great hopes of reaching the world. Forget any plans of changing society. Forget any aspirations of moving mountains. Forget all that. Just help me make it through the night!

The suffering of the broken heart.

Go with me for a moment to witness what was perhaps the foggiest night in history. The scene is very simple; you'll recognize it quickly. A grove of twisted olive trees. Ground cluttered with large rocks. A low stone fence. A dark, dark night.

Now, look into the picture. Look closely through the shadowy foliage. See that person? See that solitary figure? What's he doing? Flat on the ground. Face stained with dirt and tears. Fists pounding the hard earth. Eyes wide with a stupor of fear. Hair matted with salty sweat. Is that blood on his forehead?

That's Jesus. Jesus in the Garden of Gethsemane.

Maybe you've seen the classic portrait of Christ in the garden. Kneeling beside a big rock. Snow-white robe. Hands peacefully folded in prayer. A look of serenity on his face. Halo over his head. A spotlight from heaven illuminating his golden-brown hair.

Now, I'm no artist, but I can tell you one thing. The man who painted that picture didn't use the gospel of Mark as a pattern. Look what Mark wrote about that painful night.

When they reached a place called Gethsemane, he said to his disciples, "Sit here while I pray." And he took Peter and James and John with him. Horror and dismay came over him, and he said to them, "My heart is ready to break with grief; stop here, and stay awake." Then he went forward a little, threw himself on the ground, and prayed that, if it were possible, this hour might pass him by. "Abba, Father," he said, "all things are possible to thee; take this cup away from me. Yet not what I will, but what thou wilt."

He came back and found them asleep; and he said to Peter, "Asleep, Simon? Were you not able to keep awake for one hour? Stay awake, all of you; and pray that you may be spared the test: the spirit is willing, but the flesh is weak." Once more he went away and prayed. On his return he found them asleep again, for their eyes were heavy; and they did not know how to answer him.

The third time he came and said to them, "Still sleeping?

Still taking your ease? Enough! The hour has come. The Son of Man is betrayed to sinful men. Up, let us go forward! My betrayer is upon us."[1]

Look at those phrases. *"Horror* and *dismay* came over him." "My heart is ready to *break* with grief." "He went a little forward and *threw* himself on the ground."

Does this look like the picture of a saintly Jesus resting in the palm of God? Hardly. Mark used black paint to describe this scene. We see an agonizing, straining, and struggling Jesus. We see a "man of sorrows."[2] We see a man struggling with fear, wrestling with commitments, and yearning for relief.

We see Jesus in the fog of a broken heart.

The writer of Hebrews would later pen, "During the days of Jesus' life on earth, he offered up prayers and petitions with *loud cries and tears* to the one who could save him from death."[3]

My, what a portrait! Jesus is in pain. Jesus is on the stage of fear. Jesus is cloaked, not in sainthood, but in humanity.

The next time the fog finds you, you might do well to remember Jesus in the garden. The next time you think that no one understands, reread the fourteenth chapter of Mark. The next time your self-pity convinces you that no one cares, pay a visit to Gethsemane. And the next time you wonder if God really perceives the pain that prevails on this dusty planet, listen to him pleading among the twisted trees.

Here's my point. Seeing God like this does wonders for our own suffering. God was never more human than at this hour. God was never nearer to us than when he hurt. The Incarnation was never so fulfilled as in the garden.

As a result, time spent in the fog of pain could be God's greatest gift. It could be the hour that we finally see our Maker. If it is true that in suffering God is most like man, maybe in our suffering we can see God like never before.

The next time you are called to suffer, pay attention. It may be the closest you'll ever get to God. Watch closely. It could very well be that the hand that extends itself to lead you out of the fog is a pierced one.

PÃO, SENHOR?

He couldn't have been over six years old. Dirty face, barefooted, torn T-shirt, matted hair. He wasn't too different from the other hundred thousand or so street orphans that roam Rio de Janeiro.

I was walking to get a cup of coffee at a nearby cafe when he came up behind me. With my thoughts somewhere between the task I had just finished and the class I was about to teach, I scarcely felt the tap, tap, tap on my hand. I stopped and turned. Seeing no one, I continued on my way. I'd only taken a few steps, however, when I felt another insistent tap, tap, tap. This time I stopped and looked downward. There he stood. His eyes were whiter because of his grubby cheeks and coal-black hair.

"Pão, senhor?" ("Bread, sir?")

Living in Brazil, one has daily opportunities to buy a candy bar or sandwich for these little outcasts. It's the least one can do. I told him to come with me and we entered the sidewalk cafe. "Coffee for me and something tasty for my little friend." The boy ran to the pastry counter and made his choice. Normally, these youngsters take the food and scamper back out into the street without a word. But this little fellow surprised me.

The cafe consisted of a long bar: one end for pastries and the other for coffee. As the boy was making his choice, I went to the other end of the bar and began drinking my coffee. Just as I was getting my derailed train of thought back on track, I saw him again. He was standing in the cafe entrance, on tiptoe, bread in hand, looking in at the people. "What's he doing?" I thought.

Then he saw me and scurried in my direction. He came and stood in front of me about eye-level with my belt buckle. The little Brazilian orphan looked up at the big American missionary, smiled a smile that would have stolen your heart and said, "Obrigado." (Thank you.) Then, nervously scratching the back of his ankle with his big toe, he added, *"Muito* obrigado." (Thank you very much.)

All of a sudden, I had a crazy craving to buy him the whole restaurant.

But before I could say anything, he turned and scampered out the door.

As I write this, I'm still standing at the coffee bar, my coffee is cold, and I'm late for my class. But I still feel the sensation that I felt half an hour ago. And I'm pondering this question: If I am so moved by a street orphan who says thank you for a piece of bread, how much more is God moved when I pause to thank him—really thank him—for saving my soul?

CHAPTER 27

PUPPIES, BUTTERFLIES, AND A SAVIOR

When I was ten years old, I had a puppy named Tina. You would have loved her. She was the perfect pet. An irresistible, pug-nosed Pekingese pup. One ear fell over and the other ear stood straight up. She never tired of playing and yet never got in the way.

Her mother died when she was born so the rearing of the puppy fell to me. I fed her milk from a doll bottle and used to sneak out at night to see if she was warm. I'll never forget the night I took her to bed with me only to have her mess on my pillow. We made quite a pair. My first brush with parenthood.

One day I went into the backyard to give Tina her dinner. I looked around and spotted her in a corner near the fence. She had cornered a butterfly (as much as a butterfly can be cornered) and was playfully yelping and jumping in the air trying to catch the butterfly in her mouth. Amused, I watched her for a few minutes and then called to her.

"Tina! Come here, girl! It's time to eat!"

What happened next surprised me. Tina stopped her playing

and looked at me. But instead of immediately scampering in my direction, she sat back on her haunches.

Then she tilted her head back toward the butterfly, looked back at me, then back to the butterfly, and then back to me. For the first time in her life, she had to make a decision.

Her "want to" longed to pursue the butterfly which tauntingly awaited her in midair. Her "should" knew she was supposed to obey her master. A classic struggle of the will: a war between the "want" and the "should." The same question that has faced every adult now faced my little puppy.

And do you know what she did? She chased the butterfly! Scurrying and barking, she ignored my call and chased that silly thing until it flew over the fence.

That is when the guilt hit.

She stopped at the fence for a long time, sitting back on her hind legs looking up in the air where the butterfly had made its exit. Slowly, the excitement of the chase was overshadowed by the guilt of disobedience.

She turned painfully and walked back to encounter her owner. (To be honest, I was a little miffed.) Her head was ducked as she regretfully trudged across the yard.

For the first time in her life, she felt guilty.

She had violated her "should" and had given in to her "want." My heart melted, however, and I called her name again. Sensing forgiveness, Tina darted into my hands. (I always was a softy.)

Now, I may be overdoing it a bit. I don't know if a dog can really feel guilty or not. But I do know a human can. And whether the sin is as slight as chasing a butterfly or as serious as sleeping with another man's wife, the effects are the same.

Guilt creeps in on cat's paws and steals whatever joy might have flickered in our eyes. Confidence is replaced by doubt, and honesty is elbowed out by rationalization. Exit peace. Enter turmoil. Just as the pleasure of indulgence ceases, the hunger for relief begins.

Our vision is shortsighted and our myopic life now has but one purpose—to find release for our guilt. Or as Paul questioned for all of us, "What a wretched man I am! Who will rescue me from this body of death?"[1]

That's not a new question. One hardly opens the Bible before he encounters humanity coping, or more frequently, failing to cope, with guilt. Adam and Eve's rebellion led to shame and hiding. Cain's jealousy led to murder and banishment. And before long, the entire human race was afflicted. Evil abounded and the people grew wicked. The heart of man grew so cold that he no longer sought relief for his callused conscience. And, in what has to be the most fearful Scripture in the Bible, God says that he was sorry that he had made man on earth.[2]

All of this from man's inability to cope with sin.

If only we had a guilt-kidney that would pass on our failures or a built-in eraser that would help us live with ourselves. But we don't. In fact, that is precisely the problem.

Man cannot cope with guilt alone.

When Adam was created, he was created without the ability to cope with guilt. Why? Because he was not made to make mistakes. But when he did, he had no way to deal with it. When God pursued him to help him, Adam covered his nakedness and hid in shame.

Man by himself cannot deal with his own guilt. He must have help from the outside. In order to forgive himself, he must have forgiveness from the one he has offended. Yet man is unworthy to ask God for forgiveness.

That, then, is the whole reason for the cross.

The cross did what sacrificed lambs could not do. It erased our sins, not for a year, but for eternity. The cross did what man could not do. It granted us the right to talk with, love, and even live with God.

You can't do that by yourself. I don't care how many worship services you attend or good deeds you do, your goodness is insufficient. You *can't* be good enough to deserve forgiveness. No one bats a thousand. No one bowls three hundred. No one. Not you, not me, not anyone.

That's why we have guilt in the world.

That's why we need a savior.

You can't forgive me for my sins nor can I forgive you for yours. Two kids in a mud puddle can't clean each other. They need someone clean. Someone spotless. We need someone clean too.

That's why we need a savior.

What my little puppy needed was exactly what you and I need—a master who would extend his hands and say, "Come on, that's okay." We don't need a master who will judge us on our performance, or we'll fall woefully short. Trying to make it to heaven on our own goodness is like trying to get to the moon on a moon beam; nice idea, but try it and see what happens.

Listen. Quit trying to quench your own guilt. You can't do it. There's no way. Not with a bottle of whiskey or perfect Sunday school attendance. Sorry. I don't care how bad you are. You can't be bad enough to forget it. And I don't care how good you are. You can't be good enough to overcome it.

You need a Savior.

GOD'S TESTIMONY

Though the little farm was only two hours away in mileage, it was at least a century away in time.

My friend, Sebastão, had invited me to his hometown of Marecá, a spot-in-the-road town about seventy miles from Rio de Janeiro. He was a twenty-six-year-old factory worker who had visited our congregation and was involved in a Bible study. Slow-talking, tall, gangly; this fellow was no city slicker. He was a bit too honest, simple, and quick to smile to have any roots in the urban jungle.

I welcomed the opportunity to see some of the Brazilian countryside. What I didn't know, however, was that I was about to learn a lesson on faith.

I could feel my neck muscles relax as we left Rio and her polluted war of traffic in the rearview mirror. My little VW sedan leaned in and out of the picturesque roads that wound through the hills. The scenery was not unlike bluegrass Kentucky; thick, rich green grass, generous valleys, friendly hillsides dotted with grazing Herefords.

Soon we pulled off the four-lane onto a two-lane; then, after a half dozen "bear rights" and "stay lefts" we emptied out onto a one-lane dirt road.

"Normally, I come by bus," Sebastão explained. "I usually have to walk this piece. A "piece" it was not. For at least another four miles we stirred up the rarely-driven-upon country dust. In the process we passed a younger fellow leading a mule that carried two churns of milk. "That's my cousin," Sebastão volunteered. "He comes by every morning at sunup with fresh milk." The thin road carried us through a myriad colors; the white-trunked eucalyptus trees sat like candles on a cake of dark green pasture. The Brazilian sky was brilliantly blue and the hills rustic and red.

"Stop here," I was instructed. I pulled to a stop in front of a big wooden gate suspended between two fence posts. "Just a second and I'll open the gate."

If I thought the road we had just taken was small, the one that led us from the gate to the house was invisible. I kept thinking how I needed a jeep as we bounded through the grass, slid under the bushes, crept between the trees, and finally appeared in a clearing next to an old stucco house.

Waiting for us was Sebastão's father, Senhor José. He certainly did not look his seventy plus years. Eyes shaded by an old straw hat, he smiled a toothless grin when he saw us. His barreled brown chest and narrow waist testified to thousands of hours of hoeing and planting. His flat bare feet were stained the color of the soil and his hands were crusty and thick.

"Good to have you," he welcomed. You could tell he meant it.

The little house made me think of pictures I'd seen of the United States during the Depression. Unlit kerosene lanterns (no electricity). Basins of water to wash up in (no running water). A wall lined with well-worn hoes, shovels, and picks (no modern equipment). The kitchen was a separate hut that sat next to the front door of the house. I was intrigued by the stove. It was made of hard, baked mud, molded in a long narrow piece about four feet long and three feet tall. A four or five inch trough ran down the center to hold the wood. The ever-present pots cooking the beans and rice straddled the hot trough. I felt a long way from Rio.

Senhor José took me on a tour through his segment of the world. For thirty-seven years he had plowed and tilled his two acres. It was obvious that he knew every hole and turn.

"I fed fourteen mouths off this land," he smiled, fingering a lettuce plant. "Where did you say you were from?"

"The U.S."

"What do you do here?"

I explained a bit about my work. He did not respond but led me over to a little creek where he sat on a rock and began undressing.

"Gonna take a bath, Pop?" Sebastão asked.

"Yep, it's Saturday."

"Well, we'll see you back at the house then."

Sebastão led me through a sugar cane patch where he cut a stalk, skinned it, and gave me a piece to eat. We made our way back to the house and sat down at the outdoor dinner table. The benches were worn smooth from decades of use.

About that time Senhor José appeared with clean trousers, hat removed, and hair wet.

Though we hadn't talked for half an hour, he renewed the conversation exactly where we had left it (you could tell he'd been thinking).

"A missionary, huh? Your job must be pretty easy."

"How's that?" I asked.

"I have no trouble believing in God. After I see what he has done on my little farm, year after year, it is easy to believe." He smiled another toothless grin and yelled to his wife to bring out some beans.

As we drove home, I couldn't help thinking about Senhor José. My, what a simple life. No traffic jams, airline schedules, or long lines. Far removed from Wall Street, IRS, and mortgages. Unacquainted with Johannine theology, Martin Luther, or Christian evidences.

I thought of his faith, his ability to believe, and his surprise that there were some who couldn't. I compared his faith with others I knew had more difficulty believing: a university student, a wealthy import-export man, an engineer. There was such a difference between José and the others.

His faith was rooted in the simple miracles that he witnessed every day:

A small seed becoming a towering tree.
A thin stalk pushing back the earth.
A rainbow arching in the midst of the thundercloud.

It was easy for him to believe. I can see why. Someone who witnesses God's daily display of majesty doesn't find the secret of Easter absurd. Someone who depends upon the mysteries of nature for his livelihood doesn't find it difficult to depend on an unseen God for his salvation.

"Nature," wrote Jonathan Edwards, "is God's greatest evangelist."

"Faith," wrote Paul, "does not rest in the wisdom of men, but in the power of God."[1]

"God's testimony," wrote David, "makes wise the simple."[2]

God's testimony. When was the last time you witnessed it? A stroll through knee-high grass in a green meadow. An hour listening to seagulls or looking at seashells on the beach. Or witnessing the shafts of sunlight brighten the snow on a crisp winter dawn.

Miracles that almost match the magnitude of the empty tomb happen all around us; we only have to pay attention.

The old Brazilian farmer gave me a time-tested principle to take home. He reminded me that there is a certain understanding of God on the cross that comes only with witnessing his daily testimony. There comes a time when we should lay down our pens and commentaries and step out of our offices and libraries. To really understand and believe in the miracle on the cross, we'd do well to witness God's miracles every day.

DYNAMITE
DECISIONS

I still chuckle when I think about the joke I heard about the game warden who got a quick lesson on fishing.

It seems he noticed how this one particular fellow named Sam consistently caught more fish than anyone else. Whereas the other guys would only catch three or four a day, Sam would come in off the lake with a boat full. Stringer after stringer was always packed with freshly caught trout.

The warden, curious, asked Sam his secret. The successful fisherman invited the game warden to accompany him and observe. So the next morning the two met at the dock and took off in Sam's boat. When they got to the middle of the lake, they stopped the boat and the warden sat back to see how it was done.

Sam's approach was simple. He took out a stick of dynamite, lit it, and threw it in the air. The explosion rocked the lake with such a force that dead fish immediately began to surface. Sam took out a net and started scooping them up.

Well, you can imagine the reaction of the game warden. When he recovered from the shock of it all, he began yelling at Sam. "You can't do this! I'll put you in jail, buddy! You will be paying every fine there is in the book!" Sam, meanwhile, set his net down and took out another stick of dynamite. He lit it and toed it in the lap of the game warden with these words, "Are you going to sit there all day complaining or are you going to fish?"

The poor warden was left with a fast decision to make. He was yanked, in one second, from an observer to a participant. A dynamite of a choice had to be made and be made quickly!

Life is like that. Few days go by without our coming face to face with an uninvited, unanticipated, yet unavoidable decision. Like a crashing snow bank, these decisions tumble upon us without warning. They disorientate and bewilder. Quick. Immediate. Sudden. No council, no study, no advice. Pow! All of a sudden you are hurled into the air of uncertainty and only instinct will determine if you will land on your feet.

Want a good example? Look at the three apostles in the garden. Sound asleep. Weary from a full meal and a full week, their eyelids too heavy, they are awakened by Jesus only to tumble back into dreamland. The last time, however, they were awakened by Jesus to clanging swords, bright torches, and loud voices.

"There he is!"

"Let's get him!"

A shout. A kiss. A shuffling of feet. A slight skirmish. All of a sudden it is decision time. No time to huddle. No time to pray. No time to meditate or consult friends. Decision.

Peter makes his. Out comes the sword. Off goes the ear. Jesus rebukes him. Now what?

Mark, who apparently was a young eyewitness, wrote these words, "Then everyone deserted him and fled."[1]

That's a nice way of saying they ran like scared mice. All of them? All of them. Even Peter? Yes, even Peter. James? Yes, James. John? John, his beloved one? Yes, John ran away too. They all did. The decision came upon them like a halloween ghost and they ran fast. The only thing that was moving faster than their feet was their pulse rate. All those words of loyalty and commitment were left behind in a cloud of dust.

But before we get too hard on these quick-footed followers, let's look at ourselves. Maybe you have been in the garden of decision a few times yourself. Has your loyalty ever been challenged? Have you ever passed by this trap door of the devil?

For the teenager it could be a joint being passed around the circle. For the business man it could be an offer to make a little cash "under the table." For the wife it could be a chance for her to give her "two bits" of juicy gossip. For the student it could be an opportunity to improve his grade while looking at his friend's quiz. For the husband it could mean an urge to lose his temper over his wife's spending. One minute we are in a calm boat on a lake talking about fishing, in the next we have a stick of dynamite in our hands.

More often than not, the end result is catastrophe. Rather than calmly defusing the bomb, we let it explode. We find ourselves doing the very thing we detest. The child in us lunges forward, uncontrolled and unrestrained, and the adult in us follows behind shaking his head.

Now, it doesn't have to be like that. Jesus didn't panic. He, too, heard the swords and saw the clubs, but he didn't lose his head. And it was his head that the Romans wanted!

In rereading the garden scene we can see why. One statement made by our master offers two basic tools for keeping our cool in the heat of a decision. "Watch and pray so that you will not fall into temptation."[2]

The first tool: "Watch." They don't come any more practical than that. Watch. Stay alert. Keep your eyes open. When you see sin coming, duck. When you anticipate an awkward encounter, turn around. When you sense temptation, go the other way.

All Jesus is saying is, "Pay attention." You know your weaknesses. You also know the situations in which your weaknesses are most vulnerable. *Stay out of those situations.* Back seats. Late hours. Night clubs. Poker games. Bridge parties. Movie theaters. Whatever it is that gives Satan a foothold in your life, stay away from it. Watch out!

Second tool: "Pray." Prayer isn't telling God anything new. There is not a sinner nor a saint who would surprise him. What prayer does is invite God to walk the shadowy pathways of life with us. Prayer is asking God to watch ahead for falling trees and tumbling boulders and to bring up the rear, guarding our backside from the poison darts of the devil.

"Watch and pray." Good advice. Let's take it. It could be the difference between a peaceful day on the lake and a stick of dynamite blowing up in our faces.

WHAT DID YOU EXPECT?

My first rub with expectations came when I was a red-headed, freckle-faced fourth grader. It all had to do with my first girlfriend, Marlene. Man, was I high on Marlene! She was the Queen's queen. She could turn my head and accelerate my pulse rate like no one else. She must have been part hypnotist, because when I was with her all I could do was grin. Stare and grin. No words. No dialogue. Just a gawking, drooling ten-year-old "in love."

Then one day she consented to "go with me" (or, in adult terms, be my girlfriend). Wow! Fireworks, music, stars. Strike up the band. "I'm yours, your Highness."

There was only one problem. I'd never had a girlfriend before. Maybe that's why a well-meaning friend gave me some advice during recess one day. "A boyfriend is supposed to do things for his girl."

"Like what?"

"Like walk her to class, dummy! Sit with her at the lunch table. That kind of stuff."

So that day at lunch, I waited at the cafeteria door for her to arrive. When she appeared, I gentlemanly took her books, extended my arm, and walked her to the lunch line. Prince Charles and Lady Diana never looked so eloquent.

All was fine and good until the next day after school. Her best friend came up to me and broke the news, "Marlene wants to break up." I was dumbfounded. "What for?" "Because you didn't sit with her at lunch today."

What had I done?

I had my first questions about women that day. I would later learn, however, that the problem was not a female problem; it was and is a human problem.

It is the problem of expectations. You see, Marlene now had certain expectations of me. I sat with her at lunch one day, therefore I should sit with her at lunch every day. Though nothing was ever stated, the perception was there. Though no agreement was ever made, the assumption was just as strong. She *expected* me to be there. I let her down. (We broke up.)

Sound familiar? How about your experience with expectations? They can get serious, you know. They've been known to do a lot more than just mess up a fourth grade romance. Divorce, job tension, poor self-image, family dissension, world wars, embittered friendships—all these can be caused by this same little culprit, expectations.

Expectations are like rifles. Used correctly and appropriately, they are valuable and necessary. But, oh, how quickly are they misused. How quickly do we load their chambers, cock their triggers, and draw a bead on those we love. Quietly we pull the trigger. "You let me down." And we both fall victim to the bullet of expectation.

Ever caught yourself using these tell-tale words of unhealthy expectations? How about with your children?

"Now, your big brother made an A in chemistry, and we know you'll do just as well."

"When I was your age, son, I made the *varsity* football team."

"Are you going to be a smart doctor just like your dad?"

"Now, honey, don't even think about that university. When you graduate you're going to our alma mater. I'm already saving for your tuition!"

Or maybe these with your spouse:

"If you had a better salary, John, we could afford that house."

"Honey, I promised Paul I'd play golf next Saturday. You don't mind, do you?"

"It's not my fault that the kitchen is a mess. It's the wife's job to keep the house."

Or, at work:

"Eric, I've got high hopes for you in this company. Don't let me down."

"I know it's after 5:00 P.M. But I thought you wouldn't mind if we saw one more client."

"I know you haven't had a vacation, Phil. But those who really care about this firm are willing to sacrifice."

Expectations. They create conditional love. "I love you, but I'll love you even more *if*. . . "

Now, I know what you're thinking. Shouldn't we expect the best out of each other? Shouldn't we encourage each other to strive for excellence and never settle for anything else?

Absolutely.

But it was Christ on the cross who taught us how to use expectations. Does he demand a lot? You better believe it. Does he expect much? Only our best. Does he have expectations? Just that we leave everything, deny all, and follow him.

The difference? Jesus couched his expectations with two important companions. Forgiveness and acceptance.

Study attentively these words written by Paul: "While we

were still sinners, Christ died for us."[1] When did he die for us? When we reached perfection? No. When we overcame all temptation? Hardly. When we mastered the Christian walk? Far from it. Christ died when we were still sinners. His sacrifice, then, was not dependent on our performance.

When we love with expectations, we say, "I love you. But I'll love you even more if . . . "

Christ's love had none of this. No strings, no expectations, no hidden agendas, no secrets. His love for us was, and is, up front and clear. "I love you," he says. "Even if you let me down. I love you in spite of your failures."

One step behind the expectations of Christ come his forgiveness and tenderness. Tumble off the tightrope of what our Master expects and you land safely in his net of tolerance.

Expectations. Alone, they are bullets that can kill; but buffered by acceptance and forgiveness, they can bring out the best. Even in preteen romances.

COME HOME

The practice of using earthly happenings to clarify heavenly truths is no easy task. Yet, occasionally, one comes across a story, legend, or fable that conveys a message as accurately as a hundred sermons and with ten times the creativity. Such is the case with the reading below. I heard it first told by a Brazilian preacher in São Paulo. And though I've shared it countless times, with each telling I am newly warmed and reassured by its message.

The small house was simple but adequate. It consisted of one large room on a dusty street. Its red-tiled roof was one of many in this poor neighborhood on the outskirts of the Brazilian village. It was a comfortable home. Maria and her daughter, Christina, had done what they could to add color to the gray walls and warmth to the hard dirt floor: an old calendar, a faded photograph of a relative, a wooden crucifix. The furnishings were modest: a pallet on either side of the room, a washbasin, and a wood-burning stove.

Maria's husband had died when Christina was an infant. The young mother, stubbornly refusing opportunities to remarry, got a job and set out to raise her young daughter. And now, fifteen years later, the worst years were over. Though Maria's salary as a maid afforded few luxuries, it was reliable and it did provide food and clothes. And now Christina was old enough to get a job to help out.

Some said Christina got her independence from her mother. She recoiled at the traditional idea of marrying young and raising a family. Not that she couldn't have had her pick of husbands. Her olive skin and brown eyes kept a steady stream of prospects at her door. She had an infectious way of throwing her head back and filling the room with laughter. She also had that rare magic some women have that makes every man feel like a king just by being near them. But it was her spirited curiosity that made her keep all the men at arm's length.

She spoke often of going to the city. She dreamed of trading her dusty neighborhood for exciting avenues and city life. Just the thought of this horrified her mother. Maria was always quick to remind Christina of the harshness of the streets. "People don't know you there. Jobs are scarce and the life is cruel. And besides, if you went there, what would you do for a living?"

Maria knew exactly what Christina would do, or would *have* to do for a living. That's why her heart broke when she awoke one morning to find her daughter's bed empty. Maria knew immediately where her daughter had gone. She also knew immediately what she must do to find her. She quickly threw some clothes in a bag, gathered up all her money, and ran out of the house.

On her way to the bus stop she entered a drugstore to get one last thing. Pictures. She sat in the photograph booth, closed the curtain, and spent all she could on pictures of herself. With her purse full of small black-and-white photos, she boarded the next bus to Rio de Janeiro.

Maria knew Christina had no way of earning money. She also knew that her daughter was too stubborn to give up. When pride meets hunger, a human will do things that were before unthinkable. Knowing this, Maria began her search. Bars, hotels, nightclubs, any place with the reputation for street walkers or prostitutes. She went to them all. And at each place she left her picture—taped on a bathroom mirror, tacked to a hotel bulletin board, fastened to a corner phone booth. And on the back of each photo she wrote a note.

It wasn't too long before both the money and the pictures ran out, and Maria had to go home. The weary mother wept as the bus began its long journey back to her small village.

It was a few weeks later that young Christina descended the hotel stairs. Her young face was tired. Her brown eyes no longer danced with youth but spoke of pain and fear. Her laughter was broken. Her dream had become a nightmare. A thousand times over she had longed to trade these countless beds for her secure pallet. Yet the little village was, in too many ways, too far away.

As she reached the bottom of the stairs, her eyes noticed a familiar face. She looked again, and there on the lobby mirror was a small picture of her mother. Christina's eyes burned and her throat tightened as she walked across the room and removed the small photo. Written on the back was this compelling invitation. "Whatever you have done, whatever you have become, it doesn't matter. Please come home."

She did.

"The Son is the radiance of God's glory and the exact representation of his being. . . . "[1]

"Come to me, all you who are weary and burdened, and I will give you rest."[2]

CONSISTENT INCONSISTENCIES

I suspect that the most consistent thing about life has to be its inconsistency.

Choosing not to be neatly categorized, life has opted to be a tossed salad of tragedies and triumphs, profanity and purity, despair and hope. The bad is perplexingly close to the good. The just is frighteningly near to the unfair. And life? Life is always a clock's tick away from death. And evil? Evil is paradoxically close to goodness. It is as if only a sheer curtain separates the two. Given the right lure, at the right moment, aimed at the right weakness, there is not a person alive who wouldn't pull back his curtain and live out his vilest fantasy.

The inconsistency of life.

As a result, one moment can simultaneously usher in sweet victory and crushing defeat. The same day can bring both reunion and separation. The same birth can bring both pain and peace. Truth and half-truth often ride in the same saddle. (And yes, James, good and evil *can* come out of the same mouth.)

"If life was just simpler!" we reason. "More predictable!" But it isn't. Even for the best among us, life is like a wild roller coaster ride of hairpin curves and diving dips.

Maybe that is why there is within all of us just a bit of

paranoia, an unsettling insecurity. Oh, we may submerge it some with pin-striped shirts and martinis, but the anxiety of the future is still present. Don't all of us live with a fear of the unknown? Don't all of us dread the horrible day when the thin curtain that separates us from evil might be pulled back and in we would tumble? Cancer. Murder. Rape. Death. How haunting is that gnawing awareness that we are not immune to life's mishaps and perils.

It's this eerie inconsistency that keeps all of us, to one degree or another, living our lives on the edge of our chairs.

Yet, it was in this inconsistency that God had his finest hour. Never did the obscene come so close to the holy as it did on Calvary. Never did the good in the world so intertwine with the bad as it did on the cross. Never did what is right involve itself so intimately with what is wrong, as it did when Jesus was suspended between heaven and earth.

God on a cross. Humanity at its worst. Divinity at its best.

Something is said at the cross about inconsistencies. Something hopeful. Something healing. Simply stated, that which is consistent did battle with that which is inconsistent, and the consistent won.

Something is also said about God himself. God is not stumped by an evil world. He doesn't gasp in amazement at the depth of our faith or the depth of our failures. We can't surprise God with our cruelties. He knows the condition of the world . . . and loves it just the same. For just when we find a place where God would never be (like on a cross), we look again and there he is, in the flesh.

THE ROAR

The door is locked. Deadbolted. Maybe even a chair under the doorknob. Inside sit ten knee-knocking itinerants who are astraddle the fence between faith and fear. As you look around the room, you wouldn't take them for a bunch who are about to put the kettle of history on high boil. Uneducated. Confused. Callused hands. Heavy accents. Few social graces. Limited knowledge of the world. No money. Undefined leadership. And on and on.

No, as you look at this motley crew, you wouldn't wager too many paychecks on their future. But something happens to a man when he witnesses someone who has risen from the dead. Something stirs within the soul of a man who has stood within inches of God. Something stirs that is hotter than gold fever and more permanent than passion.

It all started with ten stammering, stuttering men. Though the door was locked, he still stood in their midst. "As the Father has sent me, I am sending you."[1]

And send them he did. Ports. Courtyards. Boats. Synagogues. Prisons. Palaces. They went everywhere. Their message of the Nazarene dominoed across the civilized world. They were an infectious fever. They were a moving organism. They refused to be stopped. Uneducated drifters who shook history like a housewife shakes a rug.

My, wouldn't it be great to see it happen again?

Many say it's impossible. The world is too hard. Too secular. Too post-Christian. "This is the age of information, not regeneration." So we deadbolt the door for fear of the world.

And as a result, the world goes largely untouched and untaught. Over half of the world has yet to hear the story of the Messiah, much less study it. The few believers who do go out often come home weary and wounded, numbed at the odds and frustrated at the needs.

What would it take to light the fire again? Somehow, those fellows in the upper room did it. They did it without dragging their feet or making excuses. For them it was rather obvious. "All I know is that he was dead and now he is alive."

Something happens to a man when he stands within inches of the Judaean Lion. Something happens when he hears the roar, when he touches the golden mane. Something happens when he gets so close he can feel the Lion's breath. Maybe we could all use a return visit. Maybe we all need to witness his majesty and sigh at his victory. Maybe we need to hear our own commission again. "Will you tell them?" Jesus challenged. "Will you tell them that I came back . . . and that I am coming back again?"

"We will," they nodded. And they did.

Will you?

READER'S GUIDE

FINAL WORDS, FINAL ACTS

1. *Final words. Final acts. Each one is a window through which the cross can be better understood. Each one opens a treasury of promises.*

    A. Why are the final words and actions of a dying person significant? Why are the final words and actions of Christ particularly significant?

    B. In preparation for this study read Luke's account of the betrayal, the Last Supper, Jesus' arrest and trial, and his crucifixion in chapters 22 and 23. What things surprise you? What things are hard to comprehend? Considering that these are Jesus' final hours on earth, what one word best depicts his words and actions during these hours?

    C. What do you hope to gain from this study of Christ's last words and actions? What will make the difference in how well you succeed? Write down five specific goals for the study, and at the end of the study assess to what extent you have achieved them.

2. *It's much easier to die like Jesus if you have lived like him for a lifetime.*

A. From your observation, to what extent does someone's personality change as he or she gets older? To what extent does a person's character change?

B. What do the following passages reveal about our ability to be like Jesus: John 14:5–24; 1 Corinthians 2:16? What does it mean to have the mind of Christ? What outward indications will there be when we truly live in a Christ-like manner? What does Jesus promise us when we live in a Christ-like manner?

C. What specific character trait would you want to be remembered for at your death? To what extent is that true of you now? What could you do to strengthen that characteristic in yourself?

CHAPTER 2

WORDS THAT WOUND

1. *Sometimes I wonder if we don't see Christ's love as much in the people he tolerated as in the pain he endured.*

    A. What kinds of "wounds" hurt the most? Physical abuse? Insults? Rejection? Apathy? Prejudice? Revenge? Are there others you would add to the list? Which would you rank as the most difficult to forgive? Why?

    B. Which of these wounds did Jesus experience? Give an example of each that he experienced.

    C. Read Luke's account of the crucifixion again (Luke 23:26–43), focusing on what was said to Jesus. Would you agree with Max's statement above? Why or why not?

    D. If Max's statement is true, in what way might we today cause Jesus more pain than his crucifixion did?

2. *If ever a person deserved a shot at revenge, Jesus did. But he didn't take it. Instead he died for them.*

    A. The cliche says "revenge is sweet." How would you describe revenge? Describe a time in which you took revenge. How did you feel afterwards?

B. What do the following passages teach about revenge: Ezekiel 25:15–17; Romans 12:17–21; 1 Peter 3:9–17? How are we to overcome our desire for revenge? When a person responds to injury with kindness, what benefits does it bring? What action does God take in such situations?

C. Why does revenge hurt the one who seeks it more than the one who is the intended recipient? Describe a time in which you overcame a desire for revenge. How did it make you feel? What benefits did it bring?

CHAPTER 3

VIGILANTE VENGEANCE

1. *Anger. It's a peculiar yet predictable emotion. It begins as a drop of water. . . . Yet, get enough of these seemingly innocent drops of anger and before long you've got a bucket full of rage. . . . We become walking time bombs that, given just the right tension and fear, could explode like Mr. Goetz.*

    A. How serious a problem is anger in our society? What recent examples can you give that illustrate the problem? Why do you think people are angry? Do you agree that, given the right tension and fear, we are time bombs waiting to explode?

    B. How "serious" a sin is anger, judging by Galatians 5:19–21?

    C. According to these passages, what typically accompanies anger: Proverbs 14:17, 29; Ecclesiastes 7:9; James 1:19–20? What would these passages indicate as antidotes to anger? In view of these passages, would you say "counting to ten" has some value?

2. *Uncontrolled anger won't better our world, but sympathetic understanding will. Once we see the world and ourselves for what we are, we can help.*

A. What makes you angry? Have you ever been uncontrollably angry? How does it feel? What helps you control your anger?

B. When Stephen was stoned to death, he uttered a similar statement to Jesus' statement. Read Acts 6:8–15 and 7:54–8:1. What parallels are there between Jesus' nature and Stephen's? How did their words at their death affect those around them?

C. Goetz prepared for a situation that made him angry by carrying a gun. What "weapons" could you arm yourself with so that you would be able to handle a difficult situation with understanding instead of anger?

CHAPTER 4

THE TALE OF THE CRUCIFIED CROOK

1. *You are valuable just because you exist. Not because of what you do or what you have done, but simply because you are.*

A. To what extent are people valued in today's culture? What gives a person value, according to today's standards? What affects society's view of the worth of the individual?

B. What do the following passages teach about the value God places upon people: Romans 5:8; Ephesians 2:4–5; Titus 3:4–7; 1 John 4:9–10?

C. Do we behave as if we have intrinsic value? If people truly believed they had intrinsic value, what problems in society would no longer exist?

2. *It makes me smile to think that there is a grinning ex-con walking the golden streets who knows more about grace than a thousand theologians.*

A. What do you think is most significant about the story of the crucified crook?

B. Read Luke 23:32–43. What can you learn about the two criminals from this brief episode? Why do you think Jesus gave this criminal a promise of paradise?

C. How do you think the crucified crook would explain grace in one sentence?

CHAPTER 5

LEAVING
IS LOVING

1. *What kind of God would give you families and then ask you to leave them? What kind of God would give you friends and then ask you to say good-bye?*

   A. Do you know someone who has had to choose between family or friends and a commitment to God? What sacrifices were made? What was the result?

   B. What do you think Jesus meant in Matthew 19:28–29? In what way do Matthew 6:33 and Matthew 12:46–50 shed light on his meaning?

   C. In what way did Jesus live by this principle?

2. *John fastened his arm around Mary a little tighter. Jesus was asking him to be the son that a mother needs and that in some ways he never was.*

   A. Considering all the physical and spiritual struggles surrounding the crucifixion, why do you think this personal story about Jesus' mother was recorded for us?

B. Read John 19:25–27. How does this event indicate Jesus' love for his family? What does it indicate about his relationship with his friends? How do you reconcile his love for his family and friends with his statement in Matthew 19:28–29?

C. What did Paul say in 1 Timothy 5:8 about caring for one's family? How would you explain the balance in our responsibility to our family and to our faith?

THE CRY
OF LONELINESS

1. *I'm writing to those of you who can find a lonely person simply by looking in the mirror.*

    A. How would you describe loneliness? When are people most susceptible to loneliness? What antidotes to loneliness do we use?

    B. Read Psalm 139:1–18 and Acts 17:24–28. In what way do they offer comfort to someone who feels lonely?

    C. Are there people you know who are lonely? Which groups within the church are particularly vulnerable— those who have lost loved ones, the elderly, those who are away from their family and friends, missionaries supported by your church? Are there others? In what specific ways could you help dispel their loneliness?

2. *And although he may offer no answer, although he may solve no dilemma, although the question may freeze painfully in midair, he who also was once alone, understands.*

A. Why was it important for Jesus to be totally separated from God for a time?

B. Do you agree with Max's interpretation of this haunting passage (Matthew 27:46)? How do you understand the word "forsaken" in this passage? Of all the statements at the cross, in what way is this the most heart rending? Read Psalm 22. In what way does David's anguish parallel Jesus' anguish?

C. Can you imagine any greater pain and loneliness than Jesus suffered? How does it affect you to know that he chose to suffer that for your sake?

I THIRST

1. *Just at the right time we are reminded that the one to whom we pray knows our feelings. He knows temptation. He has felt discouraged.*

A. Why is it important to realize not only the divinity of Jesus, but also his humanity?

B. According to Hebrews 2:14–18 and Hebrews 4:14–16, in what ways can Jesus identify with us as humans? What blessings does that bring to us? How does Jesus now act on our behalf?

C. In prayer, how do you balance reverence for Jesus as God and creator of the universe with the awareness that Jesus shared in our humanity and understands our weaknesses?

2. *We are most indebted to John for choosing to include verse 28 of chapter 19. It reads simply: "I am thirsty."*

A. Why does this verse seem out of character with Jesus' other statements at the cross? What significance does it have for us?

B. Read John 19:28–29. Why did Jesus say, "I am thirsty"? Read Psalm 22 and Psalm 69:21. What parallels are there between these psalms and the events of the crucifixion?

C. How would you describe the intensity of Jesus' thirst on the cross? In Matthew 5:6, Jesus said we also should be thirsty. When were you most intensely thirsty? If you now had the same craving for righteousness as you then had for water, how would it change your life?

CREATIVE COMPASSION

1. *The ultimate act of creative compassion is revealed. God on a cross.*
The Creator being sacrificed for the creation. God convincing man
once and for all that forgiveness still follows failure.

A. What does Max mean by calling the crucifixion
the "ultimate act of creative compassion"?

B. In what way was the crucifixion of Christ the
result of mankind's greatest failure? Has there ever been
a greater need for forgiveness than for killing the Son of
God? Based on the following passages, how would you
describe God's forgiving nature: Psalm 103:1–5; Luke
6:37–38; Acts 3:19; Acts 10:42–43; 1 John 1:7–9? What
is required of those seeking forgiveness?

C. How would you assure someone about God's ability to forgive any sin?

2. *"It is finished." The mission was finished. All that the master painter needed to do was done and was done in splendor.*

A. What is your mission in life? In what ways are you in the process of accomplishing it? At what point would your mission be finished?

B. Read John 19:28–30. What did Jesus mean by "It is finished"? What was finished? What tasks had not been completed? How does his statement clarify his mission?

C. Spend some time writing down a personal mission statement. Then make a list of your priorities based on your mission statement. What changes do you want to make in view of your mission and priorities?

IT IS FINISHED

1. *Jesus didn't quit. But don't think for one minute that he wasn't tempted to.*

> A. Do you think Jesus seriously considered not dying on the cross? What do you think would have been the strongest temptation for not going through with it?

> B. In the following passages, what could have tempted Jesus to give up: Mark 9:33–41; Mark 10:32–45; Mark 14:32–42?

> C. What did Jesus do to gain the strength to continue? What are our greatest sources of strength when we are tempted to give up?

2. *God didn't call us to be successful, just faithful.*

> A. Do you agree with this statement? How would you distinguish between being successful and being faithful? Can you be successful without being faithful? Can you be faithful without being successful? Explain.

B. What do the following passages teach about faithfulness: Matthew 24:12–13; Romans 2:6–7; Colossians 1:22–23; Hebrews 12:1–12? What will characterize the person who remains faithful? Why is the analogy of the runner an apt comparison for the Christian life?

C. To what extent do we value faithfulness in our society—faithfulness to our word, to our mates, to our responsibilities, to our God? To what extent does our culture value success? How can you model greater faithfulness for those around you?

TAKE ME HOME

1. *The two are again one. The abandoned is now found. The schism is now bridged.*

> A. How would you describe the unity of God and Christ? What earthly comparisons could you make?

> B. According to these passages, how did Jesus describe his unity with God the Father: John 10:38; John 14:10–11; John 17:20–21? What was so significant about Jesus being reunited with God?

> C. At what times do you feel the greatest sense of oneness with Jesus? According to John 17:20–26, what results from a unity with Jesus?

2. *Satan's vultures have been scattered. Hell's demons have been jailed. Death has been damned.*

> A. In what way was the moment of Satan's apparent greatest triumph actually the moment of his greatest defeat?

B. Read John 12:31–33; John 14:28–31; John 16:5–11; and Hebrews 2:14–16. What do they teach about the impact of Jesus' death on the power of Satan?

C. Even though Jesus defeated Satan, in what ways do we continue to allow him to have power? According to these passages, how does he attempt to destroy our relationship with God: John 8:42–47; 2 Corinthians 11:3–4, 13–15; 1 Peter 5:8–9 ?

WHO WOULD
HAVE BELIEVED?

1. *There was something about the crucifixion that made every witness either step toward it or away from it. It simultaneously compelled and repelled.*

 A. Of the witnesses of the crucifixion, with whom do you best identify? Why?

 B. Look at some of the people who were repelled by it: Judas (Luke 22:1–6); Herod, the chief priests, the Sanhedrin, and the crowds (Luke 23:1–25). What caused them to reject Jesus' claim to be the Messiah? Which of their reasons for rejecting Jesus are still prevalent today?

 C. Look at some of the people who were compelled by it: the "crucified crook" (Luke 23:39–43); the women at the cross (John 19:25–27); Joseph of Arimathea and Nicodemus (John 19:38–42). What lessons can we learn from their examples?

2. *We can do what we want with the cross. We can examine its history. We can study its theology. We can reflect upon its prophecies. Yet the one thing we can't do is walk away in neutral.*

A. How do you respond to people who say that Jesus was merely a good man, not the Son of God? If Jesus had not been the Son of God, why would it not be accurate to say he was a good man?

B. In 1 Corinthians 15:1–20, what arguments does Paul present about the significance of Christ's resurrection from the dead? If a person doesn't accept that, what is left?

C. In what way do these Old Testament passages serve as Messianic prophecies: Isaiah 11; Micah 5:1–5; Zechariah 9:9?

D. What causes you to believe that Jesus is the Son of God? Is there one thing in particular, or is it an accumulation of evidence? Are you willing to bet your eternal destiny on the fact that Jesus is who he says he is?

CHAPTER 12

FACES IN
THE CROWD

1. *Some believe that Malchus was later numbered among the believers at Jerusalem. We don't know for sure.*

    A. If you had been given the opportunity to interview Malchus after this scene in the garden, what questions would you have asked him? What do you think happened to Malchus? Why?

    B. Read the story of Malchus in Matthew 26:47–56; Mark 14:43–52; Luke 22:47–53; and John 18:1–11. What information is unique to each account? What insights into Jesus does this incident give us?

    C. What contemporary example do you know of someone who has been "touched" by Jesus with dramatic results? Is Jesus' power to change lives today any less miraculous than his healing of Malchus? What benefit is there in telling the story of Malchus or the story of someone today who is changed by Jesus?

2. *Ironic as it may appear, one of the hardest things to do is to be saved by grace.*

    A. Do you agree with Max's statement? If so, do you agree with his explanation that pride gets in the way? How does pride hinder us? For what other reasons might people reject grace?

    B. What do the following passages indicate about our ability to earn our salvation: John 1:12–13; Romans 4:4–8, 13–16; Romans 11:5–6; Ephesians 2:8–10? Why is it difficult to accept salvation as a gift from God?

    C. What wisdom does Proverbs offer on the subject of pride in the following verses: 11:2; 16:18–20; 29:23? According to these verses, what is the opposite of pride in ourselves? How does that fit with the concept of grace?

WELL . . . ALMOST

1. *It's one thing to forgive yourself for something you did. It is something else to try to forgive yourself for something that you might have done, but didn't.*

A. Recount a time when you regretted not doing something, perhaps a missed opportunity to help someone, a relationship you let grow apart, or a time when you didn't stand up for your faith. What held you back? Do you have lingering regrets about your lack of action?

B. How seriously does God take our inaction? What indications are given in these examples: Matthew 25:14–30 and Matthew 25:31–46? Are there any more serious warnings in Scripture than these?

C. From what you see in the above passages, what expectations does God have of you?

2. *No, Jesus never had room for "almost" and he still doesn't. "Almost" may count in horseshoes and hand grenades, but with the Master, it is just as good as a "never."*

    A. Max says Jesus demands absolute obedience. How do we view "absolutes"—absolute trust, absolute truth, absolute commitment? To what are we willing to dedicate ourselves absolutely? Has "absolute" become obsolete?

    B. How do Matthew 25:1–13 and Mark 10:17–31 support Max's statement that "almost" is as good as "never"? How would you summarize the message of each account?

    C. How would you answer a non-Christian friend who said that Jesus' demand for absolute obedience was unfair or unrealistic?

CHAPTER 14

THE TEN
WHO RAN

1. *I haven't met a person yet who hasn't done the very thing he swore he would never do. We've all walked the streets of Jerusalem.*

A. What are some of the things you thought you would never do—only to find yourself doing them? Perhaps it is a parenting style you thought you would never use with your kids. Perhaps it is a sin you never thought you would be guilty of. Perhaps it is the very thing you dislike in others. Why do we do the very things we want not to do?

B. How did Paul describe this same problem in Romans 7:14–25? What caused him to be at war with himself? How did he understand the struggle? What was his salvation?

C. Are you sensing any spiritual struggles right now? What could you do to "arm" the "slave to God's law"? What could you do to "disarm" the "slave to the law of sin"?

2. *He who forgave his followers stands ready to forgive the rest of us. All we have to do is come back.*

A. The apostles had seen the miracles, had listened to the teachings, and had heard Jesus foretell his death. Why did they not understand? Why did they run?

B. We often refer to the apostle Thomas as "doubting Thomas," yet what do we learn about his faith in John 11:1–16? Like the others, Thomas left behind his faith in Jesus, at least for a time. Read John 20:19–31. How did Jesus make a special point of assuring Thomas? What reassurance does Jesus give us?

C. Luke 15:11–32 gives one of the most poignant portrayals of God's willingness to take us back if we will just come home. Read this account, putting God's name in the place of the father and your name in the place of the younger son.

CHAPTER 15

THE ONE
WHO STAYED

1. *One gets the impression that to John, Jesus was above all a loyal companion.*

A. Why do you think John refers to himself as the "disciple whom Jesus loved"? Did Jesus love John more than the other disciples?

B. Notice some of the special occasions that John shared with Jesus: Matthew 26:36–37; Luke 9:28–36; John 13:18–27; John 19:25–27. What would indicate that Jesus relied on him in particular?

C. The Gospel of John is quite different from the other gospel accounts. For one thing, John likes to record discourses of Jesus with one person at a time, such as Jesus' conversations with Nicodemus, the woman at the well, and the royal official. Devote a week to reading the Gospel of John. As the disciple perhaps closest to Jesus, does John give a more person-centered account of the events? What other insights do you gain from his unique perspective?

2. *John teaches us that the strongest relationship with Christ may not necessarily be a complicated one.*

A. Of the people you know, who would you say has the strongest relationship with Christ? How would you describe that relationship? Has it come from formal training, family training, life experiences, or personal study?

B. How did John describe the essence of relationship with Jesus in the following passages: John 14:21; 14:23; 16:27?

C. What will be the natural outgrowth of our love for Jesus according to John 15:9–17?

D. How would you condense John's message on relationship with Jesus into one sentence?

CHAPTER 16

THE HILL
OF REGRET

1. *While Jesus was climbing up the hill of Calvary, Judas was climbing another hill; the hill of regret.*

    A. How do you view the character of Judas? How could he spend all that time with Jesus and then betray him? Why did he so quickly regret his decision?

    B. Read the following accounts of Judas in Matthew 26:14–16; Matthew 26:17–30; John 12:4–6; John 13:2; and John 13:18–30. What insights do they give into Judas?

    C. Read Matthew's account of Judas's regret in Matthew 27:1–10. What further insight does it give into the character of Judas?

    D. In what way are the traits of Judas common to all of us to one degree or another?

2. *It takes just as much faith to believe that Jesus can look past my betrayals as it does to believe that he rose from the dead. Both are just as miraculous.*

A. What is the very first thing that comes to mind when you think of Jesus' miracles? Something in biblical times or something in the present? Do we tend to view any present-day occurrence as having the significance of Jesus' miracles while he was on earth? Is Jesus an active or passive participant in your life?

B. What assurances do the following passages provide about God's willingness to forgive even those who betrayed his son: Acts 2:22–47; James 4:7–10; 1 John 1:9? What blessings accompany forgiveness from God?

C. How would you counsel someone struggling to forgive himself for his sins? What verses would you direct him to?

THE GOSPEL OF THE SECOND CHANCE

1. *No wonder they call it the gospel of the second chance.*

   A. What is meant by the "gospel of the second chance"? What other names could it be given?

   B. Of all the followers who deserted Jesus, perhaps Peter's story is the most striking. Read the account of his denial of Jesus in Mark 14:27–31, 66–72 and then the angel's response after Jesus' resurrection in Mark 16:1–7. Also read Luke 24:33–34 and John 21:15–19. What message is conveyed in Peter's being singled out? What seems to be Jesus' attitude toward Peter—frustration, disappointment, concern, love?

   C. On what other occasions had Peter been given a second chance? Read Matthew 14:22–33 and 17:1–8. In what way did Jesus give him additional chances? What appears to be Jesus' attitude toward Peter on each occasion?

D. What do you think is Jesus' attitude about giving you a second chance, or a third chance, or a fourth? Would he do any less for you than for Peter?

2. *It's not every day that you find someone who will give you a second chance—much less someone who will give you a second chance every day.*

A. Can you think of a time you were given a second chance? How did it affect you? How willing are you to offer others a second chance?

B. What does Matthew 18:21–35 say about second chances? What does Psalm 78 say about God's willingness to provide second chances? How many instances of a second chance does the psalm record? What does Job 33:12–30 teach about God's active role in second chances?

C. As a reminder that he is the God of second chances, write out Lamentations 3:19–26 and place it where you can read it every morning.

LEAVE ROOM
FOR THE MAGIC

1. *We make the same mistake that Thomas made: we forget that "impossible" is one of God's favorite words.*

    A. What "impossibilities" had Thomas witnessed? Why do you think he doubted that Jesus had risen from the dead?

    B. What assurance does Ephesians 3:20 give us that God is still in the "impossible" business? Is this verse true for believers today as it was for the original recipients of the letter? What is "his power that is at work within us"?

    C. What goal has seemed too impossible for even God to fulfill? What could you begin specifically praying for in order to reach that goal? What additional steps could you begin taking toward the goal?

2. *Anytime you mix loyalty with a little imagination, you've got a man of God on your hands.*

A. Do you know some people who, like Thomas, exemplify a mixture of loyalty and imagination in serving God? Give an example. What makes them effective servants?

B. Look at these examples of people who were loyal and imaginative in serving God: Moses' mother (Exodus 1:22–2:10); Abigail (1 Samuel 25:1–35); and the friends of the paralytic (Mark 2:1–12). How was each loyal to God? How was each imaginative? What good resulted in each case?

C. How would you rate your "loyalty quotient"? How would you rate your "imagination quotient"? What cues could you take from Thomas and the others about how to increase both?

CHAPTER 19

A CANDLE
IN THE CAVERN

1. *Jesus had no room for those who specialized in making religion a warlord, and faith a footrace. No room at all.*

A. With whom was Jesus most patient during his time on earth? With whom was he least tolerant? Whom do you think Jesus would be least tolerant of if he had been born into our world today?

B. Read Matthew 23. Whom is he talking about in this chapter? What was their role in Jewish society? Make a list of the practices for which he condemns them.

C. To what extent do each of those problems exist in religion today?

2. *And it is still often the case that one has to find faith in spite of the church instead of in the church.*

A. To what extent would you agree with Max's statement? Why do you think it is true, or not true?

B. Notice some of the people Jesus praised for their faith: the Canaanite woman (Matthew 15:21–28 and Mark 7:24–30); the Roman centurion (Luke 7:1–10); and, as is implied by Jesus' actions, the thief on the cross (Luke 23:39–43). In each case, how was faith found in an unexpected place?

C. What lesson is there for us in these examples? Do we ignore people that we consider unlikely candidates for faith in Jesus? Where could you invest greater efforts in the future?

MINIATURE MESSENGERS

1. *It's not just tears that are the issue, it's what they represent. They represent the heart, the spirit and the soul of a person. To put a lock and key on your emotions is to bury part of your Christlikeness!*

A. How comfortable are we with showing our emotions? Why are we reluctant to publicly display our emotions? To what extent do we attribute a show of emotion to gender or personality type as opposed to being a natural and necessary part of every person?

B. What emotions does Christ reveal in these passages: seeing Jerusalem (Luke 19:41–44); on the Mount of Olives (Luke 22:39–46); the death of Lazarus (John 11:17–36)?

C. What physical price do we pay when we bottle up our emotions? What spiritual price do we pay when we suppress our emotions?

2. *You can't go to the cross with just your head and not your heart.*

A. Do you agree with Max's statement? What is the danger in having a religion that is totally heart and no head? What is the danger in having a religion that is totally head and no heart?

B. What emotions were displayed by those who witnessed the death and resurrection of Jesus: those who followed him (Mark 16:9–10; John 20:19–20); the eye-witnesses to the crucifixion (Luke 23:47–49); the people on the road to Emmaus (Luke 24:13–32)?

C. Should our emotions be any different than theirs? How can we prevent becoming jaded by the familiarity of the story?

CHAPTER 21

ALIVE!

1. In this chapter, it is as if Max captures freeze frames of the events from the Garden of Gethsemane to the resurrection. What is the effect of these quick images?

2. Look at each event. Which word in each paragraph best depicts it?

3. What other words would you add to each event?

4. Read the account of these events, this time from the Gospel of Matthew (26:36–28:10). What other images do you see in Matthew's account?

CHAPTER 22

OPEN ARMS

1. *The reassuring lesson is clear. God used (and uses!) people to change the world. People! Not saints or super humans or geniuses, but people. . . . And what they may lack in perfection, God makes up for in love.*

A. Who would you list in a "Who's Who" of the five most outstanding men and women of the Bible other than Jesus? What strengths did each possess? What weaknesses did each possess? How was each person used to change the world?

B. How does God use our weaknesses for his purpose, according to 2 Corinthians 4 and 2 Corinthians 12:7–10?

C. If Satan were to try to convince you that you were of no special value to the Lord, how might he do it? How would you answer him?

2. *Look at the forgiveness found in those open arms and take courage.*

    A. How do you picture God? Do you picture him with open arms?

    B. As you read the following passages, make a list of the ways God's love and forgiveness for his followers is described: Exodus 34:6–7; Psalm 32; Psalm 103:1–18; Isaiah 44:21–22; 1 John 1:7–9.

    C. Read again the description in Luke 15:20 of the father's reaction when he saw his son returning home. The next time you need to ask God's forgiveness, imagine him reacting to you in the same way—running to meet you, being filled with compassion, throwing his arms around you, and kissing you. What kind of courage does it take to talk to a father like that?

A Street Vendor Named Contentment

1. *An hour of contentment. An hour when deadlines are forgotten and strivings have ceased. An hour when what we have overshadows what we want.*

A. How would you define contentment? How is it different from happiness? What is necessary in order to be content?

B. Read Philippians 4:11–13 where Paul says he has found the secret of contentment in all circumstances. What was that secret? What kind of circumstances had Paul been in, according to 2 Corinthians 11:23–28?

C. How rare is contentment? What words would best describe most of us on a normal day: worried, hurried, busy, frustrated, tired, anxious, discouraged—or—peaceful, serene, content, happy, relaxed? What advice might Paul give us to increase our contentment?

2. *People seem strangely proud of their ulcers and headaches.*

A. In what way is that a true statement for many people? What makes stress and pressure virtual hallmarks of success?

B. According to Luke 12:22–34, what should be the hallmarks of our lives in Christ? To what does Jesus compare us? What do we compare our lives to—a rat race, swimming with the sharks? What contrasts are evident?

C. What does your physical health tell you about your sense of peace and contentment? What does it say about your worry level? To what extent are you doctoring the symptoms instead of addressing the problem?

CLOSE TO THE CROSS— BUT FAR FROM CHRIST

1. *So close to the cross but so far from the Christ.*

    A. In what ways are we like the soldiers at the foot of the cross? Where are our eyes focused—up on the crucified Son of God or down on our possessions? Like they, in what way are we calloused to the sight of the crucifixion?

    B. In what ways do we focus on the trivialities of religion and ignore the heart of the matter? What did Jesus say in Matthew 23:23–24 to those who focused on the more trivial issues of religion? How does Micah 6:8 define the "heart of the matter"?

    C. What issues do you see churches arguing and dividing over today that you think Jesus would consider "tithing mint and cumin"? What would you consider the "more important matters" to be today?

2. *What about you? Can you build a bridge? Toss a rope? Span a chasm? Pray for oneness?*

    A. How much unity is possible among religious groups? To what extent can churches have differences and still be unified?

    B. From what you see in Jesus' prayer in John 17:11, 20–23, what is the appropriate basis for unity in the church today?

    C. What can we do as individuals to increase unity among believers? What could your church do to increase unity with other churches?

THE FOG OF THE BROKEN HEART

1. *Seeing God like this does wonders for our own suffering. God was never more human than at this hour. God was never nearer to us than when he hurt.*

    A. How does it help to understand that Jesus in his humanity suffered in the Garden of Gethsemane?

    B. Reread the account in Mark 14:32–42 or in one of the other Gospels. What about Jesus' behavior seems very "human" to you? What about these events is surprising?

    C. If this were the only passage available to a non-Christian, what basic principles of the gospel could be taught from it? In what way can this passage serve as an example and as encouragement when you pray amidst the "fog"?

2. *If it is true that in suffering God is most like man, maybe in our suffering we can see God like never before.*

    A. In times of suffering, is your vision of God better or worse? Under what circumstances do you turn to God? Under what circumstances do you turn away from him?

    B. How do the following passages assure us that God not only understands but cares about our sufferings: Matthew 10:28–31; John 14:1–3; Romans 8:28–39?

    C. How can times of suffering ultimately be a blessing? Read Luke 6:20–22; 2 Corinthians 4:7–5:11; and 2 Thessalonians 1:3–10.

PÃO, SENHOR?

1. *Living in Brazil, one has daily opportunities to buy a candy bar or sandwich for these little outcasts. It's the least one can do.*

   A. Have you ever had an experience like Max's? What do you do when you are confronted by a beggar, the homeless, a request for a donation from a charity?

   B. How did Jesus say we were to treat others in Matthew 10:40–42 and Matthew 25:31–46? What did James say about it in James 2:14–17?

   C. How would you summarize the commands embodied in the above passages? What kind of rationalizations can most easily keep Christians from actually doing what we are told to do?

2. *If I am so moved by a street orphan who says thank you for a piece of bread, how much more is God moved when I pause to thank him—really thank him—for saving my soul?*

   A. Do we sometimes take our blessings, and particularly our salvation, for granted? Why?

B. What do the following passages teach about expressing gratitude toward God: Ephesians 5:19–20; Colossians 1:10–14; Colossians 3:15–17; 1 Thessalonians 5:16–18? For what are we to give thanks? When?

C. To what extent are praise and gratitude a part of your prayers? How do they compare to your petitions to God? When was the last time you truly thanked God for saving your soul?

PUPPIES, BUTTERFLIES, AND A SAVIOR

1. *Guilt creeps in on cat's paws and steals whatever joy might have flickered in our eyes.*

    A. Max compares guilt to a cat stealing our joy. What other ways could you describe guilt's effects?

    B. How do these Scriptures describe the effects of guilt: Psalm 31:9–10; Psalm 38; Psalm 51? What insights do they offer into the cure for guilt?

    C. Can joy exist alongside guilt? Which is the stronger emotion? What advice would you give for replacing guilt with peace and joy?

2. *Quit trying to quench your own guilt. You can't do it. There's no way. Not with a bottle of whiskey or perfect Sunday school attendance.*

    A. How do we try to quench the feelings of guilt? How do we try to rationalize it away?

B. In your own words explain the message of the following verses: Isaiah 43:25; Hebrews 10:22; 1 John 1:7–9.

C. When is guilt a necessary and healthy emotion? When is guilt an unhealthy emotion? When is it unhealthy not to feel guilt? How would you summarize what part guilt plays in the Christian's life?

CHAPTER 28

GOD'S TESTIMONY

1. *I thought of his faith, his ability to believe, and his surprise that there were some who couldn't.*

    A. Generally speaking, who has an easier time believing—those who have a little education or those who have a lot of education? What potential dangers are there in being too "sophisticated" in knowledge?

    B. What do Acts 14:15–17 and Romans 1:18–20 teach about people's ability to see the existence of God?

    C. Restate in your own words the definition of faith in Hebrews 11:1–3.

    D. Which is harder for you to believe—that there is a God or that there isn't? How would you explain your reasons for faith to someone who didn't believe in God?

2. *To really understand and believe in the miracle on the cross, we'd do well to witness God's miracles every day.*

    A. What daily evidence of God's presence is most compelling to you? Does it ever become so commonplace that you take it for granted?

    B. What evidences of God does the psalmist celebrate in Psalm 19:1–4 and Psalm 33:6–15?

    C. If you were to write a psalm about the daily miracles of God, what miracles would you include?

Chapter 29

Dynamite
Decisions

1. *One statement made by our master offers two basic tools for keeping our cool in the heat of a decision. "Watch and pray so that you will not fall into temptation."*

A. Have you ever been in the "garden of decision" yourself? In what way has your loyalty been challenged? When you are suddenly laced with a decision, how do you tend to react?

B. Reread the account in Mark 14:32–52 of the garden scene. How do we see Jesus using these tools? What was the result? What was the result of the disciples not using them?

C. How would you restate the following passages in modern terms: Proverbs 4:23–27; 1 Corinthians 16:13; 1 Peter 5:8?

D. It is said that a person's character is revealed in moments of crisis. What specific suggestions can you make for preparing ahead of time so that a Christlike character is revealed in moments of crisis and sudden decisions?

2. *Second tool: "Pray." Prayer isn't telling God anything new. There is not a sinner nor a saint who would surprise him. What prayer does is invite God to walk the shadowy pathways of life with us.*

A. Do you agree with Max's statements on prayer? How could you expand on the idea that it invites God to walk with us?

B. Read Luke 18:1–8. What lesson is Jesus teaching about prayer? What additional insights into prayer do these verses offer: Ephesians 6:18; Colossians 4:2–4; Hebrews 4:16? For what are we to pray? What is to be our attitude in prayer?

C. What specific things are you praying for in regard to yourself? What specific things are you praying for in regard to others? In what other areas might you want to invite God to walk with you?

WHAT DID
YOU EXPECT?

1. *Expectations. They create conditional love.*

   A. What is the problem with conditional love? What does it do to marriages? to children? to faith?

   B. In what way did Jesus fail to meet the people's expectations of the Messiah? What did the people expect him to do? According to Matthew 11:1–6 and John 6:35–66, how did even those close to Jesus have wrong expectations? What happened when their expectations were not met?

   C. What expectations do we have of Jesus? What happens when he fails to meet our expectations? For instance, what happens to your faith and love for Jesus when he fails to answer a prayer as you expect?

2. *Jesus couched his expectations with two important companions. Forgiveness and acceptance.*

   A. Within this study what are some examples of Jesus' expectations not being met? How did he respond?

Take, for example, the disciples in the Garden of Gethsemane.

B. Look at these instances in which people did not meet Jesus' expectations: Peter (Matthew 16:21–23); the disciples (Matthew 17:14–21; Mark 8:1–21); Judas (Matthew 26:47–50). In each case, what did Jesus expect of them, why did people fail to meet his expectations, and how did he treat them?

C. Spend some time in prayer, asking forgiveness for failing to meet Jesus' expectations of you and praising him for accepting you despite your failures. Also pray for the strength to be more Christlike in forgiving and accepting others who fail to meet your expectations.

COME HOME

1. *When pride meets hunger, a human will do things that were before unthinkable.*

    A. Do you agree with Max that, given the right circumstances, "a human will do things that were before unthinkable"? To what degree are each of us capable of the most heinous sins?

    B. How would you describe humanity's condition—basically good, basically evil, a product of the environment, a product of genetics? What do the following passages teach about the sinfulness of humanity: Ecclesiastes 7:20; Isaiah 64:6; Romans 3:9–23?

    C. Why is it good for each of us to recognize our sinfulness? How does it affect our perspective on Christ's sacrifice for us? How does it affect our understanding and forgiveness of other people?

2. *"Whatever you have done, whatever you have become, it doesn't matter. Please come home."*

   A. In what way does Jesus make the same statement to us?

   B. For you, which images in the following passages best illustrate a sinner's journey and homecoming: Deuteronomy 4:29–31; Deuteronomy 30; Luke 15:3–10? How do they describe the sinner's attitude? How do they describe God's reception?

   C. Describe a special homecoming you have experienced. What memories of it are most vivid? If an earthly homecoming can be so powerful, can you imagine what a heavenly homecoming is like?

CONSISTENT INCONSISTENCIES

1. *Evil is paradoxically close to goodness.*

    A. What examples can you give of Max's statement? Ministers dedicated to their flock but neglecting their family? Friendship becoming an affair? A desire for "good works" denying God's grace?

    B. The Bible is full of examples of good intentions leading to evil results and evil intentions masquerading as good. How were the Pharisees caught up in this paradox? Read Matthew 23:1–12, 15, 23–24, 27–28. How had good become perverted into evil? According to 2 Corinthians 11:13–15, how does evil masquerade as good?

    C. How can we discern good from evil, according to Romans 12 and 1 John 4:1–3? Make a list of the practical indicators of the godly life listed in Romans 12.

2. *Never did what is right involve itself so intimately with what is wrong, as it did when Jesus was suspended between heaven and earth.*

A. How was the crucifixion the greatest, and ultimate, battle between good and evil? In what way were good and evil closely connected?

B. Look back at Matthew's account of the crucifixion, beginning with 26:1 and ending with 27:56. Draw a line vertically down a piece of paper and on the left side list the significant nouns and verbs within that reading that describe the forces of wrong that precipitated the crucifixion. On the right side of the line list the nouns and verbs that describe Jesus during those events.

C. How do you react to that list? In one sentence summarize the message of the list. In what way is it the message of this book? In what way is it the message of the Bible itself?

THE ROAR

1. *Over half of the world has yet to hear the story of the Messiah, much less study it.*

    A. What opportunities are there to take the story to places in the world where it has previously been denied? What is your church doing to take advantage of these opportunities?

    B. How would you answer those who believe they are not articulate enough to present the gospel? What encouragement is found in Romans 1:16–17; 1 Corinthians 1:20–2:5; Ephesians 1:13–14; Colossians 1:3–6?

    C. What are the essential matters in telling the story of the Messiah? What is not essential?

2. *Maybe we all need to witness his majesty and sigh at his victory. Maybe we need to hear our own commission again.*

    A. In what way is this a fitting chapter to conclude the book? In your opinion, what was Max's purpose in writing this book? For you, has it been achieved? What is your response to the Savior he has presented?

B. What is the commission that Jesus gave in Matthew 28:18–20? Why is it often called the "Great Commission"? What are we commissioned to do in Romans 10:9–17?

C. How are you participating in taking the story of the Messiah to those who have not heard it? What could you do to be more actively involved? Could 1 Corinthians 9:16 become your marching orders?

D. At the beginning of this study you wrote five goals for the study. Look at those goals again. To what extent have you accomplished them? Are there ones that you would like to continue to pursue?

NOTES

The Part That Matters

    1. 1 Corinthians 15:3–5, RSV, italics mine.

Chapter 2

    1. 1 Peter 2:23

    2. Luke 23:34

Chapter 3

    1. Romans 7:15, author's paraphrase.

Chapter 4

    1. Walter Kaufman, ed., *Existentialism from Dostoyevsky to Sartre* (New York: Meridian Books, 1956), 294–295.

Chapter 5

    1. Acts 20:35

    2. Luke 9:24

    3. Matthew 13:57

Chapter 6

    1. Madeleine Blais, "Who's Going to Love Judy Bucknell?" (Part 1), Tropic Magazine, *Miami Herald,* 12 October 1980.

    2. Ibid.

    3. Ibid.

4. Ibid.

5. Matthew 27:46, TEV

6. Leviticus 16:20–22, author's paraphrase.

Chapter 8

1. Genesis 1:1, italics mine.

2. Hebrews 1:1–2, italics mine.

Chapter 9

1. "The Boxer" by Paul Simon © 1968.

2. Ibid.

3. Matthew 10:22

4. James 1:2–3

5. Hebrews 12:12–13, RSV

6. Galatians 6:9

7. 2 Timothy 4:7–8

8. James 1:12

Chapter 12

1. Luke 23:47

Chapter 13

1. Luke 23:4, 7, 16, 20, 22

2. Matthew 27:19, RSV

Chapter 16

1. Romans 7:24

2. Frederick Buechner, *The Sacred Journey* (Harper and Row, 1982), 52.

Chapter 18

1. John 14:5

2. John 11:16, author's paraphrase.

3. John 20:25, author's paraphrase.

4. Ephesians 3:20
5. John 20:28

Chapter 19
1. Matthew 23

Chapter 22
1. Genesis 12:10–20
2. Genesis 20:2

Chapter 25
1. Mark 14:32–42, NEB
2. Isaiah 53:3
3. Hebrews 5:7, italics mine.

Chapter 27
1. Romans 7:24
2. Genesis 6:6

Chapter 28
1. 1 Corinthians 2:5, author's paraphrase.
2. Psalm 19:7, author's paraphrase

Chapter 29
1. Mark 14:50
2. Mark 14:38

Chapter 30
1. Romans 5:8

Chapter 31
1. Hebrews 1:3
2. Matthew 11:28

Chapter 33
1. John 20:21

SIX HOURS ONE FRIDAY

CHRONICLES OF THE CROSS

MAX LUCADO

THOMAS NELSON
Since 1798

NASHVILLE   DALLAS   MEXICO CITY   RIO DE JANEIRO   BEIJING

Published in Nashville, Tennessee, by Thomas Nelson. Thomas Nelson is a registered trademark of Thomas Nelson, Inc.

Thomas Nelson, Inc., titles may be purchased in bulk for educational, business, fund-raising, or sales promotional use. For information, please e-mail SpecialMarkets@ThomasNelson.com.

Unless otherwise indicated, all Scripture references are from the *Holy Bible, New International Version,* © 1973, 1978, 1984 by the International Bible Society. Used by permission of Zondervan Bible Publishers.

Scripture references marked TLB are from *The Living Bible,* © 1971 by Tyndale House Publishers, Wheaton, Ill. Used by permission.

Scripture references marked JERUSALEM BIBLE are from *The New Jerusalem Bible,* © 1985 by Darton, Longman & Todd, Ltd., and Doubleday Co., Inc.

Library of Congress Cataloging-in-Publication Data:

Lucado, Max.
    Six hours one Friday / by Max Lucado.
        p. cm.
    Originally published: Portland, Or. : Multnomah, ©1989.
    ISBN 978-0-8499-0857-6 (tradepaper)
    ISBN 978-0-8499-1816-2 (hardcover)
    ISBN 978-0-8499-2096-7 (SE)
    1. Jesus Christ—Passion—Meditations. I Title.
    BT431.3.L86 2004
    232.96—dc22

                                                                2003022809

Printed in the United States of America

for
Jacquelyn, Joan, and Dee
from
your baby brother

CONTENTS

ACKNOWLEDGMENTS

This book was begun on one side of the equator and finished on the other. I've got people to thank in both places.

To the Christians in Rio de Janeiro, Brazil—Thanks for five thrilling years. Obrigado por tudo!

To the Christians at Oak Hills—Your faith and devotion are inspiring.

To Jim Toombs, Mike Cope, Rubel Shelly, Randy Mayeux, and Jim Woodroof—I appreciate the warm words and good advice.

To Ron Bailey—You gave the right counsel at the right time. Thanks.

To my relentless editor, Liz Heaney—I don't know how you do it, but you have a way of turning coal into diamonds.

To my secretary, Mary Stain—What would we do without you at the helm? Thanks for typing and typing and typing and…

To Marcelle Le Gallo and Kathleen McCleery—Thank you for doing Mary's work so she could do mine.

And a special thanks to my wife, Denalyn—You make coming home the highlight of my day.

INTRODUCTION

Millions saw the space boot of Neil Armstrong leave an imprint on the virgin surface of the moon. Thousands watched the first American soldier leave a mark in the mud of Normandy. Dozens witnessed the footprint of Columbus on the sandy beach of a new world.

But did anyone notice when the sandaled foot of the Nazarene stepped away from the shop and toward the cross?

With nail apron removed and tools stored, he stepped from the shadow of the shop into the light of the sun and began his solitary trek. Over the next three years he'd take countless steps and walk many roads, but follow his footprints through the sands of Galilee or down the streets of Jerusalem; trace his trail through the crusty desert of the Dead Sea or over the cobblestones of Philippi and you'll note one compelling truth. Each step he took carried him one step closer to the cross. Every setting of the sun found him closer to the cross than the one before.

Jesus walked the hospitals and convalescent homes of his day—but he didn't stay there.

He frequented the houses of worship. But he didn't stay there.

He walked the path of service. When the disciples were in the storm, he rescued them. When the multitudes were hungry, he fed them. When the wedding needed wine, he provided it. Jesus walked into the arena of service, but he didn't stay there.

He also walked into the classroom of instruction. His followers called him "teacher." One of his biographers wrote that Jesus "was teaching daily" (Lk. 19:47). The practical teaching of Jesus changed more lives than that of any other teacher. He could have ended his life in the classroom. But he didn't. He didn't stay there.

Nor did he remain in the garden of prayer. More than once the disciples awoke to find his pallet empty and knees bent. Jesus prayed. He prayed near Galilee. He prayed on the mountain. He prayed in a cemetery for the bereaved and he prayed in Gethsemane for his own strength. But he didn't stay there.

The garden of prayer, the hallways of service, the rooms of instruction: all mattered to his ministry, but none were the aim of his ministry. They fell short of a higher call:

"The Son of Man did not come to be served. He came to serve others and give his life as a ransom for many people" (Mark 10:45).

"The Son of Man came to find lost people and save them" (Luke 19:9).

The calling of Christ was the cross of Christ. He left the Nazareth carpentry shop with one ultimate aim—six hours, one Friday on the hill of Calvary.

If the calling of Christ was nothing short of the cross, what is the calling of his followers? Shouldn't we have as our daily aim, his daily aim—to be closer to the cross?

Following in his steps will lead us many places. Some of us will walk among the sick. Others will walk among the needy. Some will teach and all will worship and pray. But the path does not stop there. The path only stops at the foot of the cross.

My prayer is that the words of volume will aid you on your journey. I deeply appreciate my friends at W Publishing Group for reissuing this book. These chapters have a special place in my heart. Many of them originated as sermons presented during my first year of ministry at the church where I serve in San Antonio, Texas. Now, sixteen years and thousands of lessons later, these messages stir fond memories.

May they stir, within you, a deep love. May you step closer and closer to the cross of Christ until you, as did your Master, take your final breath on the hill of Calvary.

Hurricane Warnings

Labor Day weekend, 1979. Throughout the nation people were enjoying their last waltz with summertime. Weekend reunions, camping trips, picnics.

Except in Miami.

While the rest of the nation played, the Gold Coast of south Florida watched. Hurricane David was whirling through the Caribbean, leaving a trail of flooded islands and homeless people.

Floridians don't have to be told to duck when a hurricane is on the warpath. Windows were taped up, canned goods were bought, flashlights were tested. David was about to pounce.

On the Miami River a group of single guys was trying to figure out the best way to protect their houseboat. Not that it was much of a vessel. It was, at best, a rustic cabin on a leaky barge. But it was home. And if they didn't do something, their home was going to be at the bottom of the river.

None of the fellows had ever lived on a boat before, much less weathered a hurricane. Any sailor worth his salt would have had a good laugh watching those landlubbers.

It was like a *McHale's Navy* rerun. They bought enough rope to tie up the *Queen Mary*. They had their boat tied to trees, tied to moorings, tied to herself. When they were through, the little craft looked as if she'd been caught in a spider's web. They were so busy tying her to everything, it's a wonder one of the guys didn't get tied up.

How was I privy to such a fiasco? You guessed it. The houseboat was mine.

Don't ask what I was doing with a houseboat. Part adventure and part bargain, I guess. But that Labor Day weekend was more adventure than I'd bargained for. I had owned the boat for three monthly payments, and now I was about to have to sacrifice her to the hurricane! I was desperate. *Tie her down!* was all I could think.

I was reaching the end of my rope, in more ways than one, when Phil showed up. Now Phil knew boats. He even looked boat-wise.

He was born wearing a suntan and dock-siders. He spoke the lingo and knew the knots. He also knew hurricanes. Word on the river had it that he had ridden one out for three days in a ten-foot sailboat. They made him a living legend.

He felt sorry for us, so he came to give some advice . . . and it was sailor-sound. "Tie her to land and you'll regret it. Those trees are gonna get eaten by the 'cane. Your only hope is to anchor deep," he said. "Place four anchors in four different locations, leave the rope slack, and pray for the best."

Anchor deep. Good advice. We took it and . . . well, before I tell you whether or not we handled the hurricane, let's talk about anchor points.

Chances are someone reading these words is about to get caught in a storm. The weather is brewing and the water is rising and you can see the trees beginning to bend.

You've done everything possible, but your marriage still won't stand. It's just a matter of time.

You bit off more than you could chew. You never should have agreed to take on an assignment like that. There is no way you can meet the deadline. And when that due date comes and you don't produce . . .

You've been dreading this meeting all week. They've already laid off several men. Why else would the personnel director need to talk to you? And with a newborn at home.

Perhaps the winds have already reached gale force and you're holding on for your life.

"Why our son?" are the only words you can muster. The funeral is over and the words of comfort have been politely said. Now it is just you, your memories, and your question, "Why me?"

"The tests were positive. The tumor is malignant." Just when you thought the biggest struggle was over. More surgery.

"They took the other bid." That sale was your last hope. To be outbid could mean you'll have to shut down the shop. That client would have been just enough to keep the business afloat for another quarter. But now?

Waves that suck our joy out to sea. Winds that rip out our hopes by their roots. Rising tides that seep under the doors of our lives and cover the floors of our hearts.

I got caught in a hurricane as this chapter was being completed. The warning came in a telephone call during a meeting. The forecaster with the grim news was my wife. "Max, your sister just called. Your mother is going to have quadruple bypass

223

surgery at eight o'clock tomorrow morning." A few quick calls to the airlines. Clothes thrown in a bag. A race to the airport in time to grab the last seat on the last flight.

No time to develop a personal philosophy on pain and suffering. No time to analyze the mystery of death. No time to set anchors. Time only to sit tight and trust the anchor points.

Anchor points. Firm rocks sunk deeply in a solid foundation. Not casual opinions or negotiable hypotheses, but iron-clad undeniables that will keep you afloat. How strong are yours? How sturdy is your life when faced with one of these three storms?

Futility. You're riding high and getting higher. You should be content. You should be pleased. You are doing what you set out to do. You have a house. You have a job. You have security. You have two cars in the garage and a CD in the bank. By everyone's estimations you should be pleased.

Then why are you so unhappy? Is it because you know that every tide that rises also falls? Is it because your degree and promotion don't answer the questions that keep you awake at night? "What's it for, anyway?" "Who will know what I did?" "Who cares who I am?" "What is the purpose of it all?"

Failure. You can't hide it anymore. You blew it. You were wrong. You let everyone down. Instead of standing tall, you fell short. Instead of stepping out, you stepped back. The very thing you swore you'd never do is exactly what you did.

Your anchors drag through sand, finding no rocks. Unless a solid point is found soon, the hull of your heart will be splintered.

Finality. The scene repeats itself thousands of times each day in America. Folding chairs on manicured grass. Nicely dressed people under a canvas canopy. Kleenexes. Tears. Words. Metal casket. Flowers. Dirt. Open grave.

It's the wave of finality.

Though it has slapped the beach countless times, you never considered it would hit you, but it did. Uninvited and unexpected, it hit with tidal force, washing away your youth, your innocence, your mate, your friend. And now you're soaked and shivering, wondering if you will be next.

Futility,

 failure,

  finality.

You don't have to face these monsters alone. Listen to Phil's advice. It's sailor-sound both in and out of the water: Anchor deep.

Got any hurricanes coming your way?

This book examines three anchor points. Three boulders which can stand against any storm. Three rocks that repel the tallest of waves. Three petrified ledges to which you can hook your anchors. Each anchor point was planted firmly in bedrock two thousand years ago by a carpenter who claimed to be the Christ. And it was all done in the course of a single day. A single Friday. All done during six hours, one Friday.

———

To the casual observer there was nothing unusual about these six hours. To the casual observer this Friday was a normal Friday. Six hours of routine. Six hours of the expected.

Six hours. One Friday.

Enough time for

 a shepherd to examine his flocks,

 a housewife to clean and organize her house,

 a physician to receive a baby from a mother's womb

and cool the fever of one near death.

Six hours. From 9:00 A.M. to 3:00 P.M.

Six hours. One Friday.

Six hours filled with, as are all hours, the mystery of life.

————

The bright noonday sun casts a common shadow for the Judean countryside. It's the black silhouette of a shepherd standing near his fat-tailed flock. He stares at the clear sky, searching for clouds. There are none.

He looks back at his sheep. They graze lazily on the rocky hillside. An occasional sycamore provides shade. He sits on the slope and places a blade of grass in his mouth. He looks beyond the flock at the road below.

For the first time in days the traffic is thin. For over a week a river of pilgrims has streamed through this valley, bustling down the road with animals and loaded carts. For days he has watched them from his perch. Though he couldn't hear them, he knew they were speaking a dozen different dialects. And though he didn't talk to them, he knew where they were going and why.

They were going to Jerusalem. And they were going to sacrifice lambs in the temple.

The celebration strikes him as ironic. Streets jammed with people. Marketplaces full of the sounds of the bleating of goats and the selling of birds.

Endless observances.

The people relish the festivities. They awaken early and retire late. They find strange fulfillment in the pageantry.

Not him.

What kind of God would be appeased by the death of an animal?

Oh, the shepherd's doubts are never voiced anywhere except on the hillside. But on this day, they shout.

It isn't the slaughter of the animals that disturbs him. It is the endlessness of it all. How many years has he seen the people come and go? How many caravans? How many sacrifices? How many bloody carcasses?

Memories stalk him. Memories of uncontrolled anger . . . uncontrolled desire . . . uncontrolled anxiety. So many mistakes. So many stumbles. So much guilt. God seems so far away. *Lamb after lamb, Passover after Passover. Yet I still feel the same.*

He turns his head and looks again at the sky. Will the blood of yet another lamb really matter?

———

The wife sits in her house. It's Friday. She's alone. Her husband, a priest, is at the temple. It's time for lunch, but she has no appetite. Besides, it's hardly worth the trouble to prepare a meal for one. So, she sits and looks out the window.

The narrow street in front of her house is thick with people. Were she younger, she would be out there. Even if she had no reason to go on the streets, she would go. There was a time when she was energized by such activity. Not now. Now her hair is gray. Her face is wrinkled, and she is tired.

For years she has observed the holidays. For years she has watched the people. Many summers have passed, taking with them her youth and leaving only the perplexities that hound her.

As a young woman she was too busy to ponder. She had children to raise. Meals to prepare. Schedules to keep. She brushed away the riddles like she brushed back her hair. But now her home is empty. Those who needed her have others who need them.

Now, the questions are relentless. Who am I? Where did I come from? Where am I going? Why is it all happening?

The house is alive with excitement. In one room a man paces. In another a woman pushes. Sweat beads glisten on her forehead. Her eyes close, then open. She laughs, then groans. The young doctor encourages her. "Not much more. Don't give up." With a deep breath she leans forward and exerts her last ounce of energy. Then she leans back, pale and spent.

"You have a son." She raises her head just enough to see the red infant cradled in the broad palms of the physician.

Delighted with his task, the doctor cleans the eyes and smiles as he watches them fight to open. The child, freshly welcomed from the womb, is returned to his mother.

The next house he visits is quiet. Outside the bedroom a white-haired wife sits. Inside is the frail frame of her husband, hot with fever. Nothing can be done. The doctor is helpless as the man takes his last breath. It's deep—his bony, bare chest rises. His mouth opens wide, so wide that his lips whiten. Then he dies.

The same hands that cleansed the eyes of the infant now close the eyes of the dead. All during a period of six hours on one Friday.

He fights off the questions. He hasn't time to hear them today. But they are stubborn and demand to be heard.

Why heal the sick only to postpone death?

Why give strength only to see it ebb away?

Why be born and then begin to die?

Who points the crooked finger at death's next victim?

Who is this one that with such regular randomness separates soul from body?

He shrugs and places the sheet over the ashening face.

Six hours, one Friday.

To the casual observer the six hours are mundane. A shepherd with his sheep, a housewife with her thoughts, a doctor with his patients. But to the handful of awestruck witnesses, the most maddening of miracles is occurring.

God is on a cross. The creator of the universe is being executed.

Spit and blood are caked to his cheeks, and his lips are cracked and swollen. Thorns rip his scalp. His lungs scream with pain. His legs knot with cramps. Taut nerves threaten to snap as pain twangs her morbid melody. Yet, death is not ready. And there is no one to save him, for he is sacrificing himself.

It is no normal six hours. . . . it is no normal Friday.

Far worse than the breaking of his body is the shredding of his heart.

His own countrymen clamored for his death.

His own disciple planted the kiss of betrayal.

His own friends ran for cover.

And now his own father is beginning to turn his back on him, leaving him alone.

A witness could not help but ask: Jesus, do you give no thought to saving yourself? What keeps you there? What holds you to the cross? Nails don't hold gods to trees. What makes you stay?

———

The shepherd stands staring at the now blackened sky. Only seconds before he had stared at the sun. Now there is no sun.

The air is cool. The sky is black. No thunder. No lightning. No clouds. The sheep are restless. The feeling is eerie. The shepherd stands alone, wondering and listening.

What is this hellish darkness? What is this mysterious eclipse? What has happened to the light?

There is a scream in the distance. The shepherd turns toward Jerusalem.

A soldier, unaware that his impulse is part of a divine plan, plunges the spear into the side. The blood of the Lamb of God comes forth and cleanses.

The woman has scarcely lit the lamp when her husband rushes in the door. The reflection of the lamp's flame dances wildly in his wide eyes. "The temple curtain . . . ," he begins breathlessly, "torn! Ripped in two from top to bottom!"

The black angel hovers over the one on the center cross.

No delegation for this death, no demon for this duty. Satan has reserved this task for himself. Gleefully he passes his hand of death over these eyes of life.

But just when the last breath escapes, the war begins.

The pit of the earth rumbles. The young physician nearly loses his balance.

It is an earthquake—a rock-splitting rumble. A stampedelike vibration, as if prison doors have been opened and the captives are thundering to freedom. The doctor fights to keep his balance as he hurries back to the room of the one who has just died.

The body is gone.

Six hours. One Friday.

Let me ask you a question: What do you do with that day in history? What do you do with its claims?

If it really happened . . . if God did commandeer his own crucifixion . . . if he did turn his back on his own son . . . if he did storm Satan's gate, then those six hours that Friday were packed with tragic triumph. If that was God on that cross, then the hill called Skull is granite studded with stakes to which you can anchor.

Those six hours were no normal six hours. They were the most critical hours in history. For during those six hours on that Friday, God embedded in the earth three anchor points sturdy enough to withstand any hurricane.

ANCHOR POINT #1—*My life is not futile.* This rock secures the hull of your heart. Its sole function is to give you something which you can grip when facing the surging tides of futility and relativism. It's a firm grasp on the conviction that there is truth. Someone is in control and you have a purpose.

ANCHOR POINT #2—*My failures are not fatal.* It's not that he loves what you did, but he loves who you are. You are his. The one who has the right to condemn you provided the way to acquit you. You make mistakes. God doesn't. And he made you.

ANCHOR POINT #3—*My death is not final.* There is one more stone to which you should tie. It's large. It's round. And it's heavy. It blocked the door of a grave. It wasn't big enough, though. The tomb that it sealed was the tomb of a transient. He only went in to prove he could come out. And on the way out he took the stone with him and turned it into an anchor point. He dropped it deep into the uncharted waters of death. Tie to his rock and the typhoon of the tomb becomes a spring breeze on Easter Sunday.

There they are. Three anchor points. The anchor points of the cross.

Oh, by the way, Hurricane David never made it to Miami. Thirty minutes off the coast he decided to bear north. The worst damage my boat suffered were some rope burns inflicted by her overzealous crew.

I hope your hurricane misses you, too. But in case it doesn't, take the sailor's advice. "Anchor deep, say a prayer, and hold on." And don't be surprised if someone walks across the water to give you a hand.

My Life Is Not Futile

CHAPTER 2

GOD'S FORMULA FOR FATIGUE

It's late. It's past the bedtime hour. They think I'm studying. They think I think they're going to sleep. I know better. Too many giggles. Too many whispers. Too many trips to the closet to get another doll. Too many dashes in the dark to trade pillows.

It's late. It's time for little girls to be going to sleep. But for four-year-old Jenna and two-year-old Andrea, sleep is the last item on their list of things to do.

Here's the list.

Andrea still needs to flip on her back and let her feet hang out the crib a bit.

Jenna will fluff her pillow, then fluff her pillow and, well, it still needs a little fluffing.

Andrea will scoot from one side of the bed to the other.

Jenna has yet to count her fingers in a whisper and pump her make-believe bicycle.

And before sleep settles over them, more juice will be requested, another song will be sung, and a story will be told.

I love it. It's a game. The contestants? Childhood joy and sleepy eyes. The name of the game? Catch-me-if-you-can.

Sleep is determined to bring the day to a close, and joy is determined to stretch the day out as long as possible. One last enchanted kingdom. One last giggle. One last game.

Maybe you are like that. Maybe, if you had your way, your day would never end. Every moment demands to be savored. You resist sleep as long as possible because you love being awake so much. If you are like that, congratulations. If not, welcome to the majority.

Most of us have learned another way of going to bed, haven't we? It's called crash and burn. Life is so full of games that the last thing we want is another one as we are trying to sleep. So, for most of us, it's good-bye world, hello pillow. Sleep, for many, is not a robber but a refuge—eight hours of relief for our wounded souls.

And if you are kept awake, it's not by counting your fingers but by counting your debts, tasks, or even your tears.

You are tired.

You are weary.

Weary of being slapped by the waves of broken dreams.

Weary of being stepped on and run over in the endless marathon to the top.

Weary of trusting in someone only to have that trust returned in an envelope with no return address.

Weary of staring into the future and seeing only futility.

What steals our childhood zeal? For a child, the possibilities are limitless.

Then weariness finds us. Sesame Street gets traffic-jammed.

Dreams of Peter Pan are buried with Grandpa. And Star Trek's endless horizon gets hidden behind smog and skyscrapers.

What is the source of such weariness? What are the names of these burdens?

In this book we are looking at three. Futility, failure, and finality. The three Fs on the human report card. The three burdens that are too big for any back, too heavy for any biceps. Three burdens that no man can carry alone.

Let's look at futility. Few things can weary you more than the fast pace of the human race. Too many sprints for success. Too many laps in the gray-flannel fast lane. Too many nine-to-five masquerade parties. Too many days of doing whatever it takes eventually take their toll. You are left gasping for air, holding your sides on the side of the track.

And it isn't the late night reports or countless airports that sap your strength as much as it is the question you dare not admit you are asking yourself. *Is it worth it? When I get what I want, will it be worth the price I paid?*

Perhaps those were the thoughts of a San Antonio lawyer I read about recently. Successful, well paid, with a new wife and a remodeled house. But apparently it wasn't enough. One day he came home, took a gun out of his vault, climbed into a sleeping bag, and took his life. His note to his bride read, "It's not that I don't love you. It's just that I'm tired and I want to rest."

It is this weariness that makes the words of the carpenter so compelling. Listen to them. "Come to me, all you who are weary and burdened, and I will give you rest."[1]

Come to me. . . . The invitation is to come to him. Why him?

He offers the invitation as a penniless rabbi in an oppressed nation. He has no political office, no connections with the authorities in Rome. He hasn't written a best-seller or earned a diploma.

Yet, he dares to look into the leathery faces of farmers and tired faces of housewives and offer rest. He looks into the disillusioned eyes of a preacher or two from Jerusalem. He gazes into the cynical stare of a banker and the hungry eyes of a bartender and makes this paradoxical promise: "Take my yoke upon you and learn from me, for I am gentle and humble in heart, and you will find rest for your souls."[2]

The people came. They came out of the cul-de-sacs and office complexes of their day. They brought him the burdens of their existence, and he gave them not religion, not doctrine, not systems, but rest.

As a result, they called him Lord.

As a result, they called him Savior.

Not so much because of what he said, but because of what he did.

What he did on the cross during six hours, one Friday.

On the following pages you will see several people. They may be new to you, or they may be old acquaintances. They have one thing in common—they came to Jesus weary with the futility of life. A rejected woman. A confused patriarch. Disoriented disciples. A discouraged missionary.

They all found rest. They found anchor points for their storm-tossed souls. And they found that Jesus was the only man to walk God's earth who claimed to have an answer for man's burdens. "Come to me," he invited them.

My prayer is that you, too, will find rest. And that you will sleep like a baby.

CHAPTER 3

TWO
TOMBSTONES

I had driven by the place countless times. Daily I passed the small plot of land on the way to my office. Daily I told myself, *Someday I need to stop there.*

Today, that "someday" came. I convinced a tight-fisted schedule to give me thirty minutes, and I drove in.

The intersection appears no different from any other in San Antonio: a Burger King, a Rodeway Inn, a restaurant. But turn northwest, go under the cast-iron sign, and you will find yourself on an island of history that is holding its own against the river of progress.

The name on the sign? Locke Hill Cemetery.

As I parked, a darkened sky threatened rain. A lonely path invited me to walk through the two-hundred-plus tombstones. The fatherly oak trees arched above me, providing a ceiling for the solemn chambers. Tall grass, still wet from the morning dew, brushed my ankles.

The tombstones, though weathered and chipped, were alive with yesterday.

Ruhet in herrn accents the markers that bear names like Schmidt, Faustman, Grundmeyer, and Eckert.

Ruth Lacey is buried there. Born in the days of Napoleon—1807. Died over a century ago—1877.

I stood on the same spot where a mother wept on a cold day some eight decades past. The tombstone read simply, "Baby Boldt—Born and died December 10, 1910."

Eighteen-year-old Harry Ferguson was laid to rest in 1883 under these words, "Sleep sweetly tired young pilgrim." I wondered what wearied him so.

Then I saw it. It was chiseled into a tombstone on the northern end of the cemetery. The stone marks the destination of the body of Grace Llewellen Smith. No date of birth is listed, no date of death. Just the names of her two husbands, and this epitaph:

Sleeps, but rests not.
Loved, but was loved not.
Tried to please, but pleased not.
Died as she lived—alone.

Words of futility.

I stared at the marker and wondered about Grace Llewellen Smith. I wondered about her life. I wondered if she'd written the words . . . or just lived them. I wondered if she deserved the pain. I wondered if she was bitter or beaten. I wondered if she was plain. I wondered if she was beautiful. I wondered why some lives are so fruitful while others are so futile.

I caught myself wondering aloud, "Mrs. Smith, what broke your heart?"

Raindrops smudged my ink as I copied the words.

Loved, but was loved not . . .

Long nights. Empty beds. Silence. No response to messages left. No return to letters written. No love exchanged for love given.

Tried to please, but pleased not . . .

I could hear the hatchet of disappointment.

"How many times do I have to tell you?" Chop.

"You'll never amount to anything." Chop. Chop.

"Why can't you do anything right?" Chop, chop, chop.

Died as she lived—alone.

How many Grace Llewellen Smiths are there? How many people will die in the loneliness in which they are living? The homeless in Atlanta. The happy-hour hopper in L.A. A bag lady in Miami. The preacher in Nashville. Any person who doubts whether the world needs him. Any person who is convinced that no one really cares.

Any person who has been given a ring, but never a heart; criticism, but never a chance; a bed, but never rest.

These are the victims of futility.

And unless someone intervenes, unless something happens, the epitaph of Grace Smith will be theirs.

That's why the story you are about to read is significant. It's the story of another tombstone. This time, however, the tombstone doesn't mark the death of a person—it marks the birth.[1]

Her eyes squint against the noonday sun. Her shoulders stoop under the weight of the water jar. Her feet trudge, stirring dust on the path. She keeps her eyes down so she can dodge the stares of the others.

She is a Samaritan; she knows the sting of racism. She is a

woman; she's bumped her head on the ceiling of sexism. She's been married to five men. Five. Five different marriages. Five different beds. Five different rejections. She knows the sound of slamming doors.

She knows what it means to love and receive no love in return. Her current mate won't even give her his name. He only gives her a place to sleep.

If there is a Grace Llewellen Smith in the New Testament, it is this woman. The epitaph of insignificance could have been hers. And it would have been, except for an encounter with a stranger.

On this particular day, she came to the well at noon. Why hadn't she gone in the early morning with the other women? Maybe she had. Maybe she just needed an extra draw of water on a hot day. Or maybe not. Maybe it was the other women she was avoiding. A walk in the hot sun was a small price to pay in order to escape their sharp tongues.

"Here she comes."

"Have you heard? She's got a new man!"

"They say she'll sleep with anyone."

"Shhh. There she is."

So she came to the well at noon. She expected silence. She expected solitude. Instead, she found one who knew her better than she knew herself.

He was seated on the ground: legs outstretched, hands folded, back resting against the well. His eyes were closed. She stopped and looked at him. She looked around. No one was near. She looked back at him. He was obviously Jewish. What was he doing here? His eyes opened and hers ducked in embarrassment. She went quickly about her task.

Sensing her discomfort, Jesus asked her for water. But she was too streetwise to think that all he wanted was a drink. "Since when does an uptown fellow like you ask a girl like me for water?" She wanted to know what he really had in mind. Her intuition was partly correct. He was interested in more than water. He was interested in her heart.

They talked. Who could remember the last time a man had spoken to her with respect?

He told her about a spring of water that would quench not the thirst of the throat, but of the soul.

That intrigued her. "Sir, give me this water so that I won't get thirsty and have to keep coming here to draw water."

"Go, call your husband and come back."

Her heart must have sunk. Here was a Jew who didn't care if she was a Samaritan. Here was a man who didn't look down on her as a woman. Here was the closest thing to gentleness she'd ever seen. And now he was asking her about . . . that.

Anything but that. Maybe she considered lying. "Oh, my husband? He's busy." Maybe she wanted to change the subject. Perhaps she wanted to leave—but she stayed. And she told the truth.

"I have no husband." (Kindness has a way of inviting honesty.)

You probably know the rest of the story. I wish you didn't. I wish you were hearing it for the first time. For if you were, you'd be wide eyed as you waited to see what Jesus would do next. Why? Because you've wanted to do the same thing.

You've wanted to take off your mask. You've wanted to stop pretending. You've wondered what God would do if you opened your cobweb-covered door of secret sin.

This woman wondered what Jesus would do. She must have wondered if the kindness would cease when the truth was revealed. *He will be angry. He will leave. He will think I'm worthless.*

If you've had the same anxieties, then get out your pencil. You'll want to underline Jesus' answer.

"You're right. You have had five husbands and the man you are with now won't even give you a name."

No criticism? No anger? No what-kind-of-mess-have-you-made-of-your-life lectures?

No. It wasn't perfection that Jesus was seeking, it was honesty. The woman was amazed.

"I can see that you are a prophet." Translation? "There is something different about you. Do you mind if I ask you something?"

Then she asked the question that revealed the gaping hole in her soul.

"Where is God? My people say he is on the mountain. Your people say he is in Jerusalem. I don't know where he is."

I'd give a thousand sunsets to see the expression on Jesus' face as he heard those words. Did his eyes water? Did he smile? Did he look up into the clouds and wink at his father? Of all the places to find a hungry heart—Samaria?

Of all the Samaritans to be searching for God—a woman?

Of all the women to have an insatiable appetite for God—a five-time divorcée?

And of all the people to be chosen to personally receive the secret of the ages, an outcast among outcasts? The most "insignificant" person in the region?

Remarkable. Jesus didn't reveal the secret to King Herod. He didn't request an audience of the Sanhedrin and tell them the news. It wasn't within the colonnades of a Roman court that he announced his identity.

No, it was in the shade of a well in a rejected land to an ostracized woman. His eyes must have danced as he whispered the secret.

"I am the Messiah."

The most important phrase in the chapter is one easily overlooked. "Then, leaving her water jar, the woman went back to the town and said to the people, 'Come, see a man who told me everything I ever did. Could this be the Christ?'"[2]

Don't miss the drama of the moment. Look at her eyes, wide with amazement. Listen to her as she struggles for words. "Y-y-y-you a-a-a-are the M-m-m-messiah!" And watch as she scrambles to her feet, takes one last look at this grinning Nazarene, turns and runs right into the burly chest of Peter. She almost falls, regains her balance, and hotfoots it toward her hometown.

Did you notice what she forgot? She forgot her water jar. She left behind the jug that had caused the sag in her shoulders. She left behind the burden she brought.

Suddenly the shame of the tattered romances disappeared. Suddenly the insignificance of her life was swallowed by the significance of the moment. "God is here! God has come! God cares . . . for me!"

That is why she forgot her water jar. That is why she ran to the city. That is why she grabbed the first person she saw and announced her discovery, "I just talked to a man who knows everything I ever did . . . and he loves me anyway!"

The disciples offered Jesus some food. He refused it—he was too excited! He had just done what he does best. He had taken a life that was drifting and given it direction.

He was exuberant!

"Look!" he announced to the disciples, pointing at the woman who was running to the village. "Vast fields of human souls are ripening all around us, and are ready now for the reaping."[3]

Who could eat at a time like this?

———

For some of you the story of these two women is touching but distant. You belong. You are needed and you know it. You've got more friends than you can visit and more tasks than you can accomplish.

Insignificance will not be chiseled on your tombstone.

Be thankful.

But others of you are different. You paused at the epitaph because it was yours. You see the face of Grace Smith when you look into the mirror. You know why the Samaritan woman was avoiding people. You do the same thing.

You know what it's like to have no one sit by you at the cafeteria. You've wondered what it would be like to have one good friend. You've been in love and you wonder if it is worth the pain to do it again.

And you, too, have wondered where in the world God is.

I have a friend named Joy who teaches underprivileged children in an inner city church. Her class is a lively group of nine-year-olds who love life and aren't afraid of God. There is one exception, however—a timid girl by the name of Barbara.

Her difficult home life had left her afraid and insecure. For the weeks that my friend was teaching the class, Barbara never spoke. Never. While the other children talked, she sat. While the others sang, she was silent. While the others giggled, she was quiet.

Always present. Always listening. Always speechless.

Until the day Joy gave a class on heaven. Joy talked about seeing God. She talked about tearless eyes and deathless lives.

Barbara was fascinated. She wouldn't release Joy from her stare.

She listened with hunger. Then she raised her hand. "Mrs. Joy?"

Joy was stunned. Barbara had never asked a question. "Yes, Barbara?"

"Is heaven for girls like me?"

Again, I would give a thousand sunsets to have seen Jesus' face as this tiny prayer reached his throne. For indeed that is what it was—a prayer.

An earnest prayer that a good God in heaven would remember a forgotten soul on earth. A prayer that God's grace would seep into the cracks and cover one the church let slip through. A prayer to take a life that no one else could use and use it as no one else could.

Not a prayer from a pulpit, but one from a bed in a convalescent home. Not a prayer prayed confidently by a black-robed seminarian, but one whispered fearfully by a recovering alcoholic.

A prayer to do what God does best: take the common and make it spectacular. To once again take the rod and divide the sea. To take a pebble and kill a Goliath. To take water and make sparkling wine. To take a peasant boy's lunch and feed a multitude. To take mud and restore sight. To take three spikes and a wooden beam and make them the hope of humanity. To take a rejected woman and make her a missionary.

There are two graves in this chapter. The first is the lonely one in the Locke Hill Cemetery. The grave of Grace Llewellen Smith. She knew not love. She knew not gratification. She knew only the pain of the chisel as it carved this epitaph into her life.

247

Sleeps, but rests not.
Loved, but was loved not.
Tried to please, but pleased not.
Died as she lived—alone.

That, however, is not the only grave in this story. The second is near a water well. The tombstone? A water jug. A forgotten water jug. It has no words, but has great significance—for it is the burial place of insignificance.

CHAPTER 4

LIVING
PROOF

J enna, wake up. It's time to go to school." She will hear those words a thousand times in her life. But she heard them for the first time this morning.

I sat on the edge of her bed for a while before I said them to her. To tell the truth, I didn't want to say them. I didn't want to wake her. A queer hesitancy hung over me as I sat in the early morning blackness. As I sat in the silence, I realized that my words would awaken her to a new world.

For four lightning-fast years she'd been ours, and ours alone. And now that was all going to change.

We put her to bed last night as "our girl"—exclusive property of Mommy and Daddy. Mommy and Daddy read to her, taught her, listened to her. But beginning today, someone else would, too.

Until today, it was Mommy and Daddy who wiped away the tears and put on the Band-Aids. But beginning today, someone else would, too.

I didn't want to wake her.

Until today, her life was essentially us—Mom, Dad, and baby sister Andrea. Today that life would grow—new friends, a teacher. Her world was this house—her room, her toys, her swing set. Today her world would expand. She would enter the winding halls of education—painting, reading, calculating . . . becoming.

I didn't want to wake her. Not because of the school. It's a fine one. Not because I don't want her to learn. Heaven knows I want her to grow, to read, to mature. Not because she doesn't want to go. School has been all she could talk about for the last week!

No, I didn't want to wake her up because I didn't want to give her up.

But I woke her anyway. I interrupted her childhood with the inevitable proclamation, "Jenna, wake up. . . . It's time to go to school."

It took me forever to get dressed. Denalyn saw me moping around and heard me humming "Sunrise, Sunset" and said, "You'll never make it through her wedding." She's right.

We drove to school in two cars so I could go directly to work. I asked Jenna to ride with me. I thought I should give her a bit of fatherly assurance. As it turned out, I was the one needing assurance.

For one dedicated to the craft of words, I found very few to share with her. I told her to enjoy herself. I told her to obey her teacher. I told her, "If you get lonely or afraid, tell your teacher to call me and I'll come and get you." "Okay," she smiled. Then she asked if she could listen to a tape with kids' music. "Okay," I said.

So while she sang songs, I swallowed lumps. I watched her as she sang. She looked big. Her little neck stretched as high as it could to look over the dash. Her eyes were hungry and bright. Her hands were folded in her lap. Her feet, wearing brand new turquoise and pink tennis shoes, barely extended over the seat.

"Denalyn was right," I mumbled to myself. "I'll never make it through the wedding."

What is she thinking? I wondered. *Does she know how tall this ladder of education is that she will begin climbing this morning?*

No, she didn't. But I did. How many chalkboards will those eyes see? How many books will those hands hold? How many teachers will those feet follow and—gulp—imitate?

Were it within my power, I would have, at that very instant, assembled all the hundreds of teachers, instructors, coaches, and tutors she would have over the next eighteen years and announced, "This is no normal student. This is my child. Be careful with her!"

As I parked and turned off the engine, my big girl became small again. And it was a voice of a very little girl that broke the silence. "Daddy, I don't want to get out."

I looked at her. The eyes that had been bright were now fearful. The lips that had been singing were now trembling.

I fought a Herculean urge to grant her request. Everything within me wanted to say, "Okay, let's forget it all and get out of here." For a brief, eternal moment I considered kidnapping my own daughters, grabbing my wife, and escaping these horrid paws of progress to live forever in the Himalayas.

But I knew better. I knew it was time. I knew it was right. And I knew she would be fine. But I never knew it would be so hard to say, "Honey, you'll be all right. Come on, I'll carry you."

And she was all right. One step into the classroom and the cat of curiosity pounced on her. And I walked away. I gave her up. Not much. And not as much as I will have to in the future. But I gave her up as much as I could today.

As I was walking back to my truck, a verse pounced on me. It was a passage I'd studied before. Today's events took it from black-and-white theology to Technicolor reality.

"What, then, shall we say in response to this? If God is for us,

251

who can be against us? He who did not spare his own Son, but *gave him up for us all*—how will he not also, along with him, graciously give us all things?"[1]

Is that how you felt, God? Is what I felt this morning anything like what you felt when you gave up your son?

If so, it explains so much. It explains the proclamation of the angels to the shepherds outside Bethlehem. (A proud father was announcing the birth of a son.)

It explains the voice at Jesus' baptism, "This is my son. . . . " (You did what I wanted to do, but couldn't.)

It explains the transfiguration of Moses and Elijah on the mountaintop. (You sent them to encourage him.)

And it explains how your heart must have ached as you heard the cracking voice of your son, "Father, take this cup away."

I was releasing Jenna into a safe environment with a compassionate teacher who stood ready to wipe away any tears. You released Jesus into a hostile arena with a cruel soldier who turned the back of your son into raw meat.

I said good-bye to Jenna knowing she would make friends, laugh, and draw pictures. You said good-bye to Jesus knowing he would be spat upon, laughed at, and killed.

I gave up my child fully aware that were she to need me I would be at her side in a heartbeat. You said good-bye to your son fully aware that when he would need you the most, when his cry of despair would roar through the heavens, you would sit in silence. The angels, though positioned, would hear no command from you. Your son, though in anguish, would feel no comfort from your hands.

"He gave his best," Paul reasons. "Why should we doubt his love?"

Before the day was over, I sat in silence a second time. This time not beside my daughter, but before my Father. This time not sad over what I had to give, but grateful for what I'd already received—living proof that God does care.

CHAPTER 5

FLAMING TORCHES
AND LIVING PROMISES

Doubt. He's a nosy neighbor. He's an unwanted visitor. He's an obnoxious guest. Just when you were all prepared for a weekend of relaxation . . . just when you pulled off your work clothes and climbed into your Bermuda shorts . . . just when you unfolded the lawn chair and sat down with a magazine and a glass of iced tea . . . his voice interrupted your thoughts.

"Hey, Bob. Got a few minutes? I've got a few questions. I don't mean to be obnoxious, Bob, but how can you believe that a big God could ever give a hoot about you? Don't you think you are being presumptuous in thinking God wants you in heaven?

"You may assume you are on pretty good terms with the man upstairs, but haven't you forgotten that business trip in Atlanta? You think he won't call your cards on that one?

"How do you know God gives a flip about you anyway?"

Got a neighbor like this?

He'll pester you. He'll irritate you. He'll criticize your judgment. He'll kick the stool out from under you and refuse to help you up. He'll tell you not to believe in the invisible yet offer no answer for the inadequacy of the visible.

He's a mealy-mouthed, two-faced liar who deals from the bottom of the deck. His aim is not to convince you but to confuse you. He doesn't offer solutions, he only raises questions.

Don't let him fool you. Though he may speak the current jargon, he is no newcomer. His first seeds of doubt were sown in the Garden of Eden in the heart of Eve.

There she sat, enjoying the trees, sipping on a mint julep and catching a few rays when she noticed a pair of beady eyes peering over the shrubs.

After a little small talk, he positioned himself between Eve and the sun and cast his first shadow of a doubt. "Did God really say, 'You must not eat from any tree in the garden'?"[1]

No anger. No picket signs. No "God is dead" demonstrations. Just questions.

Had any visits from this fellow lately? If you find yourself going to church in order to be saved and not because you are saved, then you've been listening to him. If you find yourself doubting God could forgive you *again* for *that,* you've been sold some snake oil. If you are more cynical about Christians than sincere about Christ, then guess who came to dinner?

I suggest you put a lock on your gate. I suggest you post a "Do Not Enter" sign on your door. I also suggest you take a look at an encounter between a fitful doubter and a faithful God.

Abraham, or Abram as he was known at the time, was finding God's promises about as easy to swallow as a chicken bone. The promise? That his descendants would be as numerous as the stars. The problem? No son. "No problem," came God's response.

Abram looked over at his wife, Sarah, as she shuffled by in her gown and slippers with the aid of a walker. The chicken bone stuck for a few minutes but eventually slid down his throat.

Just as he was turning away to invite Sarah to a candlelight dinner, he heard promise number two.

"Abram."

"Yes, Lord?"

"All this land will be yours."

Imagine God telling you that your children will someday own Fifth Avenue, and you will understand Abram's hesitation.

"On that one, Father, I need a little help."

And a little help was given.

———

It's a curious scene.

Twilight. The sky is a soft blue ceiling with starry diamonds. The air is cool. The animals in the pasture are quiet. The trees are silhouettes. Abram dozes under a tree. His sleep is fitful.

It's as if God is allowing Abram's doubt to run its course. In his dreams Abram is forced to face the lunacy of it all. The voices of doubt speak convincingly.

How do I know God is with me?

What if this is all a hoax?

How do you know that is God who is speaking?

The thick and dreadful darkness of doubt.

The same darkness you feel when you sit on a polished pew in a funeral chapel and listen to the obituary of the one you love more than life.

The same darkness you feel when you hear the words, "The tumor is malignant. We have to operate."

The same darkness that falls upon you when you realize you just lost your temper . . . again.

The same darkness you feel when you realize the divorce you never wanted is final.

The same darkness into which Jesus screamed, "My God, my God, why have you forsaken me?"

Appropriate words. For when we doubt, God seems very far away.

Which is exactly why he chose to draw so near.

God had told Abram to take three animals, cut them in half, and arrange the halves facing each other. To us the command is mysterious. To Abram, it wasn't. He'd seen the ceremony before. He'd participated in it. He'd sealed many covenants by walking through the divided carcasses and stating, "May what has happened to these animals happen also to me if I fail to uphold my word."[2]

That is why his heart must have skipped a beat when he saw the lights in the darkness passing between the carcasses. The soft golden glow from the coals in the firepot and the courageous flames from the torch. What did they mean?

The invisible God had drawn near to make his immovable promise. "To your descendants I give this land."[3]

And though God's people often forgot their God, God didn't forget them. He kept his word. The land became theirs.

God didn't give up. He never gives up.

When Joseph was dropped into a pit by his own brothers, God didn't give up.

When Moses said, "Here I am, send Aaron," God didn't give up.

When the delivered Israelites wanted Egyptian slavery instead of milk and honey, God didn't give up.

When Aaron was making a false god at the very moment Moses was with the true God, God didn't give up.

When only two of the ten spies thought the Creator was powerful enough to deliver the created, God didn't give up.

When Samson whispered to Delilah, when Saul roared after David, when David schemed against Uriah, God didn't give up.

When God's word lay forgotten and man's idols stood glistening, God didn't give up.

When the children of Israel were taken into captivity, God didn't give up.

He could have given up. He could have turned his back. He could have walked away from the wretched mess, but he didn't.

He didn't give up.

When he became flesh and was the victim of an assassination attempt before he was two years old, he didn't give up.

When the people from his own hometown tried to push him over a cliff, he didn't give up.

When his brothers ridiculed him, he didn't give up.

When he was accused of blaspheming God by people who didn't fear God, he didn't give up.

When Peter worshiped him at the supper and cursed him at the fire, he didn't give up.

When people spat in his face, he didn't spit back. When the bystanders slapped him, he didn't slap them. When a whip ripped his sides, he didn't turn and command the awaiting angels to stuff that whip down that soldier's throat.

And when human hands fastened the divine hands to a cross with spikes, it wasn't the soldiers who held the hands of Jesus steady. It was God who held them steady. For those wounded hands were the same invisible hands that had carried the firepot and the torch two thousand years earlier. They were the same hands that had brought light into Abram's thick and dreadful darkness. They had come to do it again.

So, the next time that obnoxious neighbor walks in, escort him out. Out to the hill. Out to Calvary. Out to the cross where, with holy blood, the hand that carried the flame wrote the promise, "God would give up his only son before he'd give up on you."

CHAPTER 6

ANGELIC
MESSAGES

I had every right to be angry. If you'd had a week like mine, you would have been angry, too. My problems began on Sunday night. I was still living in Brazil and was taking some relatives to southern Brazil to see the Iguaçú Falls. A canceled flight left us stranded several hours in the São Paulo airport. No warning. No explanation. Just a notification as we were landing that the plane we were going to catch was going nowhere. If we wanted, we could wait two hours and catch another one.

"If we wanted!" Grrrr.

When we got to our hotel, it was raining. It rained until the day we left.

Determined to record the falls, I carried my video camera for one mile through a rainstorm. I don't mean a drizzle or a sprinkle or a shower. I mean a blinding downpour. When I reached the falls, I realized I had left the camera turned on for the previous hour and filmed the inside of the camera bag and run down the battery.

When I got back to the hotel, I realized that the rain had ruined the camera. How much ruin? Three hundred dollars' worth of ruin. That was Wednesday. The week wasn't over yet.

When I got back to Rio, I found out Denalyn had told her

family that we were going to spend the upcoming Christmas with them. I had already told my family that we were going to spend the holidays with them.

Thursday was the clincher. Denalyn called me at home. Our car had broken down. The car that the car dealer promised was in great shape. The car that the car dealer promised was worth the extra money. The car that the car dealer had sworn was trouble free. It broke down. Downtown. Again. On my day off.

I walked to the shopping center. I spoke to no one. No one dared to speak to me.

I sat in the car and tried to start it. No luck. When I turned the key in the ignition, all I could hear were the promises of the car dealer and the jingle of the mechanic's cash register. I spent an hour tinkering with a broken-down car in a parking lot.

Finally I called the mechanic. The tow truck was busy. Could I wait a few minutes? In Brazil, the word *minutes* can better be translated *years*. So I waited. And I waited. And I waited. My children grew up and had children of their own, and still I was waiting.

Finally, as the sun was setting, the truck appeared. "Put it in neutral," I was instructed. As I climbed in the car, I thought, *Might as well try it one more time*. I turned the key in the ignition. Guess what? You got it. It started.

That should have been good news. It was, until I saw the driver of the tow truck in no hurry to leave. He wanted to be paid. "For what?" I implored. "Was it my fault your car started?" he replied. It's a good thing I didn't know how to say "smart aleck" in Portuguese. So I paid him for watching me start my car.

I immediately drove the car to the mechanic. As I drove, two devils came and perched on my shoulders. The fact that I couldn't see them didn't make them any less real. I could hear them—they spoke the language of the Liar.

One was anger. If there was anything I wasn't mad at by this point, he took care of that. My list of offenses was long and ugly.

The other was self-pity. Boy, did he find a listening ear. Not only had I had a bad week, he reminded me that I had been plagued with a bad life! Born with the handicap of freckles and red hair. Always too slow for track. Never elected "most likely to succeed." And now, a missionary suffering on foreign soil.

Anger in one ear and self-pity in the other . . . if I hadn't seen him, who knows what I would have done.

He didn't look like an angel. In fact, he looked like anything but an angel. But I know he was an angel, for only angels bring that type of a message.

He knocked on my car window.

"*Trocadinho, Senhor?*" ("Do you have any spare change, sir?")

He was, at most, nine years old. Shirtless. Barefooted. Dirty. So dirty I couldn't tell if he was wearing shorts or not. His hair was matted. His skin was crusty. I rolled down the window. The voices on my shoulders became silent.

"What's your name?" I asked.

"José."

I looked over at the sidewalk. Two other street orphans were walking towards the cars behind me. They were naked except for ragged gym shorts.

"Are they your brothers?" I asked.

"No, just friends."

"Have you collected much money today?"

He opened a dirty hand full of coins. Enough money, perhaps, for a soft drink.

I reached in my wallet and pulled out the equivalent to a dollar. His eyes brightened. Mine watered. The light changed and the cars behind me honked. As I drove away, I saw him running to tell his friends what he had received.

The voices on my shoulders didn't dare say a word. Nor did I. The three of us drove in shameful silence.

I figured I had said enough. And God had heard every word.

What if God had responded to my grumblings? What if he'd heeded my complaints? He could have. He could have answered my carelessly mumbled prayers.

And had he chosen to do so, a prototype of the result had just appeared at my door.

"Don't want to mess with airlines? This boy doesn't have that problem. Frustrated with your video camera? That's one headache this boy doesn't have. He may have to worry about tonight's dinner, but he doesn't have to worry about video cameras. And family? I'm sure this orphan would gladly take one of your families if you are too busy to appreciate them. And cars? Yes, they are a hassle, aren't they? You should try this boy's mode of transportation— bare feet."

God sent the boy with a message. And the point the boy made was razor sharp.

"You cry over spilled champagne."

Ouch.

"Your complaints are not over the lack of necessities but the abundance of benefits. You bellyache over the frills, not the basics; over benefits, not essentials. The source of your problems is your blessings."

José gave me a lot for my dollar; he gave me a lesson on gratitude.

Gratitude. More aware of what you have than what you don't. Recognizing the treasure in the simple—a child's hug, fertile soil, a golden sunset. Relishing in the comfort of the common—a warm bed, a hot meal, a clean shirt.

And no one has more reason to be grateful than the one who has been reminded of God's gift by one of God's angels. I was. And so was Franciszek Gajowniczek. His story is moving.

It's difficult to find beauty in death. It's even more difficult to find beauty in a death camp. Especially Auschwitz. Four million Jews died there in World War II. A half-ton of human hair is still preserved. The showers that sprayed poison gas still stand.

But for all the ugly memories of Auschwitz there is one of beauty. It's the memory Gajowniczek has of Maximilian Kolbe.

In February 1941 Kolbe was incarcerated at Auschwitz. He was a Franciscan priest. In the harshness of the slaughterhouse he maintained the gentleness of Christ. He shared his food. He gave up his bunk. He prayed for his captors. One could call him the "Saint of Auschwitz."

In July of that same year there was an escape from the prison. It was the custom at Auschwitz to kill ten prisoners for every one who escaped. All the prisoners would be gathered in the courtyard, and the commandant would randomly select ten men from the ranks. These victims would be immediately taken to a cell where they would receive no food or water until they died.

The commandant begins his selection. At each selection another prisoner steps forward to fill the sinister quota. The tenth name he calls is Gajowniczek.

As the SS officers check the numbers of the condemned, one of the condemned begins to sob. "My wife and my children," he weeps.

The officers turn as they hear movement among the prisoners. The guards raise their rifles. The dogs tense, anticipating a command to attack. A prisoner has left his row and is pushing his way to the front.

It is Kolbe. No fear on his face. No hesitancy in his step. The capo shouts at him to stop or be shot. "I want to talk to the commander," he says calmly. For some reason the officer doesn't club or kill him. Kolbe stops a few paces from the commandant, removes his hat, and looks the German officer in the eye.

"Herr Commandant, I wish to make a request, please."

That no one shot him is a miracle.

"I want to die in the place of this prisoner." He points at the sobbing Gajowniczek. The audacious request is presented without stammer.

"I have no wife and children. Besides, I am old and not good for anything. He's in better condition." Kolbe knew well the Nazi mentality.

"Who are you?" the officer asks.

"A Catholic priest."

The block is stunned. The commandant, uncharacteristically speechless. After a moment, he barks, "Request granted."

Prisoners were never allowed to speak. Gajowniczek says, "I could only thank him with my eyes. I was stunned and could hardly grasp what was going on. The immensity of it: I, the condemned, am to live and someone else willingly and voluntarily offers his life for me—a stranger. Is this some dream?"

The Saint of Auschwitz outlived the other nine. In fact, he didn't die of thirst or starvation. He died only after carbolic acid was injected into his veins. It was August 14, 1941.

Gajowniczek survived the Holocaust. He made his way back to his hometown. Every year, however, he goes back to Auschwitz. Every August 14 he goes back to say thank you to the man who died in his place.

In his backyard there is a plaque. A plaque he carved with his own hands. A tribute to Maximilian Kolbe—the man who died so he could live.[1]

There are times that it takes an angel to remind us about what we have.

There aren't very many similarities between Franciszek Gajowniczek and Max Lucado. We speak two different languages. We salute two different flags. We know two different homelands. But we do have three things in common.

We both had an angel set us free from a prison. We both had a Jewish teacher die in our place. And we both learned that what we already have is far greater than anything we might want.

CHAPTER 7

REMEMBER

On the evening of that first day of the week,
when the disciples were together,
with the doors locked for fear of the Jews . . .
JOHN 20:19

The church of Jesus Christ began with a group of frightened men in a second-floor room in Jerusalem.

Though trained and taught, they didn't know what to say. Though they'd marched with him for three years, they now sat . . . afraid. They were timid soldiers, reluctant warriors, speechless messengers.

Their most courageous act was to get up and lock the door.

Some looked out the window, some looked at the wall, some looked at the floor, but all looked inside themselves.

And well they should, for it was an hour of self-examination. All their efforts seemed so futile. Nagging their memories were the promises they'd made but not kept. When the Roman soldiers took Jesus, Jesus' followers took off. With the very wine of the covenant on their breath and the bread of his sacrifice in their bellies, they fled.

All those boasts of bravado? All those declarations of devotion? They lay broken and shattered at the gate of Gethsemane's garden.

We don't know where the disciples went when they fled the garden, but we do know what they took: a memory. They took a heart-stopping memory of a man who called himself no less than God in the flesh. And they couldn't get him out of their minds. Try as they might to lose him in the crowd, they couldn't forget him. If they saw a leper, they thought of his compassion. If they heard a storm, they would remember the day he silenced one. If they saw a child, they would think of the day he held one. And if they saw a lamb being carried to the temple, they would remember his face streaked with blood and his eyes flooded with love.

No, they couldn't forget him. As a result, they came back. And, as a result, the church of our Lord began with a group of frightened men in an upper room.

Sound familiar? Things haven't changed much in two thousand years, have they? How many churches today find themselves paralyzed in the upper room?

How many congregations have just enough religion to come together, but not enough passion to go out? If the doors aren't locked, they might as well be.

Upper-room futility. A little bit of faith but very little fire.

"Sure, we're doing our part to reach the world. Why, just last year we mailed ten correspondence courses. We're anticipating a response any day now."

"You bet we care that the world is reached! We send $150 a month to . . . uh, well . . . ol' what's-his-name down there in . . . uh, well, oh, I forget the place, but . . . we pray for it often."

"World hunger? Why, that's high on our priority list! In

fact, we have plans to plan a planning session. At least, that is what we are planning to do."

Good people. Lots of ideas. Plenty of good intentions. Budgets. Meetings. Words. Promises. But while all this is going on, the door remains locked and the story stays a secret.

You don't turn your back on Christ, but you don't turn toward him either. You don't curse his name, but neither do you praise it. You know you should do something, but you're not sure what. You know you should come together, but you're not sure why.

Upper-room futility. Confused ambassadors behind locked doors. What will it take to unlock them? What will it take to ignite the fire? What will it take to restore the first-century passion? What will have to happen before the padlocks of futility tumble from our doors and are trampled under the feet of departing disciples?

More training? That's part of it. Better strategies? That would help. A greater world vision? Undoubtedly. More money? That's imperative. A greater dependence on the Holy Spirit? Absolutely.

But in the midst of these items there is one basic ingredient that cannot be overlooked. There is one element so vital that its absence ensures our failure. What is needed to get us out is exactly what got the apostles out.

Picture the scene. Peter, John, James. They came back. Banking on some zany possibility that the well of forgiveness still had a few drops, they came back. Daring to dream that the master had left them some word, some plan, some direction, they came back.

But little did they know their wildest dream wasn't wild enough. Just as someone mumbles, "It's no use," they hear a noise. They hear a voice.

"Peace be with you."[1]

Every head lifted. Every eye turned. Every mouth dropped open. Someone looked at the door.

It was still locked.

It was a moment the apostles would never forget, a story they would never cease to tell. The stone of the tomb was not enough to keep him in. The walls of the room were not enough to keep him out.

The one betrayed sought his betrayers. What did he say to them? Not "What a bunch of flops!" Not "I told you so." No "Where-were-you-when-I-needed-you?" speeches. But simply one phrase, "Peace be with you." The very thing they didn't have was the very thing he offered: peace.

It was too good to be true! So amazing was the appearance that some were saying, "Pinch me, I'm dreaming" even at the ascension.[2] No wonder they returned to Jerusalem with great joy![3] No wonder they were always in the temple praising God![4]

A transformed group stood beside a transformed Peter as he announced some weeks later: "Therefore let all Israel be assured of this: God has made this Jesus, whom you crucified, both Lord and Christ."[5]

No timidity in his words. No reluctance. About three thousand people believed his message.

The apostles sparked a movement. The people became followers of the death-conqueror. They couldn't hear enough or say enough about him. People began to call them "Christ-ians." Christ was their model, their message. They preached "Jesus Christ and him crucified," not for the lack of another topic, but because they couldn't exhaust this one.

What unlocked the doors of the apostles' hearts?

Simple. They saw Jesus. They encountered the Christ. Their

sins collided with their Savior and their Savior won! What lit the boiler of the apostles was a red-hot conviction that the very one who should have sent them to hell, went to hell for them and came back to tell about it.

A lot of things would happen to them over the next few decades. Many nights would be spent away from home. Hunger would gnaw at their bellies. Rain would soak their skin. Stones would bruise their bodies. Shipwrecks, lashings, martyrdom. But there was a scene in the repertoire of memories that caused them never to look back: the betrayed coming back to find his betrayers, not to scourge them, but to send them. Not to criticize them for forgetting, but to commission them to remember. *Remember* that he who was dead is alive and they who were guilty have been forgiven.

Think about the first time you ever saw him. Think about your first encounter with the Christ. Robe yourself in that moment. Resurrect the relief. Recall the purity. Summon forth the passion. Can you remember?

I can. 1965. A red-headed ten-year-old with a tornado of freckles sits in a Bible class on a Wednesday night. What I remember of the class are scenes—school desks with initials carved in them. A blackboard. A dozen or so kids, some listening, some not. A teacher wearing a suit coat too tight to button around his robust belly.

He is talking about Jesus. He is explaining the cross. I know I had heard it before, but that night I heard it for sure. "You can't save yourself; you need a savior." I can't explain why it connected that night as opposed to another, but it did. He simply articulated what I was beginning to understand—I was lost—and he explained what I needed—a redeemer. From that night on, my heart belonged to Jesus.

Many would argue that a ten-year-old is too young for such a decision. And they may be right. All I know is that I never made a more earnest decision in my life. I didn't know much about God, but what I knew was enough. I knew I wanted to go to heaven. And I knew I couldn't do it alone.

No one had to tell me to be happy. No one had to tell me to tell others. They couldn't keep me quiet. I told all my friends at school. I put a bumper sticker on my bicycle. And though I'd never read 2 Corinthians 4:13, I knew what it meant. "I believed; therefore I have spoken." Pardon truly received is pardon powerfully proclaimed.

There is a direct correlation between the accuracy of our memory and the effectiveness of our mission. If we are not teaching people how to be saved, it is perhaps because we have forgotten the tragedy of being lost! If we're not teaching the message of forgiveness, it may be because we don't remember what it was like to be guilty. And if we're not preaching the cross, it could be that we've subconsciously decided that—God forbid—somehow we don't need it.

In what was perhaps the last letter Paul ever wrote, he begged Timothy not to forget. In a letter written within earshot of the sharpening of the blade that would sever his head, he urged Timothy to remember. "Remember Jesus Christ. . . ."[6] You can almost picture the old warrior smiling as he wrote the words. "Remember Jesus Christ, raised from the dead, descended from David. This is my gospel. . . ."

When times get hard, remember Jesus. When people don't listen, remember Jesus. When tears come, remember Jesus. When disappointment is your bed partner, remember Jesus. When fear pitches his tent in your front yard. When death looms, when anger singes, when shame weighs heavily. Remember Jesus.

Remember holiness in tandem with humanity. Remember the sick who were healed with callused hands. Remember the dead called from the grave with a Galilean accent. Remember the eyes of God that wept human tears. And, most of all, remember this descendant of David who beat the hell out of death.

Can you still remember? Are you still in love with him? Remember, Paul begged, remember Jesus. Before you remember anything, remember him. If you forget anything, don't forget him.

Oh, but how quickly we forget. So much happens through the years. So many changes within. So many alterations without. And, somewhere, back there, we leave him. We don't turn away from him . . . we just don't take him with us. Assignments come. Promotions come. Budgets are made. Kids are born, and the Christ . . . the Christ is forgotten.

Has it been a while since you stared at the heavens in speechless amazement? Has it been a while since you realized God's divinity and your carnality?

If it has, then you need to know something. He is still there. He hasn't left. Under all those papers and books and reports and years. In the midst of all those voices and faces and memories and pictures, he is still there.

Do yourself a favor. Stand before him again. Or, better, allow him to stand before you. Go into your upper room and wait. Wait until he comes. And when he appears, don't leave. Run your fingers over his feet. Place your hand in the pierced side. And look into those eyes. Those same eyes that melted the gates of hell and sent the demons scurrying and Satan running. Look at them as they look at you. You'll never be the same.

A man is never the same after he simultaneously sees his utter despair and Christ's unbending grace. To see the despair without the grace is suicidal. To see the grace without the despair is upper-room futility. But to see them both is conversion.

My Failures
Are Not Fatal

CHAPTER 8

FATAL
ERRORS

T he handwriting was shaky. The stationery was lined, loose-leaf paper. The ink was black and the tone desperate. The note was dated February 6, 1974, and was addressed to the U.S. government.

"I am sending ten dollars for blankets I stole while in World War II. My mind could not rest. Sorry I'm late." It was signed, "an ex-GI." Then there was this postscript, "I want to be ready to meet God."

This recruit was not alone in his guilt. His letter is one of literally tons of letters that have been sent to the U.S. government since it began collecting and storing the letters in 1811. Since that time $3,500,000 has been deposited in what is called the Conscience Fund.

An average of $45,000 per year is received. The biggest year was 1950 in which $350,000 was collected.

One man writing from Brazil sent fifty dollars to cover the cost of two pair of cavalry boots, two pair of trousers, one case of KC rations and thirty pounds of frozen meat he stole from the army between 1943 and 1946.

In some instances the amounts are small; only the remorse is big. One Colorado woman sent in two eight-cent stamps to make up for having used one stamp twice (which for some reason had not been canceled). A former IRS employee mailed in one dollar for four ballpoint pens she had never returned to the office.

A Salem, Ohio, man submitted one dollar with the following note, "When a boy, I put a few pennies on the railroad track and the train flattened them. I also used a dime or a quarter in a silver-coating experiment in high school. I understand there is a law against defacing our money. I have not seen it but I desire to be a law-abiding citizen."

Anxiety over a thirty-year-old mistake? Regret over mashed pennies? A guilty conscience because of ballpoint pens? If the struggle to have a clean conscience wasn't so common, the letters would be funny. But the struggle is common.

What do you do with your failures? Our mistakes come to us as pebbles, small stones that serve as souvenirs of our stumbles. We carry them in our hands, and soon our hands are full. We put them in our pockets, and soon our pockets bulge. We place them in a bag and put it over our shoulder; the burlap scratches and chaps. And soon the bag of yesterday's failures is so heavy we drag it.

Here are some failures that have been dragged into my office.

Unfaithfulness. He wanted to try again. She said, "No way." He wanted a second chance. She said, "You blew your chance." He admitted he made a mistake by seeing another woman. He sees now that the mistake was fatal to his marriage.

Homosexuality. His wrists bore the scars of a suicide attempt. His arms had tracks from countless needles. His eyes reflected the spirit of one hellbent on self-destruction. His words were those of a prisoner grimly resigned to the judge's sentence. "I'm gay. My dad says I'm a queer. I guess he's right."

Division. A church leadership demanded submission. A membership demanded a louder voice. It was a bomb waiting to explode. The eruption resulted in a half-empty building of walking wounded.

Immorality. She came to church with a pregnant womb and a repentant spirit. "I can't have a child," she pleaded. "We'll find a home for it," she was assured. She agreed. Then she changed her mind. Her boyfriend funded the abortion. "Can God ever forgive me?" she asked.

Nothing drags more stubbornly than a sack of failures.

Could you do it all over again, you'd do it differently. You'd be a different person. You'd be more patient. You'd control your tongue. You'd finish what you started. You'd turn the other cheek instead of slapping his. You'd get married first. You wouldn't marry at all. You'd be honest. You'd resist the temptation. You'd run with a different crowd.

But you can't. And as many times as you tell yourself, "What's done is done," what you did can't be undone.

That's part of what Paul meant when he said, "The wages of sin is death."[1] He didn't say, "The wages of sin is a bad mood." Or, "The wages of sin is a hard day." Nor, "The wages of sin is depression." Read it again. "The wages of sin is death." Sin is fatal.

Can anything be done with it?

Your therapist tells you to talk about it. So you do. You pull the bag into his office and pour the rocks out on his floor and analyze each one. And it's helpful. It feels good to talk and he's nice. But when the hour is up, you still have to carry the bag out with you.

Your friends tell you not to feel bad. "Everyone slumps a bit in this world," they say. "Not very comforting," you say.

Feel-great-about-life rallies tell you to ignore the thing and be happy! Which works—until you wipe the fog off your mirror and take an honest look. Then you see, it's still there.

Legalists tell you to work the weight off. A candle for every rock. A prayer for every pebble. Sounds logical, but what if I run out of time? Or what if I didn't count correctly? You panic.

What *do* you do with the stones from life's stumbles?

My oldest daughter, Jenna, is four years old. Some time ago she came to me with a confession. "Daddy, I took a crayon and drew on the wall." (Kids amaze me with their honesty.)

I sat down and lifted her up into my lap and tried to be wise. "Is that a good thing to do?" I asked her.

"No."

"What does Daddy do when you write on the wall?"

"You spank me."

"What do you think Daddy should do this time?"

"Love."

Don't we all want that? Don't we all long for a father who, even though our mistakes are written all over the wall, will love us anyway? Don't we want a father who cares for us in spite of our failures?

We *do* have that type of a father. A father who is at his best when we are at our worst. A father whose grace is strongest when our devotion is weakest. If your bag is big and bulky, then you're in for some thrilling news: Your failures are not fatal.

CHAPTER 9

CRISTO
REDENTOR

inety feet tall. One thousand three hundred twenty
tons of reinforced Brazilian tile. Positioned on a
mountain a mile and one-half above sea level. It's the
famous *Christ the Redeemer* statue that overlooks the city of Rio de
Janeiro, Brazil.

No tourist comes to Rio without snaking up Corcovado
Mountain to see this looming monument. The head alone is nine
feet tall. The span from fingertip to fingertip—sixty-three feet.

While living in Rio, I saw the statue dozens of times. But no
time was as impressive as the first.

I was a college student spending a summer in Brazil. Except
for scampers across the Mexican border, this was my first trip
outside the continental U.S. I had known this monument only
through *National Geographic* magazine. I was to learn that no
magazine can truly capture the splendor of *Cristo Redentor.*

Below me was Rio. Seven million people swarming on the
lush green mountains that crash into the bright blue Atlantic.
Behind me was the *Christ the Redeemer* statue. As I looked at the
towering edifice through my telephoto lens, two ironies caught
my attention.

I couldn't help but notice the blind eyes. Now, I know what

you are thinking—all statues have blind eyes. You are right, they do. But it's as if the sculptor of this statue intended that the eyes be blind. There are no pupils to suggest vision. There are no circles to suggest sight. There are only Little Orphan Annie openings.

I lowered my camera to my waist. *What kind of redeemer is this? Blind? Eyes fixated on the horizon, refusing to see the mass of people at its feet?*

I saw the second irony as I again raised my camera. I followed the features downward, past the strong nose, past the prominent chin, past the neck. My focus came to rest on the cloak of the statue. On the outside of the cloak there is a heart. A Valentine's heart. A simple heart.

A stone heart.

The unintended symbolism staggered me. *What kind of redeemer is this? Heart made of stone? Held together not with passion and love, but by concrete and mortar. What kind of redeemer is this? Blind eyes and stony heart?*

I've since learned the answer to my own question: What kind of redeemer is this? Exactly the kind of redeemer most people have.

Oh, most people would not admit to having a blind redeemer with a stone heart. But take a close look.

For some, Jesus is a good luck charm. The "Rabbit's Foot Redeemer." Pocket sized. Handy. Easily packaged. Easily understood. Easily diagramed. You can put his picture on your wall or you can stick it in your wallet as insurance. You can frame him. Dangle him from your rearview mirror or glue him to your dashboard.

His specialty? Getting you out of a jam. Need a parking place? Rub the redeemer. Need help on a quiz? Pull out the rabbit's foot. No need to have a relationship with him. No need to love him. Just keep him in your pocket next to your four-leaf clover.

For many he's an "Aladdin's Lamp Redeemer." New jobs. Pink Cadillacs. New and improved spouses. Your wish is his command. And what's more, he conveniently reenters the lamp when you don't want him around.

For others, Jesus is a "Monty Hall Redeemer." "All right, Jesus, let's make a deal. For fifty-two Sundays a year, I'll put on a costume—coat and tie, hat and hose—and I'll endure any sermon you throw at me. In exchange, you give me the grace behind pearly gate number three."

The Rabbit's Foot Redeemer. The Aladdin's Lamp Redeemer. The Monty Hall Redeemer. Few demands, no challenges. No need for sacrifice. No need for commitment.

Sightless and heartless redeemers. Redeemers without power. That's not the Redeemer of the New Testament.

Compare the blind Christ I saw in Rio to the compassionate one seen by a frightened woman early one morning in Jerusalem.[1]

It's dawn. The early morning sun stretches a golden blanket across the streets of the city. Diamonds of dew cling to blades of grass. A cat stretches as it awakens. The noises are scattered.

A rooster crows his early morning recital.

A dog barks to welcome the day.

A peddler shuffles down the street, his wares on his back.

And a young carpenter speaks in the courtyard.

Jesus sits surrounded by a horseshoe of listeners. Some nod their heads in agreement and open their hearts in obedience. They have accepted the teacher as their teacher and are learning to accept him as their Lord.

Others are curious, wanting to believe yet wary of this one whose claims so stretch the boundaries of belief.

Whether cautious or convinced, they listen keenly. They arose early. There was something about his words that was more comforting than sleep.

We don't know his topic that morning. Prayer, perhaps. Or maybe kindness or anxiety. But whatever it was, it was soon interrupted when people burst into the courtyard.

Determined, they erupt out of a narrow street and stomp toward Jesus. The listeners scramble to get out of the way. The mob is made up of religious leaders, the elders and deacons of their day. Respected and important men. And struggling to keep her balance on the crest of this angry wave is a scantily clad woman.

Only moments before she had been in bed with a man who was not her husband. Was this how she made her living? Maybe. Maybe not. Maybe her husband was gone, her heart was lonely, the stranger's touch was warm, and before she knew it, she had done it. We don't know.

But we do know that a door was jerked open and she was yanked from a bed. She barely had time to cover her body before she was dragged into the street by two men the age of her father. What thoughts raced through her mind as she scrambled to keep her feet?

Curious neighbors stuck heads through open windows. Sleepy dogs yelped at the ruckus.

And now, with holy strides, the mob storms toward the teacher. They throw the woman in his direction. She nearly falls. "We found this woman in bed with a man!" cries the leader. "The law says to stone her. What do you say?"

Cocky with borrowed courage, they smirk as they watch the mouse go for the cheese.

The woman searches the faces, hungry for a compassionate glance. She finds none. Instead, she sees accusation. Squinty eyes. Tight lips. Gritted teeth. Stares that sentence without seeing.

Cold, stony hearts that condemn without feeling.

She looks down and sees the rocks in their hands—the rocks of righteousness intended to stone the lust out of her. The men squeeze them so tightly that their fingertips are white. They squeeze them as if the rocks were the throat of this preacher they hate.

In her despair she looks at the Teacher. His eyes don't glare. "Don't worry," they whisper, "it's okay." And for the first time that morning she sees kindness.

When Jesus saw her, what did he see? Did he see her as a father sees his grown daughter as she walks down the wedding aisle? The father's mind races back through time watching his girl grow up again—from diapers to dolls. From classrooms to boyfriends. From the prom date to the wedding day. The father sees it all as he looks at his daughter.

As Jesus looked at this daughter, did his mind race back? Did he relive the act of forming this child in heaven? Did he see her as he had originally made her?

"Knitted together" is how the psalmist described the process of God making man.[2] Not manufactured or mass-produced, but knitted. Each thread of personality tenderly intertwined. Each string of temperament deliberately selected.

God as creator. Pensive. Excited. Inventive.

An artist, brush on pallet, seeking the perfect shade.

A composer, fingers on keyboard, listening for the exact chord.

A poet, pen poised on paper, awaiting the precise word.

The Creator, the master weaver, threading together the soul.

Each one different. No two alike. None identical.

On earth, Jesus was an artist in a gallery of his own paintings. He was a composer listening as the orchestra interpreted his music. He was a poet hearing his own poetry. Yet his works of art had been defaced. Creation after battered creation.

He had created people for splendor. They had settled for mediocrity. He had formed them with love. They had scarred each other with hate.

When he saw businessmen using God-given intelligence to feed Satan-given greed . . .

When he saw tongues he had designed to encourage used as daggers to cut . . .

When he saw hands that had been given for holding used as weapons for hurting . . .

When he saw eyes into which he'd sprinkled joy now burning with hatred . . .

I wonder, did it weary him to see hearts that were stained, even discarded?

Jesus saw such a heart as he looked at this woman. Her feet were bare and muddy. Her arms hid her chest, and her hands clutched each other under her chin. And her heart, her heart was ragged, torn as much by her own guilt as by the mob's anger.

So, with the tenderness only a father can have, he set out to untie the knots and repair the holes.

He begins by diverting the crowd's attention. He draws on the ground. Everybody looks down. The woman feels relief as the eyes of the men look away from her.

The accusers are persistent. "Tell us, teacher! What do you want us to do with her?"

He could have asked why they didn't bring the man. The Law indicted him as well. He could have asked why they were suddenly blowing the dust off an old command that had sat on the shelves for centuries. But he didn't.

He just raised his head and offered an invitation, "I guess if you've never made a mistake, then you have a right to stone this woman." He looked back down and began to draw on the earth again.

Someone cleared his throat as if to speak, but no one spoke. Feet shuffled. Eyes dropped. Then thud . . . thud . . . thud . . . rocks fell to the ground.

And they walked away. Beginning with the grayest beard and ending with the blackest, they turned and left. They came as one, but they left one by one.

Jesus told the woman to look up. "Is there no one to condemn you?" He smiled as she raised her head. She saw no one, only rocks—each one a miniature tombstone to mark the burial place of a man's arrogance.

"Is there no one to condemn you?" he had asked. *There is still one who can,* she thinks. And she turns to look at him.

What does he want? What will he do?

Maybe she expected him to scold her. Perhaps she expected him to walk away from her. I'm not sure, but I do know this: What she got, she never expected. She got a promise and a commission.

The promise: "Then neither do I condemn you."

The commission: "Go and sin no more."

The woman turns and walks into anonymity. She's never seen or heard from again. But we can be confident of one thing: On that morning in Jerusalem, she saw Jesus and Jesus saw her. And could we somehow transport her to Rio de Janeiro and let her stand at the base of the *Cristo Redentor,* I know what her response would be.

"That's not the Jesus I saw," she would say. And she would be right. For the Jesus she saw didn't have a hard heart. And the Jesus that saw her didn't have blind eyes.

However, if we could somehow transport her to Calvary and let her stand at the base of the cross . . . you know what she would say. "That's him," she would whisper. "That's him."

She would recognize his hands. The only hands that had held no stones that day were his. And on this day they still hold no stones. She would recognize his voice. It's raspier and weaker, but the words are the same, "Father, forgive them. . . . " And she would recognize his eyes. How could she ever forget those eyes? Clear and tear filled. Eyes that saw her not as she was, but as she was intended to be.

CHAPTER 10

THE
GOLDEN GOBLET

Flames leap from the hill. Pillows of smoke float upward. Orange tongues crack and pop.

From the midst of the blaze comes a yell—the protest of a prisoner as the dungeon door is locked; the roar of a lion as he feels the heat of the burning jungle.

The cry of a lost son as he looks for his father.

"My God, my God, why have you forsaken me?"

The words ricochet from star to star, crashing into the chamber of the King. Couriers from a bloody battlefield, they stumble into the King's presence. Bruised and broken, they plea for help, for relief.

The soldiers of the King prepare to attack. They mount their steeds and position their shields. They draw their swords.

But the King is silent. It is the hour for which he has planned. He knows his course of action. He has awaited those words since the beginning—since the first poison was smuggled into the kingdom.

It came camouflaged. It came in a golden cup with a long stem. It was in the flavor of fruit. It came not in the hands of a king, but the hands of a prince—the prince of the shadows.

Until this moment there had been no reason to hide in the

Garden. The King walked with his children and the children knew their King. There were no secrets. There were no shadows.

Then the prince of shadows entered the Garden. He had to hide himself. He was too ugly, too repulsive. Craters marred his face. So he came in darkness. He came encircled in ebony. He was completely hidden; only his voice could be heard.

"Taste it," he whispered, holding the goblet before her. "It's sweet with wisdom."

The daughter heard the voice and turned. She was intrigued. Her eyes had never seen a shadow. There was something tantalizing about his hiddenness.

The King watched. His army knew the prince of shadows would be no contest for their mighty legion. Eagerly they awaited the command to attack.

But no command was given.

"The choice is hers," the King instructed. "If she turns to us for help, that is your command to deliver her. If she doesn't turn, if she doesn't look to me—don't. The choice is hers."

The daughter stared at the goblet. Rubies embedded in gold filigree invited her touch. Wine wooed her to taste. She reached out and took the cup and drank the poison. Her eyes never looked up.

The venom rushed through her, distorting her vision, scarring her skin, and twisting her heart. She ducked into the shadow of the prince.

Suddenly she was lonely. She missed the intimacy she was made to know. Yet rather than return to the King, she chose to lure another away from him. She replenished the goblet and offered it to the son.

Once again the army snapped into position. Once again they listened for the command of the King. His words were the same.

"If he looks to me, then rush to him. If he doesn't, then don't go. The choice is his."

The daughter placed the goblet into the hands of the son. "It's all right," she assured. "It's sweet." The son looked at the delight that danced in her eyes. Behind her stood a silhouetted figure.

"Who is he?" the son asked.

"Drink it," she insisted. Her voice was husky with desire.

The goblet was cold against Adam's lips. The liquid burned his innocence. "More?" he requested as he ran his finger through the dregs on the bottom and put it to his mouth.

The soldiers looked to their King for instructions. His eyes were moist.

"Bring me your sword!" The general dismounted and stepped quickly toward the throne. He extended the unsheathed blade before the King.

The King didn't take it; he merely touched it. As the tip of his finger encountered the top of the sword, the iron grew orange with heat. It grew brighter and brighter until it blazed.

The general held the fiery sword and awaited the King's command. It came in the form of an edict.

"Their choice will be honored. Where there is poison, there will be death. Where there are goblets, there will be fire. Let it be done."

The general galloped to the Garden and took his post at the gate. The flaming sword proclaimed that the kingdom of light would never again be darkened by the passing of shadows. The King hated the shadows. He hated them because in the shadows the children could not see their King. The King hated the goblets. He hated them because they made the children forget the Father.

But outside the Garden the circle of the shadow grew larger and more empty goblets littered the ground. More faces were disfigured. More eyes saw distortedly. More souls were twisted. Purity was forgotten and all sight of the King was lost. No one remembered that once there was a kingdom without shadows.

In their hands were the goblets of selfishness.

On their lips was the litany of the liar. "Taste it; it's sweet."

And, true to the words of the King, where there was poison, there was death. Where there were goblets, there was fire. Until the day the King sent his Prince.

The same fire that ignited the sword now lit a candle and placed it amidst the shadows.

His arrival, like that of the goblet bearer, did not go unnoticed.

"A star!" was how his coming was announced. "A bright light in a dark sky." A diamond glittering in the dirt.

"Burn brightly, my Son," whispered the King.

Many times the Prince of Light was offered the goblet. Many times it came in the hands of those who'd abandoned the King. "Just a taste, my friend?" With anguish Jesus would look into the eyes of those who tried to tempt him. What is this poison that would make a prisoner try to kill the one who came to release him?

The goblet still bore the seductive flavor of promised power and pleasure. But to the Son of Light its odor was vile. The very sight of the goblet so angered the Prince that he knocked it out of the hand of the tempter, leaving the two alone, locked in an intense glare.

"I will taste the poison," swore the King's Son. "For this I have come. But the hour will be mine to choose."

Finally that hour came. The Son went for one last visit with his Father. He met Him in another garden. A garden of gnarled trees and stony soil.

"Does it have to be this way?"

"It does."

"Is there no one else who can do it?"

The King swallowed. "None but you."

"Do I have to drink from the cup?"

"Yes, my Child. The same cup."

He looked at the Prince of Light. "The darkness will be great." He passed his hand over the spotless face of his Son. "The pain will be awful." Then he paused and looked at his darkened dominion. When he looked up, his eyes were moist. "But there is no other way."

The Son looked into the stars as he heard the answer. "Then, let it be done."

Slowly the words that would kill the Son began to come from the lips of the Father.

"Hour of death, moment of sacrifice, it is your moment. Rehearsed a million times on false altars with false lambs, the moment of truth has come.

"Soldiers, you think you lead him? Ropes, you think you bind him? Men, you think you sentence him? He heeds not your commands. He winces not at your lashes. It is my voice he obeys. It is my condemnation he dreads. And it is your souls he saves.

"Oh, my Son, my Child. Look up into the heavens and see my face before I turn it. Hear my voice before I silence it. Would that I could save you and them. But they don't see and they don't hear.

"The living must die so that the dying can live. The time has come to kill the Lamb.

"Here is the cup, my Son. The cup of sorrows. The cup of sin.

"Slam, mallet! Be true to your task. Let your ring be heard throughout the heavens.

"Lift him, soldiers. Lift him high to his throne of mercy. Lift him up to his perch of death. Lift him above the people that curse his name.

"Now plunge the tree into the earth. Plunge it deep into the heart of humanity. Deep into the strata of time past. Deep into the seeds of time future.

"Is there no angel to save my Isaac? Is there no hand to redeem the Redeemer?

"Here is the cup, my Son. Drink it alone."

God must have wept as he performed his task. Every lie, every lure, every act done in shadows was in that cup. Slowly, hideously they were absorbed into the body of the Son. The final act of incarnation.

The Spotless Lamb was blemished. Flames began to lick his feet.

The King obeys his own edict. "Where there is poison, there will be death. Where there are goblets, there will be fire."

The King turns away from his Prince. The undiluted wrath of a sin-hating Father falls upon his sin-filled Son. The fire envelops him. The shadow hides him. The Son looks for his Father, but his Father cannot be seen.

"My God, my God . . . why?"

———

The throne room is dark and cavernous. The eyes of the King are closed. He is resting.

In his dream he is again in the Garden. The cool of the evening floats across the river as the three walk. They speak of the Garden—of how it is, of how it will be.

"Father . . . ," the Son begins. The King replays the word again. Father. Father. The word was a flower, petal-delicate, yet so easily crushed. Oh, how he longed for his children to call him Father again.

A noise snaps him from his dream. He opens his eyes and sees a transcendent figure gleaming in the doorway. "It is finished, Father. I have come home."

COME
HOME

E ngland. Nineteenth century. Christmas. In a small town there is the tradition of a village party where all the children receive gifts. It is a festive occasion: the bright smiles of the youngsters, a tall tree at the square, colorful packages. There is a young retarded man in the town who, because of his handicap, is the victim of many cruel jokes. The trick played on him this Christmas Day is the cruelest of all.

As the mountain of gifts becomes smaller and smaller, his face grows longer and longer. He is too old for a gift, but he doesn't know that. His childlike heart is heavy as he watches everyone receive presents except himself. Then some of the boys come to him with a gift. His is the last one under the tree. His eyes dance as he looks at the brightly wrapped package. His excitement soars as he tears away the ribbons. His fingers race to rip away the paper. But as he opens the box, his heart sinks.

It's empty.

The packaging was attractive. The ribbons were colorful. The outside was enough to get him into the inside; but when he got to the inside, the box was empty![1]

Ever been there?

Many people have—

A young mother weeps silently into her pillow. All her life she had dreamed of marriage. "If only I could have a home. If only I could have a husband and a house."

So now she's married. The honeymoon has long since ended. The tunnel she dug out of one prison only led her to another. Her Land of Oz has become a land of dirty diapers, car pools, and bills.

She shares a bed with a husband she doesn't love. She listens to the still sleep of a child she doesn't know how to raise. And she feels the sand of her youth slide through her fingers.

A middle-aged businessman sits in his plush office staring blankly out the window. A red German sports car awaits him in the parking lot. There is a gold ring on his finger and a gold card in his wallet. His name is in brass on a walnut door and a walnut desk. His suit is tailored. His shoes are hand sewn, his name well known.

He should be happy. He possesses the package he set out to get when he stood at the bottom of the ladder looking up. But now that he has what he wants, he doesn't want it. Now that he is at the top of the ladder, he sees that it is leaning against the wrong building.

He left his bride in the dust of his ambition. The kids that called him daddy don't call him daddy anymore; they have a new one. And though he has everything that success offers, he'd trade it in a heartbeat to have a home to go home to tonight.

"I've counted the holes in the ceiling tiles a hundred times." The voice shook in spite of an attempt to sound stable.

"They say I'll be in this cast for six weeks. They also say I'm lucky to be alive."

His voice was barely audible through the oxygen mask. The skin on his forehead and nose was scraped.

"They keep asking me what I remember. I don't even remember getting into the car, much less driving it. I'd never tried crack before. I guess I tried too much. I'll think before I try it again. In fact, it looks like I'm going to have plenty of time for thinking."

No games. No noise. No flashing lights. Your dreams have come true, but instead of letting you sleep, they are keeping you awake. What do you do at a time like this? Where do you go when the parade stops? Your failures suck the sandy foundation of your future out from under you. Now what do you do?

You can blame the world. The prodigal son could have done that. In fact, he probably did.[2]

The boy stared at his reflection in the muddy puddle. He questioned whether the face was really his. It didn't look like him.

The flame in the eyes had been extinguished. The smirk had been humbled. The devil-may-care attitude had been replaced with soberness.

He tumbled headlong and landed face first.

It wasn't enough to be friendless. It wasn't enough to be broke. It wasn't enough to pawn his ring, his coat, even his shoes. The long hours walking the streets didn't break him. You would think that the nights with only a bunkhouse pillow or the days lugging a bucket of pig slop would force a change of heart.

But they didn't. Pride is made of stone. Hard knocks may chip it, but it takes reality's sledgehammer to break it.

His was beginning to crack.

His first few days of destitution were likely steamy with resentment. He was mad at everyone. Everyone was to blame. His friends shouldn't have bailed out on him. And his brother should come and bail him out. His boss should feed him better, and his dad never should have let him go in the first place.

He named a pig after each one of them.

Failure invites finger pointing and buck passing. A person may be out of money, out of a job, and out of friends, but he is never out of people to blame.

Sometimes it's the family:

"If my parents had taken their job more seriously . . . "
"If my husband wasn't so selfish . . . "
"If my kids had any respect for me . . . "
"If I had been potty trained earlier . . . "

Sometimes it's the system:

"No one can make a good grade in this school!"
"If I had been given an equal shot, I would have been
    promoted."
"This whole place is rigged."
"There is no way a person can move up in this world."

Even the church has a few bucks passed its way.

"Oh, I'd attend church, but did you know I went to church
    once back in '58 and no one came to visit me?"

"That group of folks? A bunch of hypocrites."

"I plan on going back to church. Just as soon as I find one
    that is teaching the proper doctrine, housing all the
    homeless, feeding all the sick and giving green stamps
    for attendance awards, then I'll go back."

Soon you are right and everyone else is wrong. You are the victim
and the world is your enemy.

————

A second option is to continue playing the games, only this time
with a little more abandon.

My wife has a cousin named Rob. Rob is a great guy. His
good heart and friendly smile endear him to everyone. He is the
kind of fellow you call upon when you can't call on anyone else.

So when the Girl Scouts needed someone to dress up like the
Cookie Monster at a fund-raiser, who did they call? You got it.
Rob.

There were a few problems. First, no one anticipated the day
of the campaign would be so hot. Second, Rob didn't know that
the costume would be so big. Third, who would have thought
that Rob's glasses would fog up so badly he couldn't see? As he was
sitting on the stage waiting his turn to speak, the heat inside the
mask covered his glasses with fog. He couldn't wipe them off—his
paws were too big to fit in the eyehole.

He started to worry. Any minute he would be called upon to
give a talk, and he couldn't even see where the podium was!

He whispered for help. The costume was too thick, and his
cries went unheard.

He began to wave his hands. What he heard in response were

the squeals of delight from the kids. They thought he was waving at them!

As I heard this story I chuckled . . . and then I sighed. It was too familiar. Cries for help muffled behind costumed faces? Fear hidden behind a painted smile? Signals of desperation thought to be signs of joy?

Tell me that doesn't describe our world.

Ever since Eve hemmed the fig leaves to fit Adam, we have been disguising our truths.

And we've gotten better with each generation.

Michelangelo's creativity is nothing compared to a bald man's use of a few strands of hair. Houdini would stand in awe at our capacity to squeeze lumberjack waistlines into ballerina-sized pants.

We are masters of the masquerade. Cars are driven to make a statement. Jeans are purchased to portray an image. Accents are acquired to hide a heritage. Names are dropped. Weights are lifted. Yarns are spun. Toys are purchased. Achievements are professed.

And the pain is ignored. And, with time, the real self is forgotten.

The Indians used to say that within every heart there is a knife. This knife turns like the minute hand on a clock. Every time the heart lies, the knife rotates an increment. As it turns, it cuts into the heart. As it turns, it carves a circle. The more it turns, the wider the circle becomes. After the knife has rotated one full circle, a path has been carved. The result? No more hurt, no more heart.

One option the boy in the pigpen had was to walk back into the masquerade party and pretend everything was fine. He could have carved his integrity until the pain disappeared. He could have done what millions do. He could have spent a lifetime in the pigpen pretending it was a palace. But he didn't.

Something told him that this was the moment of—and for—truth.

He looked into the water. The face he saw wasn't pretty—muddy and swollen. He looked away. "Don't think about it. You're no worse off than anybody else. Things will get better tomorrow."

The lies anticipated a receptive ear. They'd always found one before. "Not this time," he muttered. And he stared at his reflection.

"How far I have fallen." His first words of truth.

He looked into his own eyes. He thought of his father. "They always said I had your eyes." He could see the look of hurt on his father's face when he told him he was leaving.

"How I must have hurt you."

A crack zigzagged across the boy's heart.

A tear splashed into the pool. Another soon followed. Then another. Then the dam broke. He buried his face in his dirty hands as the tears did what tears do so well; they flushed out his soul.

His face was still wet as he sat near the pool. For the first time in a long time he thought of home. The memories warmed him. Memories of dinner-table laughter. Memories of a warm bed. Memories of evenings on the porch with his father as they listened to the hypnotic ring of the crickets.

"Father." He said the word aloud as he looked at himself. "They used to say I looked like you. Now you wouldn't even recognize me. Boy, I blew it, didn't I?"

He stood up and began to walk.

The road home was longer than he remembered. When he

last traveled it, he turned heads because of his style. If he turned heads this time, it was because of his stink. His clothes were torn, his hair matted, and his feet black. But that didn't bother him, because for the first time in a calendar of heartaches, he had a clean conscience.

He was going home. He was going home a changed man. Not demanding that he get what he deserved, but willing to take whatever he could get. "Give me" had been replaced with "help me," and his defiance had been replaced with repentance.

He came asking for everything with nothing to give in return. He had no money. He had no excuses.

And he had no idea how much his father had missed him.

He had no idea the number of times his father had paused between chores to look out the front gate for his son. The boy had no idea the number of times his father had awakened from restless sleep, gone into the son's room, and sat on the boy's bed. And the son would have never believed the hours the father had sat on the porch next to the empty rocking chair, looking, longing to see that familiar figure, that stride, that face.

As the boy came around the bend that led up to his house, he rehearsed his speech one more time.

"Father, I have sinned against heaven and against you."

He approached the gate and placed his hand on the latch. He began to lift it, then he paused. His plan to go home suddenly seemed silly. "What's the use?" he heard himself asking himself. "What chance do I have?" He ducked, turned around, and began to walk away.

Then he heard the footsteps. He heard the slap, slap, slap of sandals. Someone was running. He didn't turn to look. *It's probably a servant coming to chase me away or my big brother wanting to know what I'm doing back home.* He began to leave.

But the voice he heard was not the voice of a servant nor the voice of his brother; it was the voice of his father.

"Son!"

"Father?"

He turned to open the gate, but the father already had. The son looked at his father standing at the entrance. Tears glistened on his cheeks as arms stretched from east to west inviting the son to come home.

"Father, I have sinned." The words were muffled as the boy buried his face in his father's shoulder.

The two wept. For a forever they stood at the gate intertwined as one. Words were unnecessary. Repentance had been made, forgiveness had been given.

The boy was home.

———

If there is a scene in this story that deserves to be framed, it's the one of the father's outstretched hands. His tears are moving. His smile is stirring. But his hands call us home. Imagine those hands. Strong fingers. Palms wrinkled with lifelines. Stretching open like a wide gate, leaving entrance as the only option.

When Jesus told this parable of the loving father, I wonder, did he use his hands? When he got to this point in the story, did he open his arms to illustrate the point?

Did he perceive the thoughts of those in the audience who were thinking, "I could never go home. Not after my life"? Did he see a housewife look at the ground and a businessman shake his head as if to say, "I can't start over. I've made too big a mess"? And did he open his arms even wider as if to say, "Yes. Yes, you can. You can come home"?

Whether he did that day or not, I don't know. But I know that he did later. He later stretched his hands as open as he could. He forced his arms so wide apart that it hurt. And to prove that those arms would never fold and those hands would never close, he had them nailed open.

They still are.

CHAPTER 12

THE FISH AND THE FALLS

A LEGEND OF GRACE

THE JOURNEY

Once upon a distant time, when time was not and rivers had no names, there was a fish.

Born in the cascading bubbles of a rocky mountain stream, this freckled fish learned early the passion of play. He was at home in the water. He raced back and forth in the harbor made by a fallen log. He dared, on occasion, to cross the rapids by darting from rock to rock.

Each morning he witnessed the sun lift the shadowy curtain of night. It was his daily invitation to dance in the clean waters. Then, as the sun climbed higher, its warmth would lull him to slowness, giving him time to stare through the waters at the tall trees that waved and the furred visitors whose tongues would drink and then disappear.

But if the day was his time to play, the night was his time to think. This young trout, not content to know so little, kept his eyes open while others closed theirs. *What is the source of this stream? Where does it go? Why is it here? Why am I here?* He pondered the questions that others never asked. And he listened at length for the answers.

Then one night he heard the roar.

The night was so bright that the moon saw herself in the stream. The fish, awake with his thoughts, recognized for the first time a noise he'd always heard.

A roar. It rumbled under the river. It vibrated the water. Suddenly the fish knew why the water was always moving.

Who is the maker of this sound? Who is the giver of this noise?

He had to know.

He swam all night without stopping, nourished by his need to know. The roar grew louder. Its thunder both frightened and compelled him.

He swam until the stars turned pale and the gray pebbles regained their colors. When he could swim no more, weariness overcame curiosity, and he stopped. He slept.

THE ENCOUNTER

The sun was warm on the trout's back. In his sleep, he dreamt he was playing again. Dashing between the rocks daring the water to catch him. He dreamt he was at home.

Then he awoke, remembering his pilgrimage.

He heard the roar. It sounded near. He opened his eyes and there it was. A wall of white foam. Water tumbling, then falling, then flying, then crashing.

It was like nothing he'd ever seen.

I will climb it and see it.

He swam to where the water crashed into the river. He attempted to swim upwards. He would ascend the falls by brute force. But the onrush of the water was too strong. Undaunted, he swam until he could swim no more, then he slept.

The next day he attempted to jump to the top. He plunged downward, deep below the churning foam. He swam deep. He swam until the water was still and dark and the roar was distant. Then he turned upward.

His fins fought from one side to the other, pushing and propelling the trout until he was swimming faster than he'd ever swum. He swam straight for the surface. Higher and higher, faster and faster. He raced through the calm waters toward the surface. He broke through the top of the water and soared high into the air. He soared so high he was sure he would land on the top of the waterfall. But he didn't. He barely rose above the foam. Then he fell.

I'll try again. Down he swam. Up he pushed. Out he flew. And down he tumbled.

He tried again. And again. And again. Ever trying to reach the top of the wall. Ever failing at his quest.

Finally night fell and the moon stood vigil over the weary young trout.

He awoke with renewed strength and a new plan. He found a safe pool off to the side of the base of the waterfall. Through the still waters he looked up. He would swim against the gentle trickle of the water as it poured over the rocks. Pleased with his wisdom, he set out. Doggedly he pushed his body to do what it wasn't made to do.

For an entire passing of the sun through the sky he struggled. He pushed on—climbing, falling; climbing, falling; climbing, falling. At one point, when his muscles begged for relief, he actually reached a ledge from which he could look out over the water below. Swollen with his achievements he leaned too far out and tumbled headfirst into the calm pool from which he began.

Wearied from his failure, he slept.

He dreamt of the roar. He dreamt of the glory of leaving the mountain stream and dwelling in the waterfall. But when he awoke, he was still at the bottom.

When he awoke, the moon was still high. It discouraged him to realize that his dream was not reality. He wondered if it was worth it. He wondered if those who never sought to know were happier.

He considered returning. The current would carry him home.

I've lived with the roar all my life and never heard it. I could simply not hear it again.

But how do you not hear the yearning of your heart? How do you turn away from discovery? How can you be satisfied with existence once you've lived with purpose?

The fish wanted nothing more than to ascend the water. But he was out of choices. He didn't know what to do. He screamed at the waterfall. "Why are you so harsh? Why are you so resistant? Why won't you help me? Don't you see I can't do it on my own? I need you!"

Just then the roar of the water began to subside. The foaming slowed. The fish looked around. The water was growing still!

Then, he felt the current again. He felt the familiar push of the rushing water. Only this time the push was from behind. The water gained momentum, slowly at first, then faster and faster until the fish found himself being carried to the tall stone wall over which had flowed the water. The wall was bare and big.

For a moment he feared he would be slammed into it. But just as he reached the rocks, a wave formed beneath him. The trout was lifted upwards. Up he went out of the water on the tip of a rising tongue. The wave elevated him up the wall.

By now the forest was silent. The animals stood still as if they witnessed majesty. The wind ceased its stirring. The moon tilted ever so slightly in an effort not to miss the miracle.

All of nature watched as the fish rode the wave of grace. All of nature rejoiced when he reached the top. The stars raced through the blackness. The moon tilted backwards and rocked in sweet satisfaction. Bears danced. Birds hugged. The wind whistled. And the leaves applauded.

The fish was where he had longed to be. He was in the presence of the roar. What he couldn't do, the river had done. He knew immediately he would spend forever relishing the mystery.

CHAPTER 13

THE ELEVENTH
HOUR GIFT

Nicodemus came in the middle of the night. The centurion came in the middle of the day. The leper and the sinful woman appeared in the middle of crowds. Zacchaeus appeared in the middle of a tree. Matthew had a party for him.

The educated. The powerful. The rejected. The sick. The lonely. The wealthy. Who would have ever assembled such a crew? All they had in common were their empty hope chests, long left vacant by charlatans and profiteers. Though they had nothing to offer, they asked for everything: a new birth, a second chance, a fresh start, a clean conscience. And without exception their requests were honored.

And now, one more beggar comes with a request. Only minutes from the death of them both, he stands before the King. He will ask for crumbs. And he, like the others, will receive a whole loaf.

Skull's hill—windswept and stony. The thief—gaunt and pale.

Hinges squeak as the door of death closes on his life.

His situation is pitiful. He's taking the last step down the spiral staircase of failure. One crime after another. One rejection after

311

another. Lower and lower he descended until he reached the bottom—a crossbeam and three spikes.

He can't hide who he is. His only clothing is the cloak of his disgrace. No fancy jargon. No impressive résumé. No Sunday school awards. Just a naked history of failure.

He sees Jesus.

Earlier he had mocked the man. When the crowd first chorused its criticism, he'd sung his part.[1] But now he doesn't mock Jesus. He studies him. He begins to wonder who this man might be.

How strange. He doesn't resist the nails; he almost invites them.

He hears the jests and the insults and sees the man remain quiet. He sees the fresh blood on Jesus' cheeks, the crown of thorns scraping Jesus' scalp, and he hears the hoarse whisper, "Father, forgive them."

Why do they want him dead?

Slowly the thief's curiosity offsets the pain in his body. He momentarily forgets the nails rubbing against the raw bones of his wrists and the cramps in his calves.

He begins to feel a peculiar warmth in his heart: he begins to care; he begins to care about this peaceful martyr.

There's no anger in his eyes, only tears.

He looks at the huddle of soldiers throwing dice in the dirt, gambling for a ragged robe. He sees the sign above Jesus' head. It's painted with sarcasm: King of the Jews.

They mock him as a king. If he were crazy, they would ignore him. If he had no followers, they'd turn him away. If he were nothing to fear, they wouldn't kill him. You only kill a king if he has a kingdom.

Could it be . . .

His cracked lips open to speak.

312

Then, all of a sudden, his thoughts are exploded by the accusations of the criminal on the other cross. He, too, has been studying Jesus, but studying through the blurred lens of cynicism.

"So you're the Messiah, are you? Prove it by saving yourself—and us, too, while you're at it!"[2]

It's an inexplicable dilemma—how two people can hear the same words and see the same Savior, and one see hope and the other see nothing but himself.

It was all the first criminal could take. Perhaps the crook who hurled the barb expected the other crook to take the cue and hurl a few of his own. But he didn't. No second verse was sung. What the bitter-tongued criminal did hear were words of defense.

"Don't you fear God?"

Only minutes before these same lips had cursed Jesus. Now they are defending him. Every head on the hill lifts to look at this one who spoke on behalf of the Christ. Every angel weeps and every demon gapes.

Who could have imagined this thief thinking of anyone but himself? He'd always been the bully, the purse-snatching brat. Who could remember the last time he'd come to someone's aid? But as the last grains of sand trickle through his hourglass, he performs man's noblest act. He speaks on God's behalf.

Where are those we would expect to defend Jesus?

A much more spiritual Peter has abandoned him.

A much more educated Pilate has washed his hands of him.

A much more loyal mob of countrymen has demanded his death.

A much more faithful band of disciples has scattered.

When it seems that everyone has turned away, a crook places himself between Jesus and the accusers and speaks on his behalf.

"Don't you even fear God when you are dying? We deserve to die for our evil deeds, but this man hasn't done one thing wrong."[3]

The soldiers look up. The priests cease chattering. Mary wipes her tears and raises her eyes. No one had even noticed the fellow, but now everyone looks at him.

Perhaps even Jesus looks at him. Perhaps he turns to see the one who had spoken when all others had remained silent. Perhaps he fights to focus his eyes on the one who offered this final gesture of love he'd receive while alive. I wonder, did he smile as this sheep straggled into the fold?

For that, in effect, is exactly what the criminal is doing. He is stumbling to safety just as the gate is closing. Lodged in the thief's statement are the two facts that anyone needs to recognize in order to come to Jesus. Look at the phrase again. Do you see them?

"We are getting what we deserve. This man has done nothing wrong."[4]

We are guilty and he is innocent.

We are filthy and he is pure.

We are wrong and he is right.

He is not on that cross for his sins. He is there for ours.

And once the crook understands this, his request seems only natural. As he looks into the eyes of his last hope, he made the same request any Christian has made.

"Remember me when you come into your kingdom."[5]

No stained-glass homilies. No excuses. Just a desperate plea for help.

At this point Jesus performs the greatest miracle of the cross. Greater than the earthquake. Greater than the tearing of the temple curtain. Greater than the darkness. Greater than the resurrected saints appearing on the streets.

He performs the miracle of forgiveness. A sin-soaked criminal is received by a blood-stained Savior.

"Today you will be with me in Paradise. This is a solemn promise."[6]

Wow. Only seconds before the thief was a beggar nervously squeezing his hat at the castle door, wondering if the King might spare a few crumbs. Suddenly he's holding the whole pantry.

Such is the definition of grace.

My Death Is Not Final

CHAPTER 14

GOD
VS.
DEATH

*"I will tell you something that has
been secret: that we are not all going to die,
but we shall all be changed."*[1]

I was only going to be in Washington, D.C., for one day, and that day was full. Still, I had to see it. I had read about it, heard about it, seen news reports and pictures of it, but I had to see it for myself.

"You'll only have about ten minutes," my host explained.

"Ten minutes is all I need," I told him.

So he pulled the car over and let me out.

A gray sky was shedding a coat of drizzle. I pulled my overcoat tighter around my neck. The barren trees and dead grass cast an appropriate backdrop for my mission. I walked a few hundred yards, descended a sloping sidewalk, and there it was. The Washington Monument to my left, the Lincoln Memorial to my back, and before me stretched the Vietnam Veterans Memorial.

The wailing wall of a generation. Black marble tablets carved with names that read like the roster of a high school football team more than a list of dead soldiers—Walter Faith, Richard Sala, Michael Andrews, Roy Burris, Emmet Stanton.

Each name a young life. Behind each name was a bereaved widow . . . an anguished mother . . . a fatherless child.

I looked down at my feet. There lay a dozen roses, soggy and frosty from the weather. It was the day after Valentine's Day. A girlfriend or wife had come to say, "I still remember. I haven't forgotten."

Next to me stood a trio. By the emotion on their faces, it was obvious they hadn't come out of curiosity. They had come out of grief. The one in the center caught my attention. He wore a green army coat. He was big. He was black. He was bearded. Angry tears steamed down his face. Twenty years of emotion still trying to find an exit.

A couple walked behind me. They were looking for a name. In their hands was a program that told them on what tablet to look. "Did you find it?" I heard the woman ask. "Every name has a number."

True, I thought. *Every name does have a number and sooner or later every number is called.*

It was then that I stopped looking at the names and stared at the monument. I relaxed my focus from the lettering and looked at the tablet. What I saw was sobering. I saw myself. I saw my own reflection. My face looked at me from the shiny marble. It reminded me that I, too, have been dying as long as I have been living. I, too, will someday have my name carved in a granite stone. Someday I, too, will face death.

Death. The bully on the block of life. He catches you in the alley. He taunts you in the playground. He badgers you on the way home: "You, too, will die someday."

You see him as he escorts the procession of hearse-led cars.

He's in the waiting room as you walk out of the double doors of the intensive care unit. He's near as you stare at the pictures of the bloated bellies of the starving in Zimbabwe. And he'll be watching your expression as you slow your car past the crunched metal and the blanketed bodies on the highway.

"Your time is coming," he jabs.

Oh, we try to prove him wrong. We jog. We diet. We pump iron. We play golf. We try to escape it, knowing all along that we will only, at best, postpone it.

"Everyone has a number," he reminds.

And every number will be called.

He'll make your stomach tighten. He'll leave you wide eyed and flat footed. He'll fence you in with fear. He'll steal the joy of your youth and the peace of your final years. And if he achieves what he sets out to do, he'll make you so afraid of dying that you never learn to live.

That is why you should never face him alone. The bully is too big for you to fight by yourself. That's why you need a big brother.

Read these words and take heart. "Since the children have flesh and blood (that's you and me), he too shared in their humanity (that's Jesus, our big brother) so that by his death he might destroy him who holds the power of death—that is, the devil—and free those who all their lives were held in slavery by their fear of death. For surely it is not angels he helps, but Abraham's descendants (that's us)."[2]

Jesus unmasked death and exposed him for who he really is—a ninety-eight-pound weakling dressed up in a Charles Atlas suit. Jesus had no patience for this impostor. He couldn't sit still while death pulled the veil over life.

In fact, if you ever want to know how to conduct yourself at a funeral, don't look to Jesus for an example. He interrupted each one he ever attended.

A lifeguard can't sit still while someone is drowning. A teacher can't resist helping when a student is confused. And Jesus couldn't watch a funeral and do nothing.

In this last section we are going to watch Jesus when he comes face to face with death. We are going to see his eyes mist as he sees his brothers and sisters bruised and beaten by the bully of death. We are going to see his fists clench as he encounters his enemy. We are going to . . . well, turn the page and you'll see for yourself.

You'll see why the Christian can face the bully nose to nose and claim the promise that echoed in the empty tomb, "My death is not final."

FANTASY
OR REALITY?

T wo crowds. One entering the city and one leaving. They couldn't be more diverse. The group arriving buzzes with laughter and conversation. They follow Jesus. The group leaving the city is solemn—a herd of sadness hypnotized by the requiem of death. Above them rides the reason for their grief—a cold body on a wicker stretcher.

The woman at the back of the procession is the mother. She has walked this trail before. It seems like just yesterday she buried the body of her husband. Her son walked with her then. Now she walks alone, quarantined in her sadness. She is the victim of this funeral.

She is the one with no arm around her shoulder. She is the one who will sleep in the empty house tonight. She is the one who will make dinner for one and conversation with none. She is the one most violated. The thief stole her most treasured diamond—companionship.

The followers of Jesus stop and step aside as the procession shadows by. The blanket of mourning muffles the laughter of the disciples. No one speaks. What could they say? They feel the same despair felt by the bystanders at any funeral. "Someday that will be me."

No one intervenes. What could they do? Their only choice is to stand and stare as the mourners shuffle past.

Jesus, however, knows what to say and what to do. When he sees the mother, his heart begins to break . . . and his lips begin to tighten. He glares at the angel of death that hovers over the body of the boy. "Not this time, Satan. This boy is mine."

At that moment the mother walks in front of him. Jesus speaks to her. "Don't cry." She stops and looks into this stranger's face. If she wasn't shocked by his presumption, you can bet some of the witnesses were.

Don't cry? Don't cry? What kind of request is that?

A request only God can make.

Jesus steps toward the bier and touches it. The pallbearers stop marching. The mourners cease moaning. As Jesus stares at the boy, the crowd is silent.

The demon had been perched spiderlike over the body. He was enjoying the parade. He was the warden. The people were the prisoners. He was marching the condemned to execution. They were watching from behind invisible bars, imprisoned by their impermanence. He had relished the fear in the faces. He had giggled at their despair.

Then he hears the voice. That voice . . . he knows the owner. His back arches and he hisses instinctively.

He turns. He doesn't see what others see. He doesn't see the face of a Nazarene. He doesn't hear the voice of a man. He sees the wrath of God. He hears the command of a King.

"Get out of here."

He doesn't have to be told twice.

Jesus turns his attention to the dead boy. "Young man," his voice is calm, "come back to life again."

The living stand motionless as the dead comes to life.

Wooden fingers move. Gray-pale cheeks blush. The dead man sits up.

Luke's description of what happens next is captivating.

"Jesus gave him back to his mother."[1]

How would you feel at a moment like this? What would you do? A stranger tells you not to weep as you look at your dead son. One who refuses to mourn in the midst of sorrow calls the devil's bluff, then shocks you with a call into the cavern of death. Suddenly what had been taken is returned. What had been stolen is retrieved. What you had given up, you are given back.

Jesus must have smiled as the two embraced. Stunned, the crowd breaks into cheers and applause. They hug each other and slap Jesus on the back. Someone proclaims the undeniable, "God has come to help his people."[2]

Jesus gave the woman much more than her son. He gave her a secret—a whisper that was overheard by us. "That," he says pointing at the cot, "that is fantasy. This," he grins, putting an arm around the boy, "this is reality."

CHAPTER 16

THE SPARKLE
FROM ETERNITY

Wallace was an important man. He was the kind of man you would find leading a prayer at the football games or serving as president of the Lion's Club. He wore a title and a collar and had soft hands with no calluses.

He had a nice office just off the sanctuary. His secretary was a bit stale but he wasn't. He had a warm smile that melted your apprehension as you walked through his office door. He sat in a leather swivel chair and had diplomas on the wall. And he had a way of listening that made you willing to tell secrets you'd never told anyone.

He was a good man. His marriage wasn't all it could be, but it was better than most. His church was full. His name was respected. He was a fifteen-handicap golfer, and the church bought him a membership at the country club to commemorate his twentieth year with the congregation. People recognized him in public and flocked to hear him on Easter and Christmas. His retirement account was growing, and he was less than a decade from hanging up the frock and settling down to an autumn of soft wine and good books.

If he committed a sin, no one knew it. If he had a fear, no one heard it—which may have been his gravest sin.

Wallace loved people. This morning, though, he doesn't want people. He wants to be alone. He rings his secretary and advises her that he is not taking any more calls for the rest of the day. She doesn't think it unusual. He's been on the phone all morning. She thinks he needs time to study. She is partly correct. He has been on the phone all morning and he does need time. Not time to study, however. Time to weep.

Wallace looks at the eight-by-ten photo that sits on the mahogany credenza behind his desk. Through watery eyes he gazes at his twelve-year-old daughter. Braces. Pigtails. Freckles. She is a reflection of his wife—blue eyes, brown hair, pug nose. The only thing she got from her father was his heart. She owns that. And he has no intention of requesting that she return it.

She isn't his only child, but she is his last. And she is his only daughter. He'd built a fence of protection around his little girl. Maybe that is why the last few days had hurt so badly. The fence had crumbled.

It began six days ago. She came home early from school feverish and irritable. His wife put her to bed, thinking it was the flu. During the night the fever rose. The next morning they rushed her to the hospital.

The doctors were puzzled. They couldn't pinpoint the problem. They could only agree on one thing—she was sick and getting sicker.

Wallace had never known such helplessness. He didn't know how to handle his pain. He was so accustomed to being strong, he didn't know how to be weak. He assured all who called that his daughter was fine. He assured all who inquired that God was a great God. He assured everyone but himself.

Inside, his emotions were a mighty river. And his dam was

beginning to crack. It was the call from the doctor this morning that broke it. "She is in a coma."

Wallace hangs up the phone and tells his secretary to hold the calls. He reaches over and takes the picture and holds it in his hands. Suddenly the words swirl in his head like a merry-go-round. "It's not fair, it's not fair."

He leans over, holds the picture to his face and weeps.

Nothing is right about it. Nothing. "Why a twelve-year-old girl? Why her, for mercy sakes?" His face hardens as he looks out his window toward the gray sky.

"Why don't you take me?" he screams.

He sits up. He walks over to the coffee table by the couch and picks up the box of tissues he keeps handy for counselees. As he's blowing his nose, he looks out the window into the courtyard of the church. An old man sits reading a paper. Another enters and sits beside him and throws bread crumbs on the cobbles. There's a rustle of wings as a covey of pigeons flutters off the roof and snatches up the food.

Don't you know my daughter is dying? How can you act as if nothing is wrong?

He's thinking about his daughter. In the springtime she used to come by every day on the way home from school. She would wait in the courtyard for him to walk her home. He would hear her chasing pigeons below and know it was time to go. He'd stop what he was doing, stand at this same window, and watch her. He'd watch her walk a tightrope on the curb around the garden. He'd watch her pick a wildflower out of the grass. He'd watch her spin around and around until she became so dizzy that she'd fall on her back and watch the clouds spin in the sky.

"Oh, Princess," he'd say. "My little girl." Then he'd stack his books and headaches on his desk and go down to meet her.

But it is not springtime and his daughter is not in the court-yard. It is winter, his little girl is nearly dead, and two old men are sitting on a bench.

"Dear, dear Princess."

Suddenly a third man enters the courtyard. He tells some-thing to the other two. Then the three hurry out. *Must be a fight,* Wallace thinks to himself. Then he remembers. *The teacher. He is here.*

He'd almost forgotten. Jesus was arriving today. As Wallace was leaving the house this morning, his neighbor had asked him if he was going to see the controversial teacher.

Inwardly he'd scoffed at the idea. "No, too busy today," he'd answered with a wave, knowing that even on a slow day he wouldn't take time to go see an itinerant preacher. Especially this one.

The journals from headquarters had branded this guy a mav-erick. Some even said he was insane. But the crowds hung around him like he was God's gift to humanity.

I'm going. Wallace replayed the neighbor's response in his head.

"Yeah," Wallace had said to himself, "you also subscribe to *National Enquirer.*"

"They say he can heal . . . ," he recalled his neighbor saying.

Wallace stood up straight. Then he relaxed. "Don't be foolish."

"Faith healers are an insult to our profession," he had declared while lecturing at the seminary last fall. "Parasites of the people, charlatans of the church, prophets for profit." He'd seen these guys on television, stuffed into double-breasted suits, wearing mannequin smiles and powdered faces. He shakes his head and walks back to his desk. He picks up the photograph.

He stares at the face of the child who is about to be taken from him. "They say he can heal. . . . "

Wallace began to weigh the options. "If I go and am recognized, it will mean my job. But if she dies and he could have done something . . . " A man reaches a point where his desperation is a notch above his dignity. He shrugs his shoulders. "What choice do I have?"

———

The events of that afternoon redirected Wallace's life. He told the story whenever he had a chance.

I circled the bus terminal three times before I found a place to park. The cold wind bit my ears as I fumbled through my pockets looking for parking meter change. I buttoned my overcoat up to the knot of my tie, turned into the wind, and walked.

I passed a pawn shop window still flocked with Season's Greetings. Someone came out of a bar as I walked by. A dozen or so teens in skintight pants leaned against a brick wall. One flipped a cigarette butt at my feet. Three men in leather jackets and jeans warmed hands over a fire in a ten-gallon drum. One of them chuckled as I walked by. "Looky there, a poodle in the pound." I didn't turn around. If he was talking about me, I didn't want to know.

I felt awkward. It had been years since I'd been on this side of town. I glanced over at my reflection in a drugstore window. Wool overcoat. Wing tip shoes. Gray suit. Red tie. No wonder I was turning heads. Their question was written in their eyes. "What brings Mr. White-collar across the tracks?" The bus station was packed. I barely squeezed through the door.

Once I got in I couldn't have gotten out. Heads bobbed and ducked like corks on a lake. Everyone was trying to get across the room to the side where the deboarded passengers entered the terminal. I managed to squeeze through ahead of them. They were just curious; I was desperate.

As I reached the window, I saw him. He stood near the bus. He had only been able to advance a couple of strides against the wall of people.

He looked too normal. He wore a corduroy jacket, the kind with patches on the elbows. His slacks weren't new, but they were nice. No tie. His hairline receded a bit before it became a flow of brown curls. I couldn't hear his voice, but I could see his face. His eyebrows were bushy. He had a gleam in his eyes and a grin on his lips—as if he were watching you unwrap the birthday present he just gave you.

He was so different from what I had anticipated I had to ask a lady next to me if that was him.

"That's him," she smiled. "That's Jesus."

He bent over and disappeared for a minute and surfaced holding a toddler. He smiled. With hands around the little boy's chest, he pushed him high into the air and held him there. The hands were rugged and slender. Someone had told me that Jesus grew up in Mississippi—the son of a mechanic in Tupelo. He brought the little boy down and began walking toward the door.

I knew if he entered the bus station, I'd never get him out. I put my hands flat against the window pane and began edging along the window. People complained but I moved anyway.

When I got to the doorway, so did Jesus. Our eyes met. I froze. I guess I hadn't considered what I would say to him. Maybe I thought he would recognize me. Maybe I thought he'd ask me if there was anything he could do. "Oh, my daughter is sick and I thought you might say a prayer. . . . "

That's not how it came out. The words logjammed in my

throat. I felt my eyes water, my chin quiver, and my knees hit the uneven pavement. "It's my daughter, my little girl. . . . She's very sick. Could you please touch her so she won't die?"

I regretted the words as soon as I said them. If he's a man, then I've asked the impossible. If he's more than a man, what right do I have to make such a request?

I didn't dare look up. I was ashamed. If the crowd was going anywhere, they were going to have to move around me. I didn't have the courage to raise my face.

I guess he knew I didn't. He did it for me.

I felt his fingers under my chin. He lifted my head. He didn't have to raise it far. He had knelt down in front of me. I looked into his eyes. The gaze of this young preacher embraced this old pastor like the arms of an old friend. I knew, then, that I knew this man. From somewhere I'd seen that look. I knew those eyes.

"Take me to her." His hand moved under my arm. He helped me stand. "Where is your car?"

"A car? This way!" I grabbed his hand and began to fight a path through the crowd. It wasn't easy. With my free hand I moved people like I was parting stalks of corn in a cornfield. Faces tumbled in on us. Young mothers wanting a blessing for their children. Old faces with caved-in mouths wanting release from pain.

Suddenly I lost his hand. It slipped out. I stopped and turned and saw him standing and looking. His abrupt stop surprised the crowd. They hushed. I noticed his face was pale. He spoke as if speaking to himself.

"Someone touched me."

"What?" one of his own men inquired.

"Someone touched me."

I thought he was telling a joke. He turned, slowly studying each face. For the life of me, I couldn't tell if he was angry or delighted. He was looking for someone he didn't know but knew he'd know when he saw her.

"I touched you." The voice was beside me. Jesus pivoted.

"It was me. I'm sorry." The curtain of the crowd parted, leaving a girl on center stage. She was thin, almost frail. I could have wrapped my hand around her upper arm and touched my finger to my thumb. Her skin was dark, and her hair was in a hundred braids with beads on each end. She was coatless. She hugged her arms to herself—hands squeezing bony elbows as much out of fear as out of cold.

"Don't be afraid," Jesus assured. "What is wrong?"

"I have AIDS."

Someone behind me gasped. Several took a step back.

Jesus stepped towards her. "Tell me about it."

She looked at him, looked around at the throng of people, swallowed, and began. "I am out of money. The doctors say it is just a matter of time. I didn't have anywhere else to go. But now . . ."

She lowered her eyes and began to smile. She smiled as if someone had just whispered some good news in her ear.

I looked back at Jesus. My lands, if he wasn't smiling too! The two stood there and stared at each other, smiling like they were the only two kids in class who knew the answer to the teacher's question.

It was then I saw the look again. The same gaze met her that only moments before met me as I looked up from the pavement. Those same eyes that I knew I'd seen I saw again. Where? Where had I seen those eyes?

I turned and looked at the girl. For a moment she looked at me. I wanted to say something to her. I think she felt the same urge. We were so different, but suddenly we had everything in common: What a strange couple we were. She with her needle-tracked arms and midnight lovers; I with my clean fingernails and sermon outlines. I had spent my life telling people not to be like her. She'd spent her life avoiding hypocrites like me. But now we were thrust together against the enemy of death, desperately hoping that this country preacher could tie a knot in the end of our frazzled ropes so we could hang on.

Jesus spoke. "It was your faith that did it. Now go and enjoy life."

She resisted all effort to hide her joy. She smiled, looked back at Jesus, and jumped up and kissed him on the cheek.

The crowd laughed, Jesus blushed, and she disappeared.

I hadn't noticed, but while Jesus was speaking, some other men had worked their way into the crowd. They were standing behind me. When I heard them speak, I immediately recognized their voices. They were from my congregation.

One put his hand on my shoulder. "There's no need to bother this teacher anymore; your daughter is dead."

The words came at me like darts, but Jesus intercepted them: "Don't be afraid; just trust me."

The next few moments were a blur of activity. We raced through the crowd, jumped in the car of the man who brought the news, and sped to the hospital.

The waiting room was chaotic. Church members, neighbors, and friends were already gathering. Several wept openly. My wife, seated in one of the chairs, was pale and speechless. Her eyes were red. Her hand trembled as she brushed away a tear.

As I entered, people came to comfort me. Jesus stepped in front of them. They stopped and stared at this stranger.

"Why are you crying?" he asked. "She isn't dead; she's only asleep."

They were stunned. They were insulted. "Of all the insensitive things to say," someone shouted. "Who are you anyway?"

"Get that joker out of here!"

But leaving was the last thing Jesus had on his agenda. He turned and within a few seconds was standing in front of my daughter's hospital room. He signaled for a few of us to follow. We did.

The six of us stood at my daughter's bedside. Her face was ashen. Her lips dry and still. I touched her hand. It was cold. Before I could say anything, Jesus' hand was on mine. With the exception of one instant he never took his eyes off my daughter. But during that instant he looked at me. He looked at me with that same look, that same slight smile. He was giving another gift and couldn't wait to see the response when it was opened.

"Princess," the words were said softly, almost in a whisper, "get up!"

Her head turned slightly as if hearing a voice. Jesus stood back. Her upper body leaned forward until she was upright in bed. Her eyes opened. She turned and put her bare feet on the floor and stood.

No one moved as my wife and I watched our girl walk toward us. We held her for an eternity—half believing it couldn't be true and half not wanting to know if it wasn't. But it was.

"Better get her something to eat," Jesus teased with a smile. "She's probably famished." Then he turned to leave.

I reached out and touched his shoulder. My willingness was in my eyes. "Let me return the favor. I'll introduce you to the right people. I'll get you speaking engagements at the right places."

"Let's keep this between us, okay?" and he and three speechless friends left the room.

For weeks after that day I was puzzled. Oh, of course I was

exuberant. But my joy was peppered with mystery. Everywhere I went I saw his face. His look followed me. Even as I write this, I can see it.

Head cocked just a bit. Tender twinkle of anticipation under bushy brows. That look that whispered, "Come here. I've got a secret."

And now I know where I'd seen it before. In fact I've seen it again—several times.

I saw it in the eyes of the cancer patient I visited yesterday. Bald from chemotherapy. Shadowed eyes from the disease. Her skin was soft and her hand bony. She recognized me when she awoke. She didn't even say hello. She just lofted her eyebrows, sparkled that sparkle, and said, "I'm ready, Wallace. I'm ready to go."

I saw it last week as I spoke at a funeral. The widower, a wrinkled-faced man with white hair and bifocals. He didn't weep like the others. In fact, at one point I think I saw him smile. I shook his hand afterwards. "Don't worry about me," he exclaimed. Then he motioned for me to lean down so he could say something in my ear. "I know where she is."

But it was this morning that I saw it the clearest. I'd wanted to ask her for days, but the right moment never came. This morning it did. At the breakfast table, just the two of us, she with her cereal, I with my paper, I turned to my daughter and asked her. "Princess?"

"Uh huh?"

"What was it like?"

"What?"

"While you were gone. What was it like?"

She didn't say anything. She just turned her head slightly and looked out the window. When she turned around again, the sparkle was there. She opened her mouth and then closed it, then opened it again. "It's a secret, Dad. A secret too good for words."

Peace where there should be pain. Confidence in the midst of crisis. Hope defying despair. That's what that look says. It is a look that knows the answer to the question asked by every mortal, "Does death have the last word?" I can see Jesus wink as he gives the answer. "Not on your life."

"LAZARUS, COME OUT!"

When the famous agnostic Robert Ingersoll died, the printed funeral program left this solemn instruction, "There will be no singing."

Few feel like singing in the face of death. Running, perhaps. Crying, probably. But singing? Not at death. Death steals our reason to sing. Death takes the songs from our lips and leaves in their place stilled tongues and tear-flooded cheeks.

There was no singing at the funeral Jesus attended either. Mourning. Weeping. Wailing. But no singing.

The house was more like a prison than a residence. People shuffled about aimlessly, their faces pasty white and their eyes full moons of fear. On their lips was no music, no laughter—only the foreboding news that reminded them of their own fate: Another prisoner had been marched from death row to the gallows. Lazarus was dead. They were in prison awaiting their turn.

Shokoi Yokoi spent twenty-eight years in a prison. Not a prison of walls, but a prison of fear. When the tide began to turn in World War II, Shokoi was a Japanese soldier on the island of Guam. Fearing that defeat meant certain capture by American forces, he ran into the jungle and hid in a cave. He later learned the war was over by reading one of the thousands of leaflets that were dropped into the jungle by American planes. Still, he feared being taken as prisoner, so he remained in his cave.

For over a quarter of a century he came out only at night. He existed on frogs, rats, roaches, and mangoes. It was only when some hunters discovered him that he was convinced it was safe to leave the jungle.

"Shocking," we say. "How could a man be so blind?"

"Tragic," we sigh. "What a waste of life."

"A pity," we lament, "that a human would be so imprisoned by fear that he would cease to live."

A life wasted pacing up and down in a self-made cell of fear. It is shocking. It is tragic. It is a pity. And it is also very common.

The fear of death has filled a thousand prisons. You can't see the walls. You can't see the warden. You can't see the locks. But you can see the prisoners. You can see them as they sit on their bunks and bemoan their fate. They want to live, but they can't because they are doomed to do what they most want to avoid— they will die.

And, oh how restrictive is the ball and chain of death. You try to run away from it—you can't. You try to run with it—it is too heavy. You try to ignore it, and it yanks you into reality.

Just yesterday I visited a home that was wearing the black wreath of death. The youngest of three daughters, a recently married twenty-two-year-old, had been killed in a collision between an eighteen-wheeler and a bus. The eyes that met me at the door were those of a prisoner. The family was held hostage by the answerless questions. Taken captive by sadness, they couldn't take a dozen steps without walking into a brick wall of disbelief.

It was enough to make you cry. It is enough to make God cry.

Jesus' throat tightened as he walked among the inmates. He gazed at the chalky faces through watery eyes. How long would they listen to Satan's lie? How long would they be in bondage? What would he have to do to convince them? Hadn't he proven it at Nain? Was the raising of Jairus's daughter not proof enough? How long would these people lock themselves into this man-made prison of fear? He had shown them the key to unlock their door. Why didn't they use it ?

"Show me the tomb."

They led him to the burial place of Lazarus. It was a cave with a stone laid across the entrance. Over the stone was spun the spider web of finality. "No more!" the stone boasted. "No more shall these hands move. No longer shall this tongue speak. No more!"

Jesus wept. He wept not for the dead but for the living. He wept not for the one in the cave of death but for those in the cave of fear. He wept for those who, though alive, were dead. He wept for those who, though free, were prisoners, held captive by their fear of death.

"Move the stone." The command was soft but firm.

"But, Jesus, it will . . . it will stink."

"Move the stone so you will see God."

Stones have never stood in God's way. They didn't in Bethany two thousand years ago. And they didn't in Europe a hundred years ago.

She was a Hanoverian countess. If she was known for anything, she was known for her disbelief in God and her conviction that no one could call life from a tomb.

Before her death, she left specific instructions that her tomb was to be sealed with a slab of granite; she asked that blocks of stone be placed around her tomb and that the corners of the blocks be fastened together and to the granite slab by heavy iron clamps.

This inscription was placed on the granite rock:

This burial place,
purchased to all eternity,
must never be opened.

All that any man could do to seal the tomb was done. The countess had insured that her tomb would serve as a mockery to the belief in the resurrection. A small birch tree, however, had other plans. Its root found its way between the slabs and grew deep into the ground. Over the years it forced its way until the iron clamps popped loose and the granite lid was raised. The stone cover is now resting against the trunk of the birch, the boastful epitaph permanently silenced by the work of a determined tree . . . or a powerful God.

"Lazarus, come out!"

It took only one call. Lazarus heard his name. His eyes opened beneath the wrap. The cloth-covered hands raised. Knees lifted, feet touched the ground, and the dead man came out.

"Take the grave clothes off of him and let him go."[1]

There is a story told in Brazil about a missionary who discovered a tribe of Indians in a remote part of the jungle. They lived near a large river. The tribe was friendly and in need of medical attention. A contagious disease was ravaging the population and people were dying daily. An infirmary was located in another part of the jungle and the missionary determined that the only hope for the tribe was to go to the hospital for treatment and inoculations. In order to reach the hospital, however, the Indians would have to cross the river—a feat they were unwilling to perform.

The river, they believed, was inhabited by evil spirits. To enter the water meant certain death. The missionary set about the difficult task of overcoming the superstition of the tribe.

He explained how he had crossed the river and arrived

unharmed. No luck. He led the people to the bank and placed his hand in the water. The people still wouldn't believe him. He walked out into the river and splashed water on his face. The people watched closely, yet were still hesitant. Finally he turned and dove into the water. He swam beneath the surface until he emerged on the other side.

Having proven that the power of the river was a farce, the missionary punched a triumphant fist into the air. He had entered the water and escaped. The Indians broke into cheers and followed him across.

Jesus saw people enslaved by their fear of a cheap power. He explained that the river of death was nothing to fear. The people wouldn't believe him. He touched a boy and called him back to life. The followers were still unconvinced. He whispered life into the dead body of a girl. The people were still cynical. He let a dead man spend four days in a grave and then called him out. Is that enough? Apparently not. For it was necessary for him to enter the river, to submerge himself in the water of death before people would believe that death had been conquered.

But after he did, after he came out on the other side of death's river, it was time to sing . . . it was time to celebrate.

CHAPTER 18

THE
CELEBRATION

A party was the last thing Mary Magdalene expected as she approached the tomb on that Sunday morning. The last few days had brought nothing to celebrate. The Jews could celebrate—Jesus was out of the way. The soldiers could celebrate—their work was done. But Mary couldn't celebrate. To her the last few days had brought nothing but tragedy.

Mary had been there. She had heard the leaders clamor for Jesus' blood. She had witnessed the Roman whip rip the skin off his back. She had winced as the thorns sliced his brow and wept at the weight of the cross.

In the Louvre there is a painting of the scene of the cross. In the painting the stars are dead and the world is wrapped in darkness. In the shadows there is a kneeling form. It is Mary. She is holding her hands and lips against the bleeding feet of the Christ.

We don't know if Mary did that, but we know she could have. She was there. She was there to hold her arm around the shoulder of Mary the mother of Jesus. She was there to close his eyes. She was there.

So it's not surprising that she wants to be there again.

In the early morning mist she arises from her mat, takes her

343

spices and aloes, and leaves her house, past the Gate of Gennath and up to the hillside. She anticipates a somber task. By now the body will be swollen. His face will be white. Death's odor will be pungent.

A gray sky gives way to gold as she walks up the narrow trail. As she rounds the final bend, she gasps. The rock in front of the grave is pushed back.

"Someone took the body." She runs to awaken Peter and John. They rush to see for themselves. She tries to keep up with them but can't.

Peter comes out of the tomb bewildered and John comes out believing, but Mary just sits in front of it weeping. The two men go home and leave her alone with her grief.

But something tells her she is not alone. Maybe she hears a noise. Maybe she hears a whisper. Or maybe she just hears her own heart tell her to take a look for herself.

Whatever the reason, she does. She stoops down, sticks her head into the hewn entrance, and waits for her eyes to adjust to the dark.

"Why are you crying?" She sees what looks to be a man, but he's white—radiantly white. He is one of two lights on either end of the vacant slab. Two candles blazing on an altar.

"Why are you crying?" An uncommon question to be asked in a cemetery. In fact, the question is rude. That is, unless the questioner knows something the questionee doesn't.

"They have taken my Lord away, and I don't know where they have put him."

She still calls him "my Lord." As far as she knows his lips were silent. As far as she knows, his corpse had been carted off by graverobbers. But in spite of it all, he is still her Lord.

Such devotion moves Jesus. It moves him closer to her. So

close she hears him breathing. She turns and there he stands. She thinks he is the gardener.

Now, Jesus could have revealed himself at this point. He could have called for an angel to present him or a band to announce his presence. But he didn't.

"Why are you crying? Who is it you are looking for?"[1]

He doesn't leave her wondering long, just long enough to remind us that he loves to surprise us. He waits for us to despair of human strength and then intervenes with heavenly. God waits for us to give up and then—surprise!

Has it been a while since you let God surprise you? It's easy to reach the point where we have God figured out.

We know exactly what God does. We break the code. We chart his tendencies. God is a computer. If we push all the right buttons and insert the right data, God is exactly who we thought he was. No variations. No alterations. God is a jukebox. Insert a tithe. Punch in the right numbers and—bam—the divine music we want fills the room.

I look across my desk and see a box of tissues. Ten minutes ago that box sat in the lap of a young woman—midthirties, mother of three. She told me of the telephone call she received from her husband this morning. He wants a divorce. She had to leave work and weep. She wanted a word of hope.

I reminded her that God is at his best when our life is at its worst. God has been known to plan a celebration in a cemetery. I told her, "Get ready, you may be in for a surprise."

Have you got God figured out? Have you got God captured on a flowchart and frozen on a flannelboard? If so, then listen. Listen to God's surprises.

Hear the rocks meant for the body of the adulterous woman drop to the ground.

Listen as Jesus invites a death-row convict to ride with him to the kingdom in the front seat of the limo.

Listen as the Messiah whispers to the Samaritan woman, "I who speak to you am he."

Listen to the widow from Nain eating dinner with her son who is supposed to be dead.

And listen to the surprise as Mary's name is spoken by a man she loved—a man she had buried.

"Miriam."[2]

God appearing at the strangest of places. Doing the strangest of things. Stretching smiles where there had hung only frowns. Placing twinkles where there were only tears. Hanging a bright star in a dark sky. Arching rainbows in the midst of thunderclouds. Calling names in a cemetery.

"Miriam," he said softly, "surprise!"

Mary was shocked. It's not often you hear your name spoken by an eternal tongue. But when she did, she recognized it. And when she did, she responded correctly. She worshiped him.

The scene has all the elements of a surprise party—secrecy, wide eyes, amazement, gratitude. But this celebration is timid in comparison with the one that is being planned for the future. It will be similar to Mary's, but a lot bigger. Many more graves will open. Many more names will be called. Many more knees will bow. And many more seekers will celebrate.

It's going to be some party. I plan to make sure my name is on the guest list. How about you?

> "No eye has seen,
> no ear has heard,
> no mind has conceived
> what God has prepared for those who love him."[3]

CHAPTER 19

THE FINAL GLANCE

"Max, your dad's awake." I had been watching a movie on television. One of those thrillers that takes you from the here and now and transports you to the somewhere and sometime. My mother's statement seemed to come from another world. The real world.

I turned toward my father. He was looking at me.

His head was all he could turn. Lou Gehrig's disease had leeched his movement, taking from him everything but his faith . . . and his eyes.

It was his eyes that called me to walk over to his bedside. I had been home for almost two weeks, on special leave from Brazil, due to his worsening condition. He had slept most of the last few days, awakening only when my mother would bathe him or clean his sheets.

Next to his bed was a respirator—a metronome of mortality that pushed air into his lungs through a hole in his throat. The bones in his hand protruded like spokes in an umbrella. His fingers, once firm and strong, were curled and lifeless. I sat on the edge of his bed and ran my hands over his barreled rib cage. I put my hand on his forehead. It was hot . . . hot and damp. I stroked his hair.

"What is it, Dad?"

He wanted to say something. His eyes yearned. His eyes refused to release me. If I looked away for a moment, they followed me and were still looking when I looked back.

"What is it?"

I'd seen that expression before. I was seven years old, eight at the most. Standing on the edge of a diving board for the first time, wondering if I would survive the plunge. The board dipped under my seventy pounds. I looked behind me at the kids who were pestering me to hurry up and jump. I wondered what they would do if I asked them to move over so I could get down. Tar and feather me, I supposed.

So caught between ridicule and a jump into certain death, I did the only thing I knew to do—I shivered.

Then I heard him, "It's all right, son. Come on in." I looked down. My father had dived in. He was treading water awaiting my jump. Even as I write, I can see his expression—tanned face, wet hair, broad smile, and bright eyes. His eyes were assuring and earnest. Had he not said a word, they would have conveyed the message. But he did speak. "Jump. It's all right."

So I jumped.

Twenty-three years later the tan was gone, the hair thin, and the face drawn. But the eyes hadn't changed. They were bold. And their message hadn't changed. I knew what he was saying. Somehow he knew I was afraid. Somehow he perceived I was shivering as I looked into the deep. And somehow, he, the dying, had the strength to comfort me, the living.

I placed my cheek in the hollow of his. My tears dripped on his hot face. I said softly what his throat wanted to, but couldn't. "It's all right," I whispered. "It's going to be all right."

When I raised my head, his eyes were closed. I would never see them open again.

He left me with a final look. One last statement of the eyes. One farewell message from the captain before the boat would turn out to sea. One concluding assurance from a father to a son, "It's all right."

———

Perhaps it was a similar look that stirred the soul of the soldier during those six hours one Friday.

He was uneasy. He had been since noon.

It wasn't the deaths that troubled him. The centurion was no stranger to finality. Over the years he'd grown callous to the screams of the crucified. He'd mastered the art of numbing his heart. But this crucifixion plagued him.

The day began as had a hundred others—dreadfully. It was bad enough to be in Judea, but it was hell to spend hot afternoons on a rocky hill supervising the death of pickpockets and rabble-rousers. Half the crowd taunted, half cried. The soldiers griped. The priests bossed. It was a thankless job in a strange land. He was ready for the day to be over before it began.

He was curious at the attention given to the flatfooted peasant. He smiled as he read the sign that would go on the cross. The condemned looked like anything but a king. His face was lumpy and bruised. His back arched slightly and his eyes faced downward. "Some harmless hick," mused the centurion. "What could he have done?"

Then Jesus raised his head. He wasn't angry. He wasn't uneasy. His eyes were strangely calm as they stared from behind the bloody mask. He looked at those who knew him—moving deliberately from face to face as if he had a word for each.

For just a moment he looked at the centurion—for a second the Roman looked into the purest eyes he'd ever seen. He didn't know what the look meant. But the look made him swallow and his stomach feel empty. As he watched the soldier grab the Nazarene and yank him to the ground, something told him this was not going to be a normal day.

As the hours wore on, the centurion found himself looking more and more at the one on the center cross. He didn't know what to do with the Nazarene's silence. He didn't know what to do with his kindness.

But most of all, he was perplexed by the darkness. He didn't know what to do with the black sky in midafternoon. No one could explain it. . . . No one even tried. One minute the sun, the next the darkness. One minute the heat, the next a chilly breeze. Even the priests were silenced.

For a long while the centurion sat on a rock and stared at the three silhouetted figures. Their heads were limp, occasionally rolling from side to side. The jeering was silent . . . eerily silent. Those who had wept, now waited.

Suddenly the center head ceased to bob. It yanked itself erect. Its eyes opened in a flash of white. A roar sliced the silence. "It is finished."[1] It wasn't a yell. It wasn't a scream. It was a roar . . . a lion's roar. From what world that roar came the centurion didn't know, but he knew it wasn't this one.

The centurion stood up from the rock and took a few paces toward the Nazarene. As he got closer, he could tell that Jesus was staring into the sky. There was something in his eyes that the soldier had to see. But after only a few steps, he fell. He stood and fell again. The ground was shaking, gently at first and now violently. He tried once more to walk and was able to take a few steps and then fall . . . at the foot of the cross.

He looked up into the face of this one near death. The King looked down at the crusty old centurion. Jesus' hands were fastened; they couldn't reach out. His feet were nailed to timber; they couldn't walk toward him. His head was heavy with pain; he could scarcely move it. But his eyes . . . they were afire.

They were unquenchable. They were the eyes of God.

Perhaps that is what made the centurion say what he said. He saw the eyes of God. He saw the same eyes that had been seen by a near-naked adulteress in Jerusalem, a friendless divorcée in Samaria, and a four-day-dead Lazarus in a cemetery. The same eyes that didn't close upon seeing man's futility, didn't turn away at man's failure, and didn't wince upon witnessing man's death.

"It's all right," God's eyes said. "I've seen the storms and it's still all right."

The centurion's convictions began to flow together like rivers. "This was no carpenter," he spoke under his breath. "This was no peasant. This was no normal man."

He stood and looked around at the rocks that had fallen and the sky that had blackened. He turned and stared at the soldiers as they stared at Jesus with frozen faces. He turned and watched as the eyes of Jesus lifted and looked toward home. He listened as the parched lips parted and the swollen tongue spoke for the last time.

"Father, into your hands I commit my spirit."[2]

Had the centurion not said it, the soldiers would have. Had the centurion not said it, the rocks would have—as would have the angels, the stars, even the demons. But he did say it. It fell to a nameless foreigner to state what they all knew.

"Surely this man was the Son of God."[3]

Six hours on one Friday. Six hours that jut up on the plain of human history like Mount Everest in a desert. Six hours that have been deciphered, dissected, and debated for two thousand years.

What do these six hours signify? They claim to be the door in time through which eternity entered man's darkest caverns. They mark the moments that the Navigator descended into the deepest waters to leave anchor points for his followers.

What does that Friday mean?

For the life blackened with failure, that Friday means forgiveness.

For the heart scarred with futility, that Friday means purpose.

And for the soul looking into this side of the tunnel of death, that Friday means deliverance.

Six hours. One Friday.

What do *you* do with those six hours on that Friday?

READER'S GUIDE

ANCHORING DEEP

Do you know many people who have intentionally turned their backs on God and stomped away in anger? Neither do I. Do you know many people who gradually lost their faith over an extended period of time? So do I.

Few abandon the faith out of anger at God or disbelief in the Scriptures. If you vacate your church pew, you probably won't do so overnight. It will be a subtle, casual abandonment. Read these words from Hebrews and see how one writer describes the process: "We must pay more careful attention, therefore, to what we have heard, so that we do not drift away" (Hebrews 2:1).

What is the danger that faces any person attempting to stay spiritually afloat? Drifting. Getting off course. Aimlessly floating. A directionless meander that leaves you in uncharted and unfamiliar waters.

If you lose your faith, you will probably do so gradually. In tiny increments you will get spiritually sloppy. You will let a few days slip by without consulting your compass. Your sails will go untrimmed. Your rigging will go unprepared. And worst of all, you will forget to anchor your boat. And, before you know it, you'll be bouncing from wave to wave in stormy seas.

And unless you anchor deep, you could go down.

How do you anchor deep? Look at the verse again.

"We must pay more careful attention, therefore, to what we have heard. . . . "

Stability in the storm comes not from seeking a new message but from understanding an old one. The most reliable anchor points are not recent discoveries, but are time-tested truths that have held their ground against the winds of change. Truths like:

> My life is not futile.
> My failures are not fatal.
> My death is not final.

Attach your soul to these boulders and no wave is big enough to wash you under.

My prayer is that *Six Hours One Friday* has been a tool to help you anchor to these rocks.

The following study guide will help you even more. It is ideal for personal devotional time, small group study, or classroom exploration. The guide invites you to reexamine each chapter of the book on three levels.

LEVEL ONE: MIND ANCHORS. This first part gleans crucial quotes from the chapter and invites you to reexamine them by answering some probing questions.

LEVEL TWO: SOUL ANCHORS. This section uses parallel Scriptures to reinforce and clarify the thrust of the chapter.

LEVEL THREE: LIFE ANCHORS. Here is where you take the message home. Want to keep from drifting? Spend some time meditating over the exercises in this section.

I am deeply indebted to Steve Halliday and Liz Heaney for their work on this study guide.

One final word. Don't be content to depend on someone else's anchor points. Don't settle for a faith inherited from your family or borrowed from your friends. Their help is important and their teaching is vital, but you never know when you'll have to face a hurricane alone. So be sure that your heart is safely secured. Take the advice of the sailor, "Anchor deep, say a prayer, and hold on!"

HURRICANE WARNINGS

MIND ANCHORS

1. *Anchor points. Firm rocks sunk deeply in a solid foundation. Not casual opinions or negotiable hypotheses, but ironclad undeniables that will keep you afloat. How strong are yours?*

> A. Why are anchor points necessary in developing a strong life of faith? What happens if you don't have them?

> B. What anchor points can you identify in your own life? How strong are they?

2. *Three anchor points were planted firmly in bedrock two thousand years ago by a carpenter who claimed to be the Christ. And it was all done in the course of a single day. A single Friday. All done during six hours, one Friday.*

> A. What does it mean that these anchor points were "planted firmly in bedrock"? What gives them such strength?

B. What set apart these six hours from any other six hours in history? Why is it remarkable that Jesus' work was accomplished in such a short time?

3. *There is one stone to which you should tie. It's large. It's round. And it's heavy. It blocked the door of a grave. It wasn't big enough, though. The tomb it sealed was the tomb of a transient. He only went in to prove he could come out.*

A. In what sense was Jesus a "transient"? What Scripture verses can you think of that would say this in another way?

B. Why was it necessary for Jesus to "prove he could come out" of the tomb? Why leave evidence?

4. *To the casual observer the six hours are mundane. . . . But to the handful of awestruck witnesses the most maddening of miracles is occurring. God is on a cross. The creator of the universe is being executed. . . . And there is no one to save him, for he is sacrificing himself.*

A. How is the crucifixion of Jesus a "miracle"? What thoughts do you imagine went through Jesus' mind during his ordeal?

B. Why is it significant that Jesus sacrificed himself? How does your answer make you feel?

SOUL ANCHORS
READ HEBREWS 12:2–13.

A. According to verses 2–3, what should Christians do to avoid growing weary or losing heart in the face of personal hurricanes? In what practical ways can this advice help you?

B. How do we sometimes "make light of" hardships or "lose heart" because of them? What use does God sometimes make of these hardships, according to verse 6?

C. What is an ultimate purpose of God in allowing "hurricanes" into our lives, according to verse 10?

D. How do we feel about these hardships, according to verse 11? Does it help to know that God understands how we feel about this? Why?

E. According to verse 11, what kind of people reap the benefits of such difficult experiences?

F. What connection is there between verse 12 and verses 2–3? What anchor points are mentioned in this passage?

LIFE ANCHORS

A. On a clean sheet of paper write down five of your personal anchor points. Put this list in a safe, accessible place and reread it when hurricanes blow into your life.

B. Think of the last time you went through a personal hurricane. How did you react? Did you rely on any anchor points? If not, why not? If so, which ones?

C. What do you think were Jesus' anchor points when he walked on this earth? Which ones do you think he relied upon while he spent those six hours on the cross?

D. Take five minutes to thank God for providing firm anchor points for your faith. If you haven't been relying on these anchor points as you should, confess it and ask the Lord to help you the next time a hurricane blows your way.

CHAPTER 2

GOD'S FORMULA
FOR FATIGUE

MIND ANCHORS

1. *You are tired. You are weary. Weary of being slapped by the waves of broken dreams. Weary of being stepped on and run over in the endless marathon to the top. Weary of trusting in someone only to have that trust returned in an envelope with no return address.*

    A. Have you ever felt this way? If so, explain. If not, think of someone you know who has felt this way. What caused such feelings?

2. *Is it worth it? When I get what I want, will it be worth the price I paid? Perhaps those were the thoughts of a San Antonio lawyer I read about recently. Apparently his success wasn't enough. One day, he came home, took a gun out of his vault, climbed into a sleeping bag, and took his life. His note to his bride read, "It's not that I don't love you, it's just that I'm tired and I want to rest."*

    A. In what ways can weariness distort one's thinking?

B. Do you think this lawyer achieved what he was after? Why?

3. *Jesus was the only man to walk God's earth who claimed to have an answer for man's burdens. "Come to me," he invited them. My prayer is that you, too, will find rest. And that you will sleep like a baby.*

A. Many groups today claim to have an answer for man's problems. How is Jesus' answer different from theirs?

B. Describe this answer that Jesus claimed to have for man's burdens. How do you evaluate his answer?

C. Does this wish for "sleeping like a baby" mean that believers are shielded from situations that rob them of sleep? Explain.

SOUL ANCHORS
READ MATTHEW 11:28–29.

A. What kind of people does Jesus invite to come to him? What does he promise them?

B. The phrase "take my yoke upon you" is unfamiliar to many of us today. Read what William Hendriksen had to say about it and then answer the questions that follow:

> In Jewish literature a "yoke" represents the sum total of obligations which, according to *the teach-*

ing of the rabbis, a person must take upon himself. . . . Because of their misinterpretation, alteration, and augmentation of God's holy law, the yoke which Israel's teachers placed upon the shoulders of the people was that of a totally unwarranted legalism. It was the system of *teaching* that stressed salvation by means of strict obedience to a host of rules and regulations. Now here in 11:29 Jesus places his own teaching over against that to which the people had become accustomed. When he says, "Take my yoke upon you and learn from me," . . . he means, "Accept my teaching, namely, that a person is saved by means of simple trust in me. . . ." Symbolically speaking, Jesus here assures the oppressed persons whom he addresses, both then and now, that his yoke, that is, the one he urges them to wear, is kindly, and his burden, that is, that which he requires of us, is light. What he is really saying, therefore, is that simple trust in him and obedience to his commands out of gratitude for the salvation already imparted by him is delightful. It brings peace and joy. The person who lives this kind of life is no longer a slave. He has become free.[1]

What "yokes" are you carrying today? How does Jesus suggest you can shed them?

READ HEBREWS 4:1–11.

    C. How does a person enjoy the rest of God?

D. How did some people in the past fail to enjoy this rest?

E. What is the link between the rest mentioned in Matthew 11:28–29 and that in Hebrews 4:1–11?

LIFE ANCHORS

A. Do you believe you normally enjoy the rest Jesus provides? Why or why not? What things keep you from enjoying it?

B. If it's your desire to enjoy Jesus' offer of rest, but you're not sure what to do, begin with these three things:

1. Reread chapter two, "God's Formula for Fatigue."
2. Read once more Matthew 11:28–29 and Hebrews 4:1–11.
3. Sit down with a piece of paper and a pencil and write out specific steps you find in these two sources which describe how to enjoy God's rest.

C. Keep a personal journal for one week, each day recording any events which keep you from enjoying the rest of Jesus. At the end of the week, do two things:

1. Pray about each of those events, asking God for his help in enjoying his rest. Be sure to thank him for those times when you did enjoy his rest.
2. Analyze the events, looking for clues which might indicate how you got off track.

CHAPTER 3

TWO TOMBSTONES

MIND ANCHORS

1. *"Sleeps, but rests not. Loved, but was loved not. Tried to please, but pleased not. Died as she lived—alone."*

    A. What for you is the most chilling phrase in this epitaph? Why?

    B. If you were to write an epitaph for yourself that expresses your current lot in life, what would it say?

2. *How many people will die in the loneliness in which they are living? The homeless in Atlanta. The happy-hour hopper in L.A. A bag lady in Miami. The preacher in Nashville. Any person who doubts whether the world needs him. Any person who is convinced that no one really cares.*

    A. How do you identify people living in loneliness? What characterizes them outwardly?

    B. What lonely people do you know?

C. Have you ever fit any of the descriptions in this passage? Which one(s)?

3. *The woman asked the question that revealed the gaping hole in her soul. "Where is God? My people say he is on the mountain. Your people say he is in Jerusalem. I don't know where he is."*

A. Have you ever met someone who was asking these kinds of questions? What did you tell him or her?

B. Have you ever asked these questions yourself? If so, what prompted the questions?

4. *Barbara's difficult home life had left her afraid and insecure. While the other children talked, she sat. While the others sang, she was silent. While the others giggled, she was quiet. Always present. Always listening. Always speechless.*

Until the day Joy gave a class on heaven. Joy talked about seeing God. She talked about tearless eyes and deathless lives. Barbara listened with hunger. Then she raised her hand. "Mrs. Joy?"

"Yes, Barbara?"

"Is heaven for girls like me?"

A. Describe the emotional impact this story has on you. Why is Barbara's question so poignant?

B. What do you think caused Barbara to ask such a question?

C. If you had been Joy, how would you have answered Barbara's question?

SOUL ANCHORS

READ JOHN 4:4–42.

A. Jews of Jesus' day avoided passing through Samaria at all costs, even taking long detours to bypass the area. Yet John 4:4 says Jesus "had" to go though Samaria. Why do you think he "had" to do so?

B. How did Jesus use his own needs as tools for evangelism (vv. 6–15)? What can we learn from this?

C. What is the "living water" Jesus talks about in verse 10? What does it do?

D. What kind of people does God seek to worship him (vv. 23–24)? Could this Samaritan woman qualify? Do you?

E. How did Jesus use his own needs as tools for teaching (vv. 31–38)? What can we learn from this?

F. How did the woman's report about Jesus affect the people of her town (vv. 39–42)? Taking into account her background (vv. 17–18), why is this remarkable?

G. Identify the single greatest lesson you have learned from this story.

LIFE ANCHORS

A. Sit down with a close friend or your spouse and write out what gives your life purpose and meaning. Be specific. The next time you are overwhelmed by the rising tides of futility, take out that list and read it.

B. Do you know any Grace Llewellen Smiths? What can you do to help make them feel more significant? Why not do it today?

LIVING PROOF

MIND ANCHORS

1. *One step into the classroom and the cat of curiosity pounced on Jenna. And I walked away. I gave my daughter up. Not much. And not as much as I will have to in the future. But I gave her up as much as I could today.*

    A. In what other ways will Jenna (or your boy or girl) have to be given up in the future?

    B. Does it help to know that all this "giving up" doesn't have to be done at once? Why?

2. *I gave up my child fully aware that were she to need me I would be at her side in a heartbeat. You, God, said good-bye to your son fully aware that when he would need you the most, when his cry of despair would roar through the heavens, you would sit in silence. The angels, though positioned, would hear no command from you. Your son, though in anguish, would feel no comfort from your hands.*

    A. Why did God give up his son so completely?

B. Imagine, if you can, what it might have been like in heaven's throne room while Christ suffered on the cross. What is the mood of the angels surrounding God? Somber? Sad? Happy? Angry? Confused?

3. *Before the day was over, I sat in silence a second time. This time not beside my daughter, but before my Father. This time not sad over what I had to give, but grateful for what I'd already received—living proof that God does care.*

A. What is the "living proof" to which this passage refers?

B. How do you respond to this "living proof"?

SOUL ANCHORS
READ ROMANS 8:32–39.

A. For what purpose did God give up his son (v. 32)?

B. Finish the following phrase, based on the second half of verse 32: "Because God was willing to give up his only son for us, we should never think that he_____

_____

_____."

C. What does it mean that Christ even now "intercedes" for us (v. 34)? How does this make you feel?

D. In a passage of Scripture aimed at helping believers understand their safe position with God, what is Paul's point in quoting a text that says, "For your sake we face death all day long; we are considered as sheep to be slaughtered"?

E. What things, according to Paul, can separate a believer from the love of Christ (vv. 35–39)?

LIFE ANCHORS

A. Think about past hurricanes in your life. What gives you "living proof" that God loves you? Make a list of these specifics.

B. Do you help others experience your love for them? Who are the significant people in your life? Think of one thing you can give them as "living proof" of your love for them, and do it.

C. If you have not been able to experience God's love for you, ask God to open your heart so that you would recognize his hand in your life. Then go to a Christian friend whom you regard as spiritually mature and ask what he or she would do in your shoes.

CHAPTER 5

FLAMING TORCHES AND LIVING PROMISES

MIND ANCHORS

1. *Had any visits from Doubt lately? If you find yourself going to church in order to be saved and not because you are saved, then you've been listening to him. If you find yourself doubting if God could forgive you again for that, you've been sold some snake oil. If you are more cynical about Christians than sincere about Christ, then guess who came to dinner.*

   A. Explain the phrase "If you find yourself going to church in order to be saved and not because you are saved, then you've been listening to him." How is this statement a reflection of doubt?

   B. To which lies of Doubt are you most susceptible?

2. *The invisible God had drawn near to Abraham to make his immovable promise: "To your descendants I give this land." And though God's people often forgot their God, God didn't forget them.*

373

He kept his word. The land became theirs. God didn't give up. He never gives up.

A. In what situations are you most likely to forget God?

B. How does it make you feel to know that God "never gives up"? At what times in your life has this knowledge been especially comforting?

3. *So, the next time that obnoxious neighbor Doubt walks in, escort him out. Out to the hill. Out to Calvary. Out to the cross where, with holy blood, the hand that carried the flame wrote the promise, "God would give up his only son before he'd give up on you."*

A. Why is Calvary a good place to put doubt to rest?

SOUL ANCHORS
READ 2 TIMOTHY 2:8–13.

A. One good way to combat doubt is to remember what things are essential. What does Paul ask Timothy to "remember" in verse 8? How is this essential?

B. Verse 11 promises that we will live with Christ if we "died with him." What does it mean to "die with him"? How do you do that?

C. How is "enduring" connected with "reigning" in verse 12? How does this idea relate to verse 10?

D. What warning is included in verse 12? How does doubt sometimes enter in here? How does Paul's warning here compare to Jesus' own words in Luke 12:8–9?

E. What great hope is found in verse 13? Upon what is this hope built?

F. What does it mean to you that God is absolutely faithful?

LIFE ANCHORS

A. This chapter has listed many times when God did not give up on his people. Think about your own life. Can you recall times when you were unfaithful but God was faithful to you? Write these down and tell a friend about them.

B. Is doubt ever a good thing? Have there been times in your life when you looked your doubts in the face and they strengthened your faith? Talk about these times with a friend or write about them. How can this encourage you the next time doubt comes your way?

C. For more insight into doubt and God's faithfulness, read *Disappointment with God* by Philip Yancey.

CHAPTER 6

ANGELIC MESSAGES

MIND ANCHORS

1. *What if God had responded to my grumblings? What if he'd heeded my complaints? He could have. He could have answered my carelessly mumbled prayers. And had he chosen to do so, a prototype of the result had just appeared at my door.*

    A. What prayers have you mumbled which you're glad God hasn't answered? Why do you think grumbling comes so easy to us?

    B. What "angels" have crossed your path recently?

2. *God sent the boy with a message. And the point the boy made was razor sharp: "You cry over spilled champagne. Your complaints are not over the lack of necessities but the abundance of benefits. You bellyache over the frills, not the basics; over benefits, not essentials. The source of your problems is your blessings."*

    A. Do you believe God would make these same statements to you? Why or why not?

B. Try to name your personal "Top Ten Blessings."

3. *Gajowniczek survived the Holocaust. He made his way back to his hometown. Every year, however, he goes back to Auschwitz. Every August 14 he goes back to say thank you to the man who died in his place. In his backyard there is a plaque. On the plaque is a tribute he carved with his own hands. A tribute to Maximilian Kolbe—the man who died so Gajowniczek could live.*

A. What makes Gajowniczek trek back to Auschwitz every August 14? If you were in his place, would you continue the trips? Why?

B. The statement about Kolbe—"he died so that I could live"—is also a good way to think about Jesus' relationship to redeemed sinners. Explain how this is so.

SOUL ANCHORS
READ JOHN 11:45–52.

A. In the verses just prior to this passage, John tells how Jesus had raised Lazarus from the dead. What happened because of this miracle (v. 45)? How did this make Lazarus an "angel" to others?

B. In what two ways did people respond to this "angel" (vv. 45–46; Luke 12:9–11)? In what ways can we respond to the "angels" God sends us?

C. What did Caiaphas mean by his speech in verses 49–50?

D. What did God mean by that same speech (vv. 51–52)?

E. How are these two interpretations of the same speech typi-cal of the way God often works (see also Acts 4:24–28)?

F. For what purpose did Jesus die, according to verses 51–52? For whom did he die? Are you included in this list? If so, how?

LIFE ANCHORS

A. Who are the people for whom you are most grate-ful? Do they know how you feel? If not, tell them of your appreciation and why they mean so much to you. Ask God to help you encourage them in both the timing and the selection of your words.

B. Take a couple of hours this week to go with a friend and visit a homeless shelter or mission. Talk to the people there, finding out who they are and what has hap-pened to them. Also talk with those who work there. What needs do their clients have? How does the commu-nity respond to the have-nots in your city? What might you do to help meet some of these needs?

CHAPTER 7

REMEMBER

MIND ANCHORS

1. *The church of Jesus Christ began with a group of frightened men in a second-floor room in Jerusalem.*

    A. What frightened these men?

    B. Why do you think modern-day disciples are frightened?

2. *The one betrayed sought his betrayers. What did he say to them? Not, "What a bunch of flops!" Not, "I told you so." No "Where-were-you-when-I-needed-you?" speeches. But simply one phrase, "Peace be with you." The very thing they didn't have was the very thing he offered: peace.*

    A. How important is it that Jesus "sought his betrayers"? What likely would have happened if he hadn't done so?

    B. What was the purpose behind Jesus' speech? Why did these men need it?

3. *What unlocked the doors of the apostles' hearts? Simple. They saw Jesus. They encountered the Christ. Their sins collided with their Savior, and their Savior won! What lit the boiler of the apostles was a red-hot conviction that the very one who should have sent them to hell went to hell for them and came back to tell about it.*

    A. Explain the phrase "Their sins collided with their Savior, and their Savior won!"

    B. What should it matter to us how Jesus interacted with a group of men two thousand years ago?

4. *Think about the first time you ever saw him. Think about your first encounter with the Christ. Robe yourself in that moment. Resurrect the relief. Recall the purity. Summon forth the passion. Can you remember?*

    A. Describe the first time you "saw Christ."

    B. How long ago did you first "see Christ"? If you could climb in a time machine and revisit that moment, would you? Why?

5. *There is a direct correlation between the accuracy of our memory and the effectiveness of our mission. If we are not teaching people how to be saved, it is perhaps because we have forgotten the tragedy of being lost! If we're not teaching the message of forgiveness, it may be because we don't remember what it was like to be guilty. And if we're not preaching the cross, it could be that we've subconsciously decided that—God forbid—somehow we don't need it.*

A. Try to recall what it was like to be "lost." Describe it. Did you feel guilt? In what way(s)?

B. Do you think you need the cross? Why?

6. *A man is never the same after he simultaneously sees his utter despair and Christ's unbending grace. To see the despair without the grace is suicidal. To see the grace without the despair is upperroom futility. But to see them both is conversion.*

A. Why are both "despair" and "grace" necessary for conversion?

SOUL ANCHORS
READ ACTS 23:6–15.

A. For what reason was Paul in custody at this time (v. 6)? Would there have been an uproar had he kept silent about Jesus? Explain.

B. What incident gave Paul great strength and courage in the midst of his hardships (v. 11)? How would this have helped?

C. Did the Lord's promise of help shield Paul from trouble (vv. 12–15)? What did the promise secure for Paul?

D. What is it about seeing Jesus that gives boldness and strength?

E. Can you "see Jesus" without having an actual vision of him? If so, how?

LIFE ANCHORS

A. Take about half an hour and meditate on the cross. You could do this in several ways—

1. Remember who you are and who Jesus is and what he did for you. What is it about Jesus that particularly amazes you?

2. Use a familiar hymnbook and focus on hymns about the cross. Try reading them aloud or singing them.

3. Ask God to fill you with awe that he—the God of the universe—would die for you. Read Psalm 22 and use it to guide your thoughts.

B. Find a partner and take turns asking the following questions. Write down your answers, but don't evaluate what was said until all questions are answered. Say what you really think, not what you believe you should think.

1. What does Jesus think about your relationship with him? How would he describe it?

2. How does he view you?

3. How do you view him?

4. Do you believe he would offer you peace as he did the disciples, or do you think he would reprimand you? Why?

Once the questions have been answered, go over them together and summarize what your answers reveal.

C. What hardships are you facing right now? Write these down and beside each note how Jesus can help you weather this storm.

CHAPTER 8

FATAL ERRORS

MIND ANCHORS

1. *Could you do it all over again, you'd do it differently. You'd be a different person. You'd be more patient. You'd control your tongue. You'd finish what you started. You'd turn the other cheek instead of slapping his. You'd get married first. You wouldn't marry at all. You'd be honest. You'd resist the temptation. You'd run with a different crowd.*

But you can't. And as many times as you tell yourself "What's done is done," what you did can't be undone.

    A. What major decisions or actions in your own life would you change if you could?

    B. What dangers are there in rehearsing past personal errors? What benefits?

2. *Don't we all long for a father who, even though our mistakes are written all over the wall, will love us anyway? Don't we want a father who cares for us in spite of our failures?*

    A. How would you answer these questions? Why would you answer like this?

3. *What kind of heavenly father do we have? A father who is at his best when we are at our worst. A father whose grace is strongest when our devotion is weakest.*

    A. What specific comfort do you receive from the thought in this passage? What does this statement mean for you?

    B. Name three instances where you experienced the truth of this passage.

Soul Anchors
Compare Acts 13:13 and 15:36–41 to 2 Timothy 4:11.

    A. Describe the failure of John Mark. How serious, in Paul's mind, was this failure?

    B. What happened in Acts 15:36–41 as a direct result of this failure?

    C. The text doesn't mention how John Mark felt about this controversy. If you were in his shoes, what might you have felt?

    D. How does 2 Timothy 4:11 show that Mark's failure was not fatal? What had changed over time?

    E. What lessons can you learn from the experience of John Mark?

LIFE ANCHORS

A. If you find it difficult to believe that God accepts your failures, begin with these two things:

1. Reread "Fatal Errors," slowly and meditatively, asking God to let the truths of the chapter sink into your soul.

2. Go back to the story of John Mark in Acts 13:13 and 15:36–41, then write out the lesson you learn from John Mark and how you can apply this lesson to your life.

B. If you have trouble experiencing God's grace, it will take time for you to feel free of your guilt. Over the next week, take time to identify those things which keep you from accepting failure as a normal part of life. Here are some things to think through and write down:

1. Do you have specific memories of times when you have failed and then been punished?

2. How have the significant people in your life affected your view of failure?

3. Can you remember times when you have failed and the results were used for good in your life?

C. Analyze how you responded to the questions above and then pray that God will renew your mind and help you see yourself as he sees you.

CHAPTER 9

CRISTO REDENTOR

MIND ANCHORS

1. *What kind of redeemer is this? I thought. Blind eyes and stony heart? I've since learned the answer to my own question: exactly the kind of redeemer most people have.*

    A. Do you agree with this observation? Explain your answer.

    B. What kind of redeemer do you think your next-door neighbor has? Your closest coworker? You?

2. *In her despair the woman looks at the Teacher. His eyes don't glare. "Don't worry," they whisper. "It's okay." And for the first time that morning she sees kindness.*

    A. Imagine you are this woman. What would you have expected to see in Jesus' eyes? What is running through your mind?

    B. Does this passage mean that Jesus winks at sin? What does it mean?

3. *On earth, Jesus was an artist in a gallery of his own paintings. He was a composer listening as the orchestra interpreted his music. He was a poet hearing his own poetry. Yet his works of art had been defaced, creation after battered creation. He had created people for splendor. They had settled for mediocrity. He had formed them with love. They had scarred each other with hate.*

    A. How are these images of "artist," "composer," and "poet" meant to remind us of Jesus? To what aspects of his personality or work do they refer?

    B. Give five specific, personally observed examples that illustrate the point of this passage.

4. *"Is there no one to condemn you?" Jesus asked. There is still one who can, she thinks. And she turns to look at him. What does he want? What will he do?*

    A. Why does the woman think, "There is still one who can"?

    B. What do you think Jesus wants of you?

5. *She would recognize his eyes. How could she ever forget those eyes? Clear and tear filled. Eyes that saw her not as she was, but as she was intended to be.*

    A. What did Jesus intend this woman to be? What does he intend you to be?

    B. Does this passage give you hope? Why?

Soul Anchors
READ LUKE 7:36–50.

A. What things does the woman in this story have in common with the woman described in John 8?

B. What do you see in the eyes of this Pharisee when he looks at the woman (see verse 39)?

C. Compare the way Jesus dealt with the woman in this passage to the way he interacted with the woman of John 8. What things did he do similarly? What did he do differently?

D. What is the point of the story Jesus tells in verses 41–43? With which character in the story do you most identify? Why?

E. How would you answer the question raised in verse 49?

F. Do you think Jesus could repeat his words found in verse 50 to you? Why or why not?

Life Anchors

A. Ask your closest friend to tell you honestly what your behavior reveals about the kind of redeemer you have. Find out why he or she says this and make any changes you see are necessary.

B. Reread the story in Luke 7:41–43. Write down the sins for which you have been forgiven—be sure to mention only those for which you have experienced God's forgiveness.

C. If you do not feel as if God has forgiven you for much, pray that he will make you sensitive to the sin in your life. If you feel that your sins are so terrible that a holy God could not forgive you, read this chapter again, putting yourself in the place of the woman.

CHAPTER 10

THE
GOLDEN GOBLET

MIND ANCHORS

1. *"The choice is hers," the King instructed. "If she turns to us for help, that is your command to deliver her. If she doesn't turn, if she doesn't look to me—don't. The choice is hers."*

    A. With help so near, why do you think the woman chose as she did?

    B. Why do you think God refused to send help unless the woman asked for it?

2. *"Their choice will be honored. Where there is poison, there will be death. Where there are goblets, there will be fire. Let it be done."*

    A. In your own words, describe the spiritual principle outlined in this passage.

3. *"I will taste the poison," swore the King's Son. "For this I have come. But the hour will be mine to choose."*

A. What did the son mean by, "I will taste the poison"? How was his "tasting" different from all those who had tasted before?

B. What was important about the son choosing the hour of his "tasting"? What is significant about the timing?

4. *"Here is the cup, my Son. Drink it alone."*

God must have wept as he performed his task. Every lie, every lure, every act done in shadows was in that cup. Slowly, hideously they were absorbed into the body of the Son. The final act of incarnation. The Spotless Lamb was blemished. Flames began to lick his feet. . . . The King turns away from his Prince. The undiluted wrath of a sin-hating Father falls upon his sin-filled Son. The fire envelops him. The shadow hides him. The Son looks for his Father, but his Father cannot be seen.

"My God, my God . . . why?"

A. What one word would you pick to describe how the son must have felt at the moment he drank the cup?

B. Do you think an answer to the son's agonized question would have eased his pain? Explain your answer.

5. *A noise snaps the King from his dream. He opens his eyes and sees a transcendent figure gleaming in the doorway. "It is finished, Father. I have come home."*

A. What emotional impact do these lines have upon you?

B. What part of this story is most memorable for you? Why?

Soul Anchors
Read 2 Corinthians 5:21.

A. Who "had no sin"? What does this mean?

B. How did this one "become sin" for us? What was the purpose?

Read Galatians 3:13–14.

C. How did Christ "redeem us from the curse of the law"? When did this happen?

D. What was the purpose for Christ's becoming a curse for us?

E. How do we receive "the promise of the Spirit"?

Read Romans 8:3–4.

F. Why was the law "powerless" to bring us to God?

G. How did God overcome this powerlessness?

H. If sinful men are unable to meet the requirements of the law, how can they be saved (v. 4)?

Life Anchors

A. "The Golden Goblet" paints a picture of the spiritual warfare that raged in Eden, but that warfare continues all around us. Are you currently engaged in a spiritual struggle? What is it? Describe it to a friend and ask for prayer that you will embrace God's help to win the battle. Ask to be held accountable.

B. Pray that God will make you more sensitive to spiritual warfare and the power of prayer to defeat Satan.

C. For more insight into spiritual warfare, read *Counterattack* by Jay Carty or *This Present Darkness* by Frank Peretti.

CHAPTER 11

COME HOME

MIND ANCHORS

1. *Pride is made of stone. Hard knocks may chip it, but it takes reality's sledgehammer to break it.*

    A. In what sense is pride "made of stone"?

    B. Why is it hard for the proud to accept the gospel?

2. *His first few days of destitution were likely steamy with resentment. He was mad at everyone. Everyone was to blame. His friends shouldn't have bailed out on him. And his brother should come and bail him out. His boss should feed him better, and his dad never should have let him go in the first place. He named a pig after each one of them.*

    A. Is it easy for you to blame others for your own mistakes? Explain.

    B. What gave the young man satisfaction in naming a pig after each one of the people mentioned? Do you ever act like this? How?

3. It is so familiar: Cries for help muffled behind costumed faces. Fear hidden behind a painted smile. Signals of desperation thought to be signs of joy. Tell me that doesn't describe our world.

    A. In what ways does this describe your world?

    B. In what ways does this describe you?

4. He was going home a changed man. Not demanding that he get what he deserved, but willing to take whatever he could get. "Give me" had been replaced with "help me," and his defiance had been replaced with repentance.

    A. What factors helped cause this man's transformation?

    B. Try to think of someone you know who has gone through a similar transformation. Describe him or her before/after.

5. Jesus stretched his hands as open as he could. He forced his arms so wide apart that it hurt. And to prove that those arms would never fold and those hands would never close, he had them nailed open. They still are.

    A. What does the last phrase mean?

    B. What significance does this passage have for you?

SOUL ANCHORS
READ LUKE 15:11–32.

    A. What drove this young man to reconsider his way of living (vv. 14–16)? How is this story often replayed in the modern world?

B. Compare what the young man says in verse 18 to what King David said in Psalm 51:4. What sentiment is the same in both?

C. How does the father in verse 20 picture our heavenly father? Do you think it is a good picture? Why?

D. Compare verses 18–19 with verse 21. Note which part of the son's prepared speech gets left off. Why do you think the son was unable to finish the whole speech?

E. Was the young man worthy of the treatment he received in verses 22–24? How is this scene a picture of grace?

F. Have you ever felt like the older brother in verses 25–30? Explain.

G. How is the father's description of his son in verse 32 a good description of every Christian?

LIFE ANCHORS

A. For the next week or so, carefully monitor what you do when you catch yourself making a mistake. Do you own up to your faults? Are you critical of yourself, or do you tend to blame others? What sort of things do you say to yourself? Write down your observations and use them to guide your prayer schedule.

B. Ask someone you trust to name which of the three characters in Luke 15:1–32 you most resemble. Have your friend describe what he or she sees in you that prompts that response. With this input, consider whether you need to make some changes in your behavior and attitude. Choose three things you can do to help make those changes.

C. Take some time this week to think about how you believe God views your failures. Here are some questions to ask yourself:

1. Do I have any failures from which I have never recovered?

2. If I were to die and go to heaven today, what would Jesus say to me about my life?

3. Can I see positive outcomes from my failures?

D. For more insight into how you can change, read *Inside Out* by Larry Crabb.

CHAPTER 12

THE FISH
AND THE FALLS

MIND ANCHORS

1. *The fish swam to where the water crashed into the river. He attempted to swim upwards. He would ascend the falls by brute force. But the onrush of the water was too strong. Undaunted, he swam until he could swim no more, then he slept.*

> A. How does this passage picture man's attempt to reach God by unaided human strength? What is the outcome?

2. *But how do you not hear the yearning of your heart? How do you turn away from discovery? How can you be satisfied with existence once you've lived with purpose?*

> A. How would you answer these questions?

> B. What purpose is there in your life?

3. *All of nature watched as the fish rode the wave of grace. All of nature rejoiced when he reached the top. The stars raced through the*

blackness. The moon tilted backwards and rocked in sweet satisfaction. Bears danced. Birds hugged. The wind whistled. And the leaves applauded. The fish was where he had longed to be. He was in the presence of the roar.

What he couldn't do the river had done. He knew immediately he would spend forever relishing the mystery.

A. How is the scene depicted here like Jesus' own statement in Luke 15:10?

B. How is the wave like God's grace? In what way is the fish like you? Where would the fish be without the wave? Where would you be without God's grace?

Soul Anchors
Read Romans 5:6–11.

A. What word does Paul use to describe our inability to save ourselves (v. 6)? Why is this tough to swallow?

B. For whom did Christ die (v. 6)? Who could be characterized like this?

C. How does Paul try to get us to see the enormity of God's sacrifice for us in verses 7–8?

D. By what are Christians "justified" (v. 9)? How does this relate to the cross?

E. From what will all Christians be saved (v. 9)? What makes this possible?

F. How does Paul teach that people can go from being God's "enemies" in verse 10 to "rejoicing in God" in verse 11? What does it mean to "rejoice in God"?

LIFE ANCHORS

A. Do you know anyone who is struggling to understand the concept of God's grace? Do you know someone who has trouble believing that God's acceptance and approval have nothing to do with our efforts? Who is that person? What can you do to be a picture of grace to him or her?

B. Think through the gospel message as clearly as you can, making sure you identify all the major parts (see especially 1 Corinthians 15:1–11; Ephesians 2:8–9). Then "borrow" a child (not your own) from a close friend or neighbor and see if you can successfully communicate this message to him or her. Do a "debriefing" session afterwards to evaluate how you did.

CHAPTER 13

THE ELEVENTH HOUR GIFT

MIND ANCHORS

1. *And now, one more beggar comes with a request. Only minutes from the death of them both, he stands before the King. He will ask for crumbs. And he, like the others, will receive a whole loaf.*

    A. What are the "crumbs" this man asked for? What was the "whole loaf" he received?

    B. Why did the beggar receive such a great gift? How is this a picture of grace?

2. *It's an inexplicable dilemma—how two people can hear the same words and see the same Savior, and one see hope and the other see nothing but himself.*

    A. Describe a contemporary example of what this passage teaches.

3. *Lodged in the thief's statement are the two facts that anyone needs to recognize in order to come to Jesus. Look at the phrase again. Do you see them?*

"We are getting what we deserve. This man has done nothing wrong."

A. Name the two facts that must be recognized in order for someone to come to Jesus.

B. What makes these two facts indispensable for coming to Jesus?

SOUL ANCHORS
READ COLOSSIANS 1:21–23.

A. Before the Colossians became Christians, what was their relationship to God (v. 22)? What areas of their lives were affected?

B. Who made the first move toward reconciliation? What was his purpose in doing so (v. 22)?

C. How did God accomplish this reconciliation? What was his purpose in doing so (v. 22)?

D. How does one gain this new relationship to God (v. 23)?

E. Paul says the gospel holds great "hope." What hope in the gospel is there for you?

F. What does Paul mean when he says that he has become a servant of the gospel? How can we follow his example?

Life Anchors

A. Who are the people God has placed in your life? Consider neighbors, friends, coworkers, relatives, and service people. What message of God's grace do they hear from you? Why not decide today to make a conscious effort to tell one of these people the hope of the gospel? Plan out how and when you will do this.

B. Think about someone in your life who has treated you poorly or unfairly. Now suppose this person has come to you to ask your forgiveness. What will you do? In order to answer honestly, ask yourself these questions:

1. Am I a forgiving person—or do I hold grudges?
2. Can I remember specific incidents when a person asked for my forgiveness? What was my response?
3. Have I ever been refused forgiveness? If so, how might this affect my ability to forgive someone else?

GOD
VS.
DEATH

MIND ANCHORS

1. *At that moment I stopped looking at the names and stared at the monument. I relaxed my focus from the lettering and looked at the tablet. What I saw was sobering. I saw myself. I saw my own reflection. My face looked at me from the shiny marble. It reminded me that I, too, have been dying as long as I have been living. I, too, will someday have my name carved in a granite stone. Someday I, too, will face death.*

    A. What circumstances or events prompt you to ponder your own death?

    B. What feelings do thoughts of your own death create in you? Why?

2. *Jesus unmasked death and exposed him for who he really is—a ninety-eight-pound weakling dressed up in a Charles Atlas suit. Jesus*

had no patience for this impostor. He couldn't sit still while death pulled the veil over life.

    A. In what way is death an "impostor"? How is it "a ninety-eight-pound weakling dressed up in a Charles Atlas suit"?

    B. Why couldn't Jesus "sit still while death pulled the veil over life"?

3. *If you ever want to know how to conduct yourself at a funeral, don't look to Jesus for an example. He interrupted each one he ever attended.*

    A. Why might this statement make you smile?

    B. What point was Jesus making by interrupting all these funerals? How was this important?

SOUL ANCHORS
READ HEBREWS 2:14–16.

    A. What two reasons are given in verses 14–15 for Christ's becoming human and dying on the cross?

    B. How is it ironic that Christ's death was God's means of destroying the devil?

    C. How does death hold people in slavery? Does it hold you? Why or why not?

D. Who is included in "Abraham's descendants" (see also Romans 4:16–17; Galatians 3:26–29)?

E. What advantage do redeemed men and women have over angels (v. 16)?

LIFE ANCHORS

A. One of the most exciting results of the gospel is that the Christian does not have to fear death. Death is an impostor. Take some time this week to delight in this truth. Look up 1 Corinthians 15:51–57. Meditate on these verses, asking God to let the wonder of his power over death encourage you.

B. If, after reading this chapter, you realize you have some fears about your own dying, try some of these ideas to help fortify your faith:

1. Talk to someone about your fears. Ask for help in sorting out the rational from the irrational. Make a list of those fears which you need to overcome.
2. Find out the name of someone who has faced death and has experienced God's peace. Ask the person how he or she feels and why. What can you learn from the person that would help you?

CHAPTER 15

FANTASY
OR REALITY?

MIND ANCHORS

1. *The followers of Jesus stop and step aside as the funeral procession shadows by. The blanket of mourning muffles the laughter of the disciples. No one speaks. What could they say? They feel the same despair felt by the bystanders at any funeral. "Someday that will be me." No one intervenes. What could they do? Their only choice is to stand and stare as the mourners shuffle past.*

    A. Think of the last funeral you attended. What parts of this description fit what you saw there?

    B. Does it bother you to ponder your own mortality? Why?

2. *How would you feel at a moment like this? What would you do? A stranger tells you not to weep as you look at your dead son. One who refuses to mourn in the midst of sorrow calls the devil's bluff, then shocks you with a call into the cavern of death. Suddenly what had been taken is returned. What had been stolen is retrieved. What you had given up, you are given back.*

A. Answer the questions in the first two sentences of the passage.

B. How do you picture Jesus' demeanor in this incident? How do you picture that of the disciples?

3. *Jesus gave the woman much more than her son. He gave her a secret—a whisper that was overheard by us. "That," he says point-ing at the cot, "that is fantasy. This," he grins, putting an arm around the boy, "this is reality."*

A. In your own words, describe the secret Jesus whispered to the woman.

SOUL ANCHORS
READ LUKE 7:11–17.

A. How did the Lord react when he saw this dis-traught mother (v. 13)? How is this typical of him?

B. Did the Lord require the mother to exercise faith before he performed the miracle?

C. The text doesn't tell us, but what do you imag-ine the young man might have said after Jesus raised him from the dead (v. 15)?

D. How did the people respond to Jesus' miracle?

E. Did the people fully understand who Jesus was? How can you tell?

F. Why is it that believers today do not seem as intent on "spreading the news" about Jesus as were the people back then (v. 17)?

LIFE ANCHORS

A. Do you know someone who is dying or who has recently lost a person he or she cared about? What can you do to encourage him or her? Here are some suggestions—

1. Read him the last section of this book.
2. Spend time with her and listen to any of her fears.
3. Pray with him about those fears.
4. Commit yourself to pray for her and to keep in contact so she doesn't feel abandoned.

B. Make a list of some practical things you could do to help someone who was dying. Some things to include are—

1. Help with meals and transportation.
2. Help with correspondence and communication.
3. Volunteer to take care of the children.
4. Offer to help make sure his or her financial affairs are in order, or identify someone who can.

Keep this list in a place of easy access so that when the time comes you are ready to help.

C. If you have never lost a loved one, you may feel uncomfortable around those who are grieving. A classic on the subject is *The Last Thing We Talk About* by Joe Bayley.

CHAPTER 16

THE SPARKLE
FROM ETERNITY

MIND ANCHORS

1. *Wallace had never known such helplessness. He didn't know how to handle his pain. He was so accustomed to being strong, he didn't know how to be weak. He assured all who called that his daughter was fine. He assured all who inquired that God was a great God. He assured everyone but himself.*

    A. Why do you think it is hard for "strong" people to show weakness? How is this sometimes a handicap?

    B. Do you ever feel that God is not as great as you say he is? Explain.

2. *Wallace began to weigh his options. Should he go to see the Teacher? "If I go and am recognized, it will mean my job. But if she dies and he could have done something . . . " A man reaches a point where his desperation is a notch above his dignity. He shrugs his shoulders. "What choice do I have?"*

A. Have you ever reached a point of desperation similar to Wallace's? What happened?

B. What is it about trying circumstances that often bring people to Jesus?

3. *This Jesus looked too normal. He wore a corduroy jacket, the kind with patches on the elbows. His slacks weren't new, but they were nice. No tie. His hairline receded a bit before it became a flow of brown curls. I couldn't hear his voice, but I could see his face. His eyebrows were bushy. He had a gleam in his eyes and a grin on his lips—as if he were watching you unwrap the birthday present he just gave you.*

A. If Jesus were to appear on earth today, do you think this description might fit him? Why or why not?

B. How do you normally picture Jesus?

4. *Wallace regretted the words as soon as he said them. If he's a man, then I've asked the impossible. If he's more than a man, what right do I have to make such a request?*

A. Where do you agree or disagree with Wallace's reasoning?

B. What would the granting of Wallace's request imply about the identity of Jesus?

5. *Peace where there should be pain. Confidence in the midst of crisis. Hope defying despair. That's what that look says. It is a look that knows the answer to the question asked by every mortal: "Does death have the last word?" I can see Jesus wink as he gives the answer. "Not on your life."*

A. Are you confident that Jesus has mastered death? Why or why not?

B. How does your answer to the previous question affect the way you live?

SOUL ANCHORS
READ MARK 5:21–43.

A. Why were large crowds always following Jesus? Had you been alive at the time, do you believe you would have been among them? Why?

B. What was important to Jesus about identifying the woman who had been healed of her affliction? Why not just overlook it?

C. What does Jesus' declaration to the woman (v. 34) have in common with his instruction to Jairus (v. 36)?

D. What reasons can you name to explain why Jesus required Jairus to show faith, but not the distraught mother of Luke 7:11–17? What might this suggest about the way God works in the world?

E. Note how Jesus gave orders for the little girl to be fed after he raised her from the dead (v. 43). What does this tell you about Jesus?

LIFE ANCHORS

A. Did you notice how Jesus responded to Jairus's request for help? Even though he was busy, Jesus didn't hesitate: "Jesus went with him" (Mark 5:24).

> How receptive are you to cries for help? Do your friends see you as a caring and compassionate person—someone they can call on if they are in need? Whom do you feel free to call on? Ask those people if they feel the same toward you, and why.

B. Look more closely at those people you cited as being willing to help. What qualities or characteristics do they have that make them approachable? Write these down and evaluate your own strengths in these areas. If you see that you need to change, you can begin the process by—

1. Praying that God will help you grow in those areas in which you are weak.

2. Choosing one or two characteristics you can begin to cultivate today. Decide how you can do that.

3. Asking someone to give you feedback on any changes he or she sees in you.

C. Why wait until someone asks you for help? What could you do today that would help or encourage someone? Go do it.

CHAPTER 17

"LAZARUS, COME OUT!"

MIND ANCHORS

1. *A life wasted pacing up and down in a self-made cell of fear. It is shocking. It is tragic. It is a pity. And it is also very common.*

    A. Give several examples of what this passage describes.

    B. Have you ever wasted part of your life "pacing up and down in a self-made cell of fear"? How did you escape?

2. *Jesus wept. He wept not for the dead but for the living. He wept not for the one in the cave of death but for those in the cave of fear. He wept for those who, though alive, were dead. He wept for those who, though free, were prisoners, held captive by their fear of death.*

    A. How can someone be "alive" yet "dead"?

    B. What does Jesus' weeping tell you about his character or personality? How does this affect your perception of him?

3. *Jesus saw people enslaved by their fear of a cheap power. He explained that the river of death was nothing to fear. The people wouldn't believe him. He touched a boy and called him back to life. The followers were still unconvinced. He whispered life into the dead body of a girl. The people were still cynical. He let a dead man spend four days in a grave and then called him out. Is that enough? Apparently not. For it was necessary for him to enter the river, to submerge himself in the water of death before people would believe that death had been conquered.*

A. How was Jesus' resurrection different from the boy's, the girl's, or Lazarus's?

B. Do you believe that Jesus has conquered death? Why or why not?

SOUL ANCHORS
READ JOHN 11:1–44.

A. How could Jesus say in verse 4, "This sickness will not end in death," when he knew very well that Lazarus would die?

B. How was Jesus glorified through this incident, as he predicted in verse 4?

C. In what way are verses 25–26 the heart of the gospel? How do you respond to Jesus' question here?

D. What was Jesus doing that caused the Jews to say of his relationship to Lazarus, "See how he loved him!" (v. 36)? How do his actions color your picture of him?

E. Compare Martha's words in verse 27 to those in verse 39. Does her faith remind you of your own at times? If so, how?

F. What is the strongest impression you get of Jesus from reading these three stories of his resurrecting the dead?

LIFE ANCHORS

A. Make an appointment to visit a funeral home. Ask the funeral director questions about how he arranges funeral details, how he deals with those in grief, the differences between "religious" and "secular" services, his personal view of death, etc. When you return home, write a page or two describing how your visit affected your views of death and Christianity.

B. The next time you see a movie or television show which includes scenes of death, ask yourself how the show's producers depict death. Do they see it as final? Triumphant? Glorious? Frightening? Then sit down with a family member or friend and try to imagine how you, as a director with a Christian viewpoint, would have staged those same scenes. What would you do differently? The same?

CHAPTER 18

THE CELEBRATION

MIND ANCHORS

1. *"Why are you crying?" An uncommon question to be asked in a cemetery. In fact, the question is rude. That is, unless the questioner knows something the questionee doesn't.*

    A. What did the questioner know that the questionee didn't?

    B. Of what significance is this knowledge?

2. *Jesus doesn't leave her wondering long, just long enough to remind us that he loves to surprise us. He waits for us to despair of human strength and then intervenes with heavenly. God waits for us to give up and then—surprise!*

    A. Why do you think Jesus "waits for us to despair of human strength"?

    B. Have you experienced any of God's surprises? Describe them.

3. *"Miriam," Jesus said softly, "surprise!"*

Mary was shocked. It's not often you hear your name spoken by an eternal tongue. But when she did, she recognized it. And when she did, she responded correctly. She worshiped him.

A. Why was worship Mary's correct response? What does it mean to worship?

B. What is the correct response to Jesus today? How are you responding to him?

SOUL ANCHORS
READ JOHN 20:1–18.

A. What was Mary's concern when she saw the stone rolled away from Jesus' tomb?

B. What was remarkable about the items Peter and John found in the tomb (vv. 5–7)? What made John "believe" (v. 8)?

C. Three times Mary expresses her belief that someone has carried away the dead body of Jesus (vv. 2, 13, 15). What makes her change her belief (v. 16)?

D. What task did Jesus give Mary to do? What did she do?

E. Are you glad that God is a God of surprises? Explain your answer.

LIFE ANCHORS

A. Since God invites us to share in his work, and since he is a God of surprises, plan and give a surprise party or event for a friend who wouldn't expect it.

B. Keep a personal journal for two weeks in which you record any surprises God springs on you during that time. At the end of the two weeks, take your journal and go someplace quiet where you can thank him for these special works in your life. Pray also that you might respond well to any surprises that aren't so welcome.

C. Celebrate the resurrection with your family or friends. Some ideas include:

1. Have communion and a time of worship.
2. Present a gift to someone who cannot return the favor.
3. Attend a theatrical performance or rent a movie that highlights Jesus' victory over death.
4. Identify an unbelieving friend and ask that person to read and give his or her reaction to one of the chapters in this section of the book.
5. Discuss as a group how your lives would be different if the resurrection had never happened.

CHAPTER 19

THE FINAL GLANCE

MIND ANCHORS

1. *My dad left me with a final look. One last statement of the eyes. One farewell message from the captain before the boat would turn out to sea. One concluding assurance from a father to a son, "It's all right."*

 A. The phrase "it's all right" pops up frequently in this book, even in this story of a dying father. What's the point?

 B. For whom does the phrase "it's all right" fit? For whom does it not fit?

2. *For a long while the centurion sat on a rock and stared at the three silhouetted figures. Their heads were limp, occasionally rolling from side to side. The jeering was silent, eerily silent. . . . Suddenly the center head ceased to bob. It yanked itself erect. Its eyes opened in a flash of white. A roar sliced the silence. "It is finished." It wasn't a yell. It wasn't a scream. It was a roar, a lion's roar. From what world that roar came the centurion didn't know, but he knew it wasn't this one.*

A. What was "finished" in this story? Why was it said so forcefully?

B. Many Christians find great hope and comfort in these three words, "It is finished." Why?

3. *Had the centurion not said it, the soldiers would have. Had the centurion not said it, the rocks would have—as would have the angels, the stars, even the demons. But he did say it. It fell to a nameless foreigner to state what they all knew. "Surely this man was the Son of God."*

A. If the centurion fully understood his words, what course of action should he have taken?

B. If it is true that Jesus is the Son of God, what course of action should you take? What is your relationship to him?

SOUL ANCHORS
READ MARK 15:33–39.

A. What statement was God making by causing darkness to fall over the land for three solid hours during the height of the afternoon?

B. Read through Psalm 22:1–18. This portion of Scripture was written hundreds of years before Christ was born, yet it contains detailed descriptions of what would happen at the crucifixion. What details presented in Psalm 22 can you match with the gospel account in Mark 15?

C. What prompted the centurion to say of Jesus, "Surely this man was the Son of God!" (v. 39)?

D. Who do you think Jesus is? On what basis do you give your answer?

LIFE ANCHORS

A. Pick a favorite spot where you can be alone and think. Go there and spend some time reflecting on how this book has challenged you to change certain aspects of your life. What specific changes is God asking you to make in:

> your family life?
> your work life?
> your church life?
> your relationship to friends?
> your reading habits?
> your recreational time?
> your spending priorities?
> your giving patterns?
> your use of time?
> your conversation or vocabulary?
> other areas?

B. Write a letter to a close friend, expressing how this book has changed your view of God. Be as personal and specific as possible.

NOTES

Chapter 2
   1. Matthew 11:28
   2. Matthew 11:29

Chapter 3
   1. This story is found in John 4:1-42.
   2. John 4:28–29
   3. John 4:35, TLB

Chapter 4
   1. Romans 8:31–32 (emphasis mine)

Chapter 5
   1. Genesis 3:1
   2. Jeremiah 34:18
   3. Genesis 15:18

Chapter 6
   1. This story is adapted from the book *A Man for Others* by Patricia Treece.

Chapter 7
   1. John 20:19
   2. Matthew 28:17
   3. Luke 24:52

4. Luke 24:53

5. Acts 2:36

6. 2 Timothy 2:8

Chapter 8

1. Romans 6:23

Chapter 9

1. John 8:1–11

2. Psalm 139:13

Chapter 11

1. This story is popularly attributed to Harry Emerson Fosdick.

2. Luke 15:11–27

Chapter 13

1. Matthew 27:44

2. Luke 23:39, TLB

3. Luke 23:40, TLB

4. Luke 23:41

5. Luke 23:42

6. Luke 23:43, TLB

Chapter 14

1. 1 Corinthians 15:51, JERUSALEM BIBLE

2. Hebrews 2:14–16 (parentheses mine)

Chapter 15

1. Luke 7:15

2. Luke 7:16

Chapter 16

1. Based on Mark 5:22–43; Matthew 9:18–26; and Luke 8:41–56

Chapter 17
    1. John 11:1–44

Chapter 18
    1. John 20:1–18
    2. "Miriam" is the Aramaic form of "Mary."
    3. 1 Corinthians 2:9

Chapter 19
    1. John 19:30
    2. Luke 23:46
    3. Mark 15:39

STUDY GUIDE

Chapter 2
    1. William Hendricksen, *The Gospel of Matthew* (Grand Rapids, Mich.: Baker Book House, 1973), 504-5.

AND
THE ANGELS
WERE
SILENT

CHRONICLES OF THE CROSS

MAX LUCADO

THOMAS NELSON
Since 1798

NASHVILLE   DALLAS   MEXICO CITY   RIO DE JANEIRO   BEIJING

Published in Nashville, Tennessee, by Thomas Nelson. Thomas Nelson is a registered trademark of Thomas Nelson, Inc.

Thomas Nelson, Inc., titles may be purchased in bulk for educational, business, fund-raising, or sales promotional use. For information, please e-mail SpecialMarkets@ThomasNelson.com.

Unless otherwise indicated, all Scripture references are from the Holy Bible: New Century Version, © 1987, 1988, 1991 by Word Publishing, Dallas, Texas 75039. Used by permission.

Scripture references marked NIV are from the Holy Bible: New International Version, © 1973, 1978, 1984 by the International Bible Society. Used by permission of Zondervan Bible Publishers.

Scripture references marked KJV are from the Holy Bible: Authorized King James Version.

Scripture references marked NEB are from The New English Bible, The Delegates of the Oxford University Press and the Syndics of the Cambridge University Press © 1961, 1970. Used by permission.

Scripture references marked RSV are from the Revised Standard Version of the Bible, © 1946, 1952, 1971, 1973, Division of Christian Education, National Council of the Churches in the USA.

Scripture references marked PHILLIPS are from the J. B. Phillips: The New Testament in Modern English, revised edition. J. B. Phillips © 1958, 1960, 1972. Used by permission of Macmillan Publishing Co., Inc.

Edited by Liz Heaney.

Library of Congress Cataloging-in-Publication Data

Lucado, Max.
    And the angels were silent / Max Lucado.
      p. cm.
    Originally published: Portland, Or. : Multnomah, 1992
    ISBN 0-8499-0858-2 (tradepaper)
    ISBN 0-8499-1815-4 (hardcover)
    ISBN 978-0-8499-2097-4 (SE)
    1. Jesus Christ—Passion—Meditations. 2. Bible. N.T. Matthew
XXVI-XXVII—Meditations. I. Title
    BT431.3.L83 2004
    232.96—dc22   2003022807

Printed in the United States of America.

*For my
father- and mother-in-law,
Charles and Romadene Preston,
for giving me such delight*

Contents

CONTENTS

ACKNOWLEDGMENTS

Here's a salute to some dear people who have made this project possible and pleasant.

To Liz Heaney. You've been more than an editor; you've been a friend.

To John Van Diest. You never forgot the highest aim of Christian publishing—God's Word put into man's heart.

For Brenda Josee. Endless energy and boundless creativity.

For the rest of the Multnomah staff, publisher of the original edition of this book: my hat is off to you guys.

A special word for my secretary, Mary Stain. Your retirement and this book deadline came the same month. I was as sorry to see you leave as I was happy to finish the book. Thanks for your tireless efforts.

To Joseph Shulam of Jerusalem. A friend, a brother, and a contagious zealot.

To the Netivyah congregation in Jerusalem. The only unhappy part of our journey to your city was the departure.

To Steve Green. For twenty years of friendship and countless more of partnership.

To the Oak Hills Church. You teach me more than I could ever teach you.

To my daughters Jenna, Andrea, and Sara. If only I could have your innocence and faith.

For my wife, Denalyn. When I come home late you don't complain. When I go on the road you don't grumble. When I write in the middle of the night you don't mind. Does every writer have an angel for a wife, or did I get the last one?

And lastly, for you, the reader. If this is your first time with one of my books, I'm honored to be with you. You are entrusting me with your time and your heart. I pledge to be a good steward of both.

If not, if we've spent time together before, it's good to be with you again. My aim in this book is the same as the others: that you will see him and him only.

May I ask something of you? Please remember our work in your prayers. Pray the prayer of Colossians 4:3–4: ". . . that God will give us an opportunity to tell people his message. Pray that we can preach the secret that God has made known about Christ . . . that I can speak in a way that will make it clear, as I should."

A WORD
BEFORE

It's early in the final week. The props and players for Friday's drama are in position. Six-inch spikes are in the bin. A cross-beam leans against a shed wall. Thorn limbs are wrapped around a trellis awaiting the weaving of a soldier's fingers.

The players are nearing the stage. Pilate is concerned at the number of Passover pilgrims. Annas and Caiaphas are restless over a volatile Nazarene. Judas views his master with furtive eyes. A centurion is available, awaiting the next crucifixions.

Players and props. Only this is no play; it's a divine plan. A plan begun before Adam felt heaven's breath and now all heaven waits and watches. All eyes are on one figure—the Nazarene.

Commonly clad. Uncommonly focused. Leaving Jericho and walking toward Jerusalem. He doesn't chatter. He doesn't pause. He is on a journey. His final journey.

Even the angels are silent. They know this is no ordinary walk. They know this is no ordinary week. For hinged on this week is the door of eternity.

Let's walk with him.

Let's see how Jesus spent his final days.

Let's see what mattered to God.

When a man knows the end is near—only the important surfaces. Impending death distills the vital. The trivial is bypassed. The unnecessary is overlooked. That which is vital remains. So, if you would know Christ, ponder his final days.

He knew the end was near. He knew the finality of Friday. He read the last chapter before it was written and heard the final chorus before it was sung. As a result, the critical was centrifuged from the casual. Distilled truths taught. Deliberate deeds done. Each step calculated. Every act premeditated.

Knowing he had just one week with the disciples, what did Jesus tell them? Knowing it would be his last time in the temple, how did he act? Conscious that the last sand was slipping through the hourglass, what mattered?[1]

Enter the holy week and observe.

Feel his passion. Laughing as children sing. Weeping as Jerusalem ignores. Scorning as priests accuse. Pleading as disciples sleep. Feeling sad as Pilate turns.

Sense his power. Blind eyes . . . seeing. Fruitless tree . . . withering. Money changers . . . scampering. Religious leaders . . . cowering. Tomb . . . opening.

Hear his promise. Death has no power. Failure holds no prisoners. Fear has no control. For God has come, God has come into your world . . . to take you home.

Let's follow Jesus on his final journey. For by observing his, we may learn how to make ours.

Too Little, Too Late, Too Good to Be True

"Those who have the last place now
will have the first place in the future."
MATTHEW 20:16

The only thing slower than Ben's walk was his drawl. "Waiell, boy," he stretched his words and waited a month between phrases, "looks like it's you and me agin."

Snowy white hair billowed from under his baseball hat. Shoulders stooped. Face leathered from seven decades of West Texas winters.

What I remember most are the eyebrows. Shaggy hedges on the crest of his forehead. Caterpillars that shifted with his eyes.

He looked at the ground a lot when he talked. He was already short. This only made him seem shorter. When he wanted to make a point he would lift his eyes and flash a glance at you through his bushy brows. He fired this look at anyone who questioned his ability to work in the oil field. But most everybody did anyway.

I owe my acquaintance with Ben to my dad, who was convinced school holidays were made for boys to earn money. Like it or not, be it Christmas, summer, or Thanksgiving, he'd wake my brother and me before the sun was up and drop us off at one of the local roustabout companies to see if we could hire on for the day.

Work in the oil field has about as many ups and downs as a drilling rig, so unless you were a company man or had your own crew, there was no guarantee of work. Roustabouts began showing up long before the boss did. Didn't make any difference who got there first, though; all that mattered was the strength of your back and the experience under your belt.

That's where Ben and I came up short. I had the good back, but not the experience; Ben had the calloused hands, but not the strength. So unless there was an especially big job that justified quantity over quality, Ben and I usually were passed over.

The elements of the morning became so predictable that now, twenty years later, I can still taste and feel them.

I can feel the bitter wind as it stung my ears in the early morning blackness. I can feel the frozen handle on the heavy metal door that opened into the work shed. I can hear Ben's gruff voice coming from the stove he had already lit and sat beside: "Shut the door, boy. It's gonna git colder 'fore it gets warmer."

I'd follow the golden light from the stove through the dark shed and turn my back to the fire and look at Ben. He'd be smoking, sitting on a fifty-gallon drum. His work boots would be a foot off the ground and the collar of his coat turned up around his neck.

"Shor do need the work, today, boy. Shor do need the work."

Other workers would begin to trickle in. Each one's arrival lessened any chance Ben and I had of going out. Soon the air would cloud with smoke and bad jokes and complaints about having to work in weather too cold for jack rabbits.

Ben never said much.

After a while the foreman would come in. Sounds funny, but I used to get a bit nervous as the boss walked into the shed to read the list. With the eloquence of a drill sergeant he would bark out what he needed and who he wanted. "Need six hands to clean a battery today," or, "Putting in a new line in the south field; gonna need eight." Then he would announce his list, "Buck, Tom, Happy, and Jack—come with me."

There was a certain honor about being chosen . . . something special about being singled out, even if it was to dig ditches. But just as there was an honor with being chosen, there was a certain shame about being left behind. Again.

The only rung lower on the oil field caste system than the roustabout was the unemployment line. If you couldn't weld, then you would roughneck. If you couldn't roughneck, then you'd service wells. If you couldn't service wells, then you'd roustabout. But if you couldn't roustabout...

More times than not, Ben and I couldn't roustabout. Those of us who went unchosen would hang around the stove for a few minutes and make excuses about how we really didn't want to go out anyway. Soon everyone would meander out leaving Ben and me alone in the work shed. We had no better place to go. Besides, you never knew when another job might surface. So we waited.

That's when Ben would talk. Weaving fact with fiction he would spin stories of wildcatting with divining rods and mules. The dawn would become day as the two of us sat on tire rims or paint buckets and walked the dusty roads of Ben's memory.

We were quite a pair. In many ways we were opposites: me barely fifteen years into the world, Ben into his seventieth winter. Me—crisp and convinced that the best was yet to come. Ben—weathered and crusty, living off of yesterday's accolades.

But we came to be friends. For in the oil field we were common cast outs. Fellow failures. The "too little, too lates."

Do you know what I'm talking about? Are you one too?

Sherri is. After three children and twelve years of marriage, her husband found a wife a bit younger. A newer model. Sherri got left behind.

Mr. Robinson is. Three decades with the same company had him one office from the top. When the executive retired, he knew it was only a matter of time. The board, however, had different ideas. They wanted youth. The one thing Robinson didn't have. He got picked over.

Manuel can tell you. At least he would if he could. It's tough being one of nine children in a fatherless home in the Rio Grande Valley. For Manuel it's even harder. He's a deaf mute. Even if there were a school for the deaf he could attend, he has no money.

"A lost ball in tall grass."

"A day late and a dollar short."

"Small guy in a tall world."

"One brick short of a load."

You pick the phrase—the result is still the same. Get told enough times that only the rotten fruit gets left in the bin, and you begin to believe it. You begin to believe you are "too little, too late."

If that describes you, then you are holding the right book at the right time. You see, God has a peculiar passion for the forgotten. Have you noticed?

See his hand on the festered skin of the leper?

See the face of the prostitute cupped in his hands?

Notice how he responds to the touch of the woman with the hemorrhage?

See him with his arm around little Zacchaeus?

Over and over again God wants us to get the message: He has a peculiar passion for the forgotten. What society puts out, God puts in. What the world writes off, God picks up. That must be why Jesus told the story of the chosen workers. It's the first story of his final week. It's the last story he will tell before entering Jerusalem. Once inside the city walls Jesus becomes a marked man. The hourglass will be turned and the final countdown and chaos will begin.

But it's not Jerusalem. And he's not addressing his enemies. It's the Jericho countryside and he's with friends. And for them he weaves this parable of grace.

A certain landowner needs workers. At 6:00 A.M. he picks his crew, they agree on a wage, and he puts them to work. At 9:00 he is back at the unemployment agency and picks a few more. At noon he is back and at 3:00 in the afternoon he is back and at 5:00, you guessed it. He's back again.

Now, the punchline of the story is the anger the twelve-hour laborers felt when the other guys got the same wage. That's a great message, but we'll save it for another book.

I want to hone in on an often forgotten scene in the story: the choosing. Can you see it? It happened at 9:00. It happened at noon. It happened at 3:00. But most passionately, it happened at 5:00.

Five in the afternoon. Tell me. What is a worker still doing in the yard at 5:00 in the afternoon? The best have long since gone. The mediocre workers went at lunch. The last string went at 3:00. What kind of worker is left at 5:00 P.M.?

All day they get passed by. They are unskilled. Untrained. Uneducated. They are hanging with one hand from the bottom of the ladder. They are absolutely dependent upon a merciful boss giving them a chance they don't deserve.

So, by the way, were we. Lest we get a bit cocky, we might take Paul's advice and look at what we were when God called us.[1] Do you remember?

Some of us were polished and sharp but papier-mâché thin. Others of us didn't even try to hide our despair. We drank it. We smelled it. We shot it. We sold it. Life was a passion-pursuit. We were on a treasure hunt for an empty chest in a dead-end canyon.

Do you remember how you felt? Do you remember the perspiration on your forehead and the crack in your soul? Do you remember how you tried to hide the loneliness until it got bigger than you and then you just tried to survive?

Hold that picture for a moment. Now answer this. Why did he

choose you? Why did he choose me? Honestly. Why? What do we have that he needs?

Intellect? Do we honestly think for one minute that we have—or ever will have—a thought he hasn't had?

Willpower? I can respect that. Some of us are stubborn enough to walk on water if we felt called to do so . . . but to think God's kingdom would have done a belly-up without our determination?

How about money? We came into the kingdom with a nice little nest egg. Perhaps that's why we were chosen. Perhaps the creator of heaven and earth could use a little of our cash. Maybe the owner of every breath and every person and the author of history was getting low on capital and he saw us and our black ink and . . .

Get the point?

We were chosen for the same reason the five o'clock workers were. You and me? We are the five o'clock workers.

That's us leaning against the orchard fence sucking cigarettes we can't afford and betting beers we'll never buy on a game of penny-toss. Migrant workers with no jobs and no futures. The tattoo on your arm reads "Betty." The one on my biceps is nameless but her hips bounce when I flex. We should have given up and gone home after the lunch whistle but home is a one-bedroom motel with a wife whose first question will be, "Did you get on or not?"

So we wait. The too little, too lates.

And Jesus? Well, Jesus is the guy in the black pickup who owns the hillside acreage. He's the fellow who noticed us as he drove by leaving us in his dust. He's the one who stopped the truck, put it in reverse, and backed up to where we were standing.

He's the one you'll tell your wife about tonight as you walk to the grocery with a jingle in your pocket. "I'd never seen this guy before. He just stopped, rolled down his window, and asked us if we wanted to work. It was already near quitting time, but he said he had some work that wouldn't wait. I swear, Martha, I only worked one hour and he paid me for the full day."

"No, I don't know his name."

"Of course, I'm gonna find out. Too good to be true, that guy."

Why did he pick you? He wanted to. After all, you are his. He made you. He brought you home. He owns you. And once upon a time, he tapped you on the shoulder and reminded you of that fact. No matter how long you'd waited or how much time you'd wasted, you are his and he has a place for you.

————

"You guys still need some work?"

Ben jumped down from the barrel and answered for both of us. "Yes sir."

"Grab your hats and lunches and get in the truck."

We didn't have to be told twice. I'd already eaten my lunch but I grabbed the pail anyway. We jumped in the back of the flatbed and leaned against the cab. Old Ben put a smoke in his mouth and cupped his hand around the match to protect it from the wind. As the truck began to rumble, he spoke. Though it's been twenty years I still can see his eyes sparkle through the furry brows.

"Shor feels good to be chosen, don't it, boy?"

Sure does, Ben. It sure does.

FROM JERICHO
TO JERUSALEM

*"They will give the Son of Man to the non-Jewish people to laugh
at him and beat him with whips and crucify him.
But on the third day,
he will be raised to life again."*
MATTHEW 20:19

As far as Father Alexander Borisov knew, he would never come back alive. The black Russian night held no assurance of safety. He hoped the police would be intimidated by his flowing black and gold vestments, but there was no guarantee.

Moscow was under siege. The hibernating bear had awakened from her winter sleep and was hungry. Precedent promised to oppress the people once more.

But Borisov dared to defy precedence. On August 20, 1991, he and a few members of the one-year-old Bible Society of the Soviet Union stalked tanks while carrying bundles of New Testaments. If crews declined face-to-face talks, the priest climbed on board the tanks and pitched the Bibles through the hatches.

"In my heart, I believed that soldiers with New Testaments in their pockets would not shoot their brothers and sisters," he later said.

Insightful. Better to go to battle with God's Word in your heart than mighty weapons in your hand.

But Moscow is far from the first demonstration of that. For the most poignant portrayal of someone marching to battle with God's truth, don't go to Russia. Don't read the Associated Press. Don't watch the six o'clock news. Go instead to Scripture and highlight a paragraph you never may have noticed.

It's easy to miss. Only three verses. Only eighty-five words. There is nothing to set them apart as unique. No dramatic lead. No bold letters. No arresting titles. So matter-of-fact is the statement that the casual reader might dismiss it as a transition. But to do so is to leave the quarry without seeing the jewel.

Only one event. It hasn't the flair of a resurrection of Lazarus. Certainly not the scale of the five thousand fed. Gone is the magic of the manger. Missing is the drama of the stilled storm. It's a quiet moment in Scripture. But don't be fooled. For at this moment no angel dared sing.

Only one road. Just fourteen miles. A half-day's journey through a treacherous canyon. But it's not the road that should capture our attention. Dusty roads were common back then. No, it's not the road; it's where it goes—and it's the man who walks it.

He is at the front of his band. Nowhere else do we find Jesus at the head. Not when he descended the mountain after the Sermon on the Mount. Not after he left Capernaum. Not as he entered the village of Nain. He usually chose to be surrounded by people rather than out in front of them.

Not this time. Mark tells us that Jesus was out in front.[1] Only one man. A young soldier marching into battle.

If you want to know someone's heart, observe that person's final journey.

The story of young Matthew Huffman came across my desk the week I was writing this chapter. He was the six-year-old son of missionaries in Salvador, Brazil. One morning he began to complain of fever. As his temperature went up, he began losing his eyesight. His mother and father put him in the car and raced him to the hospital.

As they were driving and he was lying on his mother's lap, he did something his parents will never forget. He extended his hand in the air. His mother took it and he pulled it away. He extended it again. She again took it and he, again, pulled it back and reached into the air. Confused, the mother asked her son, "What are you reaching for, Matthew?"

"I'm reaching for Jesus' hand," he answered. And with those words he closed his eyes and slid into a coma from which he never would awaken. He died two days later, a victim of bacterial meningitis.

Of all the things he didn't learn in his short life, he'd learned the most important: who to reach for in the hour of death.

You can tell a lot about a person by the way he dies. Consider the example of Jim Bonham.

Of all the heroes of the Alamo, none is better known than James Bonham, the fiery young lawyer from South Carolina. He had been in Texas for only three months, but his yearning for freedom left him no choice but to march alongside these Texans in their battle for liberty. He volunteered for service at the Alamo, a small mission near the Guadalupe River. As the Mexican army filled the horizon and the tiny bastion poised for battle, Bonham broke through the enemy cordon and galloped eastward to Goliad for help.

In his book *Texas*, James Michener imagines what the soldier's appeal must have been: "Outside were a hundred and fifty men. Santa Anna has nearly two thousand already, with more on the way. . . . What we need is for every fighting man in Texas to rush to the Alamo. Strengthen our perimeters! Give us help! Start to march now!"

No commitment was given. The only assurance Colonel Fannin gave Bonham was that he would think it over. The young Carolinian knew what that meant and he masked his anger and spurred his horse on to Victoria.

Michener imagines a conversation between Bonham and a young boy.

"Where are you going next?" the boy asks.

"To the Alamo," Bonham responds without hesitation.

"Will you go back alone?"

"I came alone."

As Bonham disappears, the boy asks his father, "If things are so bad, why does he go back in?"

To which the father responds, "I doubt if he considered any other possibility."[2]

We don't know if those words were said, but we know the trip was made. Bonham rode to battle certain it would be his last.

So did Jesus. With the final mission before him, he stopped his disciples and told them for the third time of his conclusive encounter with the enemy. "We are going to Jerusalem. The Son of Man will be turned over to the leading priests and the teachers of the law, and they will say that he must die. They will give the Son of Man to the non-Jewish people to laugh at him and beat him with whips and crucify him. But on the third day, he will be raised to life again."[3]

Note his detailed knowledge of the event. He tells who—"the leading priests and teachers of the law." He tells what—"they will give the Son of Man to the non-Jewish people to laugh at him and beat him with whips and crucify him." He tells when—"but on the third day he will be raised to life again."

Forget any suggestion that Jesus was trapped. Erase any theory that Jesus made a miscalculation. Ignore any speculation that the cross was a last-ditch attempt to salvage a dying mission.

For if these words tell us anything, they tell us that Jesus died . . . on purpose. No surprise. No hesitation. No faltering.

You can tell a lot about a person by the way he dies. And the way

Jesus marched to his death leaves no doubt: He had come to earth for this moment. Read the words of Peter. "Jesus was given to you, and with the help of those who don't know the law, you put him to death by nailing him to a cross. But this was God's plan which he had made long ago; he knew all this would happen."[4]

No, the journey to Jerusalem didn't begin in Jericho. It didn't begin in Galilee. It didn't begin in Nazareth. It didn't even begin in Bethlehem.

The journey to the cross began long before. As the echo of the crunching of the fruit was still sounding in the garden, Jesus was leaving for Calvary.

And just as Father Alexander Borisov walked into battle with the Word of God in his hand, Jesus stepped toward Jerusalem with the promise of God in his heart. The divinity of Christ assured the humanity of Christ, and Jesus spoke loud enough for the pits of hell to vibrate: "But on the third day he will be raised to life again."

Is there a Jerusalem on your horizon? Are you a brief journey away from painful encounters? Are you only steps away from the walls of your own heartache?

Learn a lesson from your master. Don't march into battle with the enemy without first claiming the courage from God's promises. May I give you a few examples?

When you are confused: "'I know what I am planning for you,' says the LORD. 'I have good plans for you, not plans to hurt you.'"[5]

If you feel weighted by yesterday's failures: "So now, those who are in Christ Jesus are not judged guilty."[6]

On those nights when you wonder where God is: "I am the Holy One, and I am among you."[7]

If you think you can fall beyond God's love: "Understand the greatness of Christ's love—how wide and how long and how high and how deep that love is. Christ's love is greater than anyone can ever know."[8]

Next time you find yourself on a Jericho road marching toward Jerusalem, put the promises of God on your lips. When the blackness of oppression settles on your city, remember the convictions of Father Borisov.

By the way, Bible Society workers in Moscow will long remember the story of one soldier who did just that. In the early hours of August 20 they offered him a colorful children's Bible since they were out of smaller New Testaments. The soldier realized he would need to hide it from his superiors if he were to take it home. But his uniform had only one pocket large enough.

The soldier hesitated, then emptied his ammunition pocket. He went on to the barricade with a Bible instead of bullets.

'Tis wise to march into Jerusalem with the promise of God in your heart. It was for Alexander Borisov. It was for Matthew Huffman. And it is for you.

CHAPTER 3

THE SACRIFICIAL GENERAL

*"In the same way, the Son of Man did not come
to be served. He came to serve others
and to give his life as a ransom
for many people."*
MATTHEW 20:28

The decision had been made. The troops had been deployed and the battleships were on their way. Nearly three million soldiers were preparing to slam against Hitler's Atlantic wall in France. D-Day was set in motion. Responsibility for the invasion fell squarely on the four-starred shoulders of General Dwight D. Eisenhower.

The general spent the night before the attack with the men of the 101st Airborne. They called themselves The Screaming Eagles. As his men prepared their planes and checked their equipment, Ike went from soldier to soldier offering words of encouragement. Many of the flyers were young enough to be his sons. He treated them as if they were. A correspondent wrote that as Eisenhower watched the C-47s take off and disappear into the darkness, his hands were sunk deeply into his pockets and his eyes were full of tears.

The general then went to his quarters and sat at his desk. He took a pen and paper and wrote a message—a message that would be delivered to the White House in the event of a defeat.

It was as brief as it was courageous. "Our landings . . . have failed . . . the troops, the Air, and the Navy did all that bravery and devotion to duty could do. If any blame or fault attaches itself to the attempt it was mine alone."[1]

It could be argued that the greatest act of courage that day was not in a cockpit or foxhole, but at a desk when the one at the top took responsibility for the ones below. When the one in charge took the blame—even before the blame needed to be taken.

Rare leader, this general. Unusual, this display of courage. He modeled a quality seldom seen in our society of lawsuits, dismissals, and divorces. Most of us are willing to take credit for the good we do. Some are willing to take the rap for the bad we do. But few will assume responsibilities for the mistakes of others. Still fewer will shoulder the blame for mistakes yet uncommitted.

Eisenhower did. As a result, he became a hero.

Jesus did. As a result, he's our Savior.

Before the war began, he forgave. Before a mistake could be made, forgiveness was offered. Before blame could be given, grace was provided.

The one at the top took responsibility for the ones at the bottom. Read how Jesus describes what he came to do.

"The Son of Man did not come to be served. He came to serve others and to give his life as a ransom for many people."[2]

The phrase "Son of Man" conjured the same images for the Jew of Christ's era that the title "general" creates for you and me. It was a statement of authority and power.

Consider all the titles Jesus could have used to define himself on earth: King of kings, the great I AM, the Beginning and the End, the Lord of All, Jehovah, High and Holy. All of these and a dozen others would have been appropriate.

But Jesus didn't use them.

Instead, he called himself the Son of Man. This title appears eighty-two times in the New Testament. Eighty-one of which are in the gospels. Eighty of which are directly from the lips of Jesus.

To understand Jesus we need to understand what this title means. If Jesus thought it important enough to use over eighty times, it is certainly important enough for us to explore.

Few would argue that the title is rooted in Daniel 7, a text which is just one frame of a cinematographic masterpiece. The seer is afforded a seat in a theater that features a peek at the future powers of the earth. The empires are portrayed as beasts: rabid, hungry, and vicious. The lion with the eagle's wings[3] stands for Babylonia, and the bear with three ribs in its mouth[4] represents Medo Persia. Alexander the Great is symbolized by a leopard with four wings and four heads,[5] and a fourth beast with iron teeth represents Rome.[6]

But as the scenes unfold the empires fade. One by one the world powers tumble. At the end the conquering God, the Ancient of Days, receives into his presence the Son of Man. To him is entrusted authority, glory, and sovereign power.[7] Picture him blazing white. Atop a gallant steed. A sword in his hand.

To the Jew the Son of Man was a symbol of triumph. The conqueror. The equalizer. The score-settler. The big brother. The intimidator. The Starship *Enterprise*. The right arm of the High and Holy. The king who roared down from the heavens in a fiery chariot of vengeance and anger toward those who have oppressed God's holy people.[8]

The Son of Man was the four-starred general who called his army to invade and led his troops to victory.

For that reason when Jesus spoke of the Son of Man in terms of power, the people cheered.

When he spoke of a new world where the Son of Man would sit on his glorious throne,[9] the people understood.

When he spoke of the Son of Man who would come on the

clouds of heaven with great power and authority,[10] the people could envision the scene.

When he spoke of the Son of Man seated at the right hand of power,[11] everyone could imagine the picture.

But when he said the Son of Man would suffer . . . the people stood silent. This didn't fit the image . . . it's not what they expected.

Put yourself in their place. You've been oppressed by the Roman government for years. Since your youth you've been taught that the Son of Man would deliver you. Now he's here. Jesus calls himself the Son of Man. He proves he is the Son of Man. He can raise the dead and still a storm. The crowds of followers are growing. You are excited. Finally, the children of Abraham will be set free.

But what's this he's saying? "The Son of Man did not come to be served. He came to serve others." Earlier he'd told them, "The Son of Man will be handed over to people, and they will kill him. After three days, he will rise from the dead."[12]

Wait a minute! That's an impossible, incredible, intolerable contradiction of terms. No wonder "the followers did not understand what Jesus meant, and they were afraid to ask him."[13] The king who came to serve? The Son of Man being betrayed? The Conqueror—killed? The Ambassador of the Ancient of Days—mocked? Spit upon?

But such is the irony of Jesus wearing the title "the Son of Man." It is also the irony of the cross. Calvary is a hybrid of God's lofty status and his deep devotion. The thunderclap that echoed when God's sovereignty collided with his love. The marriage of heaven's kingship and heaven's compassion.[14] The very instrument of the cross is symbolic, the vertical beam of holiness intersecting with the horizontal bar of love.

Jesus wears a sovereign crown but bears a father's heart.

He is a general who takes responsibility for his soldiers' mistakes.

But Jesus didn't write a note; he paid the price. He didn't just assume the blame; he seized the sin. He became the ransom. He is the

General who dies in the place of the private, the King who suffers for the peasant, the Master who sacrifices himself for the servant.

As a young boy, I read a Russian fable about a master and a servant who went on a journey to a city. Many of the details I've forgotten but the ending I remember. Before the two men could reach the destination they were caught in a blinding blizzard. They lost their direction and were unable to reach the city before nightfall.

The next morning concerned friends went searching for the two men. They finally found the master, frozen to death, face down in the snow. When they lifted him they found the servant—cold but alive. He survived and told how the master had voluntarily placed himself on top of the servant so the servant could live.

I hadn't thought of that story in years. But when I read what Christ said he would do for us, the story surfaced—for Jesus is the master who died for the servants.

He is the general who made provision for his soldiers' mistakes.

He is the Son of Man who came to serve and to give his life as a ransom . . . for you.

UGLY
RELIGION

*"Jesus felt sorry for the blind men and touched their eyes,
and at once they could see."*

MATTHEW 20:34

I t happens in business when you make products you don't market.

It happens in government when you keep departments you don't need.

It happens in medicine when your research never leaves the lab.

It happens in education when your goal is grades, not learning.

And it happened on the road to Jerusalem when Jesus' disciples wouldn't let the blind men come to Christ.

"When Jesus and his followers were leaving Jericho, a great many people followed him. Two blind men sitting by the road heard that Jesus was going by, so they shouted, 'Lord, Son of David, have mercy on us!'"[1]

The people warned the blind men to be quiet, but they called out even louder, "Lord, Son of David, have mercy on us!"

Jesus stopped and said to the blind men, "What do you want me to do for you?"

They answered, "Lord, we want to see."

Jesus "touched their eyes, and at once they could see. Then they followed Jesus."[2]

Matthew doesn't tell us why the people refused to let the blind men get close to Jesus—but it's easy to figure it out. They want to protect him. He's on a mission, a critical mission. The future of Israel is at stake. He is an important man with a crucial task. He hasn't time for indigents on the side of the road.

Besides, look at them. Dirty. Loud. Obnoxious. Embarrassing. Don't they have any sense of propriety? Don't they have any dignity? These things must be handled in the proper procedure. First talk to Nathanael who talks to John who talks to Peter who then decides if the matter is worth troubling the Master or not.

But despite their sincerity, the disciples were wrong.

And so, by the way, are we when we think God is too busy for little people or too formal for poor protocol. When people are refused access to Christ by those closest to him, the result is empty, hollow religion. Ugly religion.

A striking parallel to this occurred in a San Antonio hospital.

Paul Loetz took a bad fall that left him with a punctured lung, broken ribs, and internal bruising. Lying in an emergency room, barely conscious, he probably thought things couldn't get much worse.

They did.

As he looked up from his hospital bed, the two doctors responsible for his care began arguing over who would get to put a tube into his crushed chest. The argument became a shoving match and one doctor threatened to have the other removed by security police.

"Please, somebody save my life," Loetz pleaded as doctors fought over him.[3]

The two doctors were arguing over procedure. While they were debating, two other physicians assumed responsibility for the patient and saved his life.

Hard to believe isn't it? Needs ignored while opinions are disputed? Yet it happens—even in the church. I got a call this week from a man who listens to my radio program. He grew up in a non-Christian home. He works, however, with two Christians of two denominations. I thought it strange he called me when he had Christians as coworkers. Then he told me, "One says this and one says that. All I want to do is find Jesus."

It happens today.

It happens when a church spends more time discussing the style of its sanctuary than it does the needs of the hungry. It happens when the brightest minds of the church occupy themselves with dull controversies rather than majestic truths. It happens when a church is known more for its stance on an issue than its reliance upon God.

It happens today. And it happened then.

You see, in the eyes of those closest to Jesus, these blind men had no right to interfere with the Master. After all, he is on his way to Jerusalem. The Son of Man is going to establish the kingdom. He has no time to hear the needs of some blind beggars on the side of the road.

So, the people warned the blind men to be quiet.

They are a nuisance, these beggars. Look at the way they are dressed. Look at the way they act. Look at the way they cry for help. Jesus has more important things to do than to be bothered by such insignificant people.

Christ thought otherwise. Jesus "felt sorry for the blind men and touched their eyes, and at once they could see."

Jesus hears them in spite of the clamor. And of all the people, it is the blind who really see Jesus.

Something told these two beggars that God is more concerned with the right heart than he is the right clothes or procedure. Somehow they knew that what they lacked in method could be made up for in motive, so they called out at the top of their lungs. And they were heard.

God always hears those who seek him. May I give another case in point? Go back in history a few centuries.

Hezekiah, king of Israel, stirrer of religious revival in the land, calls upon the people to abandon false gods and return to the true God. He calls upon the people to come to Jerusalem to celebrate the Passover. But there are two problems.

One, it has been so long since the people partook of the Passover that no one is ceremonially clean. No one is prepared to partake. Even the priests have been worshiping idols and have failed to observe the necessary rituals for purity.

Two, God had commanded that the Passover be celebrated on the fourteenth day of the first month. By the time Hezekiah can assemble the people, it is the second month.

So the Passover was kept a month late by impure participants.

Hezekiah prayed for them: "'LORD, you are good. . . . Please forgive all those who try to obey you even if they did not make themselves clean as the rules of the Temple command.'"[4]

Do you see the dilemma?

What does God do when the motive is pure but the method is poor?

"The LORD listened to Hezekiah's prayer, and he healed the people."[5]

The right heart with the wrong ritual is better than the wrong heart with the right ritual.

Some time ago I was in Atlanta, Georgia, at a conference. I called home and talked to Denalyn and the girls. Jenna was about five at the time and said she had a special treat for me. She took the phone over to the piano and began to play an original composition.

From a musical standpoint, everything was wrong with the song. She pounded more than she played. There was more random than rhythm in the piece. The lyrics didn't rhyme. The syntax was sinful. Technically the song was a failure.

But to me, the song was a masterpiece. Why? Because she wrote it for me.

> *You are a great daddy.*
> *I miss you very much.*
> *When you're away I'm very sad and I cry.*
> *Please come home very soon.*

What dad wouldn't like that? What father wouldn't bask in the praise of even an off-key adulation?

Some of you are scowling. "Wait a minute, Max. Are you saying that the method we use to approach God is immaterial? Are you saying that the only thing that matters is why we go to God and that how we approach him is relative?"

No, that's not what I'm saying (but I do appreciate the question). Ideally, we approach God with the right motive and the right method. And sometimes we do. Sometimes the words of our prayer are as beautiful as the motive behind the prayer. Sometimes the way we sing is as strong as the reason we sing.

Sometimes our worship is as attractive as it is sincere.

But many times it isn't. Many times our words falter. Many times our music suffers. Many times our worship is less than what we want it to be. Many times our appeals for God's presence are about as attractive as those of the blind men on the side of the road.

"Lord, help."

And sometimes, even today, sincere disciples will tell us to be quiet until we can do it right.

Jesus didn't tell the blind men to be quiet. God didn't tell Hezekiah to shut down the celebration. I didn't tell Jenna to practice a bit and call me again after she had improved.

The blind men, Hezekiah, and Jenna all did the best they could with what they had—and that was enough.

"You will search for me," God declared. "And when you search for me with all your heart, you will find me! I will let you find me."[6]

What a promise! And with the blind beggars, he proved it.

The last scene in the story is worth capturing. The two scraggly dressed, smelly but bright-eyed beggars are walking—no, skipping—behind Jesus on the road to Jerusalem. Pointing at flowers they'd always smelled but never seen. Looking into the sun they'd always felt but never witnessed. Ironic. Of all the people on the road that day, they turned out to be the ones with the clearest vision—even before they could see.

CHAPTER 5

DON'T JUST
DO SOMETHING,
STAND THERE

"Work and get everything done during six days each week,
but the seventh day is a day of rest to honor the Lord your God."
EXODUS 20:9–10

I took my daughter Andrea on a walk some time ago. She was four and curious, so we went to explore our neighborhood. "Let's cover some new territory," I suggested. Off we went, striding confidently out of the safe harbor of our cul-de-sac and stepping into unknown regions.

Captain Kirk would have been proud.

The area was brand-new to her. We walked down streets she'd never seen and petted dogs she'd never touched. Virgin territory. Wilderness wanderings. The yards were different. The kids looked older. The houses looked bigger.

I thought all the change might trouble her. I thought the new sights and sounds might generate anxiety.

"Are you okay?" I asked.

"Sure."

"Do you know where we are?"

"No."

"Do you know how to get home?"

"No."

"And you aren't worried?"

Without slowing her pace she reached up and took my hand and said, "I don't have to know how to get home. You already do."

God once did with his children what I did with Andrea. He led them into a strange land. He marched them through a sea and guided them into unexplored territory.

They didn't know where they were. The desert was strange. The sounds were new and the scenery unfamiliar. But one thing was different: They weren't as trusting as Andrea.

"Take us back to Egypt," they demanded.

But the Father wanted his children to trust him. The Father wanted his children to take his hand and relax. The Father wanted his children to quit worrying about how and be content with who.

He liberated them from slavery and created a path through the sea. He gave them a cloud to follow in the day and a fire to see at night. And he gave them food. He met their most basic need: He filled their bellies.

Each morning the manna came. Each evening the quail appeared. "Trust me. Trust me and I will give you what you need." The people were told to take just enough for one day. Their needs would be met, one day at a time. Despite God's faithfulness in keeping his promise, the people had a hard time believing their provision was the work of God. It went against their logic to see food and not hoard it.

"What if he forgets tomorrow? What if he doesn't come back?" So they would take more than one day's share of food. Overnight the food would spoil.

"Just take enough for today," was God's message. "Let me worry about tomorrow."

The Father wanted the people to trust him.

On Friday they were told to collect a two-day's supply of food, for the next day was the Sabbath—the day God set aside for humankind to meet their Creator. On the Sabbath the food collected from the day before would not spoil.

But on the Sabbath the people had a hard time sitting still. It went against common sense to pause and listen when they could get up and work. So, in spite of God's command they went out to gather food.

(Funny how it is the weary who are most reluctant to rest.)

Note God's wisdom. We need one day in which work comes to a screeching halt. We need one twenty-four-hour period in which the wheels stop grinding and the motor stops turning. We need to stop.

The Sabbath is the day that God's children in a foreign land squeeze their Father's hand and say, "I don't know where I am. I don't know how I'll get home. But you do and that's enough."

A couple of weeks ago Andrea and I went on another adventure—this time on bicycles. She had just learned to keep her balance on a two-wheeler and was ready to leave the safety of the front street and try the hill behind our house. She'd never ridden down a hill before.

We sat atop the descent and looked down it. To her it was Everest. "You sure you want to try?" I asked.

"I think so," she gulped.

"Just put on your brakes when you want to stop. Don't forget your brakes."

"Okay."

I rode to the midway point and waited. Down she came. The bike began to pick up speed. The handlebars began to shake. Her eyes got big. Her pedals moved in a blur. As she raced past she screamed, "I can't remember how to stop pedaling!"

She crashed into the curb.

If you don't know how to stop, the result can be painful. True on bikes. True in life.

Do you remember how to stop?

Ever feel like you're racing downhill on a runaway bike and you don't remember how to brake? Ever feel the wheels of your life racing faster and faster as you speed past the people you love? Could you use a reminder on how to slow it all down?

If so, read what Jesus did during the last Sabbath of his life. Start in the Gospel of Matthew. Didn't find anything? Try Mark. Read what Mark recorded about the way Jesus spent the Sabbath. Nothing there either? Strange. What about Luke? What does Luke say? Not a reference to the day? Not a word about it? Well, try John. Surely John mentions the Sabbath. He doesn't? No reference? Hmmmm. Looks like Jesus was quiet that day.

"Wait a minute. That's it?" That's it.

"You mean with one week left to live, Jesus observed the Sabbath?" As far as we can tell.

"You mean with all those apostles to train and people to teach, he took a day to rest and worship?" Apparently so.

"You're telling me that Jesus thought worship was more important than work?" That's exactly what I'm telling you.

For such is the purpose of the Sabbath. And such was the practice of Jesus. "On the Sabbath day he went to the synagogue, *as he always did*, and stood up to read."[1] Should we do any less?

If Jesus found time in the midst of a racing agenda to stop the rush and sit in the silence, do you think we could, too?

Ahh, I know what you're thinking. I can see it in your face. There you are. Looking at me from my monitor with dubious eyes and furrowed brows. "But, Max, Sunday is the only day I have to get caught up at the office." Or, "Good idea, Max, but have you heard our preacher? He provides the rest all right—I fall asleep! But the worship?" Or, "That's easy for you to say, Max. You're a preacher. If you were a housewife like me and had four kids like mine . . ." It's not easy to slow down.

It's almost as if activity is a sign of maturity. After all, isn't there a beatitude that reads, "Blessed are the busy"? No, there isn't. But there is a verse that summarizes many lives: "Man is a mere phantom as he goes to and fro: He bustles about, but only in vain; he heaps up wealth, not knowing who will get it."[2]

Does that sound like your life? Are you so seldom in one place that your friends regard you as a phantom? Are you so constantly on the move that your family is beginning to question your existence? Do you take pride in your frenzy at the expense of your faith?

Are Andrea's words yours? "I don't remember how to stop." If so, you are headed for a crash.

Slow down. If God commanded it, you need it. If Jesus modeled it, you need it. God still provides the manna. Trust him. Take a day to say no to work and yes to worship.

One final thought.

One of the reference points of London is the Charing Cross. It is near the geographical center of the city and serves as a navigational tool for those confused by the streets.

A little girl was lost in the great city. A policeman found her. Between sobs and tears, she explained she didn't know her way home. He asked her if she knew her address. She didn't. He asked her phone number; she didn't know that either. But when he asked her what she knew, suddenly her face lit up.

"I know the Cross," she said. "Show me the Cross and I can find my way home from there."

So can you. Keep a clear vision of the cross on your horizon and you can find your way home. Such is the purpose of your day of rest: to relax your body, but more importantly to restore your vision. A day in which you get your bearings so you can find your way home.

Do yourself a favor. Reach up and take your Father's hand and say what Andrea said to me, "I'm not sure where I am. I'm not sure which is the road home. But you do and that's enough."

RISKY LOVE

"Mary brought in a pint of very expensive perfume made from pure nard. She poured the perfume on Jesus' feet, and then she wiped his feet with her hair. And the sweet smell from the perfume filled the whole house."

JOHN 12:3

Artful Eddie lacked nothing.

He was the slickest of the slick lawyers. He was one of the roars of the Roaring Twenties. A crony of Al Capone, he ran the gangster's dog tracks. He mastered the simple technique of fixing the race by overfeeding seven dogs and betting on the eighth.

Wealth. Status. Style. Artful Eddie lacked nothing.

Then why did he turn himself in? Why did he offer to squeal on Capone? What was his motive? Didn't Eddie know the sure-fire consequences of ratting on the mob?

He knew, but he'd made up his mind.

What did he have to gain? What could society give him that he didn't have? He had money, power, prestige. What was the hitch?

Eddie revealed the hitch. His son. Eddie had spent his life with the despicable. He had smelled the stench of the underground long enough. For his son, he wanted more. He wanted to give his son a name. And to give his son a name, he would have to clear his own. Eddie was willing to take a risk so that his son could have a clean slate.

Artful Eddie never saw his dream come true. After Eddie squealed, the mob remembered. Two shotgun blasts silenced him forever.

Was it worth it?

For the son it was. Artful Eddie's boy lived up to the sacrifice. His is one of the best-known names in the world.

But before we talk about the son, let's talk about the principle: risky love. Love that takes a chance. Love that goes out on a limb. Love that makes a statement and leaves a legacy. Sacrificial love.

Love which is unexpected, surprising, and stirring. Acts of love that steal the heart and leave impressions on the soul. Acts of love that are never forgotten.

Such an act of love was seen in the last week of the life of Jesus. A demonstration of devotion that the world will never forget. An act of extravagant tenderness in which Jesus wasn't the giver; he was the receiver.

————

A cluster of friends encircle Jesus. They are at the table. The city is Bethany and the house is Simon's.

He was known as Simon the leper. But not any longer. Now he is just Simon. We don't know when Jesus healed him. But we do know what he was like before Jesus healed him. Stooped shoulders. Fingerless hand. Scabbed arm and infected back draped in rags. A tattered wrap that hides all of the face except for two screaming white eyes.

But that was before Jesus' touch. Was Simon the one Jesus healed after he delivered the Sermon on the Mount? Was he the one in the ten who returned to say thank you? Was he one of the four thousand Jesus helped in Bethsaida? Or was he one of the nameless myriads the gospel writers didn't take time to mention?

We don't know. But we know he had Jesus and his disciples over for dinner.

A simple act, but it must have meant a lot to Jesus. After all, the Pharisees are already clearing him a cell on death row. Won't be long until they finger Lazarus as an accomplice. Could be that the whole lot of them will be on wanted posters by the end of the week. It takes nerve to have a wanted man in your home.

But it takes more nerve to put your hand on a leper's sore.

Simon didn't forget what Jesus had done. He couldn't forget. Where there had been a nub, there was now a finger for his daughter to hold. Where there had been ulcerous sores, there was now skin for his wife to stroke. And where there had been lonely hours in quarantine, there were now happy hours such as this—a house full of friends, a table full of food.

No, Simon didn't forget. Simon knew what it was like to stare death in the face. He knew what it was like to have no home to call your own and he knew what it was like to be misunderstood. He wanted Jesus to know that if he ever needed a meal and a place to lay his head, there was one house in Bethany to which he could go.

Other homes will not be as gracious as Simon's. Before the week is up, Jesus will spend some time in the high priest's house, the nicest in Jerusalem. Three barns in the back and a beautiful view of the valley. But Jesus won't see the view; he'll see only the false witnesses, hear the lies, and feel the slaps on his face.

He won't find hospitality in the home of the high priest.

Before the week is up, Jesus will visit the chambers of Herod. Elegant chambers. Plenty of servants. Perhaps there is fruit and wine on the table. But Herod won't offer any to Jesus. Herod wants a trick. A sideshow. "Show me a miracle, country-boy," he will jab. The guards will snicker.

Before the week is up, Jesus will visit the home of Pilate. Rare opportunity to stand before the couch of the procurator of all Israel. Should be an honor. Should be a moment to remember, but it won't be. It's a moment the world would rather forget. Pilate has an opportunity to perform the world's greatest act of mercy—and he doesn't. God is in his house and Pilate doesn't see him.

We can't help but wonder, *What if?* What if Pilate had come to the defense of the innocent? What if Herod had asked Jesus for help and not entertainment? What if the high priest had been as concerned with truth as he was his position? What if one of them had turned his back on the crowd and his face toward the Christ and made a stand?

But no one did. The mountain of prestige was too high. The fall would have been too great.

But Simon did. Risky love seizes the moment. Simon took a chance. He gave Jesus a good meal. Not much, but more than most. And when the priests accused and the soldiers slapped, perhaps Jesus remembered what Simon did and was strengthened.

And when he remembered Simon's meal, perhaps he remembered Mary's gesture. Maybe he could even smell the perfume.

Not unlikely that he could. After all, it was twelve ounces worth. Imported. Concentrated. Sweet. Strong enough to scent a man's clothes for days.

Between the lashings, I wonder, did he relive the moment? As he hugged the Roman post and braced himself for the next ripping of his back, did he remember the oil that soothed his skin? Could he, in the faces of the women who stared, see the small, soft face of Mary, who cared?

She was the only one who believed him. Whenever he spoke of his death the others shrugged, the others doubted, but Mary believed. Mary believed because he spoke with a firmness she'd heard before.

"Lazarus, come out!" he'd demanded, and her brother came out. After four days in a stone-sealed grave he walked out.

And as Mary kissed the now-warm hands of her just-dead brother, she turned and looked. Jesus was smiling. Tear streaks were dry and the teeth shone from beneath the beard. He was smiling.

And in her heart she knew she would never doubt his words.

So when he spoke of his death, she believed.

And when she saw the three together, she couldn't resist. Simon, the healed leper, head thrown back in laughter. Lazarus, the resurrected corpse, leaning in to see what Jesus has said. And Jesus, the source of life for both, beginning his joke a second time.

"Now is the right time," she told herself.

It wasn't an act of impulse. She'd carried the large vial of perfume from her house to Simon's. It wasn't a spontaneous gesture. But it was an extravagant one. The perfume was worth a year's wages. Maybe the only thing of value she had. It wasn't a logical thing to do, but since when has love been led by logic?

Logic hadn't touched Simon.

Common sense hadn't wept at Lazarus's tomb.

Practicality didn't feed the crowds or love the children. Love did. Extravagant, risky, chance-taking love.

And now someone needs to show the same to the giver of such love.

So Mary did. She stepped up behind him and stood with the jar in her hand. Within a couple of moments every mouth was silent and every eye wide as they watched her nervous fingers remove the ornate cover.

Only Jesus was unaware of her presence. Just as he noticed everyone looking behind him, she began to pour. Over his head. Over his shoulders. Down his back. She would have poured herself out for him if she could.

The fragrance rushed through the room. Smells of cooked lamb and herbs were lost in the aroma of the sweet ointment.

"Wherever you go," the gesture spoke, "breathe the aroma and remember one who cares."

On his skin the fragrance of faith. In his clothing the balm of belief. Even as the soldiers divided his garments her gesture brought a bouquet into a cemetery.

The other disciples had mocked her extravagance. They thought it foolish. Ironic. Jesus had saved them from a sinking boat in a stormy sea. He'd enabled them to heal and preach. He'd brought focus into their fuzzy lives. They, the recipients of exorbitant love, chastised her generosity.

"Why waste that perfume? It could have been sold for a great deal of money and given to the poor," they smirk.

Don't miss Jesus' prompt defense of Mary. "Why are you troubling this woman? She did an excellent thing for me."[1]

Jesus' message is just as powerful today as it was then. Don't miss it: "There is a time for risky love. There is a time for extravagant gestures. There is a time to pour out your affections on one you love. And when the time comes—seize it, don't miss it."

The young husband is packing his wife's belongings. His task solemn. His heart heavy. He never dreamed she would die so young. But the cancer came so sure, so quickly. At the bottom of the drawer he finds a box, a negligee. Unworn. Still wrapped in paper. "She was always waiting for a special occasion," he says to himself, "always waiting. . . ."

As the boy on the bicycle watches the students taunt, he churns inside. That's his little brother they are laughing at. He knows he should step in and stand up for his brother, but . . . those are his friends doing the teasing. What will they think? And because it matters what they think, he turns and pedals away.

As the husband looks in the jewelry case, he rationalizes, "Sure she would want the watch, but it's too expensive. She's a practical woman, she'll understand. I'll just get the bracelet today. I'll buy the watch . . . someday."

Someday. The enemy of risky love is a snake whose tongue has mastered the talk of deception. "Someday," he hisses.

"Someday, I can take her on the cruise."

"Someday, I will have time to call and chat."

"Someday, the children will understand why I was so busy."

But you know the truth, don't you? You know even before I write it. You could say it better than I.

Some days never come.

And the price of practicality is sometimes higher than extravagance.

But the rewards of risky love are always greater than its cost.

Go to the effort. Invest the time. Write the letter. Make the apology. Take the trip. Purchase the gift. Do it. The seized opportunity renders joy. The neglected brings regret.

The reward was great for Simon. He was privileged to give rest to the one who made the earth. Simon's gesture will never be forgotten.

Neither will Mary's. Jesus promised, "Wherever the Good News is preached in all the world, what this woman has done will be told, and people will remember her."[2]

Simon and Mary: examples of the risky gift given at the right time.

Which brings us back to Artful Eddie, the Chicago mobster who squealed on Al Capone so his son could have a fair chance. Had Eddie lived to see his son, Butch, grow up, he would have been proud.

He would have been proud of Butch's appointment to Annapolis. He would have been proud of the commissioning as a World War II Navy pilot. He would have been proud as he read of his son downing five bombers in the Pacific night and saving the lives of hundreds of crewmen on the carrier Lexington. The name was cleared. The Congressional Medal of Honor that Butch received was proof.

When people say the name O'Hare in Chicago, they don't think gangsters—they think aviation heroism. And now when you say his name, you have something else to think about. Think about the undying dividends of risky love. Think about it the next time you hear it. Think about it the next time you fly into the airport named after the son of a gangster gone good.

The son of Eddie O'Hare.

CHAPTER 7

THE GUY WITH
THE DONKEY

*"If anyone asks you why you are taking the donkeys, say that the
Master needs them, and he will send them at once."*
MATTHEW 21:3

When we all get home I know what I want to do. There's
someone I want to get to know. You go ahead and swap
stories with Mary or talk doctrine with Paul. I'll catch up
with you soon. But first, I want to meet the guy with the donkey.

I don't know his name or what he looks like. I only know one
thing: what he gave. He gave a donkey to Jesus on the Sunday he
entered Jerusalem.

"Go to the town you can see there. When you enter it, you will
quickly find a donkey tied there with its colt. Untie them and bring
them to me. If anyone asks you why you are taking the donkeys, say
that the Master needs them, and he will send them at once."[1]

When we all get to heaven I want to visit this fellow. I have several questions for him.

How did you know? How did you know it was Jesus who needed
a donkey? Did you have a vision? Did you get a telegram? Did an
angel appear in your bowl of lentils?

Was it hard to give? Was it difficult to give something to Jesus for him to use? I want to ask that question because sometimes it's hard for me. Sometimes I like to keep my animals to myself. Sometimes when God wants something, I act like I don't know he needs it.

How did it feel? How did it feel to look out and see Jesus on the back of the donkey that lived in your barn? Were you proud? Were you surprised? Were you annoyed?

Did you know? Did you have any idea that your generosity would be used for such a noble purpose? Did it ever occur to you that God was going to ride your donkey? Were you aware that all four gospel writers would tell your story? Did it ever cross your mind that a couple of millenniums later, a curious preacher in South Texas would be pondering your plight late at night?

And as I ponder yours, I ponder mine. Sometimes I get the impression that God wants me to give him something and sometimes I don't give it because I don't know for sure, and then I feel bad because I've missed my chance. Other times I know he wants something but I don't give it because I'm too selfish. And other times, too few times, I hear him and I obey him and feel honored that a gift of mine would be used to carry Jesus into another place. And still other times I wonder if my little deeds today will make a difference in the long haul.

Maybe you have those questions, too. All of us have a donkey. You and I each have something in our lives, which, if given back to God, could, like the donkey, move Jesus and his story further down the road. Maybe you can sing or hug or program a computer or speak Swahili or write a check.

Whichever, that's your donkey.

Whichever, your donkey belongs to him.

It really does belong to him. Your gifts are his and the donkey was his. The original wording of the instructions Jesus gave to his disciples is proof: "If anyone asks you why you are taking the donkey, you are to say, 'Its Lord is in need.'"

The language Jesus used is the language of a royal levy. It was an ancient law that required the citizen to render to the king any item or service he or one of his emissaries might request.[2] In making such a request, Jesus is claiming to be king. He is speaking as one in authority. He is stating that as king he has rights to any possession of his subjects.

It could be that God wants to mount your donkey and enter the walls of another city, another nation, another heart. Do you let him? Do you give it? Or do you hesitate?

That guy who gave Jesus the donkey is just one in a long line of folks who gave little things to a big God. Scripture has quite a gallery of donkey-givers. In fact, heaven may have a shrine to honor God's uncommon use of the common.

It's a place you won't want to miss. Stroll through and see Rahab's rope, Paul's bucket, David's sling, and Samson's jawbone. Wrap your hand around the staff that split the sea and smote the rock. Sniff the ointment that soothed Jesus' skin and lifted his heart. Rest your head on the same cloak that gave comfort to Christ in the boat and run your hand along the smooth wood of the manger, soft as a baby's skin. Or set your shoulder beneath the heavy Roman beam, as coarse as a traitor's kiss.

I don't know if these items will be there. But I am sure of one thing—the people who used them will.

The risk takers: Rahab who sheltered the spy. The brethren who smuggled Paul.

The conquerors: David, slinging a stone. Samson, swinging a bone. Moses, lifting a rod.

The caregivers: Mary at Jesus' feet. What she gave cost much, but somehow she knew what he would give would cost more.

The anonymous disciple in the boat. He made a bed out of the boat so God could take a nap.

And the curious pilgrim on the side of the Via Dolorosa. For all we know, he knew very little. He just knew Jesus' bloody, beaten back was weary and his own back was strong. So when the soldier pointed, this man came.

Quite a fraternity, is it not? Strong stewards who view what is theirs as his and make it available whenever he might need it. Sharecroppers of the vineyard who haven't forgotten who owns the property. Loyal students who remember who is paying the tuition.

Here's another: a nineteenth-century Sunday school teacher who led a Boston shoe clerk to Christ. The teacher's name you've never heard: Kimball. The name of the shoe clerk he converted you have: Dwight Moody.

Moody became an evangelist and had a major influence on a young preacher named Frederick B. Meyer. Meyer began to preach on college campuses and while doing so, he converted J. Wilbur Chapman. Chapman became involved in the YMCA and arranged for a former baseball player named Billy Sunday to come to Charlotte, North Carolina, for a revival. A group of Charlotte community leaders were so enthusiastic afterward that they planned another campaign and brought Mordecai Hamm to town to preach. In that revival a young man named Billy Graham yielded his life to Christ.

Did the Boston schoolteacher have any idea what would become of his conversation with the shoe salesman? No, he, like the owner of the donkey, had a chance to help Jesus journey into another heart, so he did.

Some years ago, I was on a campaign in Hawaii. (Hey, somebody has to go to those desolate places!) My job was to go door-to-door and invite people to our nightly meetings. Most of the folks were kind but not too interested. Though no one was rude, no one asked us in either. Then we came upon a lady of grace who is not mentioned in Scripture only because she was born two millenniums too late.

I don't know her name, but I remember her presence—and her presents.

She was a wisp of a lady. Small. Oriental. Shoulders hunched by the years. A woman of modest means, she worked as a maid at one of the many hotels that dot the beach. When she learned we were sharing Christ, she insisted we come into her house and see how she was trying to influence her coworkers. Into a back room we went. In it was a large table covered with decoupage material. Glue. Paint. Wooden frames.

But most of the space was taken up by pieces of wood that were carved to look like an open wooden book.

She explained that she couldn't read, so it would be difficult for her to teach. She explained that she had little income, so it would be impossible to give money. But somewhere she had learned this craft and was now using it to introduce her faith to her friends. Her plan was simple. She took the wooden book and on one side of it pasted a Polaroid picture of her friend. On the other she put a Bible verse.

Her rationale? People love to see a picture of themselves. Most of her friends were simple folks with few wall decorations. Here was a way to hang a Bible verse on their wall where they would see it every day. Would something come of it? You never know.

But God does. God uses tiny seeds to reap great harvests. It is on the backs of donkeys he rides—not steeds or chariots—just simple donkeys.

If I had asked my questions to the Hawaiian lady she would have answered, "He always needs us. We are his mouth. We are his hands." I can see her blush, honored that her gifts would be chosen by a king.

I wouldn't have had to ask, "Is it hard? Is it hard to give?" The answer was in her smile.

And that last question. No, I wouldn't have to ask it either. "Do you think that two thousand years from now . . ." She has no way of knowing. The guy with the donkey didn't. Samson didn't. Moses and

Rahab didn't. The shoe salesman didn't, and we don't either. No sower of small seeds can know the extent of his harvest.

But don't be surprised if in heaven, next to David's sling and Moses' rod and the donkey's rope, you discover a decoupaged book with a picture and a verse.

HUCKSTERS AND HYPOCRITES

"My Temple will be called a house for prayer.
But you are changing it into a '
hideout for robbers.' "
MATTHEW 21:13

S peedy Morris is the basketball coach for LaSalle University. He was shaving when his wife told him he was wanted on the phone by *Sports Illustrated.* He got so excited over the prospect of national recognition that he hurried his shave and nicked himself. Not wanting to delay the caller, he ran out of the bathroom, lost his balance, and tumbled down the stairs. Limping, with blood and lather on his face, he finally got to the phone.

"Sports Illustrated?" he panted.

Imagine Morris's disappointment when the voice on the other end droned, "Yes it is, and for seventy-five cents an issue you can get a year's subscription. . . ."[1]

It's tough to be let down. It's disappointing when you think someone is interested in you, only to find he is interested in your money. When salespeople do it, it's irritating—but when people of faith do it, it can be devastating.

It's a sad but true fact of the faith: Religion is used for profit and prestige. When it is there are two results: People are exploited and God is infuriated.

There's no better example of this than what happened at the temple. After he had entered the city on the back of a donkey, Jesus "went into the Temple. After he had looked at everything, since it was already late, he went out to Bethany with the twelve apostles."[2]

Did you catch that? The first place Jesus went when he arrived in Jerusalem was the temple. He'd just been paraded through the streets and treated like a king. It was Sunday, the first day of the Passover week. Hundreds of thousands of people packed the narrow stone streets. Rivers of pilgrims flooded the marketplace. Jesus elbowed his way through the sea of people as evening was about to fall. He walked into the temple area, looked around, and walked out.

Want to know what he saw? Then read what he did on Monday, the next morning when he returned.

> Jesus went into the Temple and threw out all the people who were buying and selling there. He turned over the tables of those who were exchanging different kinds of money, and he upset the benches of those who were selling doves. Jesus said to all the people there, "It is written in the Scriptures, 'My Temple will be called a house for prayer.' But you are changing it into a 'hideout for robbers.'"[3]

What did he see? Hucksters. Faith peddlers. What lit the fire under Jesus' broiler? What was his first thought on Monday? People in the temple making a franchise out of the faith.

It was Passover week. The Passover was the highlight of the Jewish calendar. People came from all regions and many countries to be present for the celebration. Upon arriving they were obligated to meet two requirements.

First, an animal sacrifice, usually a dove. The dove had to be perfect, without blemish. The animal could be brought in from anywhere, but odds were that if you brought a sacrifice from another place, yours would be considered insufficient by the authorities in the temple. So, under the guise of keeping the sacrifice pure, the dove sellers sold doves—at their price.

Second, the people had to pay a tax, a temple tax. It was due every year. During Passover the tax had to be rendered in local currency. Knowing many foreigners would be in Jerusalem to pay the tax, money changers conveniently set up tables and offered to exchange the foreign money for local—for a modest fee, of course.

It's not difficult to see what angered Jesus. Pilgrims journeyed days to see God, to witness the holy, to worship His Majesty. But before they were taken into the presence of God, they were taken to the cleaners. What was promised and what was delivered were two different things.

Want to anger God? Get in the way of people who want to see him. Want to feel his fury? Exploit people in the name of God.

Mark it down. Religious hucksters poke the fire of divine wrath.

"I've had enough," was written all over the Messiah's face. In he stormed. Doves flapped and tables flew. People scampered and traders scattered.

This was not an impulsive show. This was not a temper tantrum. It was a deliberate act with an intentional message. Jesus had seen the moneychangers the day before. He went to sleep with pictures of this midway and its barkers in his memory. And when he woke up the next morning, knowing his days were drawing to a close, he chose to make a point: "You cash in on my people and you've got me to answer to." God will never hold guiltless those who exploit the privilege of worship.

———

Some years ago I was in the Miami airport to pick up a friend. As I walked through the terminal, a convert of an Eastern cult got my attention.

You know the kind I'm talking about: beads, sandals, frozen smile, backpack of books.

"Sir," she said. (I should have kept walking.)

"Sir, just a moment, please." Well, I had a moment. I was early and the plane was late, so what harm? (I should have kept walking.)

I stopped and she began her spiel. She said she was a teacher and her school was celebrating an anniversary. In honor of the event, they were giving away a book which explained their philosophy. She placed a copy in my hand. It was a thick hardback with a mystic cover. A guru-looking guy was sitting cross-legged with his hands folded.

I thanked her for the book and began to walk away.

"Sir?" I stopped. I knew what was coming.

"Would you like to make a donation to our school?"

"No," I responded, "but thanks for the book."

I began to walk away. She followed me and tapped me on the shoulder.

"Sir, everyone so far has given a donation in appreciation for the gift."

"That's good," I replied, "but I don't think I will. But I appreciate the book." I turned and began to walk away. I hadn't even taken a step, however, when she spoke again. This time she was agitated.

"Sir," and she opened her purse so I could see her collection of dollars and coins. "If you were sincere in your gratitude you would give a donation in appreciation."

That was low. That was sneaky. Insulting. I'm not usually terse, but I couldn't resist. "That may be true," I responded, "but if you were sincere, you wouldn't give me a gift and then ask me to pay for it."

She reached for the book, but I tucked it under my arm and walked away.

A small victory against the mammoth of hucksterism.

Sadly, the hucksters win more than they lose. And, even more sadly, hucksters garb themselves in Christian costumes as much as those of Eastern cults.

You've seen them. The talk is smooth. The vocabulary eloquent. The appearance genuine. They are on your television. They are on your radio. They may even be in your pulpit.

May I speak candidly?

The time has come to tolerate religious hucksters no longer. These seekers of "sanctimoney" have stained the reputation of Christianity. They have muddied the altars and shattered the stained glass. They manipulate the easily deceived. They are not governed by God; they are governed by greed. They are not led by the Spirit; they are propelled by pride. They are marshmallow phonies who excel in emotion and fail in doctrine. They strip-mine faith to get a dollar and rape the pew to get a payment. Our master unveiled their scams and so must we.

How? By recognizing them. Two trademarks give them away. One, they emphasize their profit more than the Prophet.

In the church in Crete some people made a living off the gullible souls in the church. Paul had strong words about them. "These people must be stopped, because they are upsetting whole families by teaching things they should not teach, which they do to get rich by cheating people."[4]

Listen carefully to the television evangelist. Analyze the words of the radio preacher. Note the emphasis of the message. What is the burden? Your salvation or your donation? Monitor what is said. Is money always needed yesterday? Are you promised health if you give and hell if you don't? If so, ignore him.

A second characteristic of ecclesiastical con men: They build more fences than they build faith.

Medicine men tell you to stay out of the pharmacy. They don't want you trying other treatments. Neither do hucksters. They present themselves as pioneers that the mainline church couldn't stomach, but, in reality, they are lone wolves on the prowl.

They have franchised an approach and want to protect it. Their bread and butter is the uniqueness of their faith. Only they can give you what you need. Their cure-all kit is the solution to your aches. Just as the dove-sellers were intolerant of imported birds, the hucksters are wary of imported faith.

Their aim is to cultivate a clientele of loyal checkbooks.

"Look out for those who cause people to be against each other and who upset other people's faith. They are against the true teaching you learned, so stay away from them. Such people are not serving our Lord Christ but are only doing what pleases themselves. They use fancy talk and fine words to fool the minds of those who do not know about evil."[5]

Christ's passion on Monday is indignance. For that reason I make no apology about challenging you to call the cards on these guys. God has been calling a halt to babblers building towers for centuries. So should we.

If not, it could happen again.

No one ever expected it would happen the first time. Especially with this church. It was the model congregation. A heated swimming pool was made available for underprivileged kids. Horses were provided for inner-city children to ride. The church gave scholarships and provided housing for senior citizens. It even had an animal shelter and medical facility, an outpatient care facility, and a drug rehabilitation program.

Walter Mondale wrote that the pastor was an "inspiration to us all." The Secretary of Health, Education, and Welfare cited the pastor's outstanding contribution. We are told "he knew how to inspire hope. He was committed to people in need, he counseled prisoners and juvenile delinquents. He started a job placement center; he opened rest homes and homes for the retarded; he had a health clinic; he organized a vocational training center; he provided free legal aid; he founded a community center; he preached about God. He even claimed to cast out demons, do miracles, and heal."[6]

Lofty words. A lengthy résumé for what appeared to be a mighty spiritual leader and his church. Where is that congregation today? What is she doing now?

The church is dead . . . literally.

Death occurred the day the pastor called the members to the pavilion. They heard his hypnotic voice over the speaker system and from all corners of the farm they came. He sat in his large chair and spoke into a handheld microphone about the beauty of death and the certainty that they would meet again.

The people were surrounded by armed guards. A vat of cyanide-laced Kool-Aid was brought out. Most of the cult members drank the poison with no resistance. Those who did resist were forced to drink.

First, the babies and children—about eighty—were given the fatal drink. Then the adults—women and men, leaders and followers, and finally the pastor.

Everything was calm for a few minutes, then the convulsions began, screams filled the Guyana sky, mass confusion broke out. In a few minutes, it was over. The members of the Peoples Temple Christian Church were all dead. All 780 of them.

And so was their leader, Jim Jones.

Mark it down and beware: There are hucksters in God's house. Don't be fooled by their looks. Don't be dazzled by their words. Be careful. Remember why Jesus purged the temple. Those closest to it may be the farthest from it.

COURAGE TO DREAM AGAIN

"If you have faith, it will happen."

Hans Babblinger of Ulm, Germany, wanted to fly. He wanted to break the bond of gravity. He wanted to soar like a bird. Problem: He lived in the sixteenth century. There were no planes, no helicopters, no flying machines. He was a dreamer born too soon. What he wanted was impossible.

Hans Babblinger, however, made a career out of helping people overcome the impossible. He made artificial limbs. In his day amputation was a common cure for disease and injury, so he kept busy. His task was to help the handicapped overcome circumstance.

Babblinger longed to do the same for himself.

With time, he used his skills to construct a set of wings. The day soon came to try them out and he tested his wings in the foothills of the Bavarian Alps. Good choice. Lucky choice. Up currents are common in the region. On a memorable day with friends watching and sun shining, he jumped off an embankment and soared safely down.

His heart raced. His friends applauded. And God rejoiced.

How do I know God rejoiced? Because God always rejoices when we dare to dream. In fact, we are much like God when we dream. The Master exults in newness. He delights in stretching the old. He wrote the book on making the impossible possible.

Examples? Check the Book.

Eighty-year-old shepherds don't usually play chicken with Pharaohs . . . but don't tell that to Moses.

Teenage shepherds don't normally have showdowns with giants . . . but don't tell that to David.

Night-shift shepherds don't usually get to hear angels sing and see God in a stable . . . but don't tell that to the Bethlehem bunch.

And for sure don't tell that to God. He's made an eternity out of making the earthbound airborne. And he gets angry when people's wings are clipped. Such is the message of the fig tree drama, a peculiar scene involving a fruitless fig tree and a mountain in the ocean.

Jesus and his disciples walked to Jerusalem on Monday morning after spending the night in Bethany. He was hungry and saw a fig tree on the side of the road. As he approached the tree, he noticed that though it had leaves, it had no fruit. Something about a tree with no fruit reminded him of what he saw in the temple on Sunday and what he is going to do in the temple later that day.[1]

So he denounced the tree. "You will never again have fruit." The tree immediately dried up.

The next day, Tuesday, the disciples see what has happened to the tree. They are amazed. Just twenty-four hours before, the tree had been green and healthy; now it is barren and dry.

"How did the fig tree dry up so quickly?" they ask.

Jesus gives them this answer, "I tell you the truth, if you have faith and do not doubt, you will be able to do what I did to this tree and even more. You will be able to say to this mountain, 'Go, fall into the sea.' And if you have faith, it will happen. If you believe, you will get anything you ask for in prayer."[2]

You won't find the words *dream* or *fly* or *wing* in the story. But look closely and you'll see a story of a God who issues a call for the Babblingers of the world to mount the cliff and test their wings.

You'll also see a God who scorns those who put dreamers in a cage and pocket the key.

Jesus, hungry and on his way to Jerusalem, stops to see if a fig tree has figs. It doesn't. It has the appearance of nutrition but offers nothing. It's all promise and no performance. The symbolism is too precise for Jesus to ignore.

He does to the tree on Monday morning what he will do to the temple on Monday afternoon: He curses it. Note, he's not angry at the tree. He's angry at what the tree represents. Jesus is disgusted by luke-warm, placid, vain believers who have pomp but no purpose. They have no fruit. This simple act slams the guillotine on the neck of empty religion.

Want a graphic example of this? Consider the Laodicean church. This church was wealthy and self-sufficient. But the church had a problem—hollow, fruitless faith. "I know what you do," God spoke to this group, "that you are not hot nor cold. I wish that you were hot or cold! But because you are lukewarm—neither hot, nor cold—I am ready to spit you out of my mouth."3

The literal translation is "to vomit." Why does the body vomit something? Why does it recoil violently at the presence of certain sub-stances? Because they are incompatible with the body. Vomiting is the body's way of rejecting anything it cannot handle.

What's the point? God can't stomach lukewarm faith. He is angered by a religion that puts on a show but ignores the service—and that is precisely the religion he was facing during his last week. And the religion he had faced his entire ministry.

When he served they complained.

They complained that his disciples ate on the wrong day. They complained that he healed on the wrong day. They complained that he forgave the wrong people. They complained that he hung out with the wrong crowd and had the wrong influence on the children. But, still worse, every time he tried to set people free, the religious leaders attempted to tie them down. Those closest to the temple were quickest with the shackles. When a courageous soul tried to fly they were there to say it couldn't be done.

By the way, they told Hans Babblinger the same thing. Seems the king was coming to Ulm and the Bishop and the citizens wanted to impress him. Word had gotten out about Hans's flying feat so they asked him to do a loop for the king. Hans consented.

They wanted one change, however. Since the crowd would be large and the hills were difficult to climb, could Hans choose a place in the lowlands in which he could fly?

Hans chose the bluffs near the Danube. They were broad and flat and the river was a good distance below. He would jump off the edge and float down to the water.

Poor choice. The updraft in the hills was nonexistent near the river. So in front of the king, his court, and half the village, Hans jumped and fell like a rock straight into the river. The king was disappointed and the Bishop mortified.

Guess what the Bishop preached the next Sunday—"Man was not meant to fly." Hans believed him. Imprisoned by a pulpit he put his wings away and never again tried to fly. He died soon after, gripped by gravity, buried with his dreams.

The cathedral of Ulm isn't the first church to cage a flyer. Through the years pulpits have grown proficient in telling people what they can't do. They did in the day of Christ, they did in the day of Hans Babblinger, and they do today—and you can be sure it is just as nauseating to God today as it was then.

But as we are looking at religion, we would do well to look in the mirror. You see, it is convenient to point fingers at organized religion and say, "Amen. Tell 'em like it is!" It's comfortable to do that, but inadequate. While we are talking about setting people free to fly, think about yourself. How are you at giving wings? How have you been at setting people free?

That friend who offended you and needs your forgiveness?

The coworker burdened with fear of the grave?

The relative who carries the sack of yesterday's failures?

Your friend weighed down by anxiety?

Tell them about the empty tomb . . . and watch them fly.

A Hispanic member of our church married recently. She is a precious sister with a robust faith. When the time came, the minister asked, "Can you repeat the vows?" To which she answered with all sincerity, "Yes, I can, but it will be with an accent."

That is the way God intended it. He intends for all of us to live out our vows but with our own particular accent. For some, it is with an accent on the sick. For others, it is a concern for the imprisoned. Still others have a burden for scholarly research or giving. But whatever our accent the message is still the same.

The message of the fig tree is not for all of us to have the same fruit. The message is for us to have some fruit. Not easy. Jesus knows that. "If you have faith and do not doubt, you will be able to do what I did to this tree and even more."

Faith in whom? Religion? Hardly. Religion is the hoax Jesus is out to disclose. In fact, when Jesus said, "You will be able to say to this mountain, 'Go, fall into the sea,'" he was probably looking up from the Kidron Valley to the Temple Mount—the temple known to many as Mount Zion. If that is the case, you have reason to smile as Jesus tells you what to do with the church that tries to cage your flight, "Tell it to jump into the lake."

No, the faith is not in religion; the faith is in God. A hardy, daring faith that believes God will do what is right, every time. And that God will do what it takes—whatever it takes—to bring his children home.

He is the shepherd in search of his lamb. His legs are scratched, his feet are sore and his eyes are burning. He scales the cliffs and traverses the fields. He explores the caves. He cups his hands to his mouth and calls into the canyon.

And the name he calls is yours.

He is the housewife in search of the lost coin. No matter that he has nine others, he won't rest until he has found the tenth. He searches the house. He moves furniture. He pulls up rugs. He cleans out the shelves. He stays up late. He gets up early. All other tasks can wait. Only one matters. The coin is of great value to him. He owns it. He will not stop until he finds it.

The coin he seeks is you.

God is the father pacing the porch. His eyes are wide with his quest. His heart is heavy. He seeks his prodigal. He searches the horizon. He examines the skyline, yearning for the familiar figure, the recognizable gait. His concern is not his business, his investments, his ownings. His concern is the son who wears his name, the child who bears his image. You.

He wants you home.

It is only in light of such passion that we can understand this incredible promise: "If you believe, you will get anything you ask for in prayer."[4]

Don't reduce this grand statement to the category of new cars and paychecks. Don't limit the promise of this passage to the selfish pool of perks and favors. The fruit God assures is far greater than earthly wealth. His dreams are much greater than promotions and proposals.

God wants you to fly. He wants you to fly free of yesterday's guilt. He wants you to fly free of today's fears. He wants you to fly free of tomorrow's grave. Sin, fear, and death. These are the mountains he has moved. These are the prayers he will answer. That is the fruit he will grant. This is what he longs to do: He longs to set you free so you can fly . . . fly home.

One final word about the church of Ulm. It's empty. Now most of its visitors are tourists. And how do most of the tourists travel to Ulm? They fly.

CHAPTER 10

OF CALLUSES
AND COMPASSION

*"The kingdom of God will be taken away from you and given to
people who do the things God wants in his kingdom."*
MATTHEW 21:43

Peculiar, this childhood church memory of mine.

For many, early church recollections are made of zippered Bibles, patent leather Easter shoes, Christmas pageants, or Sunday schools. Mine is not so religious. Mine is comprised of calluses, straight pins, and dull sermons.

There I sit, all six years of me, flat-topped and freckled. My father's hand in my lap. It is there to keep me from squirming. A robust preacher is behind the pulpit, one of God's kindest but most monotonous servants. Bored, I turn my attention to my father's hand.

If you didn't know he was a mechanic, one look at his hands would tell you as much. Thick, strong, scrubbed clean but still bearing traces of last week's grease.

I'm intrigued as I run my fingers over the calluses. They rise on the palm like a ridge of hills. Calluses. Layer upon layer of nerveless skin. The hand's defense against hours of squeezing wrenches and twisting screwdrivers.

On the back of the pew in front of me is a collection of attendance cards. At the top of each card is a red ribbon for the visitors to wear. The ribbon is attached to the card by a straight pin.

I have an idea. *I wonder how thick those calluses are? . . .*

I take the pin, and with the skill of a surgeon I begin the insertion. (I told you it was peculiar.) I look up at Dad. He doesn't move. I go deeper. No response. Another eighth of an inch. No flinch. While the rest of the church is intent on the words of a preacher, I'm fascinated by the depth of a callus. I decide to give it a final shove.

"Umph," he grunts, yanking his hand away, closing his fist which only pushes the pin further. His glares at me, my mother turns, and my brother giggles. Something tells me that the same hand will be used later that Sunday to make another point.

Peculiar, this childhood memory. But, even more peculiar is that three decades later, I find myself doing the same thing I did at age six: in church, trying to penetrate calluses with a point. Only now I'm in the pulpit, not the pew. And my tool is truth, not a pin. And the calluses are not on the hand, but on the heart.

Thick, dead skin wrapped around the nerves of the soul. The result of hours of rubbing against the truth without receiving it. Toughened, crusty, lifeless tissue that defies feeling and ignores touch.

The calloused heart.

To such hearts Jesus spoke on his last Tuesday. With the persistence of a man with one final message, his point was intended to prick the soul.

He told two stories that contain a common thread, crimson with guilt: the proclivity of people to reject God's invitation not once or twice, but time and time again.

The first story was that of the landowner.[1] He leased a vineyard to some sharecroppers and, at harvest, sent his servants to collect his share of the grapes. "But the farmers grabbed the servants, beat one, killed another, and then killed a third servant with stones."

The second is the story of the king who prepared a wedding feast for his son.[2] "When the feast was ready, the king sent his servants to tell the people, but they refused to come."

A landowner whose servants are beaten and killed? A king whose messengers are ignored? Surely the landowner and the king will wash their hands of these people. No doubt they will send the police and the military next.

Wrong.

In both cases they send more emissaries. "So the [landowner] sent some other servants to the farmers, even more than he sent the first time. But the farmers did the same thing to the servants that they had done before."

"Then the king sent other servants, saying, 'Tell those who have been invited that my feast is ready.' "

What surprising tolerance! What unexpected patience! Servant after servant. Messenger after messenger. Jesus verbally painting the picture of a determined God.

When our oldest daughter, Jenna, was two, I lost her in a department store. One minute she was at my side and the next she was gone. I panicked. All of a sudden only one thing mattered—I had to find my daughter. Shopping was forgotten. The list of things I came to get was unimportant. I yelled her name. What people thought didn't matter. For a few minutes, every ounce of energy had one goal—to find my lost child. (I did, by the way. She was hiding behind some jackets!)

No price is too high for a parent to pay to redeem his child. No energy is too great. No effort too demanding. A parent will go to any length to find his or her own.

So will God.

Mark it down. God's greatest creation is not the flung stars or the gorged canyons; it's his eternal plan to reach his children. Behind his pursuit of us is the same brilliance behind the rotating seasons and

494

the orbiting planets. Heaven and earth know no greater passion than God's personal passion for you and your return. Through holy surprises he has made his faithfulness clear.

Noah saw it as the clouds opened and the rainbow appeared. Abraham felt it as he placed his hand on aging Sarah's belly. Jacob found it through failure. Joseph experienced it in prison. Pharaoh heard it through Moses.

"Let my people go."

But Pharaoh refused. As a result, he was given a front-row seat in the arena of divine devotion. Water became blood. The day became night. Locusts came. Children died. The Red Sea opened. The Egyptian army drowned.

Listen to these seldomread but impassioned words of Moses as he speaks to the Israelites.

> Nothing like this has ever happened before! Look at the past, long before you were even born. Go all the way back to when God made humans on the earth, and look from one end of heaven to the other. Nothing like this has ever been heard of! No other people have ever heard God speak from a fire and have still lived. But you have. No other god has ever taken for himself one nation out of another. But the LORD your God did this for you in Egypt, right before your own eyes. He did it with tests, signs, miracles, war, and great sights, by his great power and strength.[3]

Moses' message? God will change the world to reach the world. God is tireless, relentless. He refuses to quit.

Listen as God articulates his passion: "My heart beats for you, and my love for you stirs up my pity. I won't punish you in my anger, and I won't destroy Israel again. I am God and not a human; I am the Holy One, and I am among you."[4]

Before you read any further, reflect on those last four words, "I am among you." Do you believe that? Do you believe God is near? He wants you to. He wants you to know he is in the midst of your world. Wherever you are as you read these words, he is present. In your car. On the plane. In your office, your bedroom, your den. He's near.

And he is more than near. He is active. Noah's God is your God. The promise given to Abram is given to you. The finger witnessed in Pharaoh's world is moving in yours.

God is in the thick of things in your world. He has not taken up residence in a distant galaxy. He has not removed himself from history. He has not chosen to seclude himself on a throne in an incandescent castle.

He has drawn near. He has involved himself in the carpools, heartbreaks, and funeral homes of our day. He is as near to us on Monday as on Sunday. In the schoolroom as in the sanctuary. At the coffee break as much as the communion table.

Why? Why did God do it? What was his reason?

Some time ago Denalyn was gone for a couple of days and left me alone with the girls. Though the time was not without the typical children's quarrels and occasional misbehavior, it went fine.

"How were the girls?" Denalyn asked when she got home.

"Good. No problem at all."

Jenna overheard my response. "We weren't good, Daddy," she objected. "We fought once; we didn't do what you said once. We weren't good. How can you say we were good?"

Jenna and I had different perceptions of what pleases a father. She thought it depended upon what she did. It didn't. We think the same about God. We think his love rises and falls with our performance. It doesn't. I don't love Jenna for what she does. I love her for whose she is. She is mine.

God loves you for the same reason. He loves you for whose you are; you are his child.[5] It was this love that pursued the Israelites. It was this love that sent the prophets. It was this love that wrapped itself in human flesh and descended the birth canal of Mary. It was this love that walked the hard trails of Galilee and spoke to the hard hearts of the religious.

"This is not normal, Lord GOD," David exclaimed as he considered God's love.[6] You are right, David. God's love is not normal love. It's not normal to love a murderer and adulterer, but God did when he loved David. It isn't normal to love a man who takes his eyes off you, but such was God's love for Solomon.[7] It isn't normal to love people who love stone idols more than they love you, but God did when he refused to give up on Israel.

And it was this love that Jesus was describing on his last Tuesday. The same love that, on Friday, would take him to the cross.

The cross, the zenith of history. All of the past pointed to it and all of the future would depend upon it. It's the great triumph of heaven: God is on the earth. And it is the great tragedy of earth: Man has rejected God.

The religious leaders knew Jesus was speaking about them. Just as their fathers had rejected the prophets, now they were rejecting the Prophet—God himself.

Jesus spoke to those who had turned their backs on history. He spoke to those who had blatantly ignored sign after sign, servant after servant. It wasn't as if they had just skipped a paragraph or missed a punchline. It wasn't as if they had misunderstood a chapter. They had missed the whole book. God had come into their city, walked down their street, knocked on their door, and they refused to let him in.

For that reason—because they had refused to believe—Jesus speaks the most sobering words in the Gospel of Matthew: "The kingdom of God will be taken away from you and given to people who do the things God wants in his kingdom."[8]

God is intolerant of the calloused heart.

He is patient with our mistakes. He is longsuffering with our stumbles. He doesn't get angry at our questions. He doesn't turn away when we struggle. But when we repeatedly reject his message, when we are insensitive to his pleadings, when he changes history itself to get our attention and we still don't listen, he honors our request.

"You refuse to listen," Paul said to the Jews. "You are judging yourselves not worthy of having eternal life! So we will now go to the people of other nations."[9]

Note it was not God who made the people unworthy. It was their refusal to listen that excluded them from grace. Jesus condemns the cold heart, the soul so overgrown with self and selfishness that it would blaspheme the source of hope, the heart so evil that it would see the Prince of Peace and call him the Lord of the Flies.[10]

Such blasphemy is unforgivable, not because of God's unwillingness to forgive, but man's unwillingness to seek forgiveness. The calloused heart is the cursed heart. The calloused heart represents the eyes that won't see the obvious and the ears that won't hear the plain. As a result, they do not seek God and pardon will not be given because pardon will not be sought.

Perhaps my childhood memory is not so peculiar after all. In a way it is the story of the gospel: Jesus piercing his hands in order to prick our hearts. Why did God pierce his hands? Why has he been so devoted? Why has he delivered his children and rescued his people?

Let two men who wrote at two ends of your Bible answer that question. First, Moses. You've already read his answer, "So you would know that the LORD is God."[11] Thousands of years, hundreds of messengers, countless miracles, and one bloodstained cross later, the apostle Paul says the same thing: "God is kind to you so you will change your hearts and lives."[12]

The purpose of his patience? Our repentance.

We began this chapter with one childhood church memory; we'll conclude with another. It is the memory I have of Holman Hunt's painting of Jesus. Perhaps you've seen it. Stone archway . . . ivy-covered bricks . . . Jesus standing before a heavy wooden door.

It was in a Bible I often held as a young boy. Beneath the painting were the words, "Behold, I stand at the door, and knock: if any man hear my voice, and open the door, I will come in to him."[13]

Years later I read about a surprise in the painting. Holman Hunt had intentionally left out something that only the most careful eye would note as missing. I had not noticed it. When I was told about it I went back and looked. Sure enough, it wasn't there. There was no doorknob on the door. It could be opened only from the inside. Hunt's message was the same as this chapter's. The same as God's. The same as all of history.

God comes to your house, steps up to the door, and knocks. But it's up to you to let him in.

CHAPTER 11

You're Invited

"Come to the wedding feast."
MATTHEW 22:4

I am writing this as I sit in a large room in the county courthouse of San Antonio, Texas. I am here by invitation. A summons to jury duty. It wasn't too personal. It wasn't very fancy. Just a simple card with my name and directions to the courthouse. But it was an invitation for me and about a hundred other folks to visit the judge.

This certainly isn't the most meaningful invitation in my life, but still it's an invitation. It makes me think of some others in which I've played a part.

Some years back I offered a person a very special invitation. I asked Denalyn to marry me. Being that marriage proposals are not something you give every day, I tried to make the event memorable.

I began by ordering Chinese food from our favorite Chinese restaurant. I ordered our favorite meal—sweet and sour pork. I put in a special request for extra fortune cookies. While the food was being delivered to my apartment, I took a small strip of paper and printed my proposal. When the food arrived I put the paper in the cookie, set the table, put on my best clothes, and waited for Denalyn.

The night was wrapped in romance. Soft music. Candlelight. When she saw the cloth napkins she knew I had something special in mind, but she wasn't sure what. I ate little. The butterflies in my stomach left little room for food. I couldn't wait to get to the dessert, for in the dessert awaited the invitation.

When the moment came for the cookies, she said she wasn't hungry. I had to beg her to take a cookie. I told her if she didn't eat it, at least read her fortune. She did. She opened the cookie and read the words I'd written on the piece of paper.

She began to cry.

I was devastated: I thought I had offended her. I thought I had insulted her. I don't know how I expected her to react, but I never expected her to cry. (That shows how little I knew about women. I now understand that crying is the utility infielder of the emotion—it covers all bases: sorrow, happiness, excitement.)

Happily, hers were tears of excitement. And she said yes. (She has since, however, been reluctant to open any more fortune cookies.)

Invitations are special. Some are casual such as asking for a date. Some are significant such as offering someone a job. Others are permanent, such as proposing marriage. But all are special.

Invitations. Words embossed on a letter: "You are invited to a gala celebrating the grand opening of . . ." Requests received in the mail: "Mr. and Mrs. John Smith request your presence at the wedding of their daughter . . ." Surprises over the phone: "Hey, Joe. I've got an extra ticket to the game. Interested?"

To receive an invitation is to be honored—to be held in high esteem. For that reason all invitations deserve a kind and thoughtful response.

But the most incredible invitations are not found in envelopes or fortune cookies, they are found in the Bible. You can't read about God without finding him issuing invitations. He invited Eve to marry Adam, the animals to enter the ark, David to be king, Israel to leave bondage, Nehemiah to rebuild Jerusalem. God is an inviting God. He invited Mary to birth his son, the disciples to fish for men, the adulterous woman to start over, and Thomas to touch his wounds. God is the King who prepares the palace, sets the table, and invites his subjects to come in.

In fact, it seems his favorite word is *come*.

"*Come*, let us talk about these things. Though your sins are like scarlet, they can be as white as snow."[1]

"All you who are thirsty, *come* and drink."[2]

"*Come* to me, all of you who are tired and have heavy loads, and I will give you rest."[3]

"*Come* to the wedding feast."[4]

"*Come* follow me, and I will make you fish for people."[5]

"Let anyone who is thirsty *come* to me and drink."[6]

God is a God who invites. God is a God who calls. God is a God who opens the door and waves his hand pointing pilgrims to a full table.

His invitation is not just for a meal, however, it is for life. An invitation to come into his kingdom and take up residence in a tearless, graveless, painless world. Who can come? Whoever wishes. The invitation is at once universal and personal.

In the last week of his life, Jesus offered two stories about urgent invitations.

The first is about two sons whose father invites them to work in the vineyard.[7] Their invitations are identical; their responses opposite. One says no, then changes his mind and goes. The other says yes, then changes his mind and stays.

The second story is about a king who prepares a wedding feast for his son.[8] He invites the people to come, but they don't. Some ignore the invitation; some give excuses about being too busy; others actually kill the servants bearing the invitation.

Have you ever wondered how Jesus felt as he told these stories? If you've ever had a personal invitation ignored, you know how he felt. Most people don't reject Jesus . . . they just don't give his invitation serious thought.

Imagine my feelings had Denalyn responded to me the way many respond to God. What if she had been vague and noncommittal? Imagine me on the edge of my seat watching her read the proposal in the amber of the candlelight. What if, instead of tears, she had given me idle talk.

"Oh, marriage has been in our family for years."

"What?"

"Marriage has been in our family for years. My uncle got married. My aunt got married. My mom and dad. I even have a sister . . ."

"Wait, wait, wait. What does this have to do with us? I'm talking about you and me."

"Well, Max, like I say, I'm all in favor of marriage. I think it's a wonderful idea, a terrific institution."

"But I'm not asking for your opinion on an institution, I'm asking for your hand in marriage."

It must sadden the Father when we give him vague responses to his specific invitation to come to him. "How kind of you to invite me, Jesus. You know my family has always been religious. In fact we trace our roots back to the Huguenot revolution. You probably remember my great-great-uncle Horace? He was a priest and real popular with the Indians."

"What?"

"Like I say, our family has been pro-religion for years. My Aunt Macy sang in the choir at First Baptist and my cousin Arnold is a deacon at . . ."

It was to such ramblings that God spoke these words in Jeremiah 7:13: "I spoke to you again and again, but you did not listen to me. I called you, but you did not answer."

What if Denalyn had said, "Max, you are very kind to think of me, but could we talk about this tomorrow? There is a movie coming on TV in a few minutes that I really want to see."

Or, even worse.

"Marriage? Well, you know, Max, we ought to discuss that some-day. Let me see, I've got an opening next . . . no that's not a good day . . . how about two weeks from Tuesday? You give me a call and we'll set up a time."

Oh, that would hurt. You see, it's one thing to be rejected. It's another not to be taken seriously. Nothing stabs deeper than to give a once-in-a-million, for-your-eyes-only invitation and have it relegated to a list of decisions to be made next week.

Jesus gives the invitation. "Here I am! I stand at the door and knock."[9] To know God is to receive his invitation. Not just to hear it, not just to study it, not just to acknowledge it, but to receive it. It is possible to learn much about God's invitation and never respond to it personally.

Yet his invitation is clear and nonnegotiable. He gives all and we give him all. Simple and absolute. He is clear in what he asks and clear in what he offers. The choice is up to us.

Isn't it incredible that God leaves the choice to us? Think about it. There are many things in life we can't choose. We can't, for example, choose the weather. We can't control the economy.

We can't choose whether or not we are born with a big nose or blue eyes or a lot of hair. We can't even choose how people respond to us.

But we can choose where we spend eternity. The big choice, God leaves to us. The critical decision is ours.

What are you doing with God's invitation?

What are you doing with his personal request that you live with him forever?

That is the only decision that really matters. Whether or not you take the job transfer is not critical. Whether or not you buy a new car is not crucial. What college you choose or what profession you select is important, but not compared to where you spend eternity. That is the decision you will remember.

What are you doing with his invitation?

As I said earlier, I write as I wait in a large room of our county courthouse. I am here by invitation. As I look around me, I see a hundred or so strangers who also received the same jury summons. They read magazines. They flip through newspapers. They stand and stretch. They do office work. And I ponder the irony of finishing a chapter on God's invitation in a room where I wait for the judge to call my name.

Every few minutes the muffled conversations are silenced by an official-looking gentleman who will enter the room and call names: Yvonne Campbell, Johnny Solis, Thomas Adams. Those he calls will be given instructions and the rest of us return to our activities.

I'm apprehensive about the interview: I don't know what the judge will do. I don't know what the judge will ask. I don't know what the judge will require. I don't know what the outcome will be. I don't even know who the judge is.

So, I'm a bit anxious.

However this isn't my first invitation to appear before a judge. I have another summons, "It is appointed for men to die once, and after that comes judgment."[10] But I don't feel the same anxiety about that appointment.

For I know what the judge will do. I know what the outcome will be. And most of all, I know who the judge is . . . he's my Father.

MOUTH-TO-MOUTH MANIPULATION

*"Then the Pharisees left that place and made plans
to trap Jesus in saying something wrong."*
MATTHEW 22:15

I n the coral reefs of the Caribbean lives a small fish known as the Kissing Fish. It's only about two to three inches long. It's bright blue and quick and a delight to behold. Most fascinating is its kiss. It's not uncommon to see two of these fish with lips pressed and fins thrashing. They give the appearance of serious underwater romance.

You would think the species would be an aquarium lover's dream. They look energetic, vivid, illuminant, and affectionate. But looks can be deceiving. For what appears to be a gentle friend in the sea is actually a pint-sized bully of the deep.

Ferociously territorial, the Kissing Fish has laid claim to its camp and wants no visitors. His square foot of coral is his and no one else's. He found it, he staked it out, and he wants no other of his kind near it.

Challenge his boundaries and he'll take you on, jaw to jaw. What appears to be a tryst is actually underwater martial arts. Mouth pushing. Liplocking. Literal jawboning. Power moves with the tongue.

Sounds funny, doesn't it?

Sounds familiar, doesn't it?

We don't have to go to the Caribbean to see that type of power struggle. Mouth-to-mouth manipulation isn't limited to the Caribbean.

Look closely at the people in your world (or the person in your mirror). You might be surprised how fishy things get when people demand their way. Kissing Fish aren't the first to use their mouths to make their point.

In frontier days disputes were settled with quick fists; today we use a more sophisticated tool: the tongue. Just like the Kissing Fish we disguise our fights. We call it debating, challenging the status quo. In reality, it's nothing more than stubbornly defending our territory.

Such was the case on Tuesday during the last week in the life of Jesus. Long before the whips snapped, words were hurled. Long before the nails were hammered, accusations were made. Long before Jesus had to bear the cross, he had to bear the acid tongues of the religious leaders.

The dialogue appears innocent. No swords were drawn. No arrests were made. But don't let the apparent innocence fool you. Like the Kissing Fish the accusers were out for blood.

There were three encounters.

CASE ONE:
SHOW ME YOUR DIPLOMA PLEASE

The procedure for being recognized as a religious teacher in Palestine was simple. Originally, rabbinical candidates had been ordained by a leading rabbi whom they respected and under whose teaching they served. This, however, led to variance in qualifications and teachings as well as widespread abuses. So the high Jewish council, the Sanhedrin, took over the responsibility for ordination.

At his ordination a man was declared to be a rabbi, elder, and judge and was given authority to teach, express wisdom, and render verdicts.

Fair procedure. Necessary safeguard. And so we aren't surprised that the religious leaders asked Jesus, "What authority do you have to do these things? Who gave you this authority?"[1] Had their questions stemmed from concern for the purity of the temple and the integrity of the position, there would have been no problem. But they wanted their territory: "We are afraid of what the crowd will do."[2]

Had they really cared about the future of the nation, they wouldn't have worried about what the people thought. They would have taken the matter of the rabbi into their own hands rather than worm away from him and eventually turn him over to a foreign government. They hadn't learned the first lesson of leadership. "A man who wants to lead the orchestra must turn his back on the crowd."

By the way, there is something odd in this picture. Do you see it? The created are asking the Creator about his credentials. The pot is asking the Potter for his I.D. No reference is made to the miracles. No question is raised about his teaching. They want to know about his ordination. Did he come out of the right seminary? Is he a member of the right denomination? Does he have the proper credentials?

Incredible. Cross-examining God. Now I see why powerful people often wear sunglasses—the spotlight blinds them to reality. They suffer from a delusion that power means something (it doesn't). They suffer from the misconception that titles make a difference (they don't). They are under the impression that earthly authority will make a heavenly difference (it won't).

Can I prove my point? Take this quiz.

Name the ten wealthiest men in the world.
Name the last ten Heisman trophy winners.
Name the last ten winners of the Miss America contest.

Name eight people who have won the Nobel or Pulitzer prize.
How about the last ten Academy Award winners for best picture or the last decade's worth of World Series winners?

How did you do? I didn't do well either. With the exception of you
trivia hounds, none of us remember the headliners of yesterday too
well. Surprising how quickly we forget, isn't it? And what I've mentioned above are no second-rate achievements. These are the best in
their fields. But the applause dies. Awards tarnish. Achievements are
forgotten. Accolades and certificates are buried with their owners.

Here's another quiz. See how you do on this one.

Think of three people you enjoy spending time with.
Name ten people who have taught you something worthwhile.
Name five friends who have helped you in a difficult time.
List a few teachers who have aided your journey through school.
Name half a dozen heroes whose stories have inspired you.

Easier? It was for me, too. The lesson? The people who make a difference are not the ones with the credentials, but the ones with the
concern.

CASE TWO:
THE SWORD IN THE STUDDED SCABBARD

"The Pharisees . . . made plans to trap Jesus in saying something
wrong. . . . 'Teacher, we know that you are an honest man and that
you teach the truth about God's way. You are not afraid of what other
people think about you, because you pay no attention to who they
are. So tell us what you think. Is it right to pay taxes to Caesar or
not?'"[3]

Chances are that when a man slaps you on the back he wants you to cough up something. This is no exception. The Pharisees are doing some heavy backslapping in this verse. Though their question is valid, their motive is not. Of all the texts that drip with manipulation, this is the worst.

Like the Kissing Fish, the Pharisees appear gentle. But also like the Kissing Fish, something smells fishy.

God has made it clear that flattery is never to be a tool of the sincere servant. Flattery is nothing more than fancy dishonesty. It wasn't used by Jesus, nor should it be used by his followers.

"May the Lord cut off all flattering lips," affirmed the psalmist.[4]

"He who rebukes a man will in the end gain more favor than he who has a flattering tongue," agreed Solomon.[5]

"Beware of the man with sweet words and wicked deeds," learned Lucy.

The psalmist you've read. Solomon you've admired. But Lucy? She learned about flattery the hard way. Here's her story:

It's Washington, D.C., in the 1860s. The nation is ravaged by war. The country is divided with strife. But for young Lucy the greatest war is in her heart.

Lucy Lambert Hale was the younger daughter of John P. Hale, one of New Hampshire's Civil War senators. She was one of the most ravishing bachelorettes in our nation's capital. Her long list of suitors was testimony to her popularity. The list of those aspiring her heart was not only long, it was historical. More than one of her young loves grew to be national figures.

As early as the age of twelve she was receiving flowers from Will Chandler, a Harvard freshman. Lucy was fond of the young man, but, after all, she was only twelve. Will became Secretary of the Navy and eventually a United States senator.

Then there was Oliver. Only two years her senior, he thought he had found his true love. She disagreed. Though he never got Lucy's hand, Oliver Wendell Holmes did get a seat on the Supreme Court.

But there was another man who, for a time, did occupy a place in her heart. And it is this man whose legacy in history is one of kind words and deadly deeds. His name was John.

While the war was raging in the nation, their love was raging in Washington. And while the nation was at odds, they, too, were often at odds. What confused Lucy about this most recent boyfriend was his inconsistency. He would state one thing and live another. His promises and performance didn't match. He would woo her with his words and bewilder her with his actions.

Consider this, the first letter he ever sent her, on Valentine's day, 1862.

My Dear Miss Hale,

Were it not for the License which a time-honored observance of this day allows, I had not written you this poor note.

You resemble in a most remarkable degree a lady, very dear to me, now dead, and your close resemblance to her surprised me the first time I saw you. This must be my apology for any apparent rudeness noticeable—To see you has indeed afforded me a melancholy pleasure, if you can conceive of such and should we never meet nor I see you again—believe me, I shall always associate you in my memory, with her, who was very beautiful, and whose face, like your own I trust, was a faithful index of gentleness and amiability.

With a thousand wishes for your future happiness I am, to you—

a Stranger

With words as sweet as molasses and determination as fierce as a bull, John made sure that he didn't remain too long a stranger. And with time, he and Lucy became engaged. That's when the war broke out— not in the country, but between John and Lucy.

He was insanely jealous. They quarreled incessantly. They argued as they listened to President Lincoln's second inaugural address. They quarreled the next night when John found Lucy dancing with the president's eldest son, Robert. They quarreled when the president appointed Lucy's father as ambassador to Spain. And John exploded when Lucy decided to break the engagement and go with her father to Spain.

John was kind with words, but possessive and jealous with actions. Lucy learned from John that a person can have words of honey and hands of steel. For that reason she left him. Ironically, she eventually married the man who had sent her flowers at the age of twelve, Will Chandler.

But though she lived a long and happy life, she would never forget the stormy romance with the man of kind words and harsh deeds. Nor would the rest of the world forget John Wilkes Booth.[6]

Now, I'm sure there was more to this story than a romance with a young girl, but for our case both the similarity and the lesson are significant. The words Jesus heard that day were just as kind. Who would have imagined they came from the lips of murderers? But therein lies the lesson of flattery. Treat it as cautiously as you would a jewel-embedded scabbard, for within both are found a sword.

CASE THREE:
MYOPIC MEANDERINGS

Enter: the Sadducees. "In this corner, weighing heavy on opinion and weak on balance, the aristocrats of Jerusalem, the Ivy Leaguers of Israel, the far left of the liberals—the Sadducees!"

This small band of leaders loved Greek philosophy and poo-pooed traditional Torah teaching as too rigid, too conservative. They were pro-Roman. The Pharisees were not—they were country club. The Sadducees were common—they thought there was no afterlife.

The Pharisees could tell you what you were going to wear in the after-life.

Normally, these two never would have been on the same side. But their fear of Jesus united them. The Sadducees made their money from the money-changing and dove-selling in the temple. Monday's temple cleansing convinced them they needed to send this fellow back to the sticks with his tail between his legs.

So, the Sadducees use the third trick of the tongue: hypothetical meandering. If this and that happens with this occurring before that . . . Their ploy is to create an extreme version of an unlikely incident and trap Jesus in his response.

If you want the long version of their question, read Matthew 22:24–28. If you want the short version and my interpretation, here it is. "Teacher, Moses said if a married man dies without having children, his brother must marry the widow and have the children for him. Once there were seven brothers among us, blah, blah, blah, blah, blah. . . ."

Just like the Kissing Fish, the Sadducees stubbornly protected tiny patches of territory. They, like the Kissing Fish, had limited vision. They battled over a little piece of ground. They fought over tiny territory in a great ocean.

There are those in the church who find a small territory and become obsessed with it. There are those in God's family who find a controversy and stake their claim to it. Every church has at least one stubborn soul who has mastered a minutiae of the message and made a mission out of it.

Myopic creatures fighting battles over needless turf.

Jesus' response is worth underlining. "You are way off." Now, your translation doesn't use those words and neither does mine. But it could. A fair translation of the Greek would be: "You are off base. You are missing the point. You are chasing a rabbit down a dead-end trail."

Some time ago I came across a song by Dennis Tice that shows the absurdity of fighting over futile territory. With his permission, I share it with you. You'll love the title; it's called "Did Adam and Eve Have Navels?"

> Did Adam and Eve have navels or a blank spot where it should be?
> Do other folks lie awake at night or is it only me?
> Thinkin' about the question that plagues all mankind
> Hmmmmmmmmm
> Belly-button fuzz wuzza part of creation, how could I be so blind?'
> I think I'll start a church someday to preach this creed of mine
> 'Cause Adam and Eve had navels and I'll prove it at the end of time.
> Sure "God is love" and "Jesus saves," but what about this truth?
> I found the answer just last year in 1st John chapter 2
> Seek out the truth, the truth will set you free
> Wait upon the Lord in all sincerity
> And then you'll reach the highest level of Christianity
> When you become a Navelist, your eyes will finally see
> That Adam and Eve had navels, I'm telling you today
> Yeah, I'm splittin' hairs for Jesus and that makes it all okay
> And I'm going to take you deeper than your eyes can currently see
> I'm splittin' hairs for Jesus for more spirituality
> I shared this truth with all the land and navelism grew
> A thousand members growing strong, ('cause I preach salvation too)
> But now the church is splittin' over some technicality,
> Did their buttons go in or pop on out, how picky can they be?[7]

As long as Christians split hairs, Christians will split churches.

In his last week Jesus left a clear message: Misuse of the mouth is noticed by God. The religious leaders thought they could manipulate Jesus with their words. They were wrong.

God is not trapped by trickery, flattered by flattery, or fooled by hypothesis. He wasn't then and isn't now.

The tragedy of the Kissing Fish is that he sees so little. All his oral warfare gets him is the same view from the same patch of coral. Had I a word with him, had I a moment with the creature who is possessed with a passion to protect his own and keep out what is new . . . I would challenge him to look around.

I would say what I need someone to say to me when I get territorial about my opinions: Let go of your territory for a while. Explore some new reefs. Scout some new regions. Much is gained by closing your mouth and opening your eyes.

CHAPTER 13

WHAT MAN
DARED NOT DREAM

"What do you think about the Christ? Whose son is he?"
MATTHEW 22:42

Heroes mirror a society. Study a nation's heroes and understand the nation. We honor those who embody our dreams—gang members toast the ruthless, slaves esteem the freedom fighter, and cult members exalt the dominant. The frail lionize the strong and the oppressed hallow the courageous.

The result is a collage of world heroes as opposite as Joseph Stalin is from Florence Nightingale, Peter Pan from George Patton, and Mark Twain from Mother Teresa. Each is an index to a chapter in the book called people.

One legendary character, however, reflects more than a culture—he reflects the globe. He is known the world over. A face as easily recognizable in Nigeria as in Indiana. One immortal whose story has been written by and told to people in every land.

If it is true that legends mirror a people, then this man is a mirror of the world. And we can learn much about ourselves by learning about him.

Some call him Sinterklaas. Others Pere Noel or Papa Noel. He's been known as Hoteiosho, Sonnerklaas, Father Christmas, Jelly Belly, and to most English speakers, Santa Claus.

His original name was Nicholas, which means victorious. He was born in A.D. 280 in what is now Turkey. He was orphaned at age nine when his parents died of a plague. Though many would think Santa majored in toy making and minored in marketing, actually the original Nicholas studied Greek philosophy and Christian doctrine.

He was honored by the Catholic church by being named Bishop of Myra in the early fourth century. He held the post until his death on December 6, 343.

History recognized him as a saint, but in the third century he was a bit of a troublemaker. He was twice jailed, once by the Emperor Diocletian for religious reasons, the other for slugging a fellow bishop during a fiery debate. (So much for finding out who is naughty and nice.)

Old Nick never married. But that's not to say he wasn't a romantic. He was best known for the kindness he showed to a poor neighbor who was unable to support his three daughters or provide the customary dowry so they could attract husbands. Old Saint Nicholas slipped up to the house by night and dropped a handful of gold coins through the window so the eldest daughter could afford to get married. He repeated this act on two other nights for the other two daughters.

This story was the seed that, watered with years, became the Santa legend. It seems that every generation adorned it with another ornament until it sparkled more than a Christmas tree.

The gift grew from a handful of coins to bags of coins. Instead of dropping them through the window, he dropped them down the chimney. And rather than land on the floor, the bags of coins landed in the girls' stockings, which were hanging on the hearth to dry. (So that's where all this stocking stuff started.)

The centuries have been as good to Nicholas's image as to his deeds. Not only have his acts been embellished, his wardrobe and personality have undergone transformations as well.

As Bishop of Myra, he wore the traditional ecclesiastical robes and a mitered hat. He is known to have been slim, with a dark beard and a serious personality.

By 1300 he was wearing a white beard. By the 1800s he was depicted with a rotund belly and an ever-present basket of food over his arm. Soon came the black boots, a red cape, and a cheery stocking on his head. In the late nineteenth century his basket of food became a sack of toys. In 1866 he was small and gnomish but by 1930 he was a robust six-footer with rosy cheeks and a Coca-Cola.

Santa reflects the desires of people all over the world. With the centuries he has become the composite of what we want:

A friend who cares enough to travel a long way against all odds to bring good gifts to good people.

A sage who, though aware of each act, has a way of rewarding the good and overlooking the bad.

A friend of children, who never gets sick and never grows old.

A father who lets you sit on his lap and share your deepest desires.

Santa. The culmination of what we need in a hero. The personification of our passions. The expression of our yearnings. The fulfillment of our desires.

And . . . the betrayal of our meager expectations.

What? you say. Let me explain.

You see, Santa can't provide what we really need. For one thing, he's only around once a year. When January winds chill our souls, he's history. When December's requests become February payments, Santa's left the mall. When April demands taxes or May brings final exams, Santa is still months from his next visit. And should July find us ill or October find us alone, we can't go to his chair for comfort— it's still empty. He only comes once a year.

And when he comes, though he gives much, he doesn't take away much. He doesn't take away the riddle of the grave, the burden of mistakes, or the anxiety of demands. He's kind and quick and cute; but when it comes to healing hurts—don't go to Santa.

Now, I don't mean to be a Scrooge. I'm not wanting to slam the jolly old fellow. I am just pointing out that we people are timid when it comes to designing legends.

You'd think we could do better. You'd think that over six centuries we'd develop a hero who'd resolve those fears.

But we can't. We have made many heroes, from King Arthur to Kennedy; Lincoln to Lindbergh; Socrates to Santa to Superman. We give it the best we can, every benefit of every doubt, every supernatural strength, and for a brief shining moment we have the hero we need—the king who can deliver Camelot. But then the truth leaks and fact surfaces amid the fiction and the chinks in the armor are seen. And we realize that the heroes, as noble as they may have been, as courageous as they were, were conceived in the same stained society as you and I.

Except one. There was one who claimed to come from a different place. There was one who, though he had the appearance of a man, claimed to have the origin of God. There was one who, while wearing the face of a Jew, had the image of the Creator.

Those who saw him—really saw him—knew there was something different. At his touch blind beggars saw. At his command crippled legs walked. At his embrace empty lives filled with vision.

He fed thousands with one basket. He stilled a storm with one command. He raised the dead with one proclamation. He changed lives with one request. He rerouted the history of the world with one life, lived in one country, was born in one manger, and died on one hill.

During his final week he summarized his claims with one question. Speaking of himself he asked his disciples, "What do you think about the Christ? Whose son is he?"[1]

A probing question. A properly positioned question. The "what" is answered by the "who." What you think about the Christ is embosomed in whose son he is. Note Jesus didn't ask, "What do you think about the Christ and his teachings?" or, "What do you think about the Christ and his opinions on social issues?" or, "What do you think about the Christ and his ability to lead people?"

After three years of ministry, hundreds of miles, thousands of miracles, innumerable teachings, Jesus asks, "Who?" Jesus bids the people to ponder not what he has done but who he is.

It's the ultimate question of the Christ: Whose son is he?

Is he the son of God or the sum of our dreams? Is he the force of creation or a figment of our imagination?

When we ask that question about Santa, the answer is the culmination of our desires. A depiction of our fondest dreams.

Not so when we ask it about Jesus. For no one could ever dream a person as incredible as he is. The idea that a virgin would be selected by God to bear himself. . . . The notion that God would don a scalp and toes and two eyes. . . . The thought that the King of the universe would sneeze and burp and get bit by mosquitoes. . . . It's too incredible. Too revolutionary. We would never create such a Savior. We aren't that daring.

When we create a redeemer, we keep him safely distant in his faraway castle. We allow him only the briefest of encounters with us. We permit him to swoop in and out with his sleigh before we can draw too near. We wouldn't ask him to take up residence in the midst of a contaminated people. In our wildest imaginings we wouldn't conjure a king who becomes one of us.

But God did. God did what we wouldn't dare dream. He did what we couldn't imagine. He became a man so we could trust him. He became a sacrifice so we could know him. And he defeated death so we could follow him.

It defies logic. It is a divine insanity. A holy incredibility. Only a

God beyond systems and common sense could create a plan as absurd as this. Yet it is the very impossibility of it all that makes it possible. The wildness of the story is its strongest witness.

For only a God could create a plan this mad. Only a Creator beyond the fence of logic could offer such a gift of love.

What man can't do, God does.

So, when it comes to goodies and candy, cherub cheeks and red noses, go to the North Pole.

But when it comes to eternity, forgiveness, purpose, and truth, go to the manger. Kneel with the shepherds. Worship the God who dared to do what man dared not dream.

CHAPTER 14

THE CURSOR OR THE CROSS?

"How are you going to escape God's judgment?"
MATTHEW 23:33

What I don't like about computers is that they do what I say and not what I mean.

Example: I mean to hit the "control" button but hit the "CAPS LOCK" BUTTON AND ALL OF A SUDDEN GIANT LETTERS DOMINATE THE SCREEN. i LOOK AT THE SCREEN AND SAY, "tHAT'S NOT WHAT i MEANT!" AND i correct my mistake.

Here's another example.

I want to correct one letter but inadvertently hit the button that removes the entire word. "That's not what I meant," I mumble to the one-eyed monster, and then I correct my mistake.

Now, I know I shouldn't be so hard on the mACHINE (OOPS, DID IT AGAIN). After all, it's just a tool. It can't read my mind (though considering what it cost, it should at least keep me from making the same mistake over and over). A computer computes. It doesn't think. It doesn't question. It doesn't smile, shake its monitor, and say, "Max, Max, I know what you are trying to do. You don't intend to be hitting the delete button, removing the very letters you want to keep.

522

If you'd look at your screen you would see that. But since you won't and since you and I are good friends and you leave me plugged in, I'm going to give you what you need and not what you request."

Computers don't do that. Computers are legalists, impersonal pragmatists. Push a button and get a response. Learn the system and get the printout. Blow the system and get ready for a long night.

Computers are heartless creatures. Don't expect any compassion from your laptop. They don't call it a hard disk for nothing. (Even the shell is hard.)

Some folks have a computer theology when it comes to understanding God. God is the ultimate desktop. The Bible is the maintenance manual, the Holy Spirit is the floppy disk, and Jesus is the 1-800 service number.

Call it computerized Christianity. Push the right buttons, enter the right code, insert the correct data, and bingo, print out your own salvation.

It's professional religion. You do your part and the Divine Computer does his. No need to pray (after all, you control the keyboard). No emotional attachment necessary (who wants to hug circuits?). And worship? Well, worship is a lab exercise—insert the rituals and see the results.

Computerized religion. No kneeling. No weeping. No gratitude. No emotion. It's great—unless you make a mistake. Unless you err. Unless you enter the wrong data or forget to save the manuscript. Unless you're caught on the wrong side of a power surge. And then . . . tough luck, buddy, you're on your own.

Religion by computer. That's what happens when . . .

> you replace the living God with a cold system;
> you replace inestimable love with pro-forma budget;
> you replace the ultimate sacrifice of Christ with the puny achievements of man.

When you view God as a computer and the Christian as a

number-crunching, cursor-commanding, button pusher . . . that is religion by the computer.

God hates it. It crushes his people. It contaminates his leaders. It corrupts his children.

How do I know? He said so. Jesus condemns religion by the rules. With eyes blazing and pistols firing, Jesus rips hole after hole in the hot-air balloon of the Pharisees. His sermon on Tuesday is a one-sided shootout. The result is a permanent proclamation of God against systematic salvation.

Let me see if a simple exercise will clarify this point. How would you fill in this blank?

A person is made right with God through _____.

Simple statement. Yet don't let its brevity fool you. How you complete it is critical; it reflects the nature of your faith.

A person is made right with God through . . .

Being good. A person is made right with God through goodness. Pay your taxes. Give sandwiches to the poor. Don't drive too fast or drink too much or drink at all. Christian conduct—that's the secret.

Suffering. There's the answer. That's how to be made right with God—suffer. Sleep on dirt floors. Stalk through dank jungles. Malaria. Poverty. Cold days. Night-long vigils. Vows of chastity. Shaved heads, bare feet. The greater the pain, the greater the saint.

No, no, no. The way to be made right with God? Doctrine. Dead-center interpretation of the truth. Airtight theology that explains every mystery. The Millennium simplified. Inspiration clarified. The role of women defined once and for all. God has to save us—we know more than he does.

How are we made right with God? All of the above are tried. All are taught. All are demonstrated. But none are from God.

In fact, that is the problem. None are from God. All are from people. Think about it. Who is the major force in the above examples? Humankind or God? Who does the saving, you or him?

If we are saved by good works, we don't need God—weekly reminders of the do's and don'ts will get us to heaven. If we are saved by suffering, we certainly don't need God. All we need is a whip and a chain and the gospel of guilt. If we are saved by doctrine then, for heaven's sake, let's study! We don't need God, we need a lexicon. Weigh the issues. Explore the options. Decipher the truth.

But be careful, student. For if you are saved by having exact doctrine, then one mistake would be fatal. That goes for those who believe we are made right with God through deeds. I hope the temptation is never greater than the strength. If it is, a bad fall could be a bad omen. And those who think we are saved by suffering, take caution as well, for you never know how much suffering is required.

In fact, if you are saving yourself, you never know for sure about anything. You never know if you've hurt enough, wept enough, or learned enough. Such is the result of computerized religion: fear, insecurity, instability. And, most ironically, arrogance.

That's right—arrogance. The insecure boast the most. Those who are trying to save themselves promote themselves. Those saved by works display works. Those saved by suffering unveil scars. Those saved by emotion flash their feelings. And those saved by doctrine—you got it. They wear their doctrine on their sleeves.

Or, as was the case of the Pharisees, on their heads: "They make the boxes of Scriptures that they wear bigger."[1]

Or on their shoulders: "They make their special prayer clothes very long."[2]

Or they demand the choice seats: They "love to have the most important seats at feasts and in the synagogues."[3]

And they take great pride in titles. "They love people to greet them with respect in the marketplaces, and they love to have people call them 'Teacher.'"[4]

The Pharisees were arrogant. They were arrogant because they were self-righteous. They were self-righteous because they were trying to make themselves righteous without God. They had turned the temple into a computer network. The synagogue was a programming course, the rituals were the keyboard, and the Pharisees were the programmers. They were the authorities. They were right and they knew it.

"They do good things so that other people will see them."[5]

It made Jesus furious. So furious that his last sermon for the Pharisees was not about love or compassion or evangelism. It was about phony faith and hollow hearts. It was an in-your-face slam dunk against legalistic leadership.

Six times he called them hypocrites and five times he called them blind. He accused them of kamikaze fatalism—choosing hell over heaven and taking everybody with them. Instead of converting people to God they made clones of themselves. They complicated the gospel with odd myths and superstition. They took pride when it came to tithing, but took naps when it came to serving.[6]

Their faith was as appealing as eating out of a bowl crusty with yesterday's lentils or as aromatic as digging up last century's graves. They were about as innocent as Freddie Kruger and as sincere as a pimp.

"You are snakes," Jesus accused, seeing in their eyes the same beady blackness that Eve had seen in the garden.

What angered Jesus during his last week was not the apostles' confusion. He wasn't upset by the people's demands. He didn't lose his temper with the soldiers and their whips nor explode with Pilate and his questions. But the one thing he could not stomach was two-faced faith: Religion used for profit and religion used for prestige. This he could not tolerate.

Thirty-six verses of fire were summarized with one question: "How are you going to escape God's judgment?"[7]

Good question. Good question for the Pharisees, good question for you and me. How are we going to escape God's judgment?

That question is answered by going back to the blank and filling it in. A person is made right with God through _____.

Ironically, or appropriately, it was a Pharisee who first wrote that line. Or, at least, he used to be a Pharisee. He got his training in front of a theological terminal. He was an up-and-coming religious technician. He could answer the pickiest questions and solve the most minute riddle. But the big question, Jesus' question, he couldn't answer.

I wonder if he was present the day Jesus asked it? "How will you escape God's judgment?" Maybe he was. Maybe his young face was in the crowd. Perhaps he was there, scrolls under the arm, scowl on the face. Heir apparent to the legalistic swivel chair.

I wonder if he was there. . . .

If he was, he had no answer. No legalist does. The man who would save himself says nothing in God's presence. All of a sudden, our best efforts are pitifully puny. Dare you stand before God and ask him to save you because of your suffering or your sacrifice or your tears or your study?

Nor do I.

Nor did Paul. It took him decades to discover what he wrote in only one sentence.

"A person is made right with God through faith."[8] Not through good works, suffering, or study. All those may be the result of salvation but they are not the cause of it.

How will you escape God's judgment? Only one way. Through faith in God's sacrifice. It's not what you do; it's what he did.

———

By the way, my computer still drives me crazy. It still does WHAT i SAY, OOps, and not what I mean. I push the wrong button, I pay the price. For that reason, I refuse to call it what the manufacturer does. It is not a personal computer. It is cold, detached, and could care less about my happiness.

A personal computer would be different. In fact it wouldn't be a computer at all; it would be a friend. A friend who gives me what I need instead of what I request. A friend who knows more about me than I do. A friend who doesn't have to be turned off at night and on in the morning.

A computer like that? Too much to ask, I know.

A God like that? Still too much to ask. But that's what he is. Why else do you think he is known as your personal Savior?

CHAPTER 15

UNCLUTTERED FAITH

"So do not let anyone make rules for you."
COLOSSIANS 2:16

Bedtime is a bad time for kids. No child understands the logic of going to bed while there is energy left in the body or hours left in the day.

My children are no exception. A few nights ago, after many objections and countless groans, the girls were finally in their gowns, in their beds, and on their pillows. I slipped into the room to give them a final kiss. Andrea, the five-year-old, was still awake, just barely, but awake. After I kissed her, she lifted her eyelids one final time and said, "I can't wait until I wake up."

Oh, for the attitude of a five-year-old! That simple uncluttered passion for living that can't wait for tomorrow. A philosophy of life that reads, "Play hard, laugh hard, and leave the worries to your father." A bottomless well of optimism flooded by a perpetual spring of faith. Is it any wonder Jesus said we must have the heart of a child before we can enter the kingdom of heaven?

I like the way J. B. Phillips renders Jesus' call to childlikeness: "Jesus called a little child to his side and set him on his feet in the middle of them all. 'Believe me,' he said, 'unless you change your whole outlook and become like little children you will never enter the kingdom of Heaven.'"[1]

Note the phrase "change your whole outlook." No small command. Quit looking at life like an adult and see it through the eyes of a child.

Essential counsel for us sober-minded, serious-faced, sour-pussed adults. Necessary advice for us Charles Atlas wannabes who shoulder the world. Good words for those of us who seldom say, "I can't wait until I wake up," and more often state, "I can't wait to go to bed."

We are like children in one way. We groan about bed just like they do—only we groan about getting out of it instead of getting into it.

It's not hard to understand why.

Who gets excited about climbing into the world many wake up to? Deadlines upon traffic jams upon grumpy bosses and crowded streets. Keeping your head to the pillow is much more appealing than keeping your shoulder to the wheel.

One word summarizes the frustration of most people—confusion. Nothing seems simple. Have you attempted to understand mortgage options lately? Tried to understand the moods of your mate? Bought a new phone system for your office recently? Tried to fix a microwave or decipher a therapist's counsel? Then you know what I mean.

Enter, religion. We Christians have a solution for the confusion don't we? "Leave the cluttered world of humanity," we invite, "and enter the sane, safe garden of religion."

Let's be honest. Instead of a "sane, safe garden," how about a "wild and woolly sideshow"? It shouldn't be the case, but when you step back and look at how religion must appear to the unreligious, well, the picture of an amusement park comes to mind.

Flashing lights of ceremony and pomp. Roller-coaster thrills of emotion. Loud music. Strange people. Funny clothes.

Like barkers on a midway, preachers persuade: "Step right up to the Church of Heavenly Hope of High Angels and Happy Hearts. . . ."

"Over here, madam; that church is too tough on folks like you. Try us, we teach salvation by sanctification which leads to purification and stabilization. That is unless you prefer the track of predestination which offers . . ."

"Your attention, please sir. Try our premillennial, noncharismatic, Calvinistic Creed service on for size . . . you won't be disappointed."

A safe garden of serenity? No wonder a lady said to me once, "I'd like to try Jesus, if I could just get past the religion."

She speaks for thousands. She may speak for you. Perhaps you long to wake up to the same life my daughter does: playful, peaceful, and secure. You haven't found it in the world and you've peeked in the church doors and aren't too sure about what you see there either.

Or maybe you've done more than peek through the church doors; you've gone in and gotten to work. You've baked, visited, volunteered, and taught. But instead of rest you got stress. And now you are puzzled because Jesus said you should feel at peace and since you don't, it certainly must be your fault. God wouldn't say that and not do it, would he? So in addition to being confused by the world and the church, you are confused at your own inability to make sense out of it all.

Whew! Being a Christian is hard work!

It's not supposed to be, though. Complicated religion wasn't made by God. Reading Matthew 23 will convince you of that. It is the crackdown of Christ on midway religion.

If you've always thought of Jesus as a pale-faced, milquetoast Tiny Tim, then read this chapter and see the other side: an angry father denouncing the pimps who have prostituted his children.

Six times he calls them hypocrites. Five times he calls them blind. Seven times he denounces them and once he prophesies their ruin. Not what you would call a public relations presentation.

But in the midst of the roaring river of words there is a safe island of instruction. Somewhere between bursts of fire Jesus holsters his pistol, turns to the wide-eyed disciples, and describes the essence of simple faith. Four verses: a reading as brief as it is practical. Call it Christ's solution to complicated Christianity.

"You must not be called 'Teacher,' because you have only one Teacher, and you are all brothers and sisters together. And don't call any person on earth 'Father,' because you have one Father, who is in heaven. And you should not be called 'Master,' because you have only one Master, the Christ. Whoever is your servant is the greatest among you. Whoever makes himself great will be made humble. Whoever makes himself humble will be made great."[2]

How do you simplify your faith? How do you get rid of the clutter? How do you discover a joy worth waking up to? Simple. Get rid of the middleman.

Discover truth for yourself. "You have only one Teacher, and you are all brothers and sisters together."[3]

Develop trust for yourself. "Don't call any person on earth 'Father,' because you have one Father, who is in heaven."[4]

Discern his will for yourself. "You have only one Master, the Christ."[5]

There are some who position themselves between you and God. There are some who suggest the only way to get to God is through them. There is the great teacher who has the final word on Bible teaching. There is the father who must bless your acts. There is the spiritual master who will tell you what God wants you to do. Jesus' message for complicated religion is to remove these middlemen.

He's not saying that you don't need teachers, elders, or counselors. He is saying, however, that we are all brothers and sisters and have equal access to the Father. Simplify your faith by seeking God for yourself. No confusing ceremonies necessary. No mysterious rituals required. No elaborate channels of command or levels of access.

You have a Bible? You can study. You have a heart? You can pray. You have a mind? You can think.

One of my favorite stories concerns a bishop who was traveling by ship to visit a church across the ocean. While en route, the ship stopped at an island for a day. He went for a walk on a beach. He came upon three fishermen mending their nets.

Curious about their trade he asked them some questions. Curious about his ecclesiastical robes, they asked him some questions. When they found out he was a Christian leader, they got excited. "We Christians!" they said, proudly pointing to one another.

The bishop was impressed but cautious. Did they know the Lord's Prayer? They had never heard of it.

"What do you say, then, when you pray?"

"We pray, 'We are three, you are three, have mercy on us.'"

The bishop was appalled at the primitive nature of the prayer. "That will not do." So he spent the day teaching them the Lord's Prayer. The fishermen were poor but willing learners. And before the bishop sailed away the next day, they could recite the prayer with no mistakes.

The bishop was proud.

On the return trip the bishop's ship drew near the island again. When the island came into view the bishop came to the deck and recalled with pleasure the men he had taught and resolved to go see them again. As he was thinking, a light appeared on the horizon near the island. It seemed to be getting nearer. As the bishop gazed in wonder he realized the three fishermen were walking toward him on the water. Soon all the passengers and crew were on the deck to see the sight.

When they were within speaking distance, the fisherman cried out, "Bishop, we come hurry to meet you."

"What is it you want?" asked the stunned bishop.

"We are so sorry. We forget lovely prayer. We say, 'Our Father, who art in heaven, hallowed be your name . . .' and then we forget. Please tell us prayer again."

The bishop was humbled. "Go back to your homes, my friends, and when you pray say, 'We are three, you are three, have mercy on us.'"

––––––––

Seek the simple faith. Major in the majors. Focus on the critical. Long for God.

"I can't wait to wake up," are the words of a child's faith. The reason Andrea can say them is because her world is simple. She plays hard, she laughs much, and she leaves the worries to her father.

Let's do the same.

CHAPTER 16

SURVIVING LIFE

*"But those people who keep their faith until the end will be saved.
The Good News about God's kingdom will be preached
in all the world, to every nation.
Then the end will come."*
MATTHEW 24:13–14

Not all of you will understand this chapter. Not all of you will comprehend its message or relate to its promise. You won't understand it if:

you've never failed and are intolerant of those who have.
your life is as hygienic as a new hospital and your soul could
pass the white glove test.
you are a red-hot zealot who thinks God is lucky to have you
on his side.
you dreamed of a perfect home and got it; dreamed of the
perfect job and got it; dreamed of the problem-free life
and got it.
your pillow has never known tears, your prayers have never
known anguish, and your faith has never known doubt

If you are tearless and fearless and can't understand why others aren't, then this chapter is going to sound like a foreign language.

Why? Because this is a chapter on survival. The next few pages deal with coping with pain. The following paragraphs were not written for those on top of the world, but for those trapped under one that has collapsed. If you can relate to that description, then turn to Matthew and get ready for some assurance.

That may surprise you if you know anything about Matthew 24. You remember it as the neighborhood hangout for end-times fanatics. The camping ground for eschatological mathematicians and last-days prophets.

It deserves that reputation. This section known as the Olivet discourse is Christ's proclamation of the end times. Scholars have dedicated more than one book to this one chapter to answer one question: What is Jesus saying?

Ominous phrases lurk in the chapter: "wars and rumors of wars," "the destroying terror," and "how terrible it will be for women who are pregnant." Eerie descriptions of the sun growing dark and the moon not giving its light. Vultures hovering around bodies and lightning flashing.

How do we explain it?

Some feel the entire chapter is symbolic and mustn't be interpreted literally. Others feel it is a combination of comments equally applied to the destruction of Jerusalem and the return of Christ. Still others state that the chapter has one purpose and that is to prepare us for the final judgment.

We know two things for sure. First, Jesus is preparing his disciples for a cataclysmic future. His words of disaster rang true in A.D. 70 when Jerusalem was brought to her knees by the Romans. His words will ring true again when he comes to reclaim his own and put a period after history.

We also know, however, that cataclysms don't just occur in Jerusalem and at the end of history. Hungry bodies and cold hearts are easily found today. The counsel Jesus gives on surviving tough times is useful for more than the battles of Rome and Armageddon. It is useful for the battles of your world and mine.

So, if you are looking for my prediction of the day Christ will return, sorry. You won't find it here. He hasn't chosen to give us that date, so time spent speculating is time poorly used.

He has chosen, however, to give a manual of survival for lives under siege.

"As Jesus left the Temple and was walking away, his followers came up to show him the Temple's buildings. Jesus asked, 'Do you see all these buildings? I tell you the truth, not one stone will be left on another. Every stone will be thrown down to the ground.'"[1]

It's impossible to overstate the role of the temple in the Jewish mind. The temple was the meeting place between God and man. It represented the atonement, the sacrifice, and the priesthood. It was the structure that represented the heart of the people.

The temple was dazzling; built with white marble and plated with gold. In the sun it shone so bright as to test the eyes. The temple area was surrounded by porches and on these porches were pillars cut out of solid marble in one piece. They were thirty-seven-and-a-half feet high and so thick that three men joining hands could barely encircle one. Archaeologists have found cornerstones from the temple that measure twenty to forty feet in length and weigh more than four hundred tons.[2]

What an impressive sight this must have been for the rural followers of Jesus! Little wonder they were slack-jawed. But more stirring than what they saw was what they heard Jesus say: "I tell you the truth, not one stone will be left on another. Every stone will be thrown down to the ground."

There is pathos in the simple phrase that begins the chapter, "He was walking away from it." Jesus has turned his back on the temple.[3] The one who called for the construction of the temple is walking away from it. The Holy One has abandoned the cherished mountain.

He told them, "The whole thing will come crashing down."[4]

To say the temple would crash was to say the nation would crash. The temple was the people. For over a millennium the temple had been the heart of Israel and now Jesus was saying the heart would break. "Your house will be left completely empty,"[5] he told the Pharisees earlier in the day.

And crash it did. In A.D. 70, Titus, the Roman general, laid siege to the city. Being set on a hill, Jerusalem was difficult to take. So Titus resolved to starve it. The grim horror of the famine is a black day in Jewish history. Let the historian Josephus describe the siege:

> Then did the famine widen in its progress, and devoured people by whole houses and families; the upper rooms were full of women and children that were dying of famine; and the lanes of the city were full of dead bodies of the aged; the children also and young men wandered about the marketplaces like shadows, all swelled with famine and fell down dead wheresoever their misery seized them. . . . The famine confounded all natural passions; for those who were just going to die looked upon those who were gone to their rest before them with dry eyes and open mouths. A deep silence, also, and a kind of deadly night had seized upon the city . . . and every one of them died with their eyes fixed upon the Temple.[6]

A holocaust: 97,000 were taken captive and 1,100,000 were slain. It was this disaster that Jesus foresaw. It was for this disaster that he prepared his disciples. And it is this type of disaster that can strike your world.

Some years ago we took a family vacation to Santa Fe, New Mexico. Denalyn and I decided to be adventurous and ride the rapids of the Rio Grande. We drove to the designated spot and there met the guide and the other courageous tourists.

His instructions were foreboding.

"When you fall in the water . . ." he began.

"And when you find yourself floating in the river . . ."

"And when the boat flips over . . ."

I was beginning to get nervous. I elbowed Denalyn and whispered, "Notice he doesn't say 'if'."

Nor did Jesus. Jesus didn't say, "In this world you may have trouble" or, "In this world there are some who have trouble." No, he assured us, "In this world you will have trouble."[7] If you have a pulse, you will have pain. If you are a person, you will have problems.

In Matthew 24 Jesus prepares his disciples by telling them what will happen.

"Many will come in my name, saying, 'I am the Christ,' and they will fool many people."[8]

"You will hear about wars and stories of wars that are coming, but don't be afraid. These things must happen before the end comes."[9]

"There will be times when there is no food for people to eat, and there will be earthquakes in different places. These things are like the first pains when something new is about to be born."[10]

"Then people will arrest you, hand you over to be hurt, and kill you. They will hate you because you believe in me."[11]

Far from a pep rally, don't you think? More like a last word given by an officer before the soldiers go to battle. More like a lesson Charles Hall would give his demolition team.

Charles Hall blows up bombs for a living. He is a part of the EOD—the Explosive Ordinance Demolition. He is paid $1,500 a week to walk the sands of postwar Kuwait searching for live mines or discarded grenades.

Richard Lowther, another EOD expert, has spent years blowing up some of the thousands of sea mines left over from World Wars I and II. He said, "Every time I pick up the paper and read about a new civil war I think 'Great, as soon as it's over I'll be there.'"[12]

You and I and these EODs have a lot in common: treacherous trails through explosive territories. Problems that lay partly obscured by the sand. A constant threat of losing life or limb.

And most significant, we, like the demolition team, are called to walk through a minefield that we didn't create. Such is the case with many of life's struggles. We didn't create them, but we have to live with them.

We didn't make alcohol, but our highways have drunk drivers. We don't sell drugs, but our neighborhoods have those who do. We didn't create international tension, but we have to fear the terrorists. We didn't train the thieves, but each of us is a potential victim of their greed.

We, like the EODs, are tiptoeing through a minefield that we didn't create.

The disciples were about to do the same. The collapse of the temple wasn't their fault; they weren't to be blamed for the rejection of Christ. It wasn't because of them that Jesus said the "house will be left completely empty," but because they lived in a sinful world they would be victims of sin's consequences.

If you live on a shooting range, chances are you are going to catch a bullet. If you live on a battlefield, a cannonball will likely land in your yard. If you walk through a dark room, you may stub your toe. If you walk through a minefield, you may lose your life.

And if you live in a world darkened by sin, you may be its victim.

Jesus is honest about the life we are called to lead. There is no guarantee that just because we belong to him we will go unscathed. No promise is found in Scripture that says when you follow the king you are exempt from battle. No, often just the opposite is the case.

How do we survive the battle? How do we endure the fray?

Jesus gives three certainties. Three assurances. Three absolutes. Imagine him leaning closer and looking deeply into the wide eyes of the disciples. Knowing the jungle they are about to enter he gives them three compasses that, if used, will keep them on the right trail.

First, assurance of victory: "Those people who keep their faith until the end will be saved."[13]

He doesn't say if you succeed you will be saved. Or if you come out on top you will be saved. He says if you endure. An accurate rendering would be, "If you hang in there until the end . . . if you go the distance."

The Brazilians have a great phrase for this. In Portuguese, a person who has the ability to hang in and not give up has *garra. Garra* means "claws." What imagery! A person with *garra* has claws that burrow into the side of the cliff and keep him from falling.

So do the saved. They may get close to the edge; they may even stumble and slide. But they will dig their nails into the rock of God and hang on.

Jesus gives you this assurance. If you hang on, he'll make sure you get home.

Secondly, Jesus gives the assurance of accomplishment: "The Good News about God's kingdom will be preached in all the world, to every nation."[14]

In 1066 one of the most decisive battles in the history of the world was fought. William, Duke of Normandy, dared to invade England. The English were a formidable opponent anywhere, but next to invincible in their own land.

But William had something the English did not. He had invented a device that gave his army a heavy advantage in battle. He had an edge: the stirrup.

Conventional wisdom of the day was that a horse was too unstable a platform from which to fight. As a result soldiers would ride their horses to the battlefield and then dismount before engaging in combat. But the Norman army, standing secure in their stirrups, were able to ride down the English. They were faster and they were stronger.

The stirrup led to the conquest of England. Without it, William might never have challenged such an enemy. And this book might have been written in Old English.

Because they had a way to stand in the battle, they were victorious after the battle. Jesus' assurance of victory was daring. Look at his listeners: upcountry fishermen and laborers whose eyes bug at the sight of a big city. You'd have been hard-pressed to find anyone who would wage that the prophecy would come to pass.

But it did, just fifty-three days later. Fifty-three days later, Jews were in Jerusalem from "every country in the world."[15] Peter stood before them and told them about Jesus.

The disciples were emboldened with the assurance that the task would be completed. Because they had a way to stand in the battle, they were victorious after the battle. They had an edge . . . and so do we.

Lastly, Jesus gives us assurance of completion: "Then the end will come."[16]

An intriguing verse is found in 1 Thessalonians 4:16, "The Lord himself will come down from heaven with a loud command."

Have you ever wondered what that command will be? It will be the inaugural word of heaven. It will be the first audible message most have heard from God. It will be the word that closes one age and opens a new one.

I think I know what the command will be. I could very well be wrong, but I think the command that puts an end to the pains of the earth and initiates the joys of heaven will be two words:

"No more."

The King of kings will raise his pierced hand and proclaim, "No more."

The angels will stand and the Father will speak, "No more."

Every person who lives and who ever lived will turn toward the sky and hear God announce, "No more."

No more loneliness.

No more tears.

No more death. No more sadness. No more crying. No more pain.

As John sat on the Island of Patmos, surrounded by sea and separated from friends, he dreamed of the day when God would say, "No more."

This same disciple who, over a half a century before, had heard Jesus speak these words of assurance now knew what they meant. I wonder if he could hear the voice of Jesus in his memory.

"The end will come."

For those who live for this world, that's bad news. But for those who live for the world to come, it's an encouraging promise.

You're in a mine field, my friend, and it's only a matter of time: "For in this world you will have trouble. . . ." Next time you are tossed into a river as you ride the rapids of life, remember his words of assurance.

> *Those who endure will be saved.*
> *The gospel will be preached.*
> *The end will come.*

You can count on it.

CHAPTER 17

SAND CASTLE
STORIES

"They knew nothing about what was happening."
MATTHEW 24:39

Hot sun. Salty air. Rhythmic waves.

A little boy is on the beach. On his knees he scoops and packs the sand with plastic shovels into a bright-red bucket. Then he upends the bucket on the surface and lifts it. And, to the delight of the little architect, a castle tower is created.

All afternoon he will work. Spooning out the moat. Packing the walls. Bottle tops will be sentries. Popsicle sticks will be bridges. A sand castle will be built.

———

Big city. Busy streets. Rumbling traffic.

A man is in his office. At his desk he shuffles papers into stacks and delegates assignments. He cradles the phone on his shoulder and punches the keyboard with his fingers. Numbers are juggled and contracts are signed and much to the delight of the man, a profit is made.

All his life he will work. Formulating the plans. Forecasting the future. Annuities will be sentries. Capital gains will be bridges. An empire will be built.

———

Two builders of two castles. They have much in common. They shape granules into grandeurs. They see nothing and make something. They are diligent and determined. And for both the tide will rise and the end will come.

Yet that is where the similarities cease. For the boy sees the end while the man ignores it. Watch the boy as the dusk approaches. Each wave slaps an inch closer to his creation. Every crest crashes closer than the one before.

But the boy doesn't panic. He is not surprised. All day the pounding waves have reminded him that the end is inevitable. He knows the secret of the surging. Soon they will come and take his castle into the deep.

The man, however, doesn't know the secret. He should. He, like the boy, lives surrounded by rhythmic reminders. Days come and go. Seasons ebb and flow. Every sunrise that becomes a sunset whispers the secret, "Time will take your castles."

So, one is prepared and one isn't. One is peaceful while the other panics.

As the waves near, the wise child jumps to his feet and begins to clap. There is no sorrow. No fear. No regret. He knew this would happen. He is not surprised. And when the great breaker crashes into his castle and his masterpiece is sucked into the sea, he smiles. He smiles, picks up his tools, takes his father's hand, and goes home.

The grownup, however, is not so wise. As the wave of years collapses on his castle he is terrified. He hovers over the sandy monument to protect it. He blocks the waves from the walls he has made. Salt-water soaked and shivering, he snarls at the incoming tide.

"It's my castle," he defies.

The ocean need not respond. Both know to whom the sand belongs.

Finally the cliff of water mounts high above the man and his little empire. For just a moment he is shadowed by the wall of water . . . then it crashes. His tiny towers of triumph crumble and disperse and he is left on his knees . . . clutching muddy handfuls of yesterday.

If only he had known. If only he had listened. If only . . .

But he, like most, never listens.

Jesus describes these people, the unprepared, by saying they know nothing about what will happen. They aren't cruel. They aren't rebellious or angry at God.

But they are blind. They don't see the setting sun. And they are deaf. They don't hear the pounding waves.

During the last week of his life, Jesus took valuable time to tell us to learn the lesson of the waves and prepare for the end.

Remember, the reason we are studying the last week of Christ is to see what is on his heart. Hear what he says. See who he touches. Witness what he does. We've seen his compassion for the forgotten. We've seen his contempt for the fake. Now a third passion surfaces—his concern for our readiness. "No one knows when that day or time will be, not the angels in heaven, not even the Son. Only the Father knows."[1]

His message is unmistakable: He will return, but no one knows when. So, be ready.

It's the message of the parable of the virgins.[2]

It's the message of the parable of the talents.[3]

It's the message of the parable of the sheep and the goats.[4]

It's a message we must heed.

But it is a message often ignored.

I was reminded of this not long ago when I boarded a plane. I walked down the aisle, found my seat, and sat down next to a strange sight.

The man seated next to me was in a robe and slippers. He was dressed for the living room, not for a journey. His seat was odd, too. Whereas my seat was the cloth type you normally see, his was fine leather.

"Imported," he said, when he noticed I was looking. "Bought it in Argentina and put it on myself."

Before I could speak he pointed to some inlaid stones in the armrest. "The rubies I purchased in Africa. They cost me a fortune."

That was only the beginning. His fold-down table was of mahogany. There was a portable TV installed next to the window. A tiny ceiling fan and globed light hung above us.

I had never seen anything like it.

My question was the obvious one, "Why did you spend so much time and expense on an airline seat?"

"I live here," he explained. "I make my home on the plane."

"You never get off?"

"Never! How could I deboard and leave such comfort?"

Incredible. The man made a home out of a mode of transportation. He made a residence out of a journey. Hard to believe? You think I'm stretching the truth? Well, maybe I haven't seen such foolishness in a plane, but I have in life. And so have you.

You've seen people treat this world as if it was a permanent home. It's not. You've seen people pour time and energy into life as though it will last forever. It won't. You've seen people so proud of what they have done that they hope they will never have to leave—they will.

We all will. We are in transit. Someday the plane will stop and the deboarding will begin.

Wise are those who are ready when the pilot says to get off.

I don't know much, but I do know how to travel. Carry little. Eat light. Take a nap. And get off when you reach the city.

And I don't know much about sand castles. But children do. Watch them and learn. Go ahead and build, but build with a child's heart. When the sun sets and the tides take—applaud. Salute the process of life, take your father's hand, and go home.

CHAPTER 18

BE READY

*"So always be ready,
because you don't know the day your Lord will come."*
MATTHEW 24:42

There is a secret to wearing a vest.

It's a secret every father should tell his son. It's one of those manly things that has to be passed down from generation to generation. It rates up there with teaching your son to shave and use deodorant. It's a secret every vest wearer must know. If you own a vest, I hope you know it. If you own a vest and don't know it, here it is: Button the first button correctly.

Take your time. Don't be in a rush. Look carefully in the mirror and then match the right button with the right hole.

If you do, if you get the first button buttoned right, then the rest will follow suit (excuse the pun). If, however, you don't get the first button right, every button thereafter will be buttoned incorrectly. The result will be a lopsided vest. Put the second button in the top hole or slide the second hole over the top button and, well, it just won't work.

There are certain things in life done only one way. Buttoning a vest is one of them.

Being ready is another.

According to Jesus, being ready for his return is a vest-button principle. According to Jesus, start wrong on this first move and the rest of your life will be cockeyed.

Not everything is a vest-button truth. The church you attend isn't. The Bible translation you read isn't. The ministry you select isn't. But being ready for Jesus' return is a vest-button truth. Get this right and the rest will fall into place. Miss it and get ready for some wrinkles.

How do we know this is a vest-button principle? Jesus told us. According to Matthew, Jesus told us in the last sermon he ever preached.

It may surprise you that Jesus made preparedness the theme of his last sermon. It did me. I would have preached on love or family or the importance of church. Jesus didn't. Jesus preached on what many today consider to be old-fashioned. He preached on being ready for heaven and staying out of hell.

It's his message when he tells of the wise and the foolish servants.[1] The wise one was ready for the return of the master; the foolish one was not.

It's his message when he tells about the ten bridesmaids. Five were wise and five were foolish.[2] The wise ones were ready when the groom came and the foolish ones were at the corner store looking for more oil.

It's his message when he tells of the three servants and the bags of gold.[3] Two servants put the money to work and made more money for the master. The third hid his in a hole. The first two were ready and rewarded when the master returned. The third was unprepared and punished.

Be ready. It's a first-step, nonnegotiable, vest-button principle.

That is the theme of Jesus' last sermon, "So always be ready, because you don't know the day your Lord will come."[4] He didn't tell when the day of the Lord would be, but he did describe what the day would be like. It's a day no one will miss.

Every person who has ever lived will be present at that final gathering. Every heart that has ever beat. Every mouth that has ever spoken. On that day you will be surrounded by a sea of people. Rich, poor. Famous, unknown. Kings, bums. Brilliant, demented. All will be present. And all will be looking in one direction. All will be looking at him. Every human being.

"The Son of Man will come again in his great glory."[5]

You won't look at anyone else. No side glances to see what others are wearing. No whispers about new jewelry or comments about who is present. At this, the greatest gathering in history, you will have eyes for only one—the Son of Man. Wrapped in splendor. Shot through with radiance. Imploded with light and magnetic in power.

Jesus describes this day with certainty.

He leaves no room for doubt. He doesn't say he may return, or might return, but that he *will* return. By the way, one-twentieth of your New Testament speaks about his return. There are over three hundred references to his second coming. Twenty-three of the twenty-seven New Testament books speak of it. And they speak of it with confidence.

"You also must be ready, because the Son of Man will come at a time you don't expect him."[6]

". . . Jesus, who has been taken from you into heaven, will come back in the same way you have seen him go into heaven."[7]

". . . he will come a second time, not to offer himself for sin, but to bring salvation to those who are waiting for him."[8]

". . . the day of the Lord will come like a thief in the night."[9]

His return is certain.

His return is final.

Upon his return "he will separate them into two groups as a shepherd separates the sheep from the goats. The Son of Man will put the sheep on his right and the goats on his left."[10]

The word *separate* is a sad word. To separate a mother from a daughter, a father from a son, a husband from a wife. To separate people on earth is sorrowful, but to think of it being done for eternity is horrible.

Especially when one group is destined for heaven and the other group is going to hell.

We don't like to talk about hell, do we? In intellectual circles the topic of hell is regarded as primitive and foolish. It's not logical. "A loving God wouldn't send people to hell." So we dismiss it.

But to dismiss it is to dismiss a core teaching of Jesus. The doctrine of hell is not one developed by Paul, Peter, or John. It is taught by Jesus himself.

And to dismiss it is to dismiss much more. It is to dismiss the presence of a loving God and the privilege of a free choice. Let me explain.

We are free either to love God or not. He invites us to love him. He urges us to love him. He came that we might love him. But, in the end, the choice is yours and mine. To take that choice from each of us, for him to force us to love him, would be less than love.

God explains the benefits, outlines the promises, and articulates very clearly the consequences. And then, in the end, he leaves the choice to us.

Hell was not prepared for people. Hell "was prepared for the devil and his angels."[11] For a person to go to hell, then, is for a person to go against God's intended destiny. "God has not destined us to the terrors of judgment, but to the full attainment of salvation through our Lord Jesus Christ."[12] Hell is man's choice, not God's choice.

Consider, then, this explanation of hell: Hell is the chosen place of the person who loves self more than God, who loves sin more than his Savior, who loves this world more than God's world. Judgment is that moment when God looks at the rebellious and says, "Your choice will be honored."

To reject the dualistic outcome of history and say there is no hell leaves gaping holes in any banner of a just God. To say there is no hell is to say God condones the rebellious, unrepentant heart. To say there is no hell is to portray God with eyes blind to the hunger and evil in the world. To say there is no hell is to say that God doesn't care that people are beaten and massacred, that he doesn't care that women are raped or families wrecked. To say there is no hell is to say God has no justice, no sense of right and wrong, and eventually to say God has no love. For true love hates what is evil.

Hell is the ultimate expression of a just Creator.

The parables of the wise and loyal servant, the wise and foolish bridesmaids, and loyal and wicked servants, all point to the same conclusion: "Everyone must die once and be judged."[13] *Eternity is to be taken seriously.* A judgment is coming.

Our task on earth is singular—to choose our eternal home. You can afford many wrong choices in life. You can choose the wrong career and survive, the wrong city and survive, the wrong house and survive. You can even choose the wrong mate and survive. But there is one choice that must be made correctly and that is your eternal destiny.

It's interesting that Jesus' first and last sermons have the same message. In his first sermon, the Sermon on the Mount, Jesus calls you and me to choose between the rock and the sand,[14] the wide gate and the narrow gate, the wide road and the narrow road, the big crowd and the small crowd, the certainty of hell and the joy of heaven.[15] In his last sermon he calls us to do the same. He calls us to be ready.

While on one of his expeditions to the Antarctic, Sir Ernest Shackleton left some of his men on Elephant Island with the intent of returning for them and carrying them back to England. But he was delayed. By the time he could go back for them the sea had frozen and he had no access to the island. Three times he tried to reach them, but was prevented by the ice. Finally, on his fourth try, he broke through and found a narrow channel.

Much to his surprise, he found the crewmen waiting for him,

supplies packed and ready to board. They were soon on their way back to England. He asked them how they knew to be ready for him. They told him they didn't know when he would return, but they were sure he would. So every morning, the leader rolled up his bag and packed his gear and told the crew to do the same saying, "Get your things ready, boys. The boss may come today."[16]

The crew leader did his crew a favor by keeping them prepared.

Jesus has done us a service by urging us to do the same: Be ready. It's a vest-button principle. Get that one buttoned right today. For you don't want to be fumbling with buttons in the presence of God.

THE PEOPLE WITH
THE ROSES

"Anything you did for even the least of my people here,
you also did for me."
MATTHEW 25:40

John Blanchard stood up from the bench, straightened his Army
uniform, and studied the crowd of people making their way
through Grand Central Station. He looked for the girl whose
heart he knew, but whose face he didn't, the girl with the rose.

His interest in her had begun thirteen months before in a Florida
library. Taking a book off the shelf he found himself intrigued, not
with the words of the book, but with the notes penciled in the mar-
gin. The soft handwriting reflected a thoughtful soul and insightful
mind. In the front of the book, he discovered the previous owner's
name, Miss Hollis Maynell.

With time and effort he located her address. She lived in New
York City. He wrote her a letter introducing himself and inviting her
to correspond. The next day he was shipped overseas for service in
World War II. During the next year and one month the two grew to
know each other through the mail. Each letter was a seed falling on a
fertile heart. A romance was budding.

Blanchard requested a photograph, but she refused. She felt that if he really cared, it wouldn't matter what she looked like.

When the day finally came for him to return from Europe, they scheduled their first meeting—7:00 P.M. at the Grand Central Station in New York. "You'll recognize me," she wrote, "by the red rose I'll be wearing on my lapel."

So at 7:00 he was in the station looking for a girl whose heart he loved, but whose face he'd never seen.

I'll let Mr. Blanchard tell you what happened.

A young woman was coming toward me, her figure long and slim. Her blonde hair lay back in curls from her delicate ears; her eyes were blue as flowers. Her lips and chin had a gentle firmness, and in her pale green suit she was like springtime come alive. I started toward her, entirely forgetting to notice that she was not wearing a rose. As I moved, a small, provocative smile curved her lips. "Going my way, sailor?" she murmured.

Almost uncontrollably I made one step closer to her, and then I saw Hollis Maynell.

She was standing almost directly behind the girl. A woman well past 40, she had graying hair tucked under a worn hat. She was more than plump, her thick-ankled feet thrust into low-heeled shoes. The girl in the green suit was walking quickly away. I felt as though I was split in two, so keen was my desire to follow her, and yet so deep was my longing for the woman whose spirit had truly companioned me and upheld my own.

And there she stood. Her pale, plump face was gentle and sensible, her gray eyes had a warm and kindly twinkle. I did not hesitate. My finger gripped the small worn blue leather copy of the book that was to identify me to her. This would not be love, but it would be something precious, something perhaps even better than love, a friendship for which I had been and must ever be grateful.

I squared my shoulders and saluted and held out the book to the woman, even though while I spoke I felt choked by the bitterness of my disappointment. "I'm Lieutenant John Blanchard, and you must be Miss Maynell. I am so glad you could meet me; may I take you to dinner?"

The woman's face broadened into a tolerant smile. "I don't know what this is about, son," she answered, "but the young lady in the green suit who just went by, she begged me to wear this rose on my coat. And she said if you were to ask me out to dinner, I should go and tell you that she is waiting for you in the big restaurant across the street. She said it was some kind of test!"[1]

It's not difficult to understand and admire Miss Maynell's wisdom. The true nature of a heart is seen in its response to the unattractive. "Tell me whom you love," Houssaye wrote, "and I will tell you who you are."

Hollis Maynell, however, is far from the first person to gauge a heart by a person's concern for the undesirable.

In the last sermon recorded by Matthew, Jesus does exactly that. He does it not with a parable, but with a description. He doesn't tell a story, but he describes a scene—the last scene, the final judgment. In his final discourse, he puts into words the very message he has put into actions, "Love for the least."

We saw in the last chapter the significance of the final judgment. We saw its certainty—there is no doubt as to Jesus' return. We saw its totality—everyone will be there. And we saw its finality—for on that day Jesus will separate the sheep from the goats, the good from the wicked.

On what basis will he make his selection? The answer may surprise you. "I was hungry, and you gave me food. I was thirsty, and you gave me something to drink. I was alone and away from home, and you invited me into your house. I was without clothes, and you gave me something to wear. I was sick, and you cared for me. I was in prison, and you visited me."[2]

What is the sign of the saved? Their scholarship? Their willingness to go to foreign lands? Their ability to amass an audience and preach? Their skillful pens and hope-filled volumes? Their great miracles? No.

The sign of the saved is their love for the least.

Those put on the right hand of God will be those who gave food to the hungry, drink to the thirsty, warmth to the lonely, clothing to the naked, comfort to the sick, and friendship to the imprisoned.

The sign of the saved is their love for the least.

Did you note how simple the works are? Jesus doesn't say, "I was sick and you healed me. . . . I was in prison and you liberated me. . . . I was lonely and you built a retirement home for me. . . ." He doesn't say, "I was thirsty and you gave me spiritual counsel."

No fanfare. No hoopla. No media coverage. Just good people doing good things.

For when we do good things to others we do good things to God.

When Francis of Asissi turned his back on wealth to seek God in simplicity, he stripped naked and walked out of the city. He soon encountered a leper on the side of the road. He passed him, then stopped and went back and embraced the diseased man. Francis then continued on his journey. After a few steps he turned to look again at the leper, but no one was there.

For the rest of his life, he believed the leper was Jesus Christ. He may have been right.

Jesus lives in the forgotten. He has taken up residence in the ignored. He has made a mansion amid the ill. If we want to see God, we must go among the broken and beaten and there we will see him.

"He rewards those who truly want to find him,"[3] is the promise.

"Anything you did for even the least of my people here, you also did for me,"[4] is the plan.

Perhaps you read about the fellow in Philadelphia who went to the flea market and found a frame he liked. It was only a couple of bucks, this dusty print of a country church. It was torn and faded, but the guy liked the frame so he bought it.

When he got home he opened it up and out tumbled a neatly folded sheet of paper. It was the Declaration of Independence. What everyone had thought was a two-dollar painting at a flea market actually contained one of the original one hundred copies of the Declaration of Independence printed on July 4, 1776.[5]

Valuable surprises are discovered in unlikely sources. True in flea markets and true in life. Make an investment in the people the world has cast off—the homeless, the AIDS patient, the orphan, the divorcee—and you may discover the source of your independence.

Jesus' message is stirring: "The way you treat them is the way you treat me."

Of all the teachings during the last week of Christ, this one is for me the most penetrating. I wish he hadn't said what he said. I wish he'd said that the sign of the saved is the books they have written, for I've written several. I wish he'd said the sign of the saved was the numbers of sermons they've preached, for I've preached hundreds. I wish he'd said the sign of the saved was the audiences they've amassed, for I've spoken to thousands.

But he didn't. His words reminded me that the person who sees Christ is the one who sees the hurting person. To see Jesus, go to the convalescent home, sit down beside the elderly woman, and steady her hand as she puts the spoon in her mouth. To see Jesus, go to the community hospital and ask the nurse to take you to see one who has received no visits. To see Jesus, leave your office and go down the hall and talk to the man who is regretting his divorce and missing his children. To see Jesus, go to the inner city and give a sandwich—not a sermon, but a sandwich—to the bag lady who's made a home out of an overpass.

To see Jesus . . . see the unattractive and forgotten.

You might say it is a test. A test to measure the depth of our character. The same kind of test Hollis Maynell used with John Blanchard. The rejected of the world wear the roses. Sometimes we, like John Blanchard, have to adjust our expectations. Sometimes we have to re-examine our motives.

Had he turned his back on the unattractive, he would have missed the love of his life.

If we turn our backs, we will miss even more.

CHAPTER 20

SERVED BY THE BEST

*"The master will dress himself to serve and tell
the servants to sit at the table,
and he will serve them."*
LUKE 12:37

Let's suppose something really crazy happened. Let's suppose you were invited to a dinner with the president.

There you are stacking dishes in the kitchen of the restaurant where you work the evening shift when a courier arrives at the back door.

"The owner won't be back until tomorrow," you tell him.

"I'm not looking for the owner, I'm looking for you."

"Huh?"

"I'm from the White House," he says, which explains the dark suit and briefcase.

"Are you for real?" You look twice at him and once behind him as he opens his case.

"I came to deliver this letter."

Part of you wonders what you've done wrong. Another part of you wonders if this isn't a joke your cousin Alfred is playing to get back at you for the horseradish in his car. And all of you thinks this guy has the wrong guy.

But you dry your hands on your apron and take the letter. It's a personal letter. There is an emblem on the envelope and your name is written, not typed, in cursive.

The stationery is the heavy, expensive type that blows the Cousin Alfred theory; he's too cheap to buy this. It couldn't be a bill; collectors aren't this formal. You open the letter and, well, how-do-you-do, it's a letter from the president of the United States of America.

You look up at the fellow who brought it and he's smiling as though this is the part of his job he likes the best.

You look around in the kitchen for somebody to show it to but you're alone. You think about running into the restaurant and sharing it with Alma the waitress, but you can't because you are too curious to wait. So you read the letter.

It's an invitation—an invitation to a dinner. A state dinner. A dinner given in your honor. A dinner dedicated to you.

Your ex threw you a surprise party during the first year of your marriage, but besides that you can't remember when someone has had a dinner for you. Not the kids. Not the neighbors. Not your boss . . . you don't even know if you've ever given yourself a dinner in your honor.

And now the commander in chief wants to.

"What's the catch?" you ask.

"No catch, just a request that you come to the White House. May I give the president your response?"

"Huh?"

"May I give the president your answer? Can you come to the dinner?"

"Well, of cuh-cuh-course. I'd love to go."

And so you go. On the appointed night, you put on your best and you go to Pennsylvania Avenue. You are met out front by more black suits who escort you in. Inside the doors a garcon of sorts takes over.

Your steps echo as you follow the tuxedoed guide down the tall hall lined with portraits of past presidents.

At the end of the corridor is the banquet room. In the center of the room is a long table and in the center of the table is one plate and beside the plate is one name—yours.

The attendant motions for you to sit and when you do he leaves and you do the thing you've wanted to do since you stepped in to the residence. You look around you and say, "Wow."

You've never seen a table this long. You've never seen crystal this nice. You've never seen china this valuable. You've never seen a setting with so many forks or a candelabra with so many candles.

"Wow."

Under your feet is an Oriental rug. Probably came from China. Over your head is a chandelier with a billion pieces of glass. *I bet it's German.* The table and chairs are made of polished teak. *Indian, no doubt.*

Straight ahead is a hearth with a fire and a white mantel. Above the mantel is a painting—a painting of, gulp, a painting of you! That's you up there. Same eyes, same goofy smile, same nose you wish was half the size—that's you!

"Wow."

"I keep it in here so I can remember you."

The voice from behind startles you. You don't have to turn and look to see who it is—-there is only one voice like his. You wait until he is right beside you before you look up. You know he's there because he places his hand on your shoulder.

You turn and look and there he is, the president. A bit shorter than you imagined, but every bit as authoritative. The square jaw. The deep eyes. The high cheeks. The gray suit. The red tie. The apron.

The what?

The president is wearing an apron! A common kitchen apron just like the one you wear when you work.

And, as if that isn't enough, behind him is a dinner cart. He reaches for your bread plate and gives you a dinner roll. "I'm so glad you could come and be my guest."

You know you should say something but what you were going to say is forgotten somewhere between the last "Wow" you said and the first *What's going on here* you thought.

You thought it was shocking to get the invitation. You thought it was breathtaking to see the White House. Your jaw hit the floor when you saw your picture on the wall. But all of that was nothing compared to this.

The commander in chief as a waiter? The president serving you food? The chief executive bringing wine and bread to your table? All those neatly prepared compliments and carefully rehearsed accolades are forgotten and you blurt out what is really on your mind: "Wait a minute. This isn't right. You aren't supposed to be doing this—I am. You aren't supposed to be serving me. I'm the dishwasher. I work at the diner. You're the top dog. Let me have the apron and let me put the food on the table, . . . sir."

But he won't let you. "Keep your seat," he insists. "Today I honor you."

I warned you this was a crazy story. This kind of stuff doesn't happen . . . or does it?

It does for those who see it. For those aware of it, it happens every week. In banquet halls around the world the commander honors the common. There they are—regular folk right out of the kitchens and carpools of life, seated at the chief's table.

The honored guests. VIPs. Hosted and served by the one in charge of history.

"This is my body," he says as he breaks the bread.

And you thought it was a ritual. You thought it was just an observance. You thought it was a memorial to something that was done back then. You thought it was a reenactment of a meal he had with them.

It is so much more.

It is a meal he has with you.

When I was a young boy I was a part of a church corps that took communion to the shut-ins and hospitalized. We visited those who were unable to come to church but still desired to pray and partake of communion.

I must have been ten or eleven years of age when we went to one hospital room that housed an elderly gentleman who was very weak. He was asleep, so we tried to wake him. We couldn't. We shook him, we spoke to him, we tapped him on the shoulder, but we couldn't stir him.

We hated to leave without performing our duty, but we didn't know what to do.

One of the young guys with me observed that even though the man was asleep his mouth was open. Why not? we said. So we prayed over the cracker and stuck a piece on his tongue. Then we prayed over the grape juice and poured it down his mouth.

He never woke up.

Neither do many today. For some, communion is a sleepy hour in which wafers are eaten and juice is drunk and the soul never stirs. It wasn't intended to be as such.

It was intended to be an I-can't-believe-it's-me-pinch-me-I'm-dreaming invitation to sit at God's table and be served by the King himself.

When you read Matthew's account of the Last Supper, one incredible truth surfaces. Jesus is the person behind it all. It was Jesus who selected the place, designated the time, and set the meal in order. "The chosen time is near. I will have the Passover with my followers at your house."[1]

And at the Supper, Jesus is not a guest, but the host. "And [Jesus] gave to the disciples." The subject of the verbs is the message of the event: "He took . . . he blessed . . . he broke . . . he gave. . . ."

And at the Supper, Jesus is not the served, but the servant. It is Jesus who, during the Supper, put on the garb of a servant and washed the disciples' feet.[2]

Jesus is the most active one at the table. Jesus is not portrayed as the one who reclines and receives, but as the one who stands and gives.

He still does. The Lord's Supper is a gift to you. The Lord's Supper is a sacrament,[3] not a sacrifice.[4]

Often, we think of the Supper as a performance, a time when we are on stage and God is the audience. A ceremony in which we do the work and he does the watching. That's not how it was intended. If it was, Jesus would have taken his seat at the table and relaxed.[5]

That's not what he did. He, instead, fulfilled his role as a rabbi by guiding his disciples through the Passover. He fulfilled his role as a servant by washing their feet. And he fulfilled his role as a Savior by granting them forgiveness of sins.

He was in charge. He was on center stage. He was the person behind and in the moment.

And he still is.

It is the Lord's table you sit at. It is the Lord's Supper you eat. Just as Jesus prayed for his disciples, Jesus begs God for us.[6] When you are called to the table, it might be an emissary who gives the letter, but it is Jesus who wrote it.

It is a holy invitation. A sacred sacrament bidding you to leave the chores of life and enter his splendor.

He meets you at the table.

And when the bread is broken, Christ breaks it. When the wine is poured, Christ pours it. And when your burdens are lifted, it is because the King in the apron has drawn near.

Think about that the next time you go to the table.

One last thought.

What happens on earth is just a warm-up for what will happen in heaven.[7] So the next time the messenger calls you to the table, drop what you are doing and go. Be blessed and be fed and, most importantly, be sure you're still eating at his table when he calls us home.

HE CHOSE YOU

"Sit here while I go over there and pray. . . .
My soul is overwhelmed with sorrow to the point of death."
MATTHEW 26:36, 38 NIV

"I pray for these followers, but I am also praying for all those
who will believe in me because of their teaching."
JOHN 17:20

Thursday night. Midnight.

The week has been full of finalities. The final visit to the temple. The final sermon. The final supper. And now, the most emotional hour of the week, the final prayer.

The garden is in shadows. The olive trees are knotted and gnarled. They twist five or six feet into the sky. Roots sprawl from the trunks and claw deeply into the rocky soil.

The spring moon casts the garden in silver. Constellations sparkle against the black velvet of the night sky. Fleets of clouds float. A breeze cools. Insects sing. Leaves stir.

That's him. Jesus. In the grove. On the ground. The young man. The one in the sweat-soaked garment. Kneeling. Imploring. His hair is plastered to his wet forehead. He agonizes.

A sound is heard in the trees. Snoring. Jesus looks across the garden at the dearest friends he has—they are asleep. They lean against the broad trunks and slumber. His yearnings don't stir them. His distress doesn't move them. They are tired.

He stands and walks through the shadowed trees and squats before them. "Please," he asks, "please just stay awake with me."

The Lord of the universe doesn't want to be alone.

He can understand their weariness, though. He has given them more in the last few hours than they could possibly grasp. Never had the apostles known Jesus to talk so much. Never had they seen him speak with such urgency. His words were fervent, fiery.

———

Thursday night . . . a few hours earlier.

It's nearly midnight when they leave the upper room and descend through the streets of the city. They pass the Lower Pool and exit the Fountain Gate and walk out of Jerusalem. The roads are lined with the fires and tents of Passover pilgrims. Most are asleep, heavied with the evening meal. Those still awake think little of the band of men walking the chalky road.

They pass through the valley and ascend the path that will take them to Gethsemane. The road is steep so they stop to rest. Somewhere within the city walls the twelfth apostle darts down a street. His feet have been washed by the man he will betray. His heart has been claimed by the Evil One he has heard. He runs to find Caiaphas.

The final encounter of the battle has begun.

As Jesus looks at the city of Jerusalem, he sees what the disciples can't. It is here, on the outskirts of Jerusalem, that the battle will end. He sees the staging of Satan. He sees the dashing of the demons. He sees the Evil One preparing for the final encounter. The enemy lurks as a specter over the hour. Satan, the host of hatred, has seized the heart of Judas and whispered in the ear of Caiaphas. Satan, the master of death, has opened the caverns and prepared to receive the source of light.

Hell is breaking loose.

History records it as a battle of the Jews against Jesus. It wasn't. It was a battle of God against Satan.

And Jesus knew it. He knew that before the war was over, he would be taken captive. He knew that before victory would come defeat. He knew that before the throne would come the cup. He knew that before the light of Sunday would come the blackness of Friday.

And he is afraid.

He turns and begins the final ascent to the garden. When he reaches the entry he stops and turns his eyes toward his circle of friends. It will be the last time he sees them before they abandon him. He knows what they will do when the soldiers come. He knows their betrayal is only minutes away.

But he doesn't accuse. He doesn't lecture. Instead, he prays. His last moments with his disciples are in prayer. And the words he speaks are as eternal as the stars that hear them.

Imagine, for a moment, yourself in this situation. Your final hour with a son about to be sent overseas. Your last moments with your dying spouse. One last visit with your parent. What do you say? What do you do? What words do you choose?

It's worth noting that Jesus chose prayer. He chose to pray for us. "I pray for these men. But I am also praying for all people who will believe in me because of the teaching of these men. Father, I pray that all people who believe in me can be one. . . . I pray that these people can also be one in us, so that the world will believe that you sent me."[1]

You need to note that in this final prayer, Jesus prayed for you. You need to underline in red and highlight in yellow his love: "I am also praying for all people who will believe in me because of the teaching." That is you. As Jesus stepped into the garden, you were in his prayers. As Jesus looked into heaven, you were in his vision. As Jesus dreamed of the day when we will be where he is, he saw you there.

His final prayer was about you. His final pain was for you. His final passion was you.

He then turns, steps into the garden, and invites Peter, James, and John to come. He tells them his soul is "overwhelmed with sorrow to the point of death," and begins to pray.

Never has he felt so alone. What must be done, only he can do. An angel can't do it. No angel has the power to break open hell's gates. A man can't do it. No man has the purity to destroy sin's claim. No force on earth can face the force of evil and win—except God.

"The spirit is willing, but the flesh is weak," Jesus confesses.

His humanity begged to be delivered from what his divinity could see. Jesus, the carpenter, implores. Jesus, the man, peers into the dark pit and begs, "Can't there be another way?"

Did he know the answer before he asked the question? Did his human heart hope his heavenly father had found another way? We don't know. But we do know he asked to get out. We do know he begged for an exit. We do know there was a time when, if he could have, he would have turned his back on the whole mess and gone away.

But he couldn't.

He couldn't because he saw you. Right there in the middle of a world that isn't fair. He saw you cast into a river of life you didn't request. He saw you betrayed by those you love. He saw you with a body that gets sick and a heart that grows weak.

He saw you in your own garden of gnarled trees and sleeping friends. He saw you staring into the pit of your own failures and the mouth of your own grave.

He saw you in your Garden of Gethsemane—and he didn't want you to be alone.

He wanted you to know that he has been there too. He knows what it's like to be plotted against. He knows what it's like to be confused. He knows what it's like to be torn between two desires. He knows what it's like to smell the stench of Satan. And, perhaps most of all, he knows what it's like to beg God to change his mind and to hear God say so gently, but firmly, "No."

For that is what God says to Jesus. And Jesus accepts the answer. At some moment during that midnight hour an angel of mercy comes over the weary body of the man in the garden. As he stands, the anguish is gone from his eyes. His fist will clench no more. His heart will fight no more.

The battle is won. You may have thought it was won on Golgotha. It wasn't. You may have thought the sign of victory is the empty tomb. It isn't. The final battle was won in Gethsemane. And the sign of conquest is Jesus at peace in the olive trees.

For it was in the garden that he made his decision. He would rather go to hell for you than go to heaven without you.

CHAPTER 22

WHEN YOUR WORLD TURNS AGAINST YOU

"In the future you will see the Son of Man sitting at the right hand of God."
MATTHEW 26:64

Get up, we must go. Here comes the man who has turned against me."[1]

The words were spoken to Judas. But they could have been spoken to anyone. They could have been spoken to John, to Peter, to James. They could have been spoken to Thomas, to Andrew, to Nathanael. They could have been spoken to the Roman soldiers, to the Jewish leaders. They could have been spoken to Pilate, to Herod, to Caiaphas. They could have been spoken to every person who praised him last Sunday but abandoned him tonight.

Everyone turned against Jesus that night. Everyone.

Judas did. What was your motive, Judas? Why did you do it? Were you trying to call his hand? Did you want the money? Were you seeking some attention? And why, dear Judas, why did it have to be a kiss? You could have pointed. You could have just called his name. But you put your lips to his cheek and kissed. A snake kills with his mouth.

The people did. The crowd turned on Jesus. We wonder who was in the crowd. Who were the bystanders? Matthew just says they were people. Regular folks like you and me with bills to pay and kids to raise and jobs to do. Individually they never would have turned on Jesus, but collectively they wanted to kill him. Even the instantaneous healing of an amputated ear didn't sway them. They suffered from mob blindness. They blocked each other's vision of Jesus.

The disciples did. "All of Jesus' followers left him and ran away."[2] Matthew must have written those words slowly. He was in that group. All the disciples were. Jesus told them they would scamper. They vowed they wouldn't. But they did. When the choice came between their skin and their friend, they chose to run. Oh, they stood for a while. Peter even pulled his sword, went for the neck, and got a lobe. But their courage was as fleeting as their feet. When they saw Jesus was going down, they got out.

The religious leaders did. Not surprising. Disappointing, though. They are the spiritual leaders of the nation. Men entrusted with the dispensing of goodness. Role models for the children. The pastors and Bible teachers of the community. "The leading priests and the whole Jewish council tried to find something false against Jesus so they could kill him."[3] Paint that passage black with injustice. Paint the arrest green with jealousy. Paint that scene red with innocent blood.

And paint Peter in a corner. For that's where he is. No place to go. Caught in his own mistake. Peter did exactly what he had said he wouldn't do. He had promised fervently only hours before, "Everyone else may stumble in their faith because of you, but I will not!" I hope Peter was hungry, because he ate those words.

Everyone turned against Jesus.

Though the kiss was planted by Judas, the betrayal was committed by all. Every person took a step, but no one took a stand. As Jesus left the garden he walked alone. The world had turned against him. He was betrayed.

Betray. The word is an eighth of an inch above *betroth* in the dictionary, but a world from *betroth* in life. It's a weapon found only in the hands of one you love. Your enemy has no such tool, for only a friend can betray. Betrayal is mutiny. It's a violation of a trust, an inside job.

Would that it were a stranger. Would that it were a random attack. Would that you were a victim of circumstances. But you aren't. You are a victim of a friend.

A sandpaper kiss is placed on your cheek. A promise is made with fingers crossed. You look to your friends and your friends don't look back. You look to the system for justice—the system looks to you as a scapegoat.

You are betrayed. Bitten with a snake's kiss.

It's more than rejection. Rejection opens a wound; betrayal pours the salt.

It's more than loneliness. Loneliness leaves you in the cold, betrayal closes the door.

It's more than mockery. Mockery plunges the knife; betrayal twists it.

It's more than an insult. An insult attacks your pride; betrayal breaks your heart.

As I search for betrayal's synonyms, I keep seeing betrayal's victims. That unsigned letter in yesterday's mail, "My husband just told me he had an affair two years ago," she wrote. "I feel so alone." The phone call at home from the elderly woman whose drug-addicted son had taken her money. My friend in the Midwest who moved his family to take the promised job that never materialized. The single mother whose ex-husband brings his new girlfriend to her house when he comes to get the kids for the weekend. The seven-year-old girl infected with HIV. "I'm mad at my mother," were her words.

Betrayal . . . when your world turns against you.

Betrayal . . . where there is opportunity for love, there is opportunity for hurt.

When betrayal comes, what do you do? Get out? Get angry? Get even? You have to deal with it some way. Let's see how Jesus dealt with it.

Begin by noticing how Jesus saw Judas. "Jesus answered, 'Friend, do what you came to do.'"[4]

Of all the names I would have chosen for Judas, it would not have been "friend." What Judas did to Jesus was grossly unfair. There is no indication that Jesus ever mistreated Judas. There is no clue that Judas was ever left out or neglected. When, during the Last Supper, Jesus told the disciples that his betrayer sat at the table, they didn't turn to one another and whisper, "It's Judas. Jesus told us he would do this."

They didn't whisper it because Jesus never said it. He had known it. He had known what Judas would do, but he treated the betrayer as if he were faithful.

It's even more unfair when you consider the betrayal was Judas's idea. The religious leaders didn't seek him; Judas sought them. "What will you pay me for giving Jesus to you?" he asked.[5] The betrayal would have been more palatable had Judas been propositioned by the leaders, but he wasn't. He propositioned them.

And Judas's method . . . again, why did it have to be a kiss?[6]

And why did he have to call him "Teacher"?[7] That's a title of respect. The incongruity of his words, deeds, and actions—I wouldn't have called Judas "friend."

But that is exactly what Jesus called him. Why? Jesus could see something we can't. Let me explain.

There was once a person in our world who brought Denalyn and me a lot of stress. She would call in the middle of the night. She was demanding and ruthless. She screamed at us in public. When she wanted something she wanted it immediately and she wanted it exclusively from us.

But we never asked her to leave us alone. We never told her to bug someone else. We never tried to get even.

After all, she was only a few months old.

It was easy for us to forgive our infant daughter's behavior because we knew she didn't know better.

Now, there is a world of difference between an innocent child and a deliberate Judas. But there is still a point to my story and it is this: The way to handle a person's behavior is to understand the cause of it. One way to deal with a person's peculiarities is to try to understand why he or she is peculiar.

Jesus knew Judas had been seduced by a powerful foe. He was aware of the wiles of Satan's whispers (he had just heard them himself). He knew how hard it was for Judas to do what was right.

He didn't justify what Judas did. He didn't minimize the deed. Nor did he release Judas from his choice. But he did look eye to eye with his betrayer and try to understand.

As long as you hate your enemy, a jail door is closed and a prisoner is taken. But when you try to understand and release your foe from your hatred, then the prisoner is released and that prisoner is you.

Perhaps you don't like that idea. Perhaps the thought of forgiveness is unrealistic. Perhaps the idea of trying to understand the Judases in our world is simply too gracious.

My response to you then is a question. What do you suggest? Will harboring the anger solve the problem? Will getting even remove the hurt? Does hatred do any good? Again, I'm not minimizing your hurt or justifying their actions. But I am saying that justice won't come this side of eternity. And demanding that your enemy get his or her share of pain will, in the process, be most painful to you.

May I gently but firmly remind you of something you know but may have forgotten? Life is not fair.

That's not pessimism; it's fact. That's not a complaint; it's just the way things are. I don't like it. Neither do you. We want life to be fair. Ever since the kid down the block got a bike and we didn't, we've been saying the same thing, "That's not fair."

But at some point someone needs to say to us, "Who ever told you life was going to be fair?"

God didn't. He didn't say, "*If* you have many kinds of troubles" . . . he said, "*When* you have many kinds of troubles . . ."[8] Troubles are part of the package. Betrayals are part of our troubles. Don't be surprised when betrayals come. Don't look for fairness here—look instead where Jesus looked.

Jesus looked to the future. Read his words: "In the future you will see the Son of Man coming." While going through hell, Jesus kept his eyes on heaven. While surrounded by enemies he kept his mind on his father. While abandoned on earth, he kept his heart on home. "In the future you will see the Son of Man sitting at the right hand of God, the Powerful One, and coming on clouds in the sky."[9]

I took a snow skiing lesson some time back. My instructor said I had potential but poor perspective. He said I looked at my skis too much. I told him I had to. They kept going where I didn't want them to go. "Does it help?" he asked.

"I guess not," I confessed, "I still fall a lot."

He gestured toward the splendid mountains on the horizon. "Try looking out there as you ski. Keep your eyes on the mountains and you'll keep your balance." He was right. It worked.

The best way to keep your balance is to keep your focus on another horizon. That's what Jesus did.

"My kingdom does not belong to this world," Jesus told Pilate. "My kingdom is from another place."[10]

When we lived in Rio de Janeiro, Brazil, I learned what it was like to long for home. We loved Brazil. The people were wonderful and the culture warm—but still it wasn't home.

My office was in downtown Rio, only a few blocks from the American embassy. Occasionally I would take my lunch to the embassy and eat. It was like going home for a few minutes. I would walk in the big door and greet the guards in English. I would go into the lobby and pick up an American newspaper. I'd check the box scores or the football standings. I'd chuckle at the cartoons. I even read the want ads. It felt good to think about home.

I would stroll down one of the large corridors and see the portraits of Lincoln, Jefferson, and Washington. Occasionally a worker would have time to chat and I'd get caught up on things back in the States.

The embassy was a bit of the homeland in a foreign country. Life in a distant land is made easier if you can make an occasional visit to home.

Jesus took a long look into the homeland. Long enough to count his friends. "I could ask my Father and he would give me twelve armies of angels." And seeing them up there gave him strength down here.

By the way, his friends are your friends. The Father's loyalty to Jesus is the Father's loyalty to you. When you feel betrayed, remember that. When you see the torches and feel the betrayer's kiss, remember his words: "I will never leave you; I will never forget you."[11]

When all of earth turns against you, all of heaven turns toward you. To keep your balance in a crooked world, look at the mountains. Think of home.

YOUR CHOICE

"What should I do with Jesus, the one called the Christ?"
MATTHEW 27:22

The most famous trial in history is about to begin.

The judge is short and patrician with darting eyes and expensive clothes. His graying hair trimmed and face beardless. He is apprehensive, nervous about being thrust into a decision he can't avoid. Two soldiers lead him down the stone stairs of the fortress into the broad courtyard. Shafts of morning sunlight stretch across the stone floor.

As he enters, Syrian soldiers dressed in short togas yank themselves and their spears erect and stare straight ahead. The floor on which they stand is a mosaic of broad, brown, smooth rocks. On the floor are carved the games the soldiers play while awaiting the sentencing of the prisoner.

But in the presence of the procurator, they don't play.

A regal chair is placed on a landing five steps up from the floor. The magistrate ascends and takes his seat. The accused is brought into the room and placed below him. A covey of robed religious leaders follow, walk over to one side of the room, and stand.

Pilate looks at the lone figure.

"Doesn't look like a Christ," he mutters.

Feet swollen and muddy. Hands tan. Knuckles lumpy.

Looks more like a laborer than a teacher. Looks even less like a troublemaker.

One eye is black and swollen shut. The other looks at the floor. Lower lip split and scabbed. Hair blood-matted to forehead. Arms and thighs streaked with crimson.

"Shall we remove the garment?" a soldier asks.

"No. It's not necessary."

It's obvious what the beating has done.

The procurator wouldn't have requested to see this prisoner. Experience has taught him to steer clear of the Jewish squabbles—especially religious ones. But he had to admit he's been curious why this Jesus has stirred the people so.

"They call him a rabble-rouser?" Pilate questions aloud, looking at the guards to his side, giving them permission to chuckle and snap the silence. They do. He shifts in the backless seat and leans against the wall. Were it not for the nature of the charges, Pilate would have waved the man and the matter away. But the accusations included words such as *revolt* and *taxes* and *Caesar*. So he is forced to press further.

"Are you the king of the Jews?"

For the first time, Jesus lifts his eyes. He doesn't raise his head, but he lifts his eyes. He peers at the procurator from beneath his brow. Pilate is surprised at the tone in Jesus' voice.

"Those are your words."

Before Pilate can respond, the knot of Jewish leaders mock the accused from the side of the courtroom.

"See, he has no respect."

"He stirs the people!"

"He claims to be king!"

Pilate doesn't hear them. *Those are your words.* No defense. No explanation. No panic. The Galilean is looking at the floor again.

Something about this country rabbi appeals to Pilate. He's different from the bleeding hearts who cluster outside. He's not like the leaders with the chest-length beards who one minute boast of a sovereign God and the next beg for lower taxes. His eyes are not the fiery ones of the zealots who are such a pain to the Pax Romana he tries to keep. He's different, this upcountry Messiah. As Pilate looks at him the stories begin to come to mind.

"Now, I remember," he says to himself, standing, then stepping down the steps and walking toward a balcony. He stops near the ledge and leans against it. The pigeons stir and a papery rustle of wings is heard as they flutter to the street below.

Pilate reflects on the reports. The strange story of the man over in Bethany. *Dead for, what was it? Three—no, four days. This is the rube they said called him from the grave. And that gathering at Bethsaida. Numbered up to several thousand . . . somebody in Herod's organization told about them. They wanted to make him king. Oh, yes, he fed the crowd.*

Pilate turns and looks at the children playing on the street below. Some are visiting with a guard. Wanting a handout, no doubt. The kids don't look good. Frail and thin. Hair stringy. Lice, probably. One part of Pilate is troubled because the guard is talking to them and another part is troubled that the guard doesn't help them. All of Pilate is troubled that children such as this have to get sick to begin with. But they do. They do in Rome; they do in Jerusalem.

He looks again at the stooped man who stands in his chambers. *We could use a king,* he sighs. *A king who could make sense out of this mess.*

There was a day when Pilate thought he could. He came to Jerusalem convinced that what was good north of the Mediterranean was good east of it. But that was long ago. That was another Pilate. That was when black was black and white was white. That was when his health was better and his dreams were virgin. That was before the politics. Give a little here to take a little there. Appease. Compromise. Raise taxes. Lower standards. Things were different now.

Rome and noble dreams seem faraway. Perhaps that's why he is intrigued by the rabbi. Something in him reminds him of why he came . . . of what he used to be. *They have scourged my back, too, my friend. They have scourged my back, too.*

Pilate looks at the Jewish leaders huddled in the corner across the court. Their insistence angers him. The lashes aren't enough. The mockery inadequate. *Jealous;* he wants to say it to their faces, but doesn't. *Jealous buzzards, the whole obstinate lot of you. Killing your own prophets.*

Pilate wants to let Jesus go. *Just give me a reason,* he thinks, almost aloud. *I'll set you free.*

His thoughts are interrupted by a tap on the shoulder. A messenger leans and whispers. Strange. Pilate's wife has sent word not to get involved in the case. Something about a dream she had.

Pilate walks back to his chair, sits, and stares at Jesus. "Even the gods are on your side?" he states with no explanation.

He has sat in this chair before. It's a curule seat: cobalt blue with thick, ornate legs. The traditional seat of decision. By sitting on it Pilate transforms any room or street into a courtroom. It is from here he renders decisions.

How many times has he sat here? How many stories has he heard? How many pleas has he received? How many wide eyes have stared at him, pleading for mercy, begging for acquittal?

But the eyes of this Nazarene are calm, silent. They don't scream. They don't dart. Pilate searches them for anxiety . . . for anger. He doesn't find it. What he finds makes him shift again.

He's not angry with me. He's not afraid . . . he seems to understand.

Pilate is correct in his observation. Jesus is not afraid. He is not angry. He is not on the verge of panic. For he is not surprised. Jesus knows his hour and the hour has come.

Pilate is correct in his curiosity. Where, if Jesus is a leader, are his followers? What, if he is the Messiah, does he intend to do? Why, if he is a teacher, are the religious leaders so angry at him?

Pilate is also correct in his question. "What should I do with Jesus, the one called the Christ?"[1]

Perhaps you, like Pilate, are curious about this one called Jesus. You, like Pilate, are puzzled by his claims and stirred by his passions. You have heard the stories: God descending the stars, cocooning in flesh, placing a stake of truth in the globe. You, like Pilate, have heard the others speak; now you would like for him to speak.

What do you do with a man who claims to be God, yet hates religion? What do you do with a man who calls himself the Savior, yet condemns systems? What do you do with a man who knows the place and time of his death, yet goes there anyway?

Pilate's question is yours. "What will I do with this man, Jesus?"

You have two choices.

You can reject him. That is an option. You can, as have many, decide that the idea of God's becoming a carpenter is too bizarre—and walk away.

Or you can accept him. You can journey with him. You can listen for his voice amid the hundreds of voices and follow him.

Pilate could have. He heard many voices that day—he could have heard Christ's. Had Pilate chosen to respond to this bruised Messiah, his story would have been different.

Listen to his question: "Are you the king of the Jews?" Had we been there that day we would know the tone of voice Pilate used. Mockery? (You . . . the king?) Curiosity? (Who are you?) Sincerity? (Are you really who you say you are?)

We wonder about his motive. So did Jesus.

"Is that your own question, or did others tell you about me?"[2]

Jesus wants to know why Pilate wants to know. What if Pilate had simply said, "I'm asking for myself. I want to know. I really want to know. Are you the king you claim to be?"

If he had asked, Jesus would have told him. If he had asked, Jesus would have freed him. But Pilate didn't want to know. He just turned on his heel and retorted, "I am not Jewish." Pilate didn't ask so Jesus didn't tell.

Pilate vacillates. He is a puppy hearing two voices. He steps toward one, then stops, and steps toward the other. Four times he tries to free Jesus, and four times he is swayed otherwise. He tries to give the people Barabbas; but they want Jesus. He sends Jesus to the whipping post; they want him sent to Golgotha. He states he finds nothing against this man; they accuse Pilate of violating the law. Pilate, afraid of who Jesus might be, tries one final time to release him; the Jews accuse him of betraying Caesar.

So many voices. The voice of compromise. The voice of expedience. The voice of politics. The voice of conscience.

And the soft, firm voice of Christ. "The only power you have over me is the power given to you by God."[3]

Jesus' voice is distinct. Unique. He doesn't cajole or plead. He just states the case.

Pilate thought he could avoid making a choice. He washed his hands of Jesus. He climbed on the fence and sat down.

But in not making a choice, Pilate made a choice.

Rather than ask for God's grace, he asked for a bowl. Rather than invite Jesus to stay, he sent him away. Rather than hear Christ's voice, he heard the voice of the people.

Legend has it that Pilate's wife became a believer. And legend has it that Pilate's eternal home is a mountain lake where he daily surfaces, still plunging his hands into the water seeking forgiveness. Forever trying to wash away his guilt . . . not for the evil he did, but for the kindness he didn't do.

THE GREATEST MIRACLE

*"People walked by . . . and shook their heads, saying,
You said you could destroy the Temple and build it again
in three days. So save yourself! Come down from that cross,
if you are really the Son of God!'"*
MATTHEW 27:39–40

Funny how taxes and Easter often fall on the same week. They did this year. I began this week with two major tasks: prepare an Easter sermon and pay my taxes.

With apologies to the IRS, one seems very heavenly and the other very earthly. One minute I'm at Calvary, the next at the checkbook. One hour is reverent, the next routine. One reminds me of how God paid it all, and the next reminds me of how I have a lot to pay. (Both the sermon and the tax preparation leave me grateful, however—the first for my Lord, the other for my three little tax deductions.)

I was two days into the week before it hit me. What an appropriate setting in which to study God's sacrifice! For if the cross doesn't make sense on a common week full of common tasks, when does it make sense?

That is the beauty of the cross. It occurred in a normal week involving flesh-and-blood people and a flesh-and-blood Jesus.

Of all the weeks for Jesus to display his powers, his final week would be the one. A few thousand loaves or a few dozen healings would do wonders for his image. Better still, a few Pharisees struck dumb would make life simpler.

Don't just clean the temple, Jesus; pick it up and move it to Jericho. When the religious leaders mutter, make it rain frogs. And as you are describing the end times, split the sky and show everyone what you mean.

This is the week for razzle-dazzle. This is the hour for the incredible. You can silence them all, Jesus.

But he doesn't. Not in Jerusalem. Not in the upper room. Not on the cross.

The week, in many respects, is run-of-the-mill. Yes, it's festive, but its celebrations are due to the Passover, not Jesus. The crowds are large, but not because of the Messiah.

The two miracles Jesus performs aren't intended to draw a crowd. The withered fig tree made a point, but turned few heads. The healed ear in the garden did a favor, but won no friends.

Jesus wasn't displaying his power.

It was an ordinary week.

An ordinary week packed with kids being dressed by impatient moms and dads hustling off to work. A week of dishes being washed and floors being swept.

Nature gave no clue that the week was different than any of the thousands before it or after it. The sun took its habitual route. The clouds puffed through the Judean sky. The grass was green and cattails danced in the wind.

Nature would groan before Sunday. The rocks would tumble before Sunday. The sky would put on a black robe before Sunday. But you wouldn't know that by looking at Monday, Tuesday, Wednesday, or Thursday. The week told no secrets.

The people gave no clue either. For most it was a week of anticipation; a weekend of festivities was arriving. Food to be bought.

Houses to be cleaned. Their faces gave no forecast of the extraordinary—for they knew of none.

One would think the disciples would suspect something, but they don't. Corner them and probe their knowledge. They don't know. The only thing they know for sure is that his eyes seem more focused—he seems determined . . . about what they aren't sure.

Tell them that before Friday's dawn they will abandon their only hope, and they won't believe you. Tell them that Thursday night holds betrayal and denial, and they will scoff.

"Not us," they will boast.

For them this week is like any other. The disciples give no clue. And most importantly, Jesus gives no clue. His water doesn't become wine. His donkey doesn't speak. The dead stay in the graves and those blind on Monday are still blind on Friday.

You'd think the heavens would be opened. You'd think trumpets would be sounding. You'd think angels would be summoning all the people of the world to Jerusalem to witness the event. You'd think that God himself would descend to bless his Son.

But he doesn't. He leaves the extraordinary moment draped in the ordinary. A predictable week. A week of tasks, meals, and crying babies.

A week that may be a lot like yours. Doubtful that anything spectacular has happened in your week. No great news, no horrible news. No earthquakes. No windfalls. Just a typical week of chores and children and checkout stands.

It was for the people of Jerusalem. On the edge of history's most remarkable hour was one of history's unremarkable weeks. God is in their city and most miss him.

Jesus could have used the spectacular to get their attention. Why didn't he? Why didn't he stun them with a loop-a-dee-loop or a double backflip off the temple? When they demanded, "Crucify him!" why didn't he make their noses grow? Why is the miraculous part of Christ quiet this week? Why doesn't he do something spectacular?

No angelic shield protected his back from the whip. No holy helmet shielded his brow from the thorny crown. God crawled neck deep into the mire of humanity, plunged into the darkest cave of death, and emerged—alive.

Even when he came out, he didn't show off. He just walked out. Mary thought he was a gardener. Thomas had to have hands-on (or hands-in) proof. Jesus still ate; he still talked; he still broke bread with the Emmaus-bound disciples.

Do you see the point?

God calls us in a real world. He doesn't communicate by performing tricks. He doesn't communicate by stacking stars in the heavens or reincarnating grandparents from the grave. He's not going to speak to you through voices in a cornfield or a little fat man in a land called Oz. There is about as much power in the plastic Jesus that's on your dashboard as there is in the Styrofoam dice on your rearview mirror.

It doesn't make a lick of difference if you are an Aquarius or a Capricorn or if you were born the day Kennedy was shot. God's not a trickster. He's not a genie. He's not a magician or a good-luck charm or the man upstairs. He is, instead, the Creator of the universe who is right here in the thick of our day-to-day world who speaks to you more through cooing babies and hungry bellies than he ever will through horoscopes, zodiac papers, or weeping Madonnas.

If you get some supernatural vision or hear some strange voice in the night, don't get too carried away. It could be God or it could be indigestion, and you don't want to misinterpret one for the other.

Nor do you want to miss the impossible by looking for the incredible. God speaks in our world. We just have to learn to hear him.

Listen for him amid the ordinary.

Need affirmation of his care? Let the daily sunrise proclaim his loyalty.

Could you use an example of his power? Spend an evening reading how your body works.

Wondering if his Word is reliable? Make a list of the fulfilled prophecies in the Bible and promises in your life.

In the final week those who demanded miracles got none and missed the one. They missed the moment in which a grave for the dead became the throne of a king.

Don't make their mistake.

I still think it ironic that the IRS and the empty tomb are saluted in the same week. Maybe it's appropriate. Don't they say that the only two things certain in life are death and taxes? Knowing God, he may speak through something as common as the second to give you the answer for the first.

A PRAYER OF DISCOVERY

"My God, my God, why have you abandoned me?"
MATTHEW 27:42 TEV

L ord?
> *Yes.*

I may be stepping out of line by saying this, but I need to tell you something that's been on my mind.

> *Go ahead.*

I don't like this verse: "My God, my God, why have you abandoned me?" It doesn't sound like you; it doesn't sound like something you would say.

Usually I love it when you speak. I listen when you speak. I imagine the power of your voice, the thunder of your commands, the dynamism in your dictates.

> *That's what I like to hear.*

Remember the creation song you sang into the soundless eternity? Ah, now, that's you. That was the act of a God!

And when you ordained the waves to splash and they roared, when you declared that the stars be flung and they flew, when you proclaimed that life be alive and it all began? . . . Or the whisper of breath into the clay-caked Adam? That was you at your best. That's the way I like to hear you. That's the voice I love to hear.

That's why I don't like this verse. Is that really you speaking? Are those words yours? Is that actually your voice? The voice that inflamed a bush, split a sea, and sent fire from heaven?

But this time, your voice is different.

Look at the sentence. There is a "why" at the beginning and a question mark at the end. You don't ask questions.

What happened to the exclamation point? That's your trademark. That's your signature closing. The mark as tall and strong as the words that precede it.

It's at the end of your command to Lazarus: "Come out!"[1]

It's there as you exorcise the demons: "Go!"[2]

It stands as courageously as you do as you walk on the waters and tell the followers: "Have courage!"[3]

Your words deserve an exclamation point. They are the cymbal clash of the finale, the cannon shot of victory, the thunder of the conquering chariots.

Your verbs form canyons and ignite disciples. Speak, God! You are the exclamation point of life itself. . . .

So, why the question mark hovering at the end of your words? Frail. Bent and bowed. Stooped as if weary. Would that you would straighten it. Stretch it. Make it stand tall.

And as long as I'm shooting straight with you—I don't like to see the word *abandon,* either. The source of life . . . abandoned? The giver of love . . . alone? The father of all . . . isolated?

Come on. Surely you don't mean it. Could deity feel abandoned?

Could we change the sentence a bit? Not much. Just the verb.

What would you suggest?

How about *challenge?* "My God, my God, why did you challenge me?" Isn't that better? Now we can applaud. Now we can lift banners for your dedication. Now we can explain it to our children. It makes sense now. You see, that makes you a hero. A hero. History is full of heroes.

And who is a hero but someone who survives a challenge.

Or, if that's not acceptable, I have another one. Why not *afflict?* "My God, my God, why did you afflict me?" Yes, that's it. Now you are a martyr, taking a stand for truth. A patriot, pierced by evil. A noble soldier who took the sword all the way to the hilt; bloody and beaten, but victorious.

Afflicted is much better than *abandoned.* You are a martyr. Right up there with Patrick Henry and Abraham Lincoln.

You are God, Jesus! You couldn't be abandoned. You couldn't be left alone. You couldn't be deserted in your most painful moment.

Abandonment. That is the punishment for a criminal. Abandonment. That is the suffering borne by the most evil. Abandonment. That's for the vile—not for you. Not you, the King of kings. Not you, the Beginning and the End. Not you, the One Unborn. After all, didn't John call you the Lamb of God?

What a name! That's who you are. The spotless, unblemished Lamb of God. I can hear John say the words. I can see him lift his eyes. I can see him smile and point at you and proclaim loud enough for all of Jordan to hear, "Behold, the Lamb of God. . . ."

And before he finishes his sentence, all eyes turn to you. Young, tan, robust. Broad shoulders and strong arms.

"Behold the Lamb of God. . . ."

Do you like that verse?

I sure do, God. It's one of my favorites. It's you.

What about the second part of it?

What?

The second part of the verse.

Hmmm, let me see if I remember. "Behold the Lamb of God who has come to take away the sins of the world."[4] Is that it, God?

That's it. Think about what the Lamb of God came to do.

"Who has come to take away the sins of the world." Wait a minute. "To take away the sins . . . " I'd never thought about those words.

I'd read them but never thought about them. I thought you just, I don't know, sent sin away. Banished it. I thought you'd just stood in front of the mountains of our sins and told them to begone. Just like you did to the demons. Just like you did to the hypocrites in the temple.

I just thought you commanded the evil out. I never noticed that you took it out. It never occurred to me that you actually touched it— or worse still, that it touched you.

That must have been a horrible moment. I know what it's like to be touched by sin. I know what it's like to smell the stench of that stuff. Remember what I used to be like? Before I knew you, I wallowed in that mire. I didn't just touch sin, I loved it. I drank it. I danced with it. I was in the middle of it.

But why am I telling you? You remember. You were the one who saw me. You were the one who found me. I was lonely. I was afraid. Remember? "Why? Why me? Why has all this hurt happened?"

I know it wasn't much of a question. It wasn't the right question. But it was all I knew to ask. You see, God, I felt so confused. So desolate. Sin will do that to you. Sin leaves you shipwrecked, orphaned, adrift. Sin leaves you aban—

Oh. Oh, my.

My, goodness, God. Is that what happened? You mean sin did the same to you that it did to me?

Oh, I'm sorry. I'm so sorry. I didn't know. I didn't understand. You really were alone, weren't you?

Your question was real, wasn't it, Jesus? You really were afraid. You really were alone. Just like I was. Only, I deserved it. You didn't.

Forgive me, I spoke out of turn.

CHAPTER 26

THE HIDDEN TOMB

*"He put Jesus' body in a new tomb that he had cut out of
a wall of rock, and he rolled a very large stone
to block the entrance of the tomb."*
MATTHEW 27:60

The road to Calvary was noisy, treacherous, and dangerous. And I wasn't even carrying a cross.

When I had thought of walking Christ's steps to Golgotha, I envisioned myself meditating on Christ's final hours and imagining the final turmoil. I was wrong.

Walking the Via Dolorosa is not a casual stroll in the steps of the Savior. It is, instead, an upstream struggle against a river of shoppers, soldiers, peddlers, and children.

"Watch your wallets," Joe told us.

I already am, I thought.

Joe Shulam is a Messianic Jew, raised in Jerusalem, and held in high regard by both Jew and Gentile. His rabbinic studies qualify him as a scholar. His archaeological training sets him apart as a researcher. But it is his tandem passion for the Messiah and the lost house of Israel that endears him to so many. We weren't with a guide; we were with a zealot.

And when a zealot tells you to guard your wallet, you guard your wallet.

Every few steps a street peddler would step in my path and dangle earrings or scarfs in my face. How can I meditate in this market?

For that is what the Via Dolorosa is. A stretch of road so narrow it bottlenecks body against body. When its sides aren't canyoned by the tall brick walls, they are lined with centuries-old shops selling everything from toys to dresses to turbans to compact discs. One section of the path is a butcher market. The smell turned my stomach and the sheep guts turned my eyes. Shuffling to catch up with Joe, I asked, "Was this street a meat market in the time of Christ?"

"It was," he answered. "To get to the cross he had to pass through a slaughterhouse."

It would be a few minutes before the significance of those words would register.

"Stay close," he yelled over the crowd. "The church is around the corner."

It'll be better at the church, I told myself.

Wrong again.

The Church of the Holy Sepulcher is seventeen hundred years of religion wrapped around a rock. In A.D. 326 Empress Helena, the mother of Constantine the Great, came to Jerusalem in search of the hill on which Christ was crucified. Makarios, Bishop of Jerusalem, took her to a rugged outcropping outside of the northwestern wall of the city. A twenty-foot jagged cluster of granite upon which sat a Roman-built temple to Jupiter. Surrounding the hill was a cemetery made up of other walls of rock, dotted with stone-sealed graves.

Helena demolished the pagan temple and built a chapel in its place. Every visitor since has had the same idea.

The result is a hill of sacrifice hidden in ornateness. After entering a tall entrance to the cathedral and climbing a dozen stone steps, I stood at the front of the top of the rock. A glass case covers the tip and the tip is all that is visible. Beneath an altar is a gold-plated hole in which the cross supposedly was lodged. Three crucified icons with elongated faces hang on crosses behind the altar.

Gold lanterns. Madonna statues. Candles and dim lights. I didn't know what to think. I was at once moved because of where I was standing and disturbed by what I was seeing.

I turned, descended the steps, and walked toward the tomb.

The traditional burial spot of Christ is under the same roof as the traditional Golgotha. To see it, you don't have to go outside; you do, however, have to use your imagination.

Two thousand years and a million tourists ago, this was a cemetery. Today it's a cathedral. The domes high above are covered with ornate paintings. I stopped and tried to picture it in its original state. I couldn't.

An elaborate sepulcher marks the traditional spot of Jesus' tomb. Forty-three lamps hang above the portal and a candelabra sits in front of it. It is solid marble, cornered with golden leaves.

An elevated stone path led into the doorway and a black-caped, black-bearded, black-hatted priest stood guard in front of it. His job was to keep the holy place clean. Fifty-plus people were standing in line to enter but he wouldn't let them. I didn't understand the purpose of the delay but I did understand the length of it.

"Twenty minutes. Twenty minutes."

The crowd mumbled. I mumbled. I came as close to the door as I could. The floor was inlaid with still more squares of marble and lanterns hung from the ceiling.

The sum total of the walk began to register with me. Holy road packed with peddlers. The cross hidden under an altar. The entrance to the tomb prohibited by a priest.

I had just muttered something about the temple needing another cleansing when I heard someone call. "No problem, come this way." It was Joe Shulam speaking. What he showed us next I will never forget.

He took us behind the elaborate cupola, through an indiscreet entrance and guided us into a plain room. It was dark. It was musty. It was unkempt and dusty. Obviously not a place designed for tourists.

While our eyes adjusted, he began to speak. "Six or so of these have been found, but are seldom visited." Behind him was a small opening. It was a rock-hewn tomb. Four feet high at the most. The width about the same.

"Wouldn't it be ironic," he smiled as he spoke, "if this was the place? It is dirty. It is uncared for. It is forgotten. The one over there is elaborate and adorned. This one is simple and ignored. Wouldn't it be ironic if this was the place where our Lord was buried?"

I walked over to the opening and stooped like the apostle John did to see in the tomb. And, just like John, I was amazed at what I saw. Not the huge room I'd imagined in my readings, but a small room lit with a timid lamp.

"Go in," Joe urged. I didn't have to be told twice.

Three steps across the rock floor and I was at the other side. The low ceiling forced me to squat and lean against a cold, rough wall. My eyes had to adjust a second time. As they did, I sat in the silence, the first moment of silence that day. It began to occur to me where I was: in a tomb. A tomb that could have held the body of Christ. A tomb that could have encaved the body of God. A tomb that could have witnessed history's greatest moment.

"Five people could be buried here." Joe had entered and was at my side. A couple of my cotravelers were with him. "Two or three would be laid here on the floor. And two would be slid into the holes over here."

"God put himself in a place like this," someone said softly.

He did. God put himself in a dark, tight, claustrophobic room and allowed them to seal it shut. The Light of the World was mummied in cloth and shut in ebony. The Hope of humanity was shut in a tomb.

We didn't dare speak. We couldn't.

The elaborate altars were forgotten. The priest-protected sepulcher was a world away. What man had done to decorate what God came to do no longer mattered.

All I could see at that moment, perhaps more than any moment, was how far he had come. More than the God in the burning bush. Beyond the infant wrapped in a feed trough. Past the adolescent Savior in Nazareth. Even surpassing the King of kings nailed to a tree and mounted on a hill was this: God in a tomb.

Nothing is blacker than a grave, as lifeless as a pit, as permanent as the crypt.

But into the crypt he came.

The next time you find yourself entombed in a darkened world of fear, remember that. The next time pain boxes you in a world of horror, remember the tomb. The next time a stone seals your exit to peace, think about the empty, musty tomb outside of Jerusalem.

It's not easy to find. To see it you may have to get beyond the pressures of people demanding your attention. You may have to slip past the golden altars and ornate statues. To see it, you may even have to bypass the chamber near the priest and slip into an anteroom and look for yourself. Sometimes the hardest place to find the tomb is in a cathedral.

But it's there.

And when you see it, bow down, enter quietly, and look closely. For there, on the wall, you may see the charred marks of a divine explosion.

I Reckons I Will Always Remember That Walk

"In the same way, the Son of Man did not come to be served. He came to serve others and to give his life as a ransom for many people."
Matthew 20:28

So what should I do with Jesus?" Pilate asked it first, but we've all asked it since.

It's a fair question. A necessary question. What do you do with such a man? He called himself God, but wore the clothes of a man. He called himself the Messiah, but never marshaled an army. He was regarded as king, but his only crown was of thorns. People revered him as regal, yet his only robe was stitched with mockery.

Small wonder Pilate was puzzled. How do you explain such a man?

One way is to take a walk. His walk. His final walk. And that is what we have done. We have followed his steps and stood in his shadow. From Jericho to Jerusalem. From the temple to the garden. From the garden to the trial. From Pilate's palace to Golgotha's cross. We have watched him walk—angrily into the temple, wearily into Gethsemane, painfully up the Via Dolorosa. And powerfully out of the vacated tomb.

Hopefully, as you witnessed his walk, you have reflected on your own, for all of us have our own walk to Jerusalem. Our own path through hollow religion. Our own journey down the narrow path of rejection. And each of us, like Pilate, must cast a verdict on Jesus.

Pilate heard the voice of the people and left Jesus to walk the road alone.

Will we?

May I conclude with the stories of three walks, three journeys? The stories of three slaves . . . and the paths they took to freedom.

Mary Barbour could tell you about slavery. Firsthand. She remembered the Marse and Marster. She could describe the plantation, the stick-and-mud slave house with the bunks. The long nights. Hot days. Hard whips. Isolation. Mary Barbour could tell you about it. Mary Barbour was a slave.

But she'd rather tell you about freedom. And that is what she did.

In 1935 a worker with the Federal Writers' Project knocked on her door in Raleigh, North Carolina. The Federal Writers' Project was a government-sponsored effort to record the memories of ex-slaves. Over two thousand were interviewed. These, the final voices to speak for the 246 years of bondage in America, did so with earthy eloquence.

They told how they were not allowed to read or write nor purchase or sell merchandise. They couldn't go to church unless invited. Whippings were common. Hard work was a fact of life.

And when freedom came, they weren't ready. They wandered roads looking for work. They were victimized by opportunists. Many ended up back at the same plantation.

But of all the memories, the most vivid, and the one most often shared, was the hour of freedom. The night the Yanks came. The day the Marster told them they could leave. The morning they went up to the "big house" and found it empty.

And of the stories of liberation, none were so specific as Mary Barbour's. She was ten years of age the night her father awoke her and led her to the wagon that would carry them to freedom.

Before you read her words, picture her seated on her porch in

Raleigh. It's 1935. Mary Barbour is over eighty years old. She rocks as she thinks. Her tiny body swallowed by the large chair. Her frail fingers tremble as she rubs her nose. Old but eager eyes stare out as if she is gazing into a land far on the horizon. You lean back against the pole and listen to her story.

> One of the first things that I remembers was my pappy waking me up in the middle of the night, dressing me in the dark, all the time telling me to keep quiet. One of the twins hollered some, and Pappy put his hand over its mouth to keep it quiet.
>
> After we was dressed, he went outside and peeped around for a minute, then he comed back in and got us. We snook out of the house and along the woods path, Pappy toting one of the twins and holding me by the hand and Mammy carrying the other two.
>
> I reckons I will always remember that walk, with the bushes slapping my legs, the wind sighing in the trees, and the hoot owls and the whippoorwills hollering at each other from the big trees. I was half asleep and scared stiff, but in a little while we pass the plum thicket and there am the mules and the wagon. There am the quilt in the bottom of the wagon, and on this they lays we younguns. And Pappy and Mammy gets on the board across the front and drives off down the road.
>
> I was sleepy, but I was scared too, so as we rides along, I listens to Pappy and Mammy talk. Pappy was telling Mammy about the Yankees coming to their plantation, burning the corncribs, the smokehouses and destroying everything. He says right low that they done took Marster Jordan to the rip raps down nigh Norfolk, and that he stole the mules and the wagon and escaped.[1]

Glimmerings of deliverance. Lingerings of the liberation. Six decades later the wind still sighs in the trees and the whippoorwills and hoot owls still holler at each other in Mary Barbour's memory.

The walk to freedom is never forgotten. The path taken from slavery to liberation is always vivid. It's more than a road, it's a release. The shackles are opened and, for perhaps the first time, freedom dawns. "I reckons I will always remember that walk . . . "

Do you remember yours? Where were you the night the door was opened? Do you remember the touch of the Father? Who walked with you the day you were set free? Can you still see the scene? Can you feel the road beneath your feet?

I hope so. I hope that permanently planted in your soul is the moment the Father stirred you in the darkness and led you down the path. It's a memory like no other. For when he sets you free, you are free indeed.

Ex-slaves describe well the hour of deliverance.

Can I tell you mine?

A Bible class in a small West Texas town. I don't know what was more remarkable, that a teacher was trying to teach the book of Romans to a group of ten-year-olds or that I remember what he said.

The classroom was midsized, one of a dozen or so in a small church. My desk had carving on it and gum under it. Twenty or so others were in the room, though only four or five were taken.

We all sat at the back, too sophisticated to appear interested. Starched jeans. High-topped tennis shoes. It was summer and the slow-setting sun cast the window in gold.

The teacher was an earnest man. I can still see his flattop, his belly bulging from beneath his coat that he doesn't even try to button. His tie stops midway down his chest. He has a black mole on his forehead, a soft voice, and a kind smile. Though he is hopelessly out of touch with the kids of 1965, he doesn't know it.

His notes are stacked on a podium underneath a heavy black Bible. His back is turned to us and his jacket goes up and down his beltline as he writes on the board. He speaks with genuine passion. He is not a dramatic man, but tonight he is fervent.

God only knows why I heard him that night. His text was Romans chapter six. The blackboard was littered with long words and diagrams. Somewhere in the process of describing how Jesus went into the tomb and came back out, it happened. The jewel of grace was lifted and turned so I could see it from a new angle . . . and it stole my breath.

I didn't see a moral code. I didn't see a church. I didn't see ten commandments or hellish demons. I saw what another ten-year-old—Mary Barbour—saw. I saw my Father enter my dark night, awaken me from my slumber, and gently guide me—no, carry me—to freedom.

"I reckons I will always remember that walk."

I said nothing to my teacher. I said nothing to my friends. I'm not sure I even said anything to God. I didn't know what to say. I didn't know what to do. But for all I didn't know there was one fact of which I was absolutely sure, I wanted to be with him.

I told my father that I was ready to give my life to God. He thought I was too young to make the decision. He asked what I knew. I told him Jesus was in heaven and I wanted to be with him. And for my dad, that was enough.

To this day I wonder if my love has ever been as pure as it was that first hour. I long for the certainty of my adorning faith. Had you told me that Jesus was in hell, I would have agreed to go. Public confession and baptism came as naturally for me as climbing into the wagon did for Mary Barbour.

You see, when your Father comes to deliver you from bondage, you don't ask questions; you obey instructions. You take his hand. You walk the path. You leave bondage behind. And you never, never forget.

Mary Barbour didn't. I haven't. And Tigyne didn't.

Tigyne belonged to the Wallamo tribe in interior Ethiopia. In the years preceding World War II, missionaries carried the message of

Christ to this Satan-worshiping tribe. One of the early converts was Tigyne. Raymond Davis was the missionary who knew him . . . and freed him.

Tigyne was a slave. His decision to follow Jesus displeased his master, who refused to allow Tigyne to attend Bible studies or worship. He frequently beat and humiliated Tigyne for his faith. But it was a price this young Christian was willing to pay.

There was another price, however, he could not afford. He couldn't purchase his freedom. For only twelve dollars his master would release him, but for this slave who'd never known a salary, it might as well have been a million.

When the missionaries learned that his freedom could be purchased, they talked it over, pooled some money, and bought his freedom.

Tigyne was now free—both spiritually and physically. He never outlived his gratitude to the men who had redeemed him.

Soon after his day of liberty, the missionaries were expelled from Ethiopia. Twenty-four years passed before Raymond Davis returned to Wallamo. During this quarter of a century Tigyne remained a vivid testimony to the power of freedom. He longed to see Davis again.

When he heard that his friend was coming, he went to the mission station several days in a row to wait. Dates on the calendar or time on the clock had no significance for Tigyne so he came daily to search for Davis.

Finally, Davis arrived, riding in a car driven by a fellow missionary.

When Tigyne saw the vehicle come around the corner, he ran to the window and took Davis's hand and began to kiss it again and again. The driver slowed the car so Tigyne could run beside it. As he ran he yelled to his friends, "Behold! Behold! One of those who redeemed me has returned!"

Finally the car stopped. Davis got out and Tigyne dropped to his knees, put his arms around his friend's legs, and began to kiss his dusty shoes. Davis reached down to bring him to full height and they stood with their arms around each other and wept.[2]

———————

Three ex-slaves. One freed from man, one freed from sin, and one freed from both. Three walks. One destiny—freedom.

It's a walk they will never forget.

"*I reckons I will always remember that walk....*" I pray you never forget your walk or his: Jesus' final walk from Jericho to Jerusalem. For it was this walk that promised you freedom.

His final walk through the temple of Jerusalem. For it was on this walk that he denounced hollow religion.

His final walk to the Mount of Olives. For it was there he promised to return and take you home.

And his final walk from Pilate's palace to Golgotha's cross. Bare, bloody feet struggling up a stony narrow path. But just as vivid as the pain of the beam against his raw back is his vision of you and him walking together.

He could see the hour he would come into your life, into your dark cabin to stir you out of your sleep and guide you to freedom.

But the walk isn't over. The journey isn't complete. There is one more walk that must be made.

"I will come back," he promised. And to prove it he ripped in two the temple curtain and split open the doors of death. He will come back.

He, like the missionary, will come back for his followers. And we, like Tigyne, won't be able to control our joy.

"The one who has redeemed us has returned!" we will cry.

And the journey will end and we will take our seats at his feast . . . forever.

See you at the table.

READER'S GUIDE

TOO LITTLE, TOO LATE, TOO GOOD TO BE TRUE

1. *There was a certain honor about being chosen . . . something special about being singled out, even if it was to dig ditches. But just as there was an honor with being chosen, there was a certain shame about being left behind. Again.*

A. Describe a time when you were specially chosen for some occasion. How did it feel? What do you remember most about it? Were you ever passed up for something you really wanted? If so, how did you feel at the time?

B. Read Matthew 20:1–16. Put yourself into the story. How would you feel if you were one of the workers hired at the beginning of the day? If you were hired at the eleventh hour? What point is Jesus trying to make in the landowner's speech of verses 13 through 15? How does verse 16 demonstrate the good news of the gospel?

2. *Get told enough times that only the rotten fruit gets left in the bin, and you begin to believe it. You begin to believe you are "too little, too late."*

A. Have you ever felt like "rotten fruit" or that you were "too little, too late"? What made you feel that way? What do you think Max would say about such assessments of you?

B. Read John 1:43–51. In what way did some people think of Jesus as "rotten fruit" (see verse 46)? How did Jesus react to such an assessment?

C. Read 1 Corinthians 1:26–29. What kinds of people made up the church in Corinth? What might this suggest about the way God sizes up people? According to verse 29, why does God choose to do this?

3. *God has a peculiar passion for the forgotten. Have you noticed?*

A. Have you noticed God's peculiar passion for the forgotten? If so, describe what you have noticed.

B. Read James 1:27 and 2:5. How does God demonstrate his peculiar passion for the forgotten in these two verses? What is to be our response to these people? Why?

C. Read Matthew 11:19. With what kind of people was Jesus known to associate? How does he respond to his opponents' charges? What does this tell you about God's peculiar passion for the forgotten?

4. *Why did he choose you? Why did he choose me? Honestly. Why? What do we have that he needs?*

A. Read Romans 9:10–16. According to Paul, on what basis is God's choice of Isaac made? What did Isaac have that God needed?

B. Read Deuteronomy 7:7–8. What reason does God give in this passage for his love for Israel? Why did he choose her? In what way is God's choice of Israel exactly like his choice of us?

5. *"Shor feels good to be chosen, don't it, boy?" Sure does, Ben. It sure does.*

A. If you have accepted Jesus as your Savior, have you thought much about what it means to be chosen? How does it make you feel?

B. Read Ephesians 1:11–12 and 1 Peter 2:9. What do these passages say about our being chosen by God? What difference does it make to be chosen? How is God's choice of us supposed to change the way we live? Does it change the way you live? Why or why not?

CHAPTER 2

FROM JERICHO TO JERUSALEM

1. *Better to go to battle with God's Word in your heart than mighty weapons in your hand.*

   A. Read Matthew 20:17–19. In what way does this passage say Jesus was going into battle? In what way was God's Word in his heart? How can you follow his example?

   B. Read 1 Samuel 17:45–47. How did David go into battle against Goliath with God's Word in his heart? How does David describe the contest in verse 45? How do we win any of our battles, according to verse 47? How do our daily actions prove that we either believe or disbelieve this verse? What do your daily actions demonstrate?

2. *You can tell a lot about a person by the way he dies.*

   A. Why does the way someone dies tell you a lot about him? Have you known anyone whose death told you a lot about him? Read Luke 9:51. How does this verse and Jesus' death tell you a lot about him?

   B. Read John 15:13. What does this verse tell you about Jesus' love for you? How does this make you feel?

3. *Forget any suggestion that Jesus was trapped. Erase any theory that Jesus made a miscalculation. Ignore any speculation that the cross was a last-ditch attempt to salvage a dying mission. For if these words tell us anything, they tell us that Jesus died . . . on purpose. No surprise. No hesitation. No faltering.*

A. Read Luke 18:31–34. What did Jesus tell his disciples about what was going to happen? According to verse 31, why did these things have to happen?

B. Read Acts 2:22–23 and 4:27–28. What do these verses tell you about Jesus' death? Although the disciples did not understand Jesus in Luke 18:31–34, did they understand in these passages? If so, what difference did that understanding make to them? What difference would this understanding make to you?

C. Read John 10:14–18. Who are Jesus' sheep in this passage? What does Jesus say He will do for them? What does verse 18 teach you about the crucifixion? How does this passage confirm what Max wrote in the quote above?

CHAPTER 3

THE SACRIFICIAL GENERAL

1. *Few will assume responsibilities for the mistakes of others. Still fewer will shoulder the blame for mistakes yet uncommitted. Eisenhower did. As a result, he became a hero. Jesus did. As a result, he's our Savior.*

A. Think of some leaders you have admired. Did they assume responsibility for the mistakes of others? If so, name some examples. Why is it hard for us to take responsibility for others' mistakes? How is General Eisenhower's action like that of Jesus? How is it different?

B. Read Matthew 20:25–28. According to Jesus, how do we become great? How do we become first? How did Jesus provide the greatest example of this? How are we to follow his example? Give several practical examples of how you can follow his example this week.

C. Read Romans 5:6–8. For whom did Christ die? In what way does Jesus' death demonstrate his incomprehensible love for us? How does this passage represent the epitome of Max's principle in this chapter?

2. *Calvary is a hybrid of God's lofty status and his deep devotion. The thunderclap that echoed when God's sovereignty collided with his love. The marriage of heaven's kingship and heaven's compassion. The very instrument of the cross is symbolic, the vertical beam of holiness intersecting with the horizontal bar of love.*

A. Which is easier for you to think of, God's holiness or his love? Explain your answer. How does the cross symbolize the intersection of these two characteristics?

B. Read Romans 3:25–26 and 11:22. How do these passages confirm Max's quote above? How does the cross satisfy both God's justice and his love?

3. *Jesus didn't write a note; he paid the price. He didn't just assume the blame; he seized the sin. He became the ransom. He is the General who dies in the place of the private, the King who suffers for the peasant, the Master who sacrifices himself for the servant.*

A. In what sense did Jesus become the ransom for us? How was his death far different from anyone else who might die for a friend?

B. Read 2 Corinthians 5:21. How does this verse fit with Max's insight in the quote above? According to this verse, why did Jesus become sin for us?

C. Read Galatians 3:13–14. How did Christ redeem us from the curse of the law? According to verse 14, why did he do this? How does this verse say we take advantage of his work on the cross? Have you taken advantage of it? Explain your answer.

CHAPTER   4

UGLY RELIGION

1. *We are wrong when we think God is too busy for little people or too formal for poor protocol. When people are refused access to Christ by those closest to him, the result is empty, hollow religion. Ugly religion.*

A. Have you ever seen ugly religion in practice? If so, what was it like? How were people affected? What impressions did it leave upon you? What, if anything, did you do about it?

B. Read Matthew 20:29–34. Why do you think the crowd rebuked the two blind men? How would you have felt had you been one of the blind men? The answer to Jesus' question seems too obvious—why do you suppose Jesus asked it? What did the blind men do after they were healed? Why do you think they did this?

C. Read Ezekiel 34:1–10. In this passage, Ezekiel uses the term *shepherds* to mean the leaders of God's people. What is wrong with the shepherds in this passage? Do they help people to get to God or do they hinder them? What is God's attitude toward these shepherds? Is it a mild reaction or a strong one?

How does this passage reinforce or contradict the above quote from Max?

2. *Something told these two beggars that God is more concerned with the right heart than he is the right clothes or procedure. Somehow they knew that what they lacked in method could be made up for in motive, so they called out at the top of their lungs. And they were heard.*

A. How are we sometimes more concerned with the right clothes or procedure than we are the right heart? Why is it so easy to fall into this trap? How can you avoid falling into it?

B. Read 2 Chronicles 30:18–20. What was the problem in this passage the people faced? What was the solution to the problem? How did God respond to the people in this instance? Why?

C. Read Isaiah 29:13. What is the Lord's complaint in this passage? How can you tell when someone's heart is far from God? How does this passage confirm what Max talked about in the quote?

D. Read Psalm 51:16–17. How is this passage a restatement of Max's quote above? What are the "sacrifices" that God desires of us? In what way is this harder than literal sacrifices? How do you comply with this desire of God's?

3. *Ironic. Of all the people on the road that day, the blind men turned out to be the ones with the clearest vision—even before they could see.*

A. What kind of vision is Max talking about in the quote above? How is your vision?

B. Compare Matthew 16:1–3 with Luke 8:10. How do these passages show that it's possible to have good physical vision but be spiritually blind? How do you improve your spiritual vision?

C. Read 1 Corinthians 1:28–29. How does this passage help explain the quote from Max? What is especially significant about verse 29? How does verse 29 help explain spiritual blindness?

CHAPTER 5

DON'T JUST DO SOMETHING, STAND THERE

1. *The Sabbath is the day that God's children in a foreign land squeeze their Father's hand and say, "I don't know where I am. I don't know how I'll get home. But you do and that's enough."*

A. What does Max mean when he says we are in a foreign land? In what way is the Sabbath a time for getting our bearings? What is to be our focus on the Sabbath?

B. Read Exodus 20:8–11. What does it mean to *keep* the Sabbath day "holy"? According to verse 11, who *made* it holy? What reason is given for not doing any work on that day? Do you make it a practice to forego work one day out of seven? Why or why not?

C. Read Psalm 122:1. Why did the psalmist "rejoice" in this verse? How does this verse relate to Max's quote above? Is the psalmist's experience your own? Why or why not?

2. *If Jesus found time in the midst of a racing agenda to stop the rush and sit in the silence, do you think we could too?*

A. Why do you think Jesus took time "in the midst of a racing agenda to stop the rush and sit in the silence"? If he needed to do so, why do we so often think we don't need to? What happens when we fail to do so? What happens to you?

B. Read Luke 4:16. According to this verse, what was it customary for Jesus to do on the Sabbath day? Is this significant for us? If so, how?

3. *Slow down. If God commanded it, you need it. If Jesus modeled it, you need it. God still provides the manna. Trust him. Take a day to say no to work and yes to worship.*

A. Is it hard for you to slow down? Explain your answer. What does Max mean when he writes that "God still provides the manna. Trust him"? Could it be that we don't take a day to say no to work and yes to worship because we don't trust God for the manna? If so, how can we change our habits?

B. Read Psalm 92:1–8. Note the title over this Psalm. For what day was it written? How is this significant? Who is the focus of this Psalm? How does that focus shape the response of the psalmist? What is your response to that focus?

C. Read Luke 10:38–42. According to verse 42, what one thing is needed? Why does Jesus call this better? Note that this must be chosen; what are you choosing? In what sense can this thing not be taken away from those who choose it?

4. *Keep a clear vision of the cross on your horizon and you can find your way home. Such is the purpose of your day of rest: to relax your body, but more importantly to restore your vision. A day in which you get your bearings so you can find your way home.*

A. Name several ways in which you can keep a clear vision of the cross on your horizon.

B. Read Hebrews 12:2–3. On what are we to fix our eyes? According to verse three, what does this accomplish? Conversely, if we fail to so fix our eyes, what two things always happen? If we have grown weary or lost heart, could this be the reason?

C. Read Psalm 62:1–2, 5–8. Where does David say he finds rest? Why does he make this so exclusive? In verse 5, whom does David exhort? Why is this significant? Why does he repeat these lines? Whom does he exhort in verse 8? What does he exhort them to do? What reason does he give them for doing so?

D. Evaluate your own experience of the Sabbath day. Are you regularly taking one day out of seven to rest and focus on God? If not, why not? If so, how does your experience compare with that of the writer of Psalm 92? Is there anything you'd like to modify in your practice of the Sabbath? If so, what?

C H A P T E R 6

RISKY LOVE

1. *The perfume was worth a year's wages. Maybe the only thing of value she had. It wasn't a logical thing to do, but since when has love been led by logic?*

A. Describe your initial reaction to this woman's action. Did you think it foolish? Exorbitant? Profound? Moving? Is love illogical? Or what does Max mean that love is not *led* by logic?

B. Read John 12:1–8. With what character in this episode do you most easily relate? Why? In what ways did Mary take a risk by doing what she did? Try to name some similar ways that we can take such risks today.

C. Read Matthew 26:6–13. In what way was the woman's action a beautiful thing? How was it symbolic of what was to happen? Why do you suppose Jesus said what he did in verse 13?

2. *There is a time for risky love. There is a time for extravagant gestures. There is a time to pour out your affections on one you love. And when the time comes—seize it, don't miss it.*

A. What are the appropriate times for risky love? Describe them. When have you chosen to demonstrate risky love? What was the outcome? Would you do it again? Why?

B. Read Proverbs 3:27–28. What do these verses say about seizing the opportunity to express risky love? If this is an area in which you could improve, how can you do so?

C. Read Philippians 2:25–30. What is the risky love described in this passage? Why was the risk taken? What was the outcome? In your opinion, was it worth it? Why?

3. *The price of practicality is sometimes higher than extravagance. But the rewards of risky love are always greater than its cost.*

A. In what way does practicality sometimes cost more than extravagance? Do you agree that "the rewards of risky love are always greater than its cost"? Why or why not?

B. Read Luke 6:32–35. List the several instances of risky love that Jesus names in this passage. Why is each one risky? Why does he encourage us to take the risk? What kind of reward are we promised if we take such risks?

4. *Go to the effort. Invest the time. Write the letter. Make the apology. Take the trip. Purchase the gift. Do it. The seized opportunity renders joy. The neglected brings regret.*

A. What opportunities exist for you right now to show risky love? List them. What's stopping you from taking the risk? What do you think of Max's statement that "the seized opportunity renders joy. The neglected brings regret"?

B. Read James 4:17. What does this verse have to do with risky love? How do you respond to it?

CHAPTER 7

THE GUY WITH THE DONKEY

1. *Sometimes I like to keep my animals to myself. Sometimes when God wants something I act like I don't know he needs it.*

A. Can you identify with what Max says in the quote above? If so, in what way? Describe a time when you felt as Max did.

B. Read Matthew 21:1–7. According to verse 3, how quickly would the owner of the donkey respond to Jesus' request? Why do you think he would respond this way? Is this the normal way you respond? Why or why not?

C. Compare Matthew 21:3 with Psalm 50:9–12 and Acts 17:24–25. According to these verses, what does God need from us? What do we have that he couldn't do without? In what sense, then, did Jesus need the donkey? In what sense does God need anything from us? Why does this make it such a great privilege to be asked to give him what we have?

2. *All of us have a donkey. You and I each have something in our lives, which, if given back to God, could, like the donkey, move Jesus and his story further down the road.*

A. Take an inventory of your donkeys. What do you have that could "move Jesus and his story further down the road"?

What talents do you have? What resources? What abilities? What gifts?

B. Read Romans 12:6–8. Note the spirit of the passage. Whatever gifts we have, Paul asks us to use them. Do you recognize any of your gifts among those listed here? Do you know what your gifts are? Are you using your gifts?

C. Read Matthew 25:14–30. With which of the three servants do you most readily identify? Why? How do the first two servants make their master feel? How does the last servant make his master feel? What is the basic lesson Jesus intended to teach with this story?

3. *It could be that God wants to mount your donkey and enter the walls of another city, another nation, another heart. Do you let him? Do you give it? Or do you hesitate?*

A. Why do we sometimes hesitate when we believe God wants to use something we have? What donkey of yours do you think God may want to mount? Describe your thoughts about this.

B. Read 2 Corinthians 9:7. How does this verse relate to giving up your donkey? What does it mean to "decide in [your] heart"? What is wrong with giving reluctantly or under compulsion? What makes God so delighted with a cheerful giver?

4. *God uses tiny seeds to reap great harvests. It is on the back of donkeys he rides—not steeds or chariots—just simple donkeys.*

A. Why do you think God chooses to use the little things to give him glory? Why not big things? Do you ever hesitate giving him little things because they don't seem important or good enough?

B. Read Jeremiah 9:23–24. Why shouldn't wise men boast of their wisdom, strong men boast of their strength, or rich men boast of their riches? How does this passage relate to Max's quote above?

C. Read Judges 7:1–8. Why do you think God whittled down the number of Gideon's troops from 32,000 to 10,000 to 300? What does God's insistence on using little things say to you?

C H A P T E R 8

HUCKSTERS AND HYPOCRITES

1. *Want to anger God? Get in the way of people who want to see him. Want to feel his fury? Exploit people in the name of God. Mark it down. Religious hucksters poke the fire of divine wrath.*

A. Try to think of a few well-known examples where religious hucksters exploited people in the name of God. What did they do? What happened to them? What happened to the people? Describe how you might have seen "the fire of divine wrath" in these instances.

B. Read Matthew 21:12–17. What made Jesus so angry in this incident? What does this tell you about Jesus? Does this have any implications for you? If so, what?

C. Read Titus 1:10–11. How does Paul characterize those who "teach . . . for the sake of dishonest gain"? What do these people do? How are we to respond?

2. Listen carefully to the television evangelist. Analyze the words of the radio preacher. Note the emphasis of the message. What is the burden? Your salvation or your donation? Monitor what is said. Is money always needed yesterday? Are you promised health if you give and hell if you don't? If so, ignore him.

A. How carefully do you analyze the religious messages you receive, whether through print, TV, radio, or in person? How can you become better at analyzing these messages? Once you recognize a harmful message, what do you normally do?

B. Read 1 Timothy 6:3–11. In verse 5, how does Paul characterize those who think that godliness is a means to financial gain? What does he say really is great gain (verse 6)? What is the problem with wanting to get rich (verse 9)? What happens to many who are eager for money (verse 10)? How are we to respond to such practices (verse 11)?

C. Read Romans 16:17–18. What is Paul's exhortation in verse 17? Do you follow his urging? How vigilant are you in this regard?

4. There are hucksters in God's house. Don't be fooled by their looks. Don't be dazzled by their words. Be careful. Remember why Jesus purged the temple. Those closest to it may be farthest from it.

A. Why do you think it's so often true that "those closest to [the temple] may be farthest from it"? When is this a personal problem for you?

B. Read 1 Thessalonians 5:21. What are we commanded to do there? How can you do it?

C. Read Acts 20:28–35. What does Paul urge the Ephesians to do in verse 28? Why does he give this warning (verse 29)? What's the best protection for God's people in this regard (verse 32)? What is one evidence Paul gives of his sincerity (verses 33–34)? How is the saying of Jesus in verse 35 an excellent guide by which to measure someone's teaching?

CHAPTER 9

COURAGE TO DREAM AGAIN

1. *God always rejoices when we dare to dream. In fact, we are much like God when we dream. The Master exults in newness. He delights in stretching the old. He wrote the book on making the impossible happen.*

    A. How practiced are you at dreaming? If it's hard for you, why do you think that is? When you dream, what do you dream about?

    B. Read Isaiah 43:18–19. What sense do you get from this passage about God's delight in new things? Why do you think he has to give us a reminder like this?

    C. Read 2 Corinthians 5:17. Why is it crucial to remember that Christians are *new* creations? What difference does it make?

2. *God can't stomach lukewarm faith. He is angered by a religion that puts on a show but ignores the service—and that is precisely the religion he was facing during his last week.*

    A. Read Matthew 21:18–22. How were Israel's religious leaders like the fig tree in verses 18–19? Was there ever a time when you could have been so characterized? What kind of fig tree are you right now?

    B. Read Luke 18:9–14. Which man in Jesus' story had a lukewarm faith? Which was robust? What did Jesus say about each man? With which man do you most easily identify?

C. Read Revelation 3:15–16. What is Jesus' reaction to a lukewarm church? Why do you think he is so graphic in this passage? What signs accompany someone who's lukewarm in his faith?

3. *The faith is not in religion; the faith is in God. A hardy, daring faith that believes God will do what is right, every time. And that God will do what it takes—whatever it takes—to bring his children home.*

A. What is the difference between faith in faith and faith in God?

B. Read Genesis 18:23–25. Note Abraham's question in verse 25. What answer is he expecting? Do you expect the same answer? Based on this question, how do you expect God to act in your life?

C. Read Job 19:25–27. Even though Job is in agony of soul, what is his firm expectation? Who is at the center of his hope? How does that hope transform his outlook?

D. Read 2 Timothy 4:7–8. Describe Paul's great hope as he neared the end of his life. Who is at the center of his hope? Did he expect to be brought home? Is this your expectation as well?

4. *God wants you to fly. He wants you to fly free of yesterday's guilt. He wants you to fly free of today's fears. He wants you to fly free of tomorrow's grave.*

A. Do any of the fears listed in the quote from Max above keep you tightly bound? If so, which ones? What would it take for you to begin to fly free of them?

B. Read Hebrews 2:14–15. According to this verse, why did Jesus take on human form? What kind of freedom did he win for us (verse 15)?

C. Read Matthew 11:28. To what place does this verse instruct us to fly? How can you do this, practically speaking? Are you doing it now? Why or why not?

CHAPTER 10

OF CALLUSES AND COMPASSION

1. *No price is too high for a parent to pay to redeem his child. No energy is too great. No effort too demanding. A parent will go to any length to find his or her own. So will God.*

A. If you have children, what price would you be willing to pay to redeem them? What kind of effort would you put out? To what lengths would you go?

B. Read Matthew 18:12–14. What kind of effort is Jesus describing in this story? How does he relate his story to what God actually does (verse 14)?

C. Read 1 John 3:16. How does John define love in this verse? How does it fit with Max's quote above?

2. *God is in the thick of things in your world. He has not taken up residence in a distant galaxy. He has not removed himself from history. He has not chosen to seclude himself on a throne in an incandescent castle. He has drawn near.*

A. Describe your current image of God. Has that image always been the same? If it has changed, describe how it has

626

changed. Was there a time when you felt God was far away? If so, how did your perception change?

B. Read Psalm 139:1–12. How close is God to you right now, according to this passage? How does this make you feel?

C. Read Hebrews 10:19–23. How is it that we can have confidence to draw near to God (verse 19)? In what manner can we draw near to God through Jesus (verse 22)? Why can we "hold unswervingly to the hope we profess" (verse 23)?

3. *God is patient with our mistakes. He is longsuffering with our stumbles. He doesn't get angry at our questions. He doesn't turn away when we struggle. But when we repeatedly reject his message, when we are insensitive to his pleadings, when he changes history itself to get our attention and we still don't listen, he honors our request.*

A. How do we repeatedly reject God's message? In what way are we insensitive to his pleadings? What does Max mean that God honors our request?

B. Read Psalm 103:8–14. What does this passage say about the way God responds to our mistakes? How does verse 14 help explain verse 10? Now read Psalm 130:3–4. If God kept a record of your sins, would you be able to stand? According to this passage, why should we fear God?

C. Read Matthew 21:33–46. Would you describe the landowner in this parable as a patient man? Why or why not? What is the main point Jesus is trying to convey through this story? Why do you think the chief priests and Pharisees understood Jesus was telling this story about them (verse 45)?

4. *God comes to your house, steps up to the door, and knocks. But it's up to you to let him in.*

A. Why do you think God doesn't just knock the door down?

B. Read Ezekiel 33:11. What is God's desire for the wicked as reflected in this verse? Whose job is it to turn from their wicked ways? What is the result of this turning? What happens when they don't turn?

C. Read James 4:8. What does James say is our part in the process he describes? What is God's part? What is the result?

CHAPTER 11

YOU'RE INVITED

1. *God is a God who invites. God is a God who calls. God is a God who opens the door and waves his hand, pointing pilgrims to a full table. His invitation is not just for a meal, however. It is for life.*

A. Read Matthew 22:1–14. Count how many times a word such as *invite* or *call* is used. What does that tell you about the point of the parable? Who is doing the inviting? Whom does he represent?

B. Read Deuteronomy 30:15–16, 19–20. What choices did God set before the Israelites? What were the consequences for each? Which choice did he clearly want them to make?

2. *It must sadden the Father when we give him vague responses to his specific invitation to come to him.*

A. How do you think the Father feels when we give him vague responses to his invitation? How would you feel to get such a response? How would you react to such a response?

B. Read Luke 14:16–24. What were the excuses given in this story for not coming to the banquet? Do any of them sound familiar in your own life or acquaintance? What excuses do we make for not accepting God's invitations? How did the master in this story react to those who rejected his invitations? What point was Jesus trying to make?

3. *To know God is to receive his invitation. Not just to hear it, not just to study it, not just to acknowledge it, but to receive it. It is possible to learn much about God's invitation and never respond to it personally.*

A. In what way does receiving God's invitation allow you to know him? What prevents people from responding to God's invitation?

B. Read 2 Timothy 3:7. How does this verse relate to the quote above? Give several examples of the situation described by Paul.

C. Read Matthew 7:24–27 and James 1:22–25. What is the main point of both passages? Why is it so easy to fall into the trap these passages describe? Have you ever fallen into such a trap? If so, how did you get out?

4. *We can choose where we spend eternity. The big choice, God leaves to us. The critical decision is ours. What are you doing with God's invitation?*

A. Answer Max's question: What are you doing with God's invitation?

B. Read Isaiah 55:1–3, 6–7. What is God's invitation in this passage? Who is invited? What is the offer? What are the benefits? Have you responded to this invitation?

C. Read Romans 10:9–13. What is the invitation in this passage? How does one accept this invitation? What are the benefits of accepting it? Who may accept the invitation? Have you accepted this invitation?

MOUTH-TO-MOUTH MANIPULATION

1. *They hadn't learned the first lesson of leadership. "A man who wants to lead the orchestra must turn his back on the crowd."*

    A. What does the maxim quoted above mean to you? Does it make sense? Why or why not?

    B. Read Matthew 21:23–27. How does verse 26 illustrate the truth of the maxim quoted above?

    C. Read John 12:42–43. What was the main problem of the leaders described in this passage? Did they heed the advice of the maxim quoted above? What was the result of their action?

    D. Read 1 Corinthians 11:1. Where is Paul's attention fixed as he writes these words? Is his back to the audience or the orchestra? When you take leadership—whether at home, at work, or in another environment—do you keep this verse in mind? How would it change the way you lead?

2. *God has made it clear that flattery is never to be a tool of the sincere servant. Flattery is nothing more than fancy dishonesty. It wasn't used by Jesus, nor should it be used by his followers.*

    A. What is the basic problem with flattery? How do you feel when people use it to try to get from you what they want?

B. Read Matthew 22:15–22. Why is verse 16 an example of pure, unadulterated flattery? How did Jesus respond to it? Why did he use the term *hypocrite* to describe these people?

C. Read Psalm 12:3 and Proverbs 28:23. What is the Lord's opinion of flattery in these passages? Why does God think rebuke is better than flattery?

3. *There are those in the church who find a small territory and become obsessed with it. There are those in God's family who find a controversy and stake their claim to it. Every church has at least one stubborn soul who has mastered a minutiae of the message and made a mission out of it.*

A. Have you ever run into the kind of situation Max describes? If so, explain the situation. What happened?

B. Read Romans 14:19–22. What is the main problem with picking a fight over a disputable issue (verse 20)? What are we to do with our small territories (verse 22)? What is to be our general outlook on such issues (verse 19)?

C. Read 1 Corinthians 1:10–17. How did the Corinthians fall into the trap Max describes in the quote above? What happens when we allow little controversies to divide the body of Christ (verse 17)? How does this happen?

4. *Let go of your territory for a while. Explore some new reefs. Scout some new regions. Much is gained by closing your mouth and opening your eyes.*

A. Is it difficult for you to let go of your territory for a while? If so, why? What can you do to make this easier for you?

B. Read Proverbs 10:19 and James 1:19. What similar advice do Solomon and James give? How are you at following their advice? What can you do to better follow their advice?

C. Read Romans 14:1. How are we instructed to deal with those whom we perceive as being weaker in faith? What are we not to do? Paul assumes in this verse that there will be disputable matters; do we? What kind of issues most often fit this category?

CHAPTER 13

WHAT MAN DARED NOT DREAM

1. *God did what we wouldn't dare dream. He did what we couldn't imagine. He became a man so we could trust him. He became a sacrifice so we could know him. And he defeated death so we could follow him.*

A. When was the last time God did something in your life that completely surprised you? Describe the incident.

B. Read Matthew 22:41–46. What in Jesus' question so completely startled the Pharisees? Why was the question so hard to answer? Why do you think nobody dared to ask him questions after this incident?

C. Read 1 Corinthians 2:9. What is the point of this verse? To whom are these divine surprises given? Do you qualify for any of these surprises?

2. *Only a God could create a plan this mad. Only a Creator beyond the fence of logic could offer such a gift of love.*

A. Why does Max call God's plan "mad"? Do you agree with him? Why or why not?

B. Read 1 Corinthians 1:18–25. Why does Paul call the preaching of the gospel "foolishness"? What is the main point of this passage (verse 25)? Why does God's plan seem like foolishness to human wisdom?

3. *What man can't do, God does.*

    A. Describe any incidents in your life in which what was impossible for you, God did.

    B. Read Job 42:2, Jeremiah 32:17, Matthew 19:26, and Luke 1:37. What is the consistent message of all four verses? What confidence does this give you?

4. *When it comes to eternity, forgiveness, purpose, and truth, go to the manger. Kneel with the shepherds. Worship the God who dared to do what man dared not dream.*

    A. How is the manger a symbol of eternity, forgiveness, purpose, and truth? Why would kneeling with the shepherds be appropriate?

    B. Read Romans 8:3. According to this verse, what did God do that was otherwise impossible? What did he accomplish? How did he do it?

    C. Read Ephesians 3:20–21. According to this verse, what is God able to accomplish? How is he able to accomplish it? Where is such power at work? What is the result of these accomplishments? How long does this result last? How does this passage strengthen your confidence in God?

CHAPTER 14

THE CURSOR OR THE CROSS?

1. *Computerized religion. No kneeling. No weeping. No gratitude. No emotion. It's great—unless you make a mistake.*

A. Have you ever dabbled in computerized religion? If so, how does it leave you feeling? What did it accomplish? How and why did you abandon it?

B. Read Matthew 23:1–36. Identify each of the "computerized" errors Jesus confronts. Do any of these ever give you problems? Which ones? How do you escape from their grip?

2. *How would you fill in this blank? A person is made right with God through* _____.

A. Fill in the blank as you think appropriate.

B. Read Ephesians 2:8–9. With what is faith contrasted in this verse? What is the problem with works? Why is boasting so terrible?

C. Read Galatians 2:15–16. What is the key element in making a person right with God? How many people will be made right by observing the law? On what are you counting to be made right with God?

3. *Thirty-six verses of fire were summarized with one question: How are you going to escape God's judgment? Good question. Good question for the Pharisees, good question for you and me.*

A. How are we going to escape God's judgment?

B. Read Romans 2:5. What characterizes those who are "storing up wrath for [themselves] for the day of God's wrath"? When will God's righteous judgment be revealed? How certain is this?

C. Read Hebrews 2:2–3; 12:25. What is the question in both passages? What is the expected answer?

4. *Why . . . do you think he is known as your personal Savior?*

A. Is Jesus your personal Savior? How do you know?

B. Read John 1:12. How does John say Jesus becomes our personal Savior?

C. Read 1 John 4:14–15. What must we do to be sure that God lives in us?

CHAPTER 15

UNCLUTTERED FAITH

1. *Oh, for the attitude of a five-year-old! That simple uncluttered passion for living that can't wait for tomorrow. A philosophy of life that reads, "Play hard, laugh hard, and leave the worries to your father."*

A. Watch children at play for half an hour. What do you observe? What elements in their play do you wish you could recapture for yourself? What stops you from recapturing them?

B. Read Matthew 18:3–4. In what ways did Jesus insist we become like children? What is the consequence if we don't?

C. Read 2 Corinthians 11:3. What was Paul's concern in this verse? Why should this always be of paramount concern to us?

2. *Complicated religion wasn't made by God. Reading Matthew 23 will convince you of that. It is the crackdown of Christ on midway religion.*

A. What does Max mean by "midway religion"? Why does Christ crack down on it?

B. Read Matthew 23:37–38. What had been Jesus' desire for Jerusalem? How had its people responded? What was the ultimate consequence?

3. *How do you simplify your faith? How do you get rid of the clutter? How do you discover a joy worth waking up to? Simple. Get rid of the middleman.*

A. What does Max mean by the middleman? Who are the middlemen in our culture?

B. Read John 10:10. According to this verse, why did Jesus come to earth? Does this sound complicated? Why or why not? Are you experiencing what Jesus talks about in this verse? Why or why not?

C. Read 1 Timothy 2:5. Who is the one-and-only mediator between God and men? What difference does this make in daily life?

4. *Seek the simple faith. Major in the majors. Focus on the critical. Long for God.*

A. Why do you think we so frequently lose track of the wisdom in Max's quote above? How do we let life and our faith get so complicated? How do you extricate yourself from unnecessary complication?

B. Read Psalm 42:1–2. Is this passage a picture of simple or cluttered faith? Does it sound appealing? Why or why not? Do you know people whose faith mirrors this passage? What do they do that nurtures such a faith?

C. Read Philippians 3:7–9. What was the driving passion of Paul's life, according to this passage? How was this passion energized? Was this a simple passion or a complex one? How does his passion compare to your own?

CHAPTER 16

SURVIVING LIFE

1. *Jesus is honest about the life we are called to lead. There is no guarantee that just because we belong to him we will go unscathed. No promise is found in Scripture that says when you follow the king you are exempt from battle. No, often just the opposite is the case.*

    A. In your own experience, does the above quote ring true? Explain your answer.

    B. Read Matthew 24:1–14. How does verse 6 stand out amid the list of coming trials? On what is this command based? How does it apply no matter what our situation may be?

    C. Read John 15:18–19 and 16:33. What promise does Jesus make in these two passages? How are we to respond to our lot in life (16:33)? How can we do so (16:33)?

    D. Read 2 Timothy 3:12. What is Paul's expectation in this verse? Who is affected? How do you deal with this promise?

2. *The saved may get close to the edge; they may even stumble and slide. But they will dig their nails into the rock of God and hang on.*

    A. Have you ever been close to the edge? What happened? How did you get pulled back to spiritual safety?

    B. Read Matthew 24:13. Do you see this verse as a promise or a threat? How do you think it's intended?

    C. Read Colossians 1:22–23. In what way is this verse simply an expansion of Matthew 24:13?

3. *The disciples were emboldened with the assurance that the task would be completed. Because they had a way to stand in the battle, they were victorious after the battle. They had an edge . . . and so do we.*

A. What was the disciples' edge? How is ours exactly the same as theirs?

B. Read Matthew 24:30–31. What encouragement does this passage give to people undergoing trials? How is it an encouragement? Does it encourage you? Why or why not?

C. Read Philippians 1:6. What promise is given in this verse? Is it conditional? How is this promise meant to help you in your walk of faith? Does it?

4. *I could very well be wrong, but I think the command that puts an end to the pains of the earth and initiates the joys of heaven will be two words: "No more."*

A. Why would the statement "No more" be appropriate for initiating the joys of heaven? If you were to guess what those final words would be, what would you guess? Why?

B. Read 1 Thessalonians 4:16–18. In what way is this passage meant to encourage us? What picture comes to mind when you read these verses? Why is it significant the Lord himself will come down from heaven?

C. Read Revelation 19:11–16. What picture do you see here of Christ? Is this an encouraging or a discouraging picture for you? Why?

CHAPTER 17

SAND CASTLE STORIES

1. *Two builders of two castles. They have much in common. They shape granules into grandeurs. They see nothing and make something. They are diligent and determined. And for both the tide will rise and the end will come.*

> A. As you look at your life, what kind of castles do you think you have been building? What attitude have you held about them? If the tide were to come in tomorrow, how would you feel?

> B. Read Luke 12:16–21. What kind of castle was the man in the story building? What kind of tide came in? What was the end result? What was Jesus' application?

> C. Read Hebrews 9:27. What is the destiny of all of us? What kind of tide is this? Are you ready for this tide?

2. *You've seen people treat this world as if it was a permanent home. It's not. You've seen people pour time and energy into life as though it will last forever. It won't. You've seen people so proud of what they have done, that they hope they will never have to leave—they will.*

> A. In what ways do we sometimes treat this world as if it were a permanent home? How do we act as though life will last forever? How often in a run-of-the-mill day do we stop to realize that one day we'll be leaving this world?

> B. Read Matthew 16:26–27. Answer the two questions in verse 26. Are you looking forward to the event described in verse 27, or are you a bit nervous about it? Why?

C. Read James 4:13–14. How would remembering the message of this passage radically change the way we do many things? Why is it that this message seems so easy to forget?

3. *I don't know much, but I do know how to travel. Carry little. Eat light. Take a nap. And get off when you reach the city.*

A. What is the quote above meant to teach us about the way we live our everyday lives?

B. Read Hebrews 11:8–10. How did Abraham practice the wisdom outlined in Max's quote above? What was the key factor in his ability to travel light? In what way is verse 10 as applicable to us as it was to Abraham? Why is it harder in some ways for us to recognize the wisdom of verse 10 than it was for Abraham?

C. Read Hebrews 11:13–16. How could this passage act as a road map for the rest of our lives? How could we be spared a lot of pain if we acted on what it teaches?

4. *Go ahead and build, but build with a child's heart. When the sun sets and the tides take—applaud. Salute the process of life, take your father's hand, and go home.*

A. What does it mean to build with a child's heart? How does the quote above relate to worship?

B. Read Luke 19:11–13. How does the command of verse 13 relate to us? What does Jesus expect us to do until he comes back? What are you doing to comply with this command?

C. Read 1 Corinthians 3:10–15. What is Paul's concern as we continue to build the church (verse 10)? What is the foundation on which we build (verse 11)? What does Paul mean by the various building materials he mentions (verse 12)? What day will bring to light how we build (verse 13)? What is the result of our building (verses 14–15)? How is your building going?

CHAPTER 18

BE READY

1. *It may surprise you that Jesus made preparedness the theme of his last sermon. It did me. I would have preached on love or family or the importance of church. Jesus didn't. Jesus preached on what many today consider to be old-fashioned. He preached on being ready for heaven and staying out of hell.*

  A. Why do you think Jesus made preparedness the theme of his last sermon? What effect does his last sermon have on you?

  B. Read Matthew 24:36–25:13. What is the consistent reason given throughout this passage for keeping watch? Are you keeping watch? If so, how? If not, why not?

2. *Jesus doesn't say he may return, or might return, but that he* will *return.*

  A. When you know something is absolutely certain to happen, how do you prepare for it? Are you preparing in the same way for the return of Christ?

  B. Read Matthew 16:27; 24:44; Luke 12:40; John 14:3. What do all these verses have in common? When something is repeated several times, what does that usually mean?

3. *Hell is the chosen place of the person who loves self more than God, who loves sin more than his Savior, who loves this world more than God's world.*

Judgment is that moment when God looks at the rebellious and says, "Your choice will be honored."

A. Do you often think of hell as a place people choose for themselves? Why or why not?

B. Read 2 Thessalonians 1:5–10. What qualifies the Thessalonians for heaven (verse 10)? Who is punished at the Lord's return (verse 8)? How are these people punished (verse 9)? Which group do you see yourself in?

4. *Our task on earth is singular—to choose our eternal home. You can afford many wrong choices in life. You can choose the wrong career and survive, the wrong city and survive, the wrong house and survive. You can even choose the wrong mate and survive. But there is one choice that must be made correctly and that is your eternal destiny.*

A. Have you made a choice about your eternal destiny? If so, what was that choice? If not, why not?

B. Read John 3:16–18. According to verse 18, what is true of someone who believes in Jesus? What is true of someone who doesn't believe in Jesus? Why did God send his Son into the world (verse 17)? Restate verse 16 in your own words.

C. Read John 20:31. Why did John write his gospel? How do we receive eternal life, according to this verse?

D. Read Acts 17:29–34. What did God overlook in the past (verse 30)? What event is yet future, according to verse 31? What reactions did people have to Paul's message (verses 32–34)? With what group do you most closely identify?

CHAPTER 19

THE PEOPLE
WITH THE ROSES

1. *The true nature of a heart is seen in its response to the unattractive. "Tell me whom you love," Houssaye wrote, "and I will tell you who you are."*

   A. What is your response to the unattractive? What do you think of Houssaye's comment?

   B. Read Matthew 25:31–46. What two groups of people are represented here? What happens to each of them? What characterizes each group? Note verse 46: What time frame is mentioned for both groups?

2. *The sign of the saved is their love for the least.*

   A. Do you agree with Max's quote above? Why or why not?

   B. Read Hebrews 13:1–3. What does it mean to keep loving each other as brothers? What is the exhortation of verse 2? How is verse 3 an application of Max's quote above?

   C. Read James 2:1–9. What is the main problem that this passage addresses? What is James's solution? How is verse 8 the heart of this passage?

3. *Jesus lives in the forgotten. He has taken up residence in the ignored. He has made a mansion amid the ill. If we want to see God, we must go among the broken and beaten and there we will see him.*

   A. When was the last time you saw Jesus among the broken and beaten? Describe your experience.

B. Read Matthew 10:42. What is one sure way to receive a reward? Is the reward based on great sacrifice? On what is it based?

C. Read Matthew 11:2–6. What was the question that John the Baptist had for Jesus? How did Jesus answer the question? What significance does this have for Max's quote above?

CHAPTER 20

SERVED BY THE BEST

1. *For some, communion is a sleepy hour in which wafers are eaten and juice is drunk and the soul never stirs. It wasn't intended to be as such. It was intended to be an I-can't-believe-it's-me-pinch-me-I'm-dreaming invitation to sit at God's table and be served by the King himself.*

A. Be honest here—what has been your attitude toward communion? How do Max's words strike you?

B. Read Matthew 26:17–30. Try to imagine what it would have been like to sit with the Savior at this meal. What are you thinking? What are you feeling? What do you think of Jesus' quote in verse 29?

2. *It is the Lord's table you sit at. It is the Lord's Supper you eat. Just as Jesus prayed for his disciples, Jesus begs God for us. When you are called to the table, it might be an emissary who gives the letter, but it is Jesus who wrote it.*

A. Who is the emissary Max mentions in the quote above? Why is it significant to remember that it's Jesus who calls you to the table?

B. Read John 17:20–23. What is the primary request Jesus makes in this passage? How is this especially relevant in talking about the Lord's Supper?

3. *What happens on earth is just a warmup for what will happen in heaven. So the next time the messenger calls you to the table, drop what you are doing and go. Be blessed and be fed and, most importantly, be sure you're still eating at his table when he calls us home.*

A. What does Max mean when he writes, "Be sure you're still eating at his table when he calls us home"? What should we be careful to do?

B. Read Luke 22:14–18. What word does Jesus use to describe his attitude about eating the Lord's Supper with his disciples? What future event is emphasized in both verse 16 and 18? Do you come to the Lord's table with this emphasis in mind?

C. Read 1 Corinthians 11:26. What does this verse add to your understanding of the Lord's Supper? How is it meant to shape the way we live our Christian lives?

CHAPTER 21

HE CHOSE YOU

1. *Jesus knew that before the war was over, he would be taken captive. He knew that before victory would come defeat. He knew that before the throne would come the cup. He knew that before the light of Sunday would come the blackness of Friday. And he is afraid.*

A. How does it make you feel to realize that Jesus was afraid? Why?

B. Read Matthew 26:36–46. How does Jesus describe his anguish of soul (verse 38)? What does his posture (verse 39) tell you? In what way were the events described in this passage like a battle?

2. *You need to note that in this final prayer, Jesus prayed for you. You need to underline in red and highlight in yellow his love, "I am also praying for all people who will believe in me because of the teaching." That is you. As Jesus stepped into the garden, you were in his prayers. As Jesus looked into heaven, you were in his vision. As Jesus dreamed of the day when we will be where he is, he saw you there.*

A. What effect does it have upon you to realize that even as Jesus prepared to go to the cross, he had you in mind?

B. Read John 17:24. What is Jesus' special request in this verse? Why does he make this request? How does this request make you feel? Why?

3. *It was in the garden that he made his decision. He would rather go to hell for you than go to heaven without you.*

A. In what way did Jesus go to hell for you? How should this knowledge affect the way we live? Does it? If so, in what way? If not, why not?

B. Read Ephesians 4:7–10. What light does this passage shed on Max's quote above? What is the significance of the phrase "in order to fill the whole universe"?

C. Read Hebrews 12:2. According to this verse, why did Jesus endure the cross, scorning its shame? What is important about his sitting down at the right hand of the throne of God?

CHAPTER 22

WHEN YOUR WORLD TURNS AGAINST YOU

1. *Betrayal is a weapon found only in the hands of one you love. Your enemy has no such tool, for only a friend can betray. Betrayal is mutiny. It's a violation of a trust, an inside job.*

A. Have you ever been betrayed? If so, what hurt the most about your situation?

B. Read Matthew 26:47–56. There are two betrayals described in this passage. Name both of them.

2. *The way to handle a person's behavior is to understand the cause of it. One way to deal with a person's peculiarities is to try to understand why they are peculiar.*

A. What are some ways you can try to understand a person's peculiarities? How can you come to at least partially understand the cause of someone's actions?

B. Read Galatians 6:2. In order to carry one another's burdens, what must you first know? How do you come to know this?

C. Read Philippians 2:19–21. Why did Paul want to send Timothy to the Philippians? What does this assume about Timothy's relationship to the Philippians?

D. Read Hebrews 12:14. What are we here commanded to do? How can we achieve this? Why is it so important to achieve?

3. *As long as you hate your enemy, a jail door is closed and a prisoner is taken. But when you try to understand and release your foe from your hatred, then the prisoner is released and that prisoner is you.*

    A. In what way does hatred make you a prisoner? Are you currently its prisoner?

    B. Read Matthew 5:43–48. What does Jesus here instruct us to do about our enemies? How can you do this in practice?

    C. Read Hebrews 12:15. What does bitterness do to a person? What does it do to others around that person? How are we instructed to deal with bitterness?

4. *To keep your balance in a crooked world, look at the mountains. Think of home.*

    A. Read John 18:36. What world was Jesus referring to? What evidence did he offer to show that this earth was not his kingdom?

    B. Read Psalm 25:15. What was the psalmist's recipe for staying upright in a crooked world?

    C. Read Psalm 73:2–5,13–20. What caused the psalmist some serious attitude problems in verses 2–5? What effect did focusing on this side of life have on him (verses 13–14)? How did he regain his spiritual equilibrium (verses 16–17)? What was his final assessment of the situation (verses 18–20)? In what way does this passage reiterate the message of Max's quote above?

YOUR CHOICE

1. *Jesus is not afraid. He is not angry. He is not on the verge of panic. For he is not surprised. Jesus knows his hour and the hour has come.*

 A. Read John 2:4; 7:6, 8, 30; 8:20; 13:1. What progression do you see in these verses? In what way do these references make it clear that Jesus was perfectly aware of his mission?

2. *Perhaps you, like Pilate, are curious about this one called Jesus. You, like Pilate, are puzzled by his claims and stirred by his passions. You have heard the stories; God descending the stars, cocooning in flesh, placing a stake of truth in the globe. You, like Pilate, have heard the others speak; now you would like for him to speak.*

 A. Are you curious about Jesus? In what ways? Does he puzzle you? How? Which stories about him are the hardest for you to accept? Why?

 B. Read Luke 22:67–70. What claim does Jesus make for himself in this passage? Why is this the most phenomenal claim of all?

3. *You have two choices. You can reject Jesus. That is an option. You can, as have many, decide that the idea of God's becoming a carpenter is too bizarre—and walk away. Or you can accept him. You can journey with him. You can listen for his voice amid the hundreds of voices and follow him.*

 A. What choice have you made about Jesus? Whose voice are you listening for amid the hundreds that vie for your attention?

B. Read John 6:60–69. Why did some disciples turn away from following Jesus? Why did Peter continue to follow him? Which decision is most like your own? Why?

4. *Pilate thought he could avoid making a choice. He washed his hands of Jesus. He climbed on the fence and sat down. But in not making a choice, Pilate made a choice.*

A. In what way did Pilate make a choice by not making a choice? How can we make exactly the same mistake?

B. Read Matthew 12:30. In what way does this verse warn against fence sitting?

C. Read John 5:22–29. How does this passage teach that it's impossible to be neutral about Jesus?

CHAPTER 24

THE GREATEST MIRACLE

1. *That is the beauty of the cross. It occurred in a normal week involving flesh-and-blood people and a flesh-and-blood Jesus.*

A. Why is it beautiful that the cross occurred in a normal week involving flesh-and-blood people? What does the normalcy of the week mean to you?

2. *God calls us in a real world. He doesn't communicate by performing tricks. He doesn't communicate by stacking stars in the heavens or reincarnating grandparents from the grave. He's not going to speak to you through voices in a cornfield or a little fat man in a land called Oz. There is about as much power in the plastic Jesus that's on your dashboard as there is the Styrofoam dice on your rearview mirror.*

A. Do you ever long for God to communicate with you through "stacking stars in the heavens" or through "voices in a cornfield"? Explain your answer. What does the Bible's emphasis on *faith* have to do with God's normal methods of communication?

B. Read 2 Corinthians 5:18–20. What did God give to us (verse 18)? To what has he committed us (verse 19)? What title has God given us (verse 20)? What is your part in this commission?

C. Acts 10 tells how an angel told Cornelius to send for Peter so that Peter could explain the gospel to the centurion. Since the angel had no trouble communicating with Cornelius, why do you think the angel himself didn't explain the gospel to Cornelius?

3. *Don't miss the impossible by looking for the incredible. God speaks in our world. We just have to learn to hear him. Listen for him amid the ordinary.*

A. Do you listen for God amid the ordinary? If so, how? What have you discovered thus far?

B. Read Psalm 19:1–4. In what ways does God continue to speak through the ordinary? How do his messages affect you?

C. Read Acts 17:26–28. What is God's direction of human affairs (verse 26) intended to accomplish (verse 27)? In what sense is God "not far from each one of us"? How does verse 28 relate to Max's quote above?

4. *In the final week those who demanded miracles got none and missed the one. They missed the moment in which a grave for the dead became the throne of a king.*

A. Is it possible for us to be so interested in the miraculous that we miss God? If so, how?

B. Read Matthew 12:39–40. What is wrong with demanding to see a miraculous sign, according to Jesus? What sign did he give the people who demanded a sign? What lesson can we learn from this encounter?

CHAPTER 25

A PRAYER OF DISCOVERY

1. *You are God, Jesus! You couldn't be abandoned. You couldn't be left alone. You couldn't be deserted in your most painful moment.*

A. Why is it so hard to accept that Jesus really was abandoned for a time on the cross? Why do you think he was abandoned?

B. Read Matthew 27:45–50. What image comes most clearly to your mind in this scene?

C. Read Psalm 22:1. What impression does it leave upon you that even the words Jesus cried out from the cross were prophesied hundreds of years before they were spoken?

2. *I thought you just sent sin away. Banished it. I thought you'd just stood in front of the mountains of our sins and told them to begone. Just like you did to the demons. Just like you did to the hypocrites in the temple. I just thought you commanded the evil out. I never noticed that you took it out. It never occurred to me that you actually touched it—or worse still, that it touched you.*

A. Why was it not possible for God simply to send sin away? Why did it have to be *taken* out?

B. Read 2 Corinthians 5:21. What did God do to him who had no sin? Who is the one who had no sin? For whom did he do this? Why did he do this? What is your reaction to this?

C. Read Galatians 3:13–14. Who redeemed us from the curse of the law? How did he do this? Why did he do this?

3. *Your question was real, wasn't it, Jesus? You really were afraid. You really were alone. Just like I was. Only, I deserved it. You didn't.*

    A. In what way did we deserve to be alone? Why did Jesus not deserve to be alone? Why did God reverse our roles?

    B. Read Isaiah 53:4–5. How many instances of this role reversal can you spot in this passage? With what main impression does this passage leave you?

    C. Read 1 Peter 3:18. For what did Christ die? What role reversal is described here? What was the purpose of this reversal? Have you personally appropriated what this verse describes?

CHAPTER 26

THE HIDDEN TOMB

1. *Shuffling to catch up with Joe, I asked, "Was this street a meat market in the time of Christ?" "It was," he answered. "To get to the cross he had to pass through a slaughterhouse."*

    A. What is especially poignant about the observation in the quote above?

    B. Read Matthew 27:26–31. In your opinion, what was the cruelest torture inflicted on Jesus? Why do you think God allowed all of this to happen?

    C. Read 1 Corinthians 5:7. What was a Passover lamb (see Exodus 12:1–13)? In what sense was Christ our Passover lamb?

2. *Wouldn't it be ironic," he smiled as he spoke, "if this was the place? It is dirty. It is uncared for. It is forgotten. The one over there is elaborate and adorned. This one is simple and ignored. Wouldn't it be ironic if this was the place where our Lord was buried?"*

653

A. What would be ironic about the state of affairs outlined above? Why would it be ironic?

B. Read Matthew 27:57–61. What details are given about the tomb? Why do you think more details are not given?

C. Compare Isaiah 52:14, Isaiah 53:2 and Luke 2:7. What do all of these verses have in common? Taken together, what do they say about God's need to do things in a flashy way? Why do you think he operates this way?

3. *God put himself in a dark, tight, claustrophobic room and allowed them to seal it shut. The Light of the World was mummied in cloth and shut in ebony. The Hope of humanity was shut in a tomb.*

A. How does the quote above make you feel? Why?

B. Read Matthew 12:40. Did Jesus expect to die? Did he expect to be buried? What attitude did he seem to take toward it in this verse?

C. Read 1 Corinthians 15:3–4. Why does Paul say that the information he conveys in this passage is "of first importance"? What crucial items does he name? Why are they all crucial?

4. *When you enter the tomb, bow down, enter quietly, and look closely. For there, on the wall, you may see the charred marks of a divine explosion.*

A. In what way could the empty tomb be considered a better symbol of the Christian faith than the cross? Which symbol better conveys God's power? Why?

B. Read Acts 2:22–24. According to verse 24, what was impossible? Why was this impossible?

C. Read 1 Corinthians 6:14. What attribute of God is stressed in this verse? What did it accomplish? What will it accomplish?

CHAPTER 27

I RECKONS I WILL ALWAYS REMEMBER THAT WALK

1. *What do you do with such a man? He called himself God, but wore the clothes of a man. He called himself the Messiah, but never marshaled an army. He was regarded as king, but his only crown was of thorns. People revered him as regal, yet his only robe was stitched with mockery.*

A. Answer the question above: What do you do with such a man?

B. Read Matthew 28:1–10. Why do you think the angel sat on the stone in verse 2? Why did he speak to the women but not the guards? How is it that the women could be both afraid and filled with joy at the same time (verse 8)?

2. *Where were you the night the door was opened? Do you remember the touch of the Father? Who walked with you the day you were set free? Can you still see the scene? Can you feel the road beneath your feet?*

A. Try to answer Max's questions above. Describe the scene if you can.

B. Read Acts 26:12–18. List the elements Paul uses in his testimony. Does the way he gives his testimony give you any ideas about the way you could give yours? Explain your answer.

3. *I told my father that I was ready to give my life to God. He thought I was too young to make the decision. He asked what I knew. I told him Jesus was in heaven and I wanted to be with him. And for my dad, that was enough.*

A. How can you tell when someone is ready to give his life to God?

B. Read Romans 10:9. How do you give your life to God, according to this verse?

C. Read 2 Corinthians 6:1–2. According to this passage, when is it appropriate to give your life to God?

4. *The journey isn't complete. There is one more walk that must be made. "I will come back," he promised. And to prove it he ripped in two the temple curtain and split open the doors of death. He will come back. He, like the missionary, will come back for his followers. And we, like Tigyne, won't be able to control our joy. "The one who has redeemed us has returned!" we will cry. And the journey will end and we will take our seats at his feast . . . forever. See you at the table.*

A. Are you looking forward to the day described in the quote above? If so, how does this expectation shape the way you live now? Do you expect to be at the table? If so, how? If not, why not?

B. Compare 1 Thessalonians 3:12–13 and 5:23–24. How does Paul connect the expectation of Christ's coming with our conduct right now? What supplies the power for godly living (5:24)?

C. Think back over the insights in this book. If you had to name one that was most meaningful to you, what would it be? Will your life be different from interacting with this insight? How?

D. Take time to pause and thank God for sending his Son to earth to die in your place. Thank him for his love. Thank him for his patience. Thank him for his provision. Spend some uninterrupted time simply basking in the gracious presence of the One who does all things well.

NOTES

A WORD BEFORE
1. I've limited this book to the events in Christ's final week as recorded by Matthew.

CHAPTER 1, Too Little, Too Late, Too Good to Be True
1. 1 Corinthians 1:26.

CHAPTER 2, From Jericho to Jerusalem
1. Mark 10:32.
2. James Michener, *Texas* (New York: Random House, 1985), 367.
3. Matthew 20:18–19.
4. Acts 2:23.
5. Jeremiah 29:11.
6. Romans 8:1.
7. Hosea 11:9b.
8. Ephesians 3:18–19.

CHAPTER 3, The Sacrificial General
1. "D-Day Recalling Military Gamble That Shaped History," *Time*, 28 May 1984, 16.
2. Matthew 20:28.
3. Daniel 7:4.
4. Daniel 7:5.
5. Daniel 7:6.
6. Daniel 7:7.
7. Daniel 7:13–14.
8. For further reference consider the Book of Enoch, an intertestamental book completed sometime around 70 B.C. This ancient manuscript tells us what picture came to the minds of people when they heard the title "the Son of Man. " Note these phrases excerpted from the Book of Enoch.

> And this Son of Man whom thou hast seen shall put down the kings
>   from their thrones,
> And shall loosen the reins of the strong
> And break the teeth of sinners.

And he shall put down the kings from their thrones and kingdoms because they do not extol and praise him . . . (Enoch 46).
When they see that Son of Man
Sitting on the throne of his glory.
And the kings and the mighty and all who possess the earth shall bless and glorify and extol him who rules over all, who was hidden.
. . . all the elect shall stand before him on that day.
And all the kings and the mighty and the exalted and those who rule the earth
Shall fall before him on their faces,
And worship and set their hope on the Son of Man,
And petition him and supplicate for mercy at their hands.
. . . he will deliver them to the angels for punishment,
to execute vengeance on them because they have oppressed his children and his elect (Enoch 62).

For that Son of Man has appeared,
And has seated himself on the throne of his glory,
And all evil shall pass away before his face,
And the word of that Son of Man shall go forth
And be strong before the Lord of Spirits (Enoch 69).

9. Matthew 19:28.
10. Matthew 24:30; Mark 13:26; Luke 17:26–30.
11. Matthew 26:64.
12. Mark 9:31.
13. Mark 9:32.
14. Matthew 20:28 isn't the only passage that speaks of the dualism of God. He is the Lord "who shows mercy, who is kind...but he does not forget to punish guilty people" (Exodus 34:6,7). He is the only "good God." At the same time he is the "Savior" (Isaiah 45:21). He is equally "full of grace and truth" (John 1:14). He is the God who in wrath can remember mercy (Habakkuk 3:2). In a precious insight Micah states to God, "You will not stay angry forever, because you enjoy being kind" (Micah 7:18). "God," states Paul, "is kind and also very strict" (Romans 11:22). He is able to "judge rightly and . . . make right any person who has faith in Jesus" (Romans 3:26).

We find it difficult to hold simultaneously in our minds a God who is the Judge who punishes and the Lover who forgives. But that is the God of Scripture. He is the God who "in a marvelous and divine way loved us even when he hated us." (John R. W. Stott, *The Cross of Christ* [Downers Grove, Ill.: InterVarsity Press, 1986], 131.) He is, at the same time, angry at our sin and touched by our plight.

CHAPTER 4, Ugly Religion
1. Matthew 20:29–30.
2. Matthew 20:34.

3. "Wilford Hall Turf Fight Puts Patients at Risk," *San Antonio Light*, 3 February 1990, A1, A16.
4. 2 Chronicles 30:18–19.
5. 2 Chronicles 30:20.
6. Jeremiah 29:13.

CHAPTER 5, Don't Just Do Something, Stand There
1. Luke 4:16, emphasis added.
2. Psalm 39:6 NIV.

CHAPTER 6, Risky Love
1. Matthew 26:10. Matthew waits until chapter 26 to tell a story that chronologically should appear in chapter 20. By referring to John's Gospel we see the anointing by Mary in Bethany occurred on Saturday night (John 12:1). Why does Matthew wait until so late to record the story? It appears that he sometimes elevates theme over chronology. The last week of Christ's life is a week of bad news. Chapters 26 and 27 sing the woeful chorus of betrayal. First the leaders, then Judas, then the apostles, Peter, Pilate, and eventually all the people turn against Jesus. Perhaps with the desire to tell one good story of faith in the midst of so many ones of betrayal, Matthew waits until Matthew 26 to tell of Simon and Mary.
2. Matthew 26:13.

CHAPTER 7, The Guy with the Donkey
1. Matthew 21:2–3.
2. Matthew 5:41-42.

CHAPTER 8, Hucksters and Hypocrites
1. *Paul Harvey's For What It's Worth*, ed. Paul Harvey, Jr. (New York: Bantam Books, 1991), 118.
2. Mark 11:11.
3. Matthew 21:12–13.
4. Titus 1:11.
5. Romans 16:17–18.
6. Mel White, *Deceived*, as quoted by John MacArthur, Jr. in *The MacArthur New Testament Commentary, Matthew 1–7* (Chicago: Moody Press, 1985), 462.

CHAPTER 9, Courage to Dream Again
1. It is obvious by comparing Matthew with Mark that the incident occurred on two days. Part on Monday and part on Tuesday. The cleansing of the temple occurred between these two parts.

Why the difference in the two accounts? Matthew chooses to describe the incident topically while Mark describes it chronologically. Mark states that Jesus cursed the tree on Monday morning (11:12–14) then cleansed the temple (11:15–19). The second part of the fig tree story—the amazement of the disciples (11:20–24)—happened on Tuesday morning as the disciples and Jesus were returning to Jerusalem.

Matthew is topical in his teaching. He groups the two events, but in doing so, doesn't contradict Mark. He wants to tell the entire story with no interruptions. He begins by saying, "Now in the morning . . ." (21:18 KJV). He doesn't say the *next* morning. And when he begins to report on the disciples' amazement, he simply says, "And when the disciples saw it . . . " (21:20).

By combining Matthew and Mark we see that the cursing of the tree took place on Monday and the commentary occurred on Tuesday. There is no conflict. One writer is topical and the other chronological. Each has it advantages. (*See* William Hendricksen, *The Gospel of Matthew* [Grand Rapids, Mich.: Baker Book House, 1973], 773.)

2. Matthew 21:21.
3. Revelation 3:15–16.
4 Matthew 21:22.

CHAPTER 10, Of Calluses and Compassion
1. Matthew 21:33–45.
2. Matthew 22:1–14.
3. Deuteronomy 4:32–34.
4. Hosea 11:8–9.
5. Romans 8:16.
6. 2 Samuel 7:19.
7. 2 Samuel 7:15.
8. Matthew 21:43.
9. Acts 13:46.
10. Matthew 12:24.
11. Deuteronomy 4:35.
12. Romans 2:4.
13. Revelation 3:20 KJV.

CHAPTER 11, You're Invited
1. Isaiah 1:18, emphasis added.
2. Isaiah 55:1, emphasis added.
3. Matthew 11:28, emphasis added.
4. Matthew 22:4, emphasis added.
5. Mark 1:17, emphasis added.
6. John 7:37, emphasis added.
7. Matthew 21:28–32.
8. Matthew 22:1–14.
9. Revelation 3:20.
10. Hebrews 9:27 RSV.

CHAPTER 12, Mouth-to-Mouth Manipulation
1. Matthew 21:23.
2. Matthew 21:26.
3. Matthew 22:15–17.
4. Psalm 12:3 NIV.

5. Proverbs 28:23 NIV.
6. Paul Aurandt, *Paul Harvey's the Rest of the Story* (New York: Bantam Books, 1977), 123.
7. Dennis Tice, "Did Adam and Eve Have Navels?" Unpublished work. Used by permission.

CHAPTER 13, What Man Dared Not Dream
1. Matthew 22:42.

CHAPTER 14, The Cursor or the Cross?
1. Matthew 23:5.
2. Matthew 23:5.
3. Matthew 23:6.
4. Matthew 23:7.
5. Matthew 23:5.
6. Matthew 23:13-32.
7. Matthew 23:33.
8. Romans 3:28.

CHAPTER 15, Uncluttered Faith
1. Matthew 18:2–3 PHILLIPS.
2. Matthew 23:8–12.
3. Matthew 23:8.
4. Matthew 23:9.
5. Matthew 23:10.

CHAPTER 16, Surviving Life
1. Matthew 24:1–2.
2. William Barclay, The Gospel of Matthew, Vol. 2, *Daily Study Bible Revised Edition*, (Philadelphia: The Westminister Press, 1975), 305.
3. The imperfect tense is used, implying a continual, unending course of action.
4. Matthew 24:2, author's paraphrase.
5. Matthew 23:38.
6. Barclay, 307.
7. John 16:33.
8. Matthew 24:5.
9. Matthew 24:6.
10. Matthew 24:7–8.
11. Matthew 24:9.
12. *The Wall Street Journal,* 15 January 1992, A-P1.
13. Matthew 24:13.
14. Matthew 24:14.
15. Acts 2:5.
16. Matthew 24:14.

CHAPTER 17, Sand Castle Stories
1. Matthew 24:36.

2. Matthew 25:1–13.
3. Matthew 25:14–30.
4. Matthew 25:31–46.

CHAPTER 18, Be Ready
1. Matthew 24:45–51.
2. Matthew 25:1–13.
3. Matthew 25:14–30.
4. Matthew 24:42.
5. Matthew 25:31.
6. Matthew 24:44.
7. Acts 1:11 NIV.
8. Hebrews 9:28.
9. 1 Thessalonians 5:2 NIV.
10. Matthew 25:32–33.
11. Matthew 25:41.
12. 1 Thessalonians 5:9 NEB.
13. Hebrews 9:27.
14. Matthew 7:24–27.
15. Matthew 7:13–14.
16. Paul Lee Tan, *Encyclopedia of 7007 Illustrations* (Rockville, Md.: Assurance Publishers, 1979), 1086.

CHAPTER 19, The People with the Roses
1. Source unknown.
2. Matthew 25:35–36.
3. Hebrews 11:6b.
4. Matthew 25:40. I like Martin Luther's commentary on this verse. "'Here below, here below,' says Christ, 'you find me in the poor: I am too high for you in heaven, you are trying to climb up there for nothing.' Thus it would be a very good idea if this high command of love were written with golden letters on all the foreheads of the poor so that we could see and grasp how near Christ is to us on this planet." S. D. Bruner, *Matthew*, vol. 2 of *The Churchbook* (Dallas: Word Publishing, 1991), 923.
5. *San Antonio Express-News*, 3 April 1991, 2.

CHAPTER 20, Served by the Best
1. Matthew 26:18.
2. John 13:5.
3. A sacrament is a gift from the Lord to his people.
4. A sacrifice is a gift of the people to the Lord.
5. There are sacrificial moments during the Supper. We offer up prayers, confessions, and thanksgivings as sacrifice. But they are sacrifices of thanksgiving for a salvation received, not sacrifices of service for a salvation desired. We don't say, "Look at what I've done." We instead, in awe, watch God and worship what he has done.

Both Luther and Calvin had strong convictions regarding the proper view of the Lord's Supper.

"Out of the sacrament and testament of God, which ought to be a good gift received, they (the religious leaders) have made up for themselves a good deed performed." (Martin Luther, *Luther's Works American Edition,* 36:49.)

"He (Jesus) bids the disciples to take: He himself, therefore, is the only one who offers. When the priests pretend that they offer Christ in the Supper, they are starting from quite another source. What a wonderful case of topsy-turvy, that a mortal man to receive the body of Christ should snatch to himself the role of offering it." (John Calvin, *A Harmony of the Gospels,* 1:133.)

(As quoted by Frederick Dale Bruner in *Matthew* vol. 2 of *The Churchbook* [Dallas: Word, Inc., 1991], 958).

6. Romans 8:34.
7. Luke 12:37.

CHAPTER 21, He Chose You
1. John 17:20–21, author's paraphrase.

CHAPTER 22, When Your World Turns against You
1. Matthew 26:46.
2. Matthew 26:56.
3. Matthew 26:59.
4. Matthew 26:50.
5. Matthew 26:15.
6. Matthew 26: 48–49.
7. Matthew 26:49.
8. James 1:2.
9. Matthew 26:64.
10. John 18:36.
11. Hebrews 13:5.

CHAPTER 23, Your Choice
1. Matthew 27:22.
2. John 18:34.
3. John 19:11.

CHAPTER 25, A Prayer of Discovery
1. John 11:43.
2. Matthew 8:32.
3. Matthew 14:27.
4. John 1:29, author's paraphrase.

CHAPTER 27, I Reckons I Will Always Remember That Walk
1. *My Folks Don't Want Me to Talk About Slavery,* ed. Belinda Hurmence (Winston-Salem, N.C.: John F. Blair Publishing, 1984), 14–15.
2. Raymond Davis, *Fire on the Mountain* (publisher information unavailable).

Max Lucado, minister for the Oak Hills Church in San Antonio, Texas, is the husband of Denalyn and father of Jenna, Andrea, and Sara. He currently has more than 40 million books in print and is America's Leading Inspirational Author.

A Life-Changing Message from America's Pastor

Embark on a journey of hope and encouragement for daily living with Max Lucado as he unpacks the timeless message of John 3:16.

If you know nothing of the Bible, start here. If you know everything in the Bible, return here. It's a twenty-six word parade of hope: beginning with God, ending with life and urging us to do the same.

He Loves.
He Gave.
We Believe.
We Live.

MAX LUCADO

NEW YORK TIMES BEST-SELLING AUTHOR

3:16

The Numbers of Hope

If 9/11 are the numbers of terror and despair, then 3:16 are the numbers of hope. Best-selling author Max Lucado leads readers through a word-by-word study of John 3:16, the passage that he calls the "Hope Diamond" of scripture. The study includes 12 lessons that are designed to work with both the trade book and the Indelible DVD for a multi-media experience.

Listen to the message of 3:16 in your home or take it on the road. This CD makes the perfect gift for the family or friends you want to hear the hope found in John 3:16.

3:16 is also available in Spanish, Portuguese, German, Swedish, Dutch, Korean, Japanese, and Chinese.

GOD'S GREAT BIG LOVE FOR ME

With colored beads built right in, this board book is the perfect book to teach the verse and meaning behind John 3:16 to preschool children.

Available February 2008

3:16 – THE NUMBERS OF HOPE
TEEN EDITION

Max offers his unique and simple storytelling for this important message while Tricia Goyer writes teen responses to Max's message, guiding teens to fully understand how this verse can impact their lives. From confession to praise, these responses are sure to bring an insightful look into the personal faith of teens.

Available February 2008

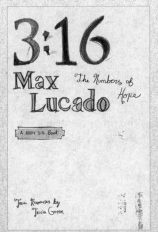

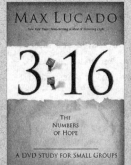

A DVD FOR SMALL GROUP STUDY

This is a kit designed and priced specifically for small groups. It will include a copy of the study guide for small groups, an evangelism booklet, the Indelible DVD, and a CD-ROM with facilitator's guide information and promotional material.